Strategic Marketing Management 1997–98
Planning and Control, Analysis and Decision

The Marketing Series is one of the most comprehensive collections of books in marketing and sales available from the UK today.

Published by Butterworth-Heinemann on behalf of The Chartered Institute of Marketing, the series is divided into three distinct groups: *Student* (fulfilling the needs of those taking the Institute's certificate and diploma qualifications); *Professional Development* (for those on formal or self-study vocational training programmes); and *Practitoner* (presented in a more informal, motivating and highly practical manner for the busy marketer).

Formed in 1911, The Chartered Institute of Marketing is now the largest professional marketing management body in Europe with over 60,000 members located worldwide. Its primary objectives are focused on the development of awareness and understanding of marketing throughout UK industry and commerce and in the raising of standards of professionalism in the education, training and practice of this key business discipline.

The CIM Workbook Series: Marketing

Certificate

Business Communications 1997–98
Misiura

Marketing Fundamentals 1997–98
Lancaster & Withey

Sales and Marketing Environment 1997–98
Oldroyd

Understanding Customers 1997–98
Phipps & Simmons

Advanced Certificate

Effective Management for Marketing 1997–98
Hatton & Worsam

Management Information for Marketing and Sales 1997–98
Hines

Marketing Operations 1997–98
Worsam

Promotional Practice 1997–98
Ace

Diploma

The Diploma Case Study Workbook 1997–98
Fifield

International Marketing Strategy 1997–98
Fifield & Lewis

Marketing Communications Strategy 1997–98
Yeshin

Strategic Marketing Management 1997–98
Fifield & Gilligan

Strategic Marketing Management 1997–98

Planning and Control, Analysis and Decision

Paul Fifield and Colin Gilligan

Published on behalf of
The Chartered Institute of Marketing

This book is dedicated to Jane and Jack, Rosie and Ben.

Butterworth-Heinemann
Linacre House, Jordan Hill, Oxford OX2 8DP
A division of Reed Educational and Professional Publishing Ltd

Ꝺ A member of the Reed Elsevier plc group

OXFORD   BOSTON   JOHANNESBURG
MELBOURNE   NEW DELHI   SINGAPORE

First published 1997

British Library Cataloguing in Publication Data
Fifield, Paul
    Strategic marketing management 1997–98: planning and
    control, analysis and decision – (The marketing series.
    Student)
    1   Marketing – Management   2   Strategic planning
    I   Title   II   Gilligan, Colin   III   Chartered Institute of
    Marketing
    658.8

ISBN 0 7506 3581 9

Set by Avocet Typeset, Brill, Aylesbury, Bucks
Printed and bound in Great Britain

Contents

A quick word from the Chief Examiner

I am delighted to recommend to you this series of CIM workbooks. All of these have been written by either the Senior Examiner or Examiners responsible for marking and set-ting the papers.

Preparing for the CIM Exams is hard work. These workbooks are designed to make that work as interesting and illuminating as possible, as well as providing you with the knowledge you need to pass. I wish you success.

Trevor Watkins
CIM Chief Examiner,
Deputy Vice Chancellor,
South Bank University

Preface

The development three years ago by The Chartered Institute of Marketing of Syllabus '94 has led to a far greater emphasis at the Diploma level upon the strategic aspects of marketing, a move which is reflected not just in the refocusing of all four of the Diploma syllabuses, but also by the way in which the Planning and Control and the Analysis and Decision examinations are now linked under the heading of Strategic Marketing Management. In writing this workbook, we have therefore paid particular attention both to the strategic aspects of the subject and to an exploration of the very strong linkages that exist – and which students are expected to demonstrate – between the Planning and Control and Analysis and Decision examination papers.

However, it needs to be recognized from the outset that candidates for the Diploma are also expected to demonstrate the depth and breadth of their understanding of marketing. This workbook alone will be insufficient to meet a candidate's needs for the Diploma examinations.

Important note

This workbook has been designed to complement, not substitute for, a wider programme of reading, research and individual study. It is for this reason that throughout the text you will find reference to two other books that you will be told to read. They are:

Strategic Marketing Management: Planning, Implementation and Control, by Wilson and Gilligan (1997), Butterworth-Heinemann

Marketing Strategy by Fifield (1992), Butterworth-Heinemann.

This workbook first appeared in 1995 and, we are pleased to say, received a very positive response both from tutors and students. However, a number of the students asked for more guidance on how to answer the sorts of questions that appear in Part B of the Planning and Control paper. In preparing this edition, the third, we have tried to address this. At the same time, and again in response to feedback from the marketplace, we have expanded the content of Units 7 and 8. Other additions to the text include an updating of some of the material and the inclusion of a greater number of examples.

We wish you success in the examinations.

Paul Fifield
Colin Gilligan

Acknowledgements

The authors would like to thank Maggie Duncan and Janice Nunn for wordprocessing the manuscript, and Richard Taylor at Butterworth-Heinemann whose increasingly frequent, and seemingly desperate, phone calls to check on the progress of the manuscript eventually forced us to sit down and make a series of revisions and additions to the second edition.

How to use your CIM workbook

The authors have been careful to structure your book with the exams in mind. Each unit, therefore, covers an essential part of the syllabus. You need to work through the complete workbook systematically to ensure that you have covered everything you need to know.

This workbook is divided into ten units. Each unit contains the following standard elements:

Objectives   tell you what part of the syllabus you will be covering and what you will be expected to know having read the unit.

Study guides   tell you how long the unit is and how long its activities take to do.

Questions   are designed to give you practice – they will be similar to those that you get in the exam.

Answers   give you a suggested format for answering exam questions. *Remember* there is no such thing as a model answer – you should use these examples only as guidelines.

Activities   give you the chance to put what you have learnt into practice.

Exam tips   are hints from the senior examiner or examiner which are designed to help you avoid common mistakes made by previous candidates.

Definitions   are used for words you must know to pass the exam.

Extending knowledge sections   are designed to help you use your time most effectively. It is not possible for the workbook to cover *everything* you need to know to pass. What you read here needs to be supplemented by your classes, practical experience at work and day-to-day reading.

Summaries   cover what you should have picked up from reading the unit.

A glossary is provided at the back of the book to help define and underpin understanding of the key terms used in each unit.

Introduction

The Strategic Marketing Management component of the Diploma in Marketing consists of two interrelated modules: Planning and Control and Analysis and Decision. In the case of Planning and Control, the syllabus has been designed to provide you with a detailed understanding of the ways in which marketing activities in a variety of types and size of organization are capable of being planned, implemented and controlled. This is achieved by examining the nature of marketing and the key issues in the strategic marketing process. The syllabus is therefore made up of five interrelated parts (the figures in brackets indicate the relative weighting that should be given to each section).

Stage one: Introduction to Planning and Control (10%)

Stage two: Where are we now? – strategic, financial and marketing analysis (25%)

Stage three: Where do we want to be? – strategic direction and strategy formulation (25%)

Stage four: How might we get there and which way is best? – strategic choice and evaluation (30%)

Stage five: How can we ensure arrival? – strategic implementation and control (10%)

These questions and themes are then developed further and emphasis given to their application within the Analysis and Decision syllabus which culminates in the case study examination.

At the same time, the content of the two modules has been designed to complement the syllabuses for the other two Diploma papers, Marketing Communications Strategy and International Marketing Strategy (see Figure 1) and to build upon material at the Certificate and Advanced Certificate levels. In working your way through the book, you should therefore actively look for and think about the sorts of interrelationships that exist throughout the Certificate, Advanced Certificate and Diploma stages; an obvious example of the way in which this might be done would be to examine how approaches to market segmentation and targeting might be applied in overseas markets. Equally, you might think about how a communications strategy needs to reflect the stage reached on the product life-cycle.

Figure 1   The Diploma in Marketing

Given this structure, and in particular the nature of the interrelationships between the two elements of Strategic Marketing Management, this workbook has been designed to provide you with a clear insight into the marketing planning and control processes and to the ways in which these can best be applied within the business and commercial world as well as, of course, to the CIM's Diploma examination papers.

In doing this, we give considerable emphasis to the three elements that underpin all of the

CIM's syllabuses: knowing, understanding and doing. Thus, in each of the units we outline and discuss the relevant concepts so that your knowledge and understanding is increased. We then address the issue of 'doing' by means of a series of exercises and questions and, of course, through the mini case study that forms Part A of the Planning and Control examination paper and the maxi case study of the Analysis and Decision examination.

It needs to be recognized from the outset, however, that a workbook cannot explore the complexity of concepts in the same way that a textbook can. For this reason, we make reference at various stages to two books that you may well find useful. These are:

Wilson, R.M.S. and Gilligan, C.T. (1997) *Strategic Marketing Management: Planning Implementation and Control*, Butterworth-Heinemann, and Fifield, P. (1992) *Marketing Strategy*, Butterworth-Heinemann.

The first of these, *Strategic Marketing Management*, was written specifically for the CIM's Planning and Control syllabus and was first published in 1992. A second edition by Professors Dick Wilson and Colin Gilligan is due for publication in 1997 shortly after this book goes to press. The references that we make within this workbook are therefore to the first edition. *Marketing Strategy* was written for a slightly different market and is part of Butterworth-Heinemann's 'Practitioner' series. Nevertheless, students of the CIM's Diploma will undoubtedly find it a very useful book, not least because of its very direct style.

Strategic Marketing Management: Planning and Control

We commented earlier that the Planning and Control syllabus focuses upon five key issues: these are illustrated in Figure 2.

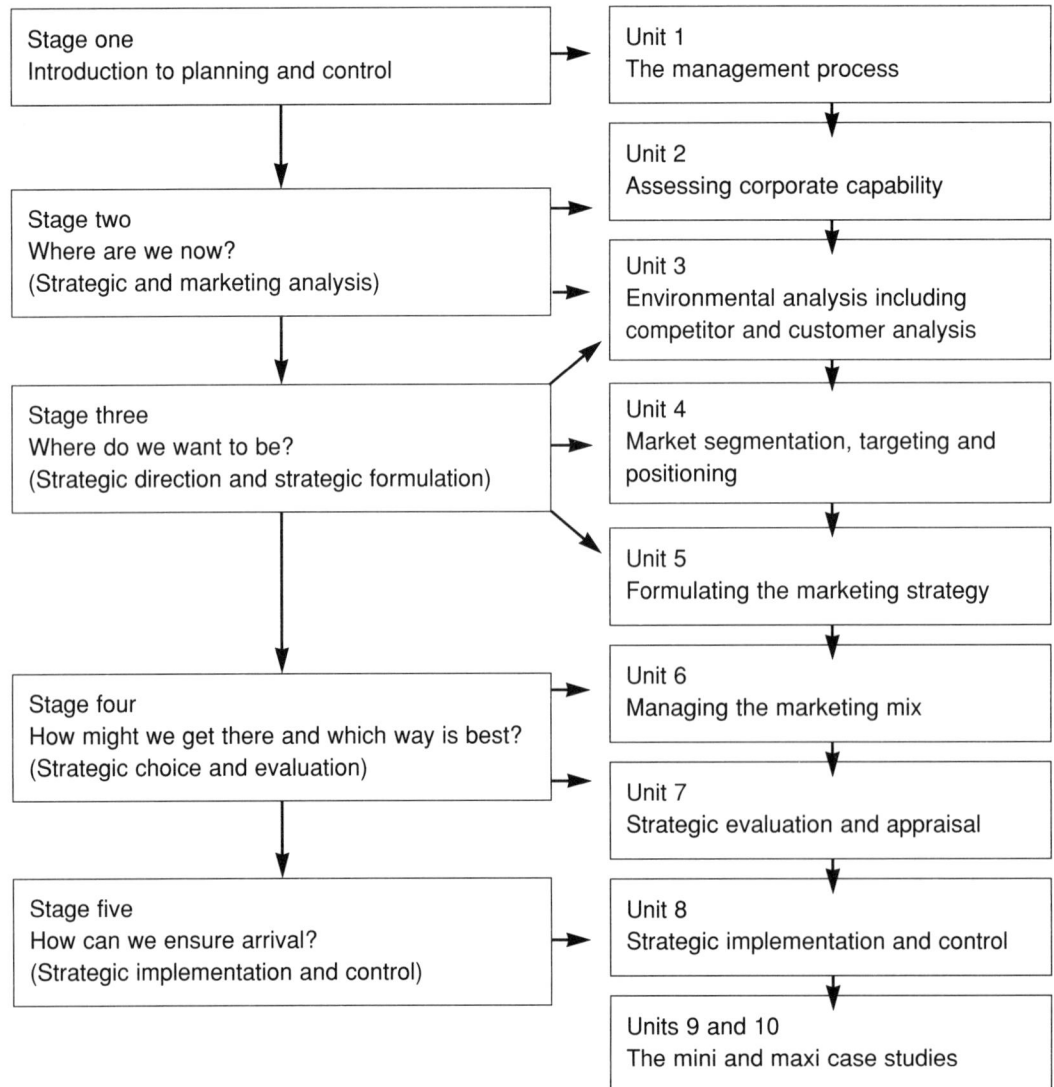

Figure 2   The Planning and Control syllabus and the structure of the book

In Unit 1 we examine a number of the dimensions of the management process and the role of marketing within this. Against this background, we then concentrate in Units 2–8 upon taking you through the most important dimensions of four major questions – Where are we now? Where do we want to be? How might we get there? and How can we ensure arrival? – as a prelude in Units 9 and 10 to an examination of the mini case study that forms the first part of the Planning and Control examination paper, and then the major case study that is the basis for the Analysis and Decision examination.

The first of the five stages of the Planning and Control syllabus is concerned with a series of background issues and, in particular, the nature of planning and the relationships that can – or should – exist between marketing management and corporate management. Unit 2 then focuses upon the various ways in which managers might identify their organization's current position and, in the light of a clear understanding of competitors and customers, assess its *true* level of marketing capability. For a variety of reasons, the assessment of capability can be seen to be one of the principal foundation stones of any strategic planning process, since it determines exactly what the organization is or should be capable of achieving. All too often, however, managers either overestimate levels of capability or fail to understand its various dimensions in sufficient detail.

Marketing capability by itself is, of course, only one part of the planning process and needs to be looked at against the background both of the organization as a whole and the nature and shape of the environment. It is for this reason that in Unit 3 we turn our attention to an analysis of the marketing environment in order to illustrate the sorts of changes that are taking place and the types of opportunities and threats that are emerging from this.

The juxtaposition of these two units is deliberate, since in recent years there has been a shift in management thinking away from the traditional idea that strategy should be environmentally-led to the view that it should be much more firmly capability-led. The two views should not, however, be viewed as bi-polar extremes, since in practice any strategy needs to reflect a clear and detailed understanding both of the environment and what the organization is capable of doing.

It is then against this background that in Unit 4 we turn to one of the other major foundation stones of any strategy, that of market segmentation, targeting and positioning. The ideas introduced within this section of the book are then developed further in Unit 5 in which we focus upon the various types of marketing strategy and how they can best be formulated. From here we go on to examine in Unit 6 the issues associated with the planning and management of the marketing mix. In Unit 7 we focus upon methods of control and appraisal and then, in Unit 8, the ways in which strategy might possibly be implemented.

Units 9 and 10 focus, in turn, upon the mini case that forms Section 1 of the Planning and Control examination and the maxi case that is the basis of the Analysis and Decision paper. The Case Study Workbook, the fourth workbook in the Diploma Series, provides further case studies for A & D candidates to explore. In both units, we have included previous cases and solutions that are designed to provide you with a clear understanding of how you should approach the answer.

Approaching the Planning and Control examination

The syllabus for Planning and Control has a number of distinct aims and objectives and is designed to ensure that students:

- Are made aware of all the major aspects of the planning and control elements of the marketing management function.
- Have an understanding of and an ability to evaluate the contribution of marketing management to corporate management.
- Examine and are familiar with all aspects of the planning process and its application to marketing.
- Are able to use the tools of analysis and decision making in the preparation of marketing plans.
- Appreciate the characteristics and planning needs of organizations in a variety of sectors so that the marketing mix can be tailored in its detail to meet the wants/needs of identified market segments and achieve specified strategic and tactical objectives.
- Have an understanding of the issues associated with the effective implementation and

control of marketing plans and how the principal barriers to implementation might possibly be overcome.

- Appreciate the need to understand the dimensions of the international environment within which marketing decisions are increasingly being made.

The learning outcomes that emerge from this mean that you should be able to:

- Understand a wide variety of marketing techniques and models.
- Apply these techniques/models to the marketing planning process in competitive and collaborative environments.
- Undertake comprehensive analyses of markets, customers and competitors.
- Conduct detailed marketing audits, both internally and externally.
- Determine marketing objectives and strategies.
- Prepare a straightforward marketing plan.
- Design appropriate marketing mixes for particular market segments.
- Initiate appraisal and control systems for marketing planning.
- Specify the marketing research needed to formulate effective marketing plans.
- Understand how the barriers to the effective implementation of marketing plans might be overcome.

After each examination the Senior Examiners write a report for the Chartered Institute in which they discuss how the students coped with the examination and highlight any particular problems that have been experienced. In looking back at the reports that I have written since taking over as the Senior Examiner for Planning and Control in 1991, there are several issues which I have referred to on almost every occasion; these, together with suggestions for the ways in which the problems might possibly be overcome are illustrated in Figure 3.

Note: Each year we are faced with several examination scripts that consist of half a page of writing and then a message to the examiner which invariably starts, 'Dear Examiner.' The message then typically goes on to say that, because of work and/or domestic pressures, the candidate has not been able to follow any sort of study programme or revise for the examination. Despite this, the candidate would be eternally grateful if the examiner could find it in his heart (author's note: never forget that we also have female examiners) to award a pass. Although examiners try to be sympathetic, you are far more likely to pass if you display real evidence of having studied the syllabus and understand the subject than if you make a plea for special treatment based on ignorance or laziness.

Approaching the Analysis and Decision examination

Unlike other Diploma subjects, the major case study paper has no formal syllabus. The examination is based on a full case study normally made up of 10–12 pages of narrative and 20–30 pages of charts, tables and appendices. The case study is sent to candidates four weeks in advance of the examination to allow time for individual and group analysis and discussion.

At the time of the examination additional information will be provided as well as three or four questions which will have to be answered in full. The examination is 'open book' which means that you will be able to take reference material with you into the examination room. You should note, however, that only material produced during the examination itself will be marked and any pre-prepared material appended to the script will be ignored by the examiner.

The major case study is designed to be a practical test of the candidate's ability to apply his or her marketing knowledge. Candidates who only reproduce theory or models which are not applied to the case situation will not gain a pass grade. Equally, the case is likely to draw from all areas of marketing and will test the candidate's ability to apply knowledge in international

What the examiners want ...	What the examiners all too often get ...	The solution
An answer to the *specific* question posed	Highly general answers that fail to tackle the specifics of the question and, instead, tell us everything that the student can vaguely remember	Read the questions and write an answer that addresses the *specific* question posed. Avoid putting down everything you know in a general and indiscriminate manner
A clear and distinct structure	Inadequate or non-existent structures and a series of generalized ramblings based on unrealistic and unsustainable assumptions	A strong and obvious structure with sub-headings and key points that have been highlighted
Answers that are written in the format that is specifically asked for, be it a report, memo, briefing paper, essay or marketing plan	Either a general essay or a series of bullet points which lack any elaboration or sense of perspective	An answer that adopts the format asked for
Examples to illustrate the points being made	A total absence of examples	Several brief, carefully chosen and appropriate examples
Reference to the appropriate literature and/or research findings	A lack of any evidence of reading or awareness of what is happening in the world of marketing	Evidence that you are aware of what has been written in the area and what is happening currently
A firm conclusion and, where asked for, an *evaluation* of the issue that is at the heart of the question	Answers that tail off or stop abruptly mid-sentence	Answers that conclude with a summary or evaluation of the key issues raised
Answers that illustrate that the candidate has a clear and detailed understanding of marketing and the marketing process	Answers that show far too little understanding of the subject	Read, practice on past papers, and THINK

Figure 3   The examinations and the scripts that we receive

as well as domestic marketing strategy. Many aspects of the entire Certificate, Advanced Certificate and Diploma syllabus may be applicable and if you have been exempted from parts of the course you should familiarize yourself with the detailed course requirements.

The rationale for the paper is:

> To extend the practice of candidates in the quantitative and qualitative analysis of marketing situations, both to develop their powers of diagnosis and to create a firm basis in decision making.

> (Tutors' guidance notes CIM)

Tackling the major case

Questions applied in the case study do not have a standardized format; they may vary in number and may emphasize different points, but will always be directed towards strategy rather than tactics. Time management in the exam is crucial. Candidates are required to answer all the questions posed and in accordance with the mark allocation stated on the paper. In every case, the candidates have a role to play and they are expected to be able to relate their answer to this role.

There are two basic questions posed in any case, and your preparation should therefore reflect this guide:

1   What is wrong?
2   What are you going to do to put it right?

The second question is critical but cannot be answered without the first. Problem identification will certainly require the application of statistical and financial analytical techniques, an organizational and behavioural understanding and marketing knowledge. Having read your answer, the examiners must know:

- What these problems are.
- What alternative solutions have been considered.
- What solution has been chosen.
- Why it has been chosen.
- How it will be implemented.

The lack of imagination by the majority of candidates in this examination is a major weakness. Marketing is creative. It is one of the means by which companies distinguish themselves and their products/services from competition. On the rare occasions that examiners are offered a creative or different approach, marks tend to soar.

Marketing is about customers first, products second. Few candidates take a truly customer-led approach to the case study. When they do, marks tend to rise dramatically.

The rules to successful case study examinations are:

- Think customer.
- Think creative.
- Think practical.
- Think application, not theory.
- Think in the role given in the case.

One of the most common examination mistakes that candidates make is to ignore the specific question posed. Always identify as clearly as possible *precisely* what the examiner is asking for and never let yourself fall into the trap of giving a general 'let me tell you everything I know or can think of' sort of answer in the hope that the person marking the paper will put it into a more structured context; they will not.

Summary

Within this introduction we have discussed the structure and purpose of the Strategic Marketing Management syllabus and made reference to the sorts of interrelationships that exist with the other papers at Diploma level. As a check on your understanding of this, consider the following questions:

- What is the structure of the Planning and Control syllabus and what is the syllabus designed to achieve?
- In what ways does the Planning and Control syllabus provide a feed-in to the Analysis and Decision examination?

Introduction to planning and control: the management process

This first part of the syllabus has been designed to help you understand the managerial context within which marketing takes place. Having worked your way through this unit, you will understand:

- The relationships between marketing planning and corporate planning.
- The basis of planning and control, the cycle of control and the nature and role of strategic, tactical and contingency planning.
- The nature of management and marketing information systems and the contribution that market research is capable of making to each stage of the planning process.
- The implications for planning and control of organizational structures and managerial cultures.

It is essential that you do not look at marketing in isolation, but that you recognize instead the sorts of interrelationships that exist between marketing planning and corporate planning. In particular, you should be aware of the sorts of constraints within which many marketing decisions are made. Although this part of the syllabus accounts for only 10 per cent of the total, it is an important underpinning for what follows, since it should help you to develop a breadth of perspective. To help with this, you should read the business press, looking for examples of how marketing decisions are influenced not just by what is happening in the environment, but also by decisions that have been taken in the past, the availability of resources, the culture of the organization, and so on. You should also talk to senior managers within your organization to gain a greater understanding of the sorts of issues that influence the marketing decisions that are taken.

In total, the unit should take you about 6 hours to complete. Suggestions for further reading appear at the end of the unit.

Although you will undoubtedly be familiar with a variety of definitions of marketing, we begin this unit by highlighting several key issues in their development.

Definitions of marketing

Definitions of marketing tend to fall into one of three distinct categories:

1 Those that focus on marketing's functional elements and activities.
2 Those concerned with marketing as a process.
3 Those that reflect the view that marketing is essentially a philosophy of how to do business.

For the most part, the functional definitions of marketing are now seen to be of little real value and so we will concentrate here upon the other two categories. In the case of process definitions, for example, it has been suggested that:

> Marketing is the process by which an organization relates creatively, productivity and profitability to the marketplace

and that:

> Marketing is a social and managerial process by which individuals and groups obtain what they need and want through creating, offering and exchanging products of value with others.

This process approach is also reflected in the definitions that have been put forward by The Chartered Institute of Marketing (CIM) and the American Marketing Association (AMA):

> Marketing is the management process for identifying, anticipating and satisfying customers profitably. (CIM)

> Marketing (management) is the process of planning and executing the conception, pricing, promotion and distribution of ideas, goods and services to create exchanges that satisfy individual and organizational objectives. (AMA)

These process views have been taken several steps further in recent years with the greater recognition that has been given to the role that *all* parts of the organization need to play in creating and maintaining high levels of customer satisfaction. The result has been a series of definitions which view marketing rather more as a *philosophy* of doing business, something which is reflected in the words of Peter Drucker in 1973:

> Marketing is so basic that it cannot be considered as a separate function on a par with others such as manufacturing or personnel. It is first a central dimension of the entire business. It is the whole business seen from the point of view of its final result, that is from the customers' point of view.

Although Drucker's definition is undoubtedly useful, since it highlights both the pivotal role of marketing within the organization and the need for managers to look at how they are operating from the customers' point of view (an outside-in approach), a series of other dimensions are typically now incorporated within any meaningful definition of the area. Perhaps the most significant of the changes that we have seen has been the far greater and more explicit recognition that is now given to the issue of *competitive position* (that is, that success comes not just from identifying customers' needs and wants, but from satisfying them more firmly than competitors) and to the broader *social role and responsibility of marketing*.

The first of these two additional dimensions is reflected in Kotler's suggestion (1991, page 16) that:

> The marketing concept hold that the key to achieving organizational goals consists in determining the needs and wants of target markets and delivering the desired satisfactions more effectively and efficiently than competitors.

The second dimension – the issue of marketing's social responsibility – is then developed in what has been labelled the *societal marketing concept.*

The question of whether marketing managers should take account of the broader social implications of their decisions has been the subject of considerable debate, with advocates of the Chicago School of Economics such as Milton Friedman arguing that the primary – and sole – responsibility of business is to maximize the return to the organization's stakeholders. However, others argue that business has a distinct responsibility to the community and that decisions taken should therefore take full account of the consequences for society of their outcome. In developing this line of argument, Kotler (1991, page 25) has suggested that:

> In recent years, some people have questioned whether the marketing concept is an appropriate organizational philosophy in an age of environmental deterioration, resource shortages, explosive population growth, world hunger and poverty, and neglected social services. The question is whether companies that do an excellent job of sensing, serving, and satisfying individual consumer wants are necessarily acting in the best long-run interests of consumers and society. The marketing concept sidesteps the potential conflicts between *consumer wants, consumer interests,* and *long-run societal welfare.*

Because of this, he argues for the adoption of the societal marketing concept which:

> holds that the organization's task is to determine the needs, wants, and interests of target markets and to deliver the desired satisfactions more effectively and efficiently than competitors in a way that preserves or enhances the consumer's and the society's well-being.

Given the nature of these comments, there are two simple matrices that help to provide an insight to an organization. The first of these (see Figure 1.1) focuses upon the management team's orientation towards customers and competitors and illustrates how this orientation can range from a myopic and firmly inwardly-focused approach through to one that is truly market-driven with full account being taken both of competitors and customers.

The degree of competitor focus

	Low	High
The degree of customer focus — **Low**	Myopic and inwardly focused	Transfixed by one or more competitors
The degree of customer focus — **High**	Preoccupied by one or more customer groups	Market-driven

Figure 1.1   The management team's customer and competitor orientations

Taking an organization with which you are familiar, where in Figure 1.1 would you position the predominant managerial orientation? What sorts of factors contribute to this positioning? What are the implications of this for how the organization interacts with the marketplace?

The second matrix that helps to provide an insight to an organization focuses upon the legality of the marketing activity and the sorts of ethics and degree of social responsibility that is reflected in the management team's decisions; this is illustrated in Figure 1.2.

	Illegal	Legal
Unethical	**Cell 1** Illegal and unethical	**Cell 3** Legal but unethical
Ethical	**Cell 2** Illegal but ethical	**Cell 4** Legal and ethical

Figure 1.2 The legal and ethical dimensions of marketing activity

Although Cell 4, in which decisions are both legal and ethical, is quite obviously the position which managers should aim for, competitive and other pressures may well force managers into other parts of the matrix.

ACTIVITY 1.2

Identify examples of products and/or services that fall into Cells 1, 2 or 3 of Figure 1.2. In what circumstances might a marketing decision be legal but unethical? Given the publicity that has been given to the apparent link between smoking and respiratory diseases, is the marketing of cigarettes ethical or unethical? Equally, is the sale of arms to a country with a civil war ethical or unethical? In what circumstances, if any, might you justify marketing an illegal product?

The relationship between marketing planning and corporate planning

It should be apparent from our comments on the ways in which definitions of marketing are changing, and in particular the emergence and acceptance of the societal marketing concept, that marketing decisions are not – or should not – be made in isolation, but with a full understanding of their consequences for a number of different stakeholder groups. At the same time, of course, marketing decisions need both to reflect and influence an organization's corporate decisions. So what then should be the relationship between marketing planning and corporate planning?

In answering this, we need to begin by clarifying what is meant by strategy and strategic decisions. In discussing this, Wilson et al (1992, pages 15–16) suggest that strategic decisions:

- Are concerned with the scope of an organization's activities, and hence with the definition of an organization's boundaries.
- Relate to the matching of the organization's activities with the opportunities of its substantive environment. Since the environment is continually changing it is necessary for this to be accommodated via adaptive decision making that anticipates outcomes – as in playing a game of chess.
- Require the matching of an organization's activities with its resources. In order to take advantage of strategic opportunities it will be necessary to have funds, capacity, and personnel available when required.

- Have major resource implications for organizations – such as acquiring additional capacity, disposing of capacity, or reallocating resources in a fundamental way.
- Are influenced by the values and expectations of those who determine the organization's strategy. Any repositioning of organizational boundaries will be influenced by managerial preferences and conceptions as much as by environmental possibilities.
- Will affect the organization's long-term direction.
- Are complex in nature since they tend to be non-routine and involve a large number of variables. As a result their implications will typically extend throughout the organization.

The relationship between an organization's marketing and corporate management has also been discussed by Greenley (1986, page 56) who has drawn a number of distinctions between marketing planning and strategic planning.

Marketing planning	Strategic planning
• Is concerned essentially with day-to-day performance and outcomes.	• Is concerned with the organization's long-term and overall direction.
• Represents just one stage in the organization's development.	• Provides the long-term framework for thinking and investment.
• Reflects a functional/professional orientation.	• Is concerned with the overall orientation that is needed to match the organization to its environment.
• The goals are sub-divided into specific targets.	• The goals and strategies need to be evaluated from an overall perspective.
• The relevance of the goals and strategies is immediately apparent.	• The relevance of the goals and strategies is often apparent only in the long term.

The Diploma syllabuses and examinations are concerned to a large extent with strategic issues. Far too many candidates confuse strategy and tactics and, as a result, lose marks. Make sure that you understand the difference between the two and that this is reflected in your answers. (To help in your understanding of strategy and tactics, refer to definitions 1.2 and 1.3.)

The position of marketing within an organization, and the extent to which a marketing culture should predominate, has been the subject of considerable discussion over the years. Marketing staff typically argue that because the marketing function is the most obvious and direct point of contact with the market, it follows that marketing decisions should be the starting point for all other organizational decisions; this is illustrated in Figure 1.3.

The three levels of strategy
Strategic decisions are taken at three levels within an organization:

1 The corporate level.
2 The business unit or divisional level.
3 The functional level.

Corporate management
Lean head office staff
A long-term perspective and a strong sense of vision
An emphasis upon proactivity and the development of long-term relationships with suppliers,
distributors and customers
A culture of excellence
Clear (and appropriate) core values
Leadership rather than management
Well developed internal and external communication patterns
A recognition that creativity is the only remaining competitive edge

Marketing	Design and Engineering	Purchasing	Production	Sales	Customers
A proactive competitive stance and an emphasis upon innovation and creativity	Rapid and constant product improvement	Zero or minimal inventory levels	Just in time and lean manufacturing	The development of long-term relationships with distributors and customers	Fast and regular customer feedback marketing in order to close the loop
An emphasis upon creating and maintaining high levels of customer satisfaction by adding value and 'delighting' the customer	Benchmarking inside and outside the industry	A policy of not compromising on quality	Zero defects and a culture of right first time, every time	Aggressive value for money offers	
A fundamental recognition of the need to build relationships with customers, suppliers, distributors and the media	Working with customers	An emphasis upon developing long-term relationships with a small number or high-quality suppliers	Zero set-up time	Low financing charges	
Innovative segmentation, targeting and positioning	Lateral thinking in the search for new ideas		A constant search for product, process and quality improvements	Customization offered where possible	
A search for new markets and opportunities			Customization offered where possible	A recognition of the need for effective customer process management	
Detailed competitor and customer analysis, with the results being fed into the strategy development process			Benchmarking inside and outside the industry	Working with customers to identify new needs and opportunities and how they might be met	
Distinctive advertising and promotional appeals			An emphasis upon best practice		
A well formulated pricing strategy and clear value for money offer					
Constant environmental analysis and interpretation					

Figure 1.3   Marketing and its contribution to effective management

It follows from this that:

Marketing strategy (is) a process of strategically analysing environmental, competitive and business factors affecting business units and forecasting future trends in business areas of interest to the enterprise. Participating in setting business objectives and formulating corporate and business unit strategy. Selecting target market strategies for; the product-markets in each business unit, establishing marketing objectives, and developing, implementing and managing program positioning strategies for meeting target market needs.

Cravens

Strategic marketing management is the analytical process of seeking differential advantage through (1) the analysis and choice of the firm's product – market relationships with a view toward developing the best yield configuration in terms of financial performance; and (2) the formulation of management strategies that create and support viable product-market relationships consistent with the enterprise capabilities and objectives.

Kerrin and Peterson

Marketing strategy reflects the company's best opinion as to how it can most profitably apply its skills and resources in the marketplace. It is inevitably broad in scope. The plan which stems from it will spell out action and timings and will contain the detailed contribution expected from each department.

Marketing strategies are the means by which marketing objectives will be achieved and are generally concerned with four major elements of the marketing mix, as follows: Product, Price, Place, Promotion.

Formulating marketing strategies is one of the most critical and difficult parts of the entire marketing process. It sets the limit of success. Communicated to all management levels, it indicates what strengths are to be developed, what weaknesses are to be remedied, and in what manner. Marketing strategies enable operating decisions to bring the company the right relationship with the emerging pattern of marketing opportunities which previous analysis has shown to offer the highest prospect of success.

McDonald

The relationship between corporate planning and marketing planning is perhaps most easily understood if you think about them in terms of a hierarchy, with corporate planning and strategy at the top and marketing planning and strategy below this. Marketing decisions are not therefore taken in a vacuum but against the background of a series of guidelines and priorities that are determined by corporate management; this is illustrated in Figure 1.4.

Figure 1.4 The corporate planning and marketing planning hierarchy

The words 'objective', 'strategies' and 'tactics' are often used in a seemingly indiscriminate way. Before we go any further, we need to clarify what the terms really mean:

Objectives represents a statement of what the organization is trying to achieve. The guidelines for setting worthwhile objectives are straightforward and highlight the need for them to be quantifiable, mutually consistent, realistic and related to a specific timescale.

The *strategy* is then the broad statement of the way in which the organization sets out to achieve these objectives. Included within this would be a series of decisions on the markets in which the organization will operate, the type of products/services it will offer and the basis of the competitive stance.

The *tactics* follow on from this and represent the detailed and day-to-day dimensions of the strategic plan.

Influences upon strategy

In developing a strategy, irrespective of whether it is the corporate strategy or a marketing strategy, managers need to take account of a variety of factors, including:

- What is happening in the organization's external environment and how the environment is likely to develop both in the short and the long term.
- What the organization is *really* capable of achieving.
- The expectations of the organization's various stakeholders.

Because the first two points are discussed in some detail in subsequent units (Units 2 and 3 respectively), we will limit ourselves at this stage to a series of comments on the significance of the various stakeholders and how their expectations need to be taken into account and reflected in the marketing planning process.

Stakeholders are groups or individuals who have a stake in, or an expectation of, the organization's performance. They include employees, managers, shareholders, suppliers, customers and the community at large. (Johnson and Scholes, 1993, pages 156–157.)

The extent to which a stakeholder's expectations need to be taken into account in the marketing planning process depends in part on the planner's understanding of these expectations and his or her perception of the stakeholder's importance. Figure 1.5 illustrates an outline stakeholder map.

ACTIVITY 1.3

Using Figure 1.5 as your initial framework, draw a stakeholder diagram for an organization with which you are familiar. In doing this, list the principal expectations of each stakeholder as you perceive them. What scope for conflict exists between these expectations? How, if at all, does the organization currently attempt to manage these conflicts?

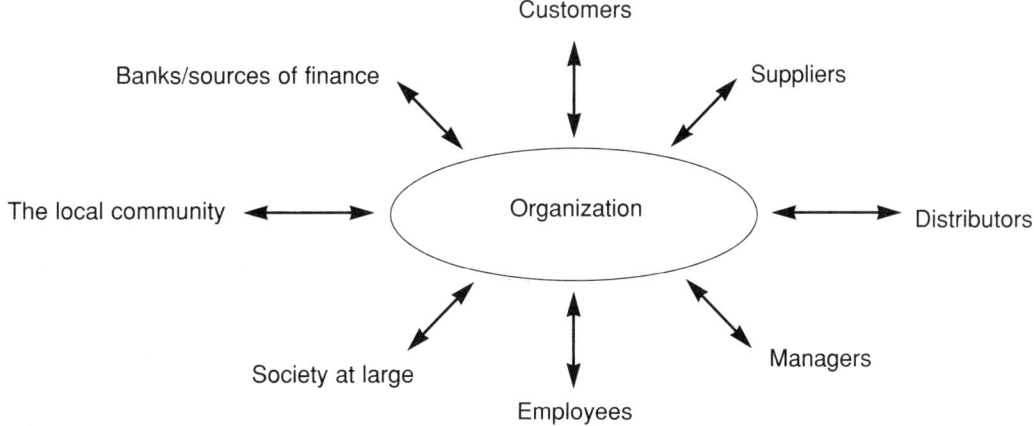

Figure 1.5 A stakeholder map

The difficulties of adopting a strategic perspective

Although the arguments for a long-term and strategic approach to marketing have an inherent logic, the reality is that in many organizations managers focus either very largely or exclusively upon the short term. There are several possible explanations for this, including the way in which relatively few managers are taught to think or act strategically and are instead measured very largely on the basis of short-term performance. Given this, there is an understandable temptation for managers to focus upon short-term and tactical issues rather than the longer-term strategic management of the marketing function. This temptation then tends to increase dramatically during periods of economic recession and when levels of competitive activity are particularly intense, and is reflected in an emphasis upon issues of *efficiency* rather than *effectiveness*.

Efficiency is concerned with how well an activity is performed, whilst *effectiveness* is concerned rather more with the appropriateness of the action. (See Figure 1.6.)

		Strategic Management	
		Ineffective	Effective
Operational Management	Inefficient	Decline quickly or die	Survive
	Efficient	Decline slowly or die	Prosper

Adapted from Christopher et al (1987, page 80)

Figure 1.6 Issues of efficiency and effectiveness

Making reference to the matrix in Figure 1.6, look at an organization with which you are familiar and plot its position. Having done this, think about the reasons for the organization being in this particular cell and, given the likely demands of the organization's marketing environment over the next few years, identify the probable consequences.

The relationship between marketing planning and corporate planning has been the focus of several examination questions over the past few years and the answers have tended to highlight the degree of confusion that exists in the minds of many students. Consider therefore the two questions below:

(i)   Evaluate the contention that marketing strategy and corporate strategy are one and the same activity (Marketing Planning and Control, December 1991, Question 4).

(ii)   The arguments in favour of a strategic perspective to marketing have been well rehearsed, although research suggests that many managers still find the adoption of a strategic perspective to be difficult. Making reference to examples in either the private or the public sectors, comment upon the problems of developing a strategic approach to marketing and how these problems might possibly be overcome (Marketing Planning and Control, June 1991, Question 3).

The role of contingency and scenario planning

Given the nature of our comments so far, it should be apparent that *strategic plans* are concerned essentially with the long term and involve a series of interrelated decisions relating to the nature of the product or service that is to be sold, the market(s) in which the organization intends operating, and the competitive stance that is to be adopted. The *tactical plans* should emerge logically from the strategic plan and relate to how the organization operates on a day-to-day basis and how it responds to short-term environmental changes and pressures. However, almost regardless of how much environmental and corporate analysis underpins the strategic and tactical plans, conditions can change – sometimes dramatically – and demand a very different sort of response from the organization. Because of this, many organizations incorporate a contingency or scenario element into the planning process so that the dangers of responding in what is almost a knee-jerk fashion to the largely unexpected are reduced. The way in which this would be manifested is that, as part of the initial planning process, managers would think not just about the sort of environmental conditions that seem most likely to prevail, but also what else might happen and how the organization might respond. Scenario planning is the more extreme of the two approaches and based on the idea of 'what if . . . ?' thinking. Examples of this would be what if . . .

- Energy prices rose by 30 per cent?
- There was a sudden change of government?
- Political factors led to the sudden closure of a major market?
- A major new competitor entered the market with a highly aggressive price-based strategy (an example of this would be the entry into various retail markets of the so-called 'category busters' who operate on a huge scale and who, by virtue of their enormous buying power and economies of scale, make the survival of all but the most efficient – and effective – competitors unlikely).

Scenario planning is therefore based very deliberately on the idea of thinking about the sorts of unexpected, sudden and dramatic changes which would demand a major response and possibly a significant change of direction on the part of the organization. The rationale for scenario planning is straightforward and based on the idea that by thinking about the unexpected, deciding what alternatives are open to the organization and then having a plan ready, the likelihood of being stampeded into what might subsequently prove to be an ill-thought out response is reduced dramatically.

Contingency planning is somewhat less extreme than this and is designed for events that may possibly happen but which, on balance, the marketing planner feels probably will not occur. An example of this would be the entry to the domestic market of an organization that is currently operating in a series of international markets and which so far has shown no interest in further expansion. Other examples might be the sudden adoption of a price-based strategy by a competitor or the development by a competitor of a new approach to distribution. Although, as we comment above, the planner believes that these sorts of changes are unlikely, they remain a possibility and so a plan – possibly outline in nature – is developed in order to help cope with the situation if it should arise.

ACTIVITY 1.5

What contingency and/or scenario planning takes place within your own organization? What assumptions are these plans based on? What additional scenarios and contingencies might be incorporated within the process?

In the light of your findings, attempt the following question:

QUESTION 1.2

Explain what is meant by strategic, tactical, scenario and contingency planning.

The planning and control cycle

> To be effective, a strategic planning system must be goal driven. The setting of objectives is therefore a key step in the marketing planning process, since unless it is carried out effectively, everything that follows will lack focus and cohesion. (Wilson et al, 1992, page 137)

Using this quotation as the foundation, we can see that planning is designed to achieve several specific purposes, including:

- It helps to co-ordinate resources and direct them towards the achievement of goals.
- It encourages or forces managers to think about the future and in this way should reduce the likelihood of the organization being taken by surprise by previously unexpected events.
- It provides managers with a sense of direction.
- It provides a subsequent basis for control.

Although planning can never guarantee success, the planning process – which involves looking in detail both at the environment and the organization's capability, as well as managerial and organizational expectations – should increase the chances of success, since it not only requires managers to identify their goals more explicitly, but also to identify and evaluate the courses of action that might lead to these goals being achieved.

Planning can therefore be seen to involve a series of decisions concerning:

- What are we trying to achieve?
- How might we achieve these objectives?
- Which strategy is the most appropriate?
- Who is to be responsible for it?
- Over what period of time and how is it to be implemented?

An important dimension of the planning process is the element of control. Having decided upon a set of objectives and how these might be achieved, the marketing planner needs to establish a series of control measures to ensure that the execution of the plan does not deviate from what was intended. These controls can be incorporated at various stages within the planning cycle, but are most obviously visible in terms of whether the goals that were set initially are ultimately achieved. However, for many organizations, and particularly those faced with an uncertain environment, this is too late a stage in the process and so a series of intermediate measures would typically be incorporated within the plan. This process of feedback is designed to provide managers with a regular update on performance and to highlight not just the extent to which the organization's performance is deviating from what was intended, but also – and very importantly – why. Given this information, managers can then decide whether corrective action is needed and, if so, what should be done; this is illustrated in Figure 1.7.

ACTIVITY 1.6

If you were to draw the planning and control cycle for your own organization, in what ways would it differ from the cycle in Figure 1.7?

Is planning worthwhile?

Although the idea of planning has an apparent inherent logic, the value of planning as it has typically been conducted has been questioned in recent years. There are several reasons for this, the most obvious of which stems from the problems and difficulties of planning in ever more uncertain and volatile environments. However, in raising this question about the value of planning, we are not arguing for planning to be dispensed with completely, but rather that the traditional model of planning that appears in Figure 1.7 (this is sometimes referred to as the logical, sequential, rational approach) be replaced with a more flexible and open approach. Amongst those to have questioned the traditional planning processes are Stacey and Arthur. In their book *Managing Chaos* (1993), they suggest that anything useful about the long-term future is essentially unknowable and that because of this regular strategic planning meetings serve a ritual rather than a functional purpose. Effective strategies are derived therefore not from traditional approaches to planning, but from the politicking and informal lobbying that is a characteristic of organizational dynamics.

ACTIVITY 1.7

What approach to marketing planning predominates within your own organization? What do you see to be its strong and its weak points? In what ways do you feel it might be improved?

Recognition of the problems associated with traditional approaches to planning has also led to what is referred to as *freewheeling opportunism* in which opportunities are evaluated not within the formal structure of an overall corporate strategy, but are instead evaluated as they emerge and then either dropped or exploited. The benefits of this approach include:

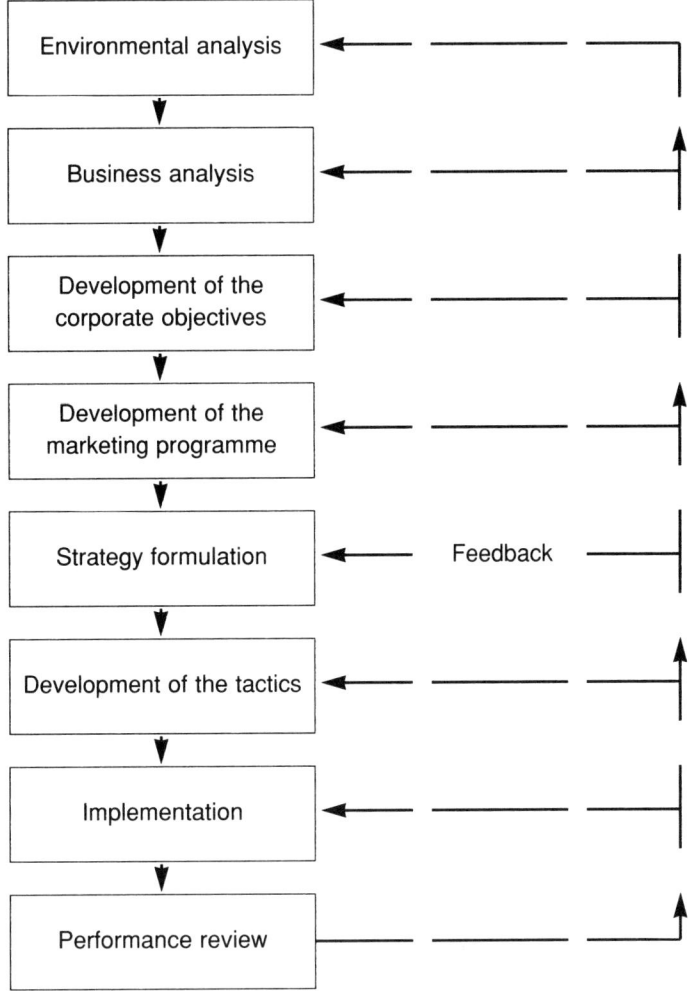

Figure 1.7 The planning and control cycle

- Opportunities are less likely to be lost as the result of the traditional planning framework.
- It is characterized by a higher degree of flexibility.
- It should lead to a higher degree of creativity amongst managers.

The obstacles to effective planning

The majority of organizations experience problems both in developing and implementing marketing plans. The most obvious causes of these problems include:

- A poor and unfocused environmental analysis that leads to the development of a plan that is based on faulty assumptions of the sort of environment the organization will face.
- An overestimation of the organization's marketing capability.
- Over-ambitious and possibly unattainable marketing objectives.
- Unrealistic timescales.
- Too much or too little detail.
- A set of objectives that are mutually inconsistent.
- An underestimation of the costs involved.
- A failure to recognize the implications of the plan for other parts of the organization and/or for distributors.
- A failure to think through in sufficient detail the issues associated with the plan's implementation.
- An 'ivory tower' syndrome in which the plan is developed by senior marketing management without making use of the knowledge and expertise of others in the marketing department. The result of this is not only that the plan fails to exploit the

full spectrum of skills available, but also that others feel no real sense of ownership of or commitment to the plan.

- A failure to take sufficient note of feedback and a lack of willingness to review and modify the plan.

Management information systems and marketing information systems

An effective marketing programme is inevitably based on a clear and detailed understanding of the market. Management and marketing information systems are therefore designed to provide this information and are a fundamental part of the 'Where are we now?' element of the planning and control process.

In developing an information system, managers must begin with a view of what information is available currently, what information gaps exist, and what additional information would be of value. It is then against this background that a worthwhile marketing information system can be developed.

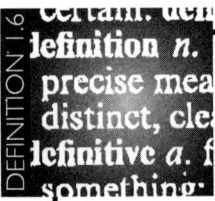

DEFINITION 1.6

definition *n.* **precise mea** **distinct, cle** **lefinitive** *a.* f **something·**

Kotler (1991, page 96) defines a marketing information system as a system which 'consists of people, equipment and procedures to gather, sort, analyse, evaluate, and distribute needed, timely, and accurate information to marketing decision makers.'

The structure of the marketing information system

In developing a marketing information system (MkIS), McDonald suggests that managers need to go through four stages:

1 Identify all the data and information that are produced currently.
2 Get managers to list the decisions they have to make, together with the information that is essential to the making of these decisions.
3 Combine these two in the most logical manner, since it is likely that there will be information gaps, information duplication and information redundancies.
4 Begin organizing a focused and cost-effective system.

One of the most common problems in developing information systems is that they simply become too complex with the result that the information that is generated is not produced in the form that is really needed or is not passed to the people who need it most. Recognizing this, any information system needs to be evaluated on a regular basis to ensure that it is achieving the results that were hoped.

So what sorts of information do marketing managers need?

Although there is perhaps an understandable temptation to respond to the question by saying 'as much as possible', the reality is that managers face the very real problem of information overload. In developing an information system, considerable thought should therefore be given to the ways any information will be used. In discussing this, Brownlie (1987, pages 100–105) has highlighted the problems that are often associated with information collection and the development of a worthwhile database. All too often, he suggests, the information that organizations collect is:

- Poorly structured.
- Available only on an irregular basis.
- Often provided by unofficial and unreliable sources.
- Qualitative in nature.
- Ambiguous in its definitions.
- Opinion based.
- Poorly qualified.
- Based on an insecure methodology.
- Likely to change.

Because of these and other problems, managers need to think in detail about their true information needs and then develop the MkIS around these. In making this comment, we are not arguing that any information that falls outside these parameters should be ignored, but that if the information that is collected on a regular basis is of the type and in the form that managers feel they need, the likelihood of it being used – and used effectively – are increased.

Aguilar (1967) has suggested that managers' information needs can generally be classified under five headings:

1 *Market tidings* market potential, structural changes, competitor and industry changes, pricing, sales negotiations and customer information.
2 *Acquisition leads* mergers, joint ventures, and acquisitions.
3 *Technical tidings* new products, new processes and technology, product problems, costs, licensing and patents.
4 *Broad issues* general conditions, and government actions and policies.
5 *Other tidings* suppliers and raw materials, resource availability, and miscellaneous information.

Looking at your own organization, what market information is collected currently? How is this information used? Do you feel that it is used as effectively as it might be? What other types of information would be useful?

ACTIVITY 1.9

Developing the information system

It can be seen from Figure 1.8 that a marketing information system has four principal components:

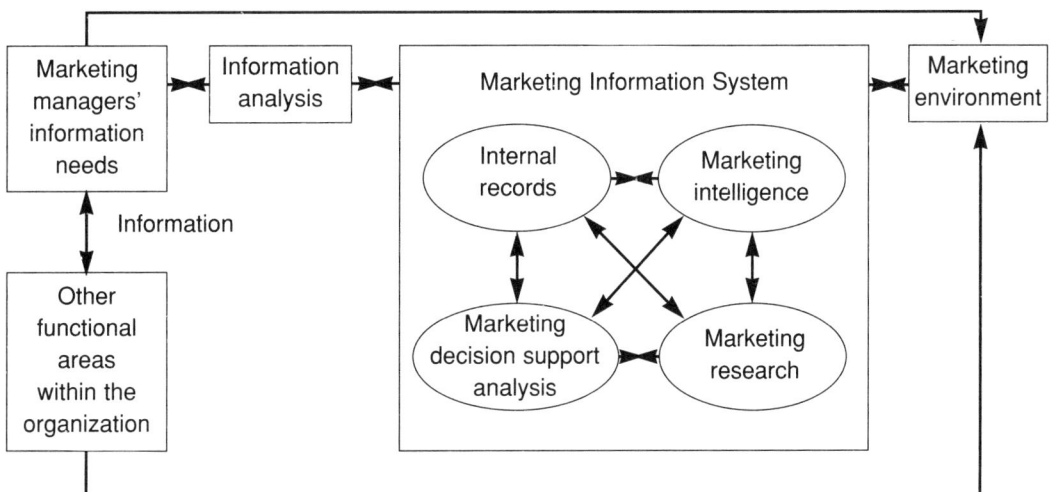

Figure 1.8 The marketing information system

15

1   *The internal records system*   which includes information on orders received, prices, inventory levels, sales patterns, and so on.

2   *The marketing intelligence system*   which provides regular information on relevant developments in the marketing environment so that managers can monitor trends and more easily identify any unexpected changes.

3   *The marketing research system*   which is concerned with the systematic collection and analysis of information that is relevant to specific marketing situations faced by the organization.

4   *The marketing decision support system*   which Kotler defines as 'a set of statistical tools and decision models with supporting hardware and software available to marketing managers to assist them in analysing data and making better marketing decisions.' (Kotler, 1991, page 114).

As part of the *marketing intelligence* and *marketing research systems* (points 2 and 3 above), managers will almost invariably need to make use of external as well as internal databases. A database is made up of files of information and data that are structured so that the user can gain access in a variety of different ways, depending upon his or her information needs. In recent years the number of commercial databases has increased enormously to the point at which virtually all product market sectors are now covered.

ACTIVITY 1.10

Go to your local business library and ask about the various databases that are available. In what ways might these databases currently supplement those used by your organization?

The characteristics of good information systems

The test of any information system must be the extent to which it contributes to the decision making process and helps managers to make better, faster and more informed decisions. The information that it contains must therefore be updated regularly, be easily accessible and in a form that managers find user-friendly. It is for this reason that we suggested earlier that in developing an information system the starting point must be a clear and detailed understanding of managers' information needs. Without this it is likely that the system will prove to be both unfocused and unwieldy. The essential ground rules that the designer of an information system needs to work with can therefore be summarized as:

- What do we need to know?
- How will the information be used?
- By whom?
- What is the preferred format?

QUESTION 1.3

Since taking over as the Senior Examiner of the Planning and Control examination in 1991, I have posed several questions on information systems and their various components. These include:

(i)   What contribution might a well-structured Marketing Information System make to the development, implementation and control of a marketing plan?

(June 1995, Question 9)

(ii)   It has been suggested that the sales force is a potentially valuable but frequently under-utilized source of marketing information. Given this, explain how a sales force might be used as a structured source of information. What types of information might they be expected to generate?

(December 1993, Question 3)

Marketing information systems were also the focus of the first of the two questions on the mini case study in the June 1994 examination; this case study (Watergate Pumps Ltd), the question and an outline answer appear in Unit 9.

The role and contribution of marketing research to effective planning

Returning for a moment to Figure 1.8 it can be seen that an important element of an MkIS is the marketing research system. This is designed to provide information on specific aspects of the marketing process and as such can be seen to include:

- *Product research*   the identification of product opportunities; customers' perceptions of existing and proposed products; comparative perceptions of competing products; positioning studies; test marketing; and packaging studies.
- *Pricing research*   perceptions of price and quality; cost analysis; price and demand elasticities; and credit related issues.
- *Promotional research*   the effectiveness of the various elements of the promotions mix; image studies; copy and media issues; sales effects; salesforce studies; and comparative studies of competitors' promotional techniques.
- *Distribution research*   distributors' perceptions, attitudes and needs; and distribution alternatives.
- *Market studies*   short- and long- term market forecasts.
- *Corporate research*   consumers', competitors' and distributors' perceptions of the organization overall and others in the market.

The market research process

Market research studies can be conducted either by an organization's own specialist staff or by an outside agency. However, irrespective of which approach is used, the market research process is broadly the same; this is illustrated in Figure 1.9.

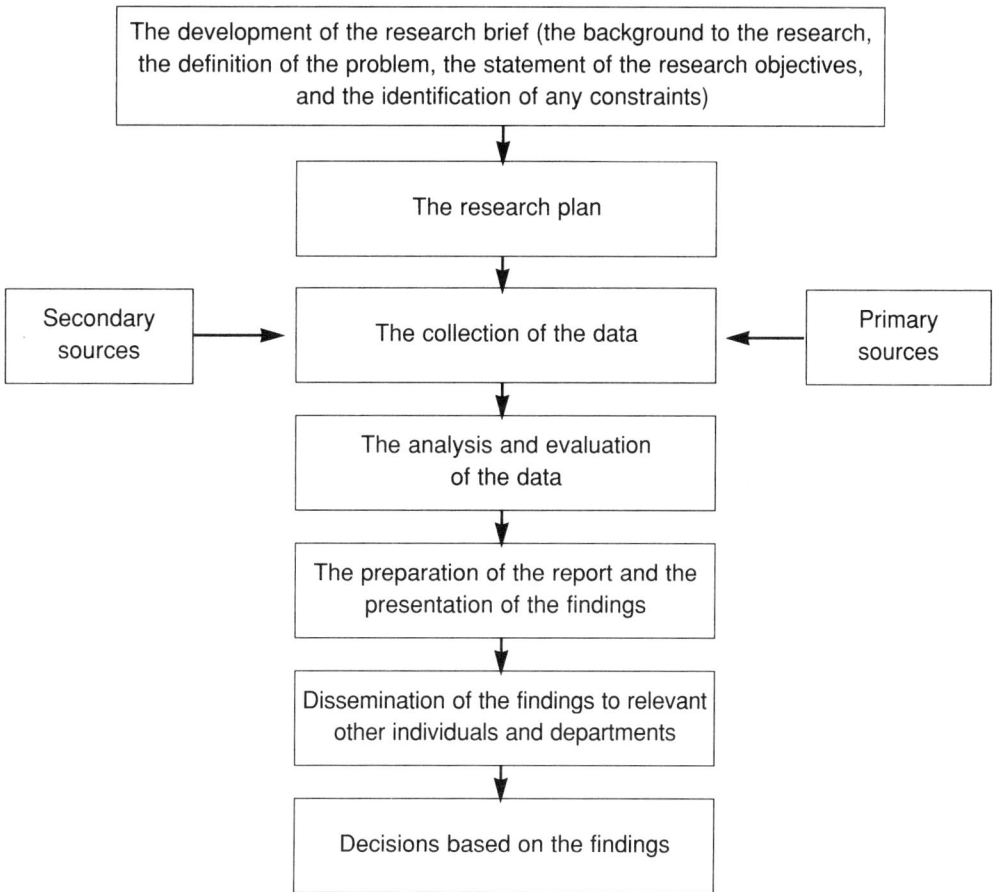

Figure 1.9   The marketing research process

In what ways might market research contribute to the effective development and management of the marketing process?

The use of secondary data

Because secondary data is generally so widely available and often relatively inexpensive, it is the obvious starting point in any data collection exercise. Although there are numerous sources of secondary information, we can identify the principal ones as being:

- Government publications
- Trade associations
- Professional and specialist journals
- Market research agencies
- Commercial publications (e.g. the Mintel and Euromonitor reports)
- Directories and yearbooks
- The national press
- Specialist libraries

There is, of course, often a trade-off involved when using secondary information in that, whilst it is generally available at a low cost, it may not be as up to date or indeed as detailed or as focused as you would like. It is because of this that secondary data often needs to be supported by more specific and focused primary data.

The use of primary data

Primary data can be collected in three main ways; these are illustrated in Figure 1.10.

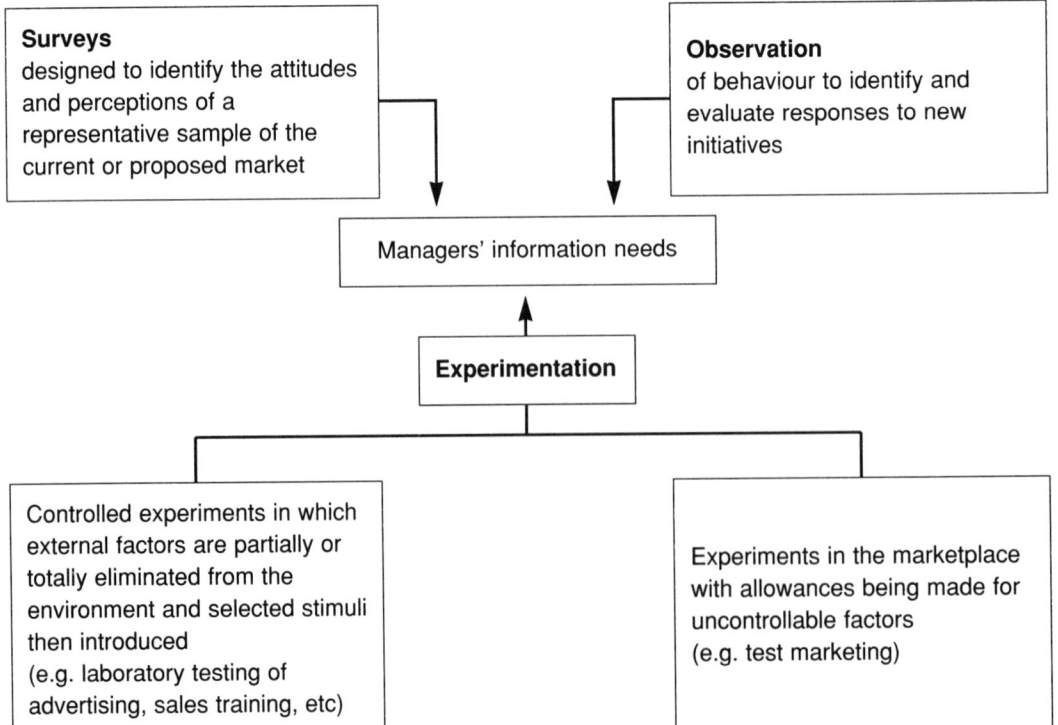

Figure 1.10 Approaches to collecting primary data

Using and choosing a market research agency

Market research can be conducted either by the organization's own specialist staff or by outside agencies. The benefits of using an outside agency are potentially significant and typically include:

- Greater specialist expertise.
- A different perspective upon the problem and, arguably, a greater degree of objectivity.
- Access to a network of other agencies.

There are several criteria that should be used in selecting an agency, the most significant of which are:

- The *type* of agency that is needed. Market research firms range from those that are capable of offering a wide range of services through to those that specialize by sector (e.g. industrial or consumer), type of market (e.g. foodstuffs, cars, drinks) and function (e.g. new product research, distribution research, advertising research). Equally, there are those that concentrate upon qualitative research and those that concentrate upon quantitative research. Others are international in their coverage, whilst some focus just upon the domestic market.
- The agency's size and the relative importance of the account to them.
- Their current and past client portfolio, since this will give an understanding not just of the breadth of their client range, but also the types of research work that they have undertaken in the past.
- Their understanding of the marketing problems faced and their views of the ways in which a programme of research might possibly contribute to their resolution.
- Their reputation.
- The nature of their pitch and the extent to which it appears to reflect an understanding of the organization and its market.
- The costs that are likely to be incurred.

An additional and possibly very important factor which should be taken into account is the *degree of empathy* which exists between the agency and the client, since it is essential that a fruitful and profitable relationship is developed. Other factors to which consideration might possibly be given include any areas of specialist expertise and their financial stability.

Your marketing director has decided to appoint an agency to carry out the market research work that previously has been conducted in-house. Prepare a short briefing paper identifying the criteria by which agencies pitching for the account should be shortlisted.

QUESTION 1.5

Organizational structures, managerial cultures and their influence upon approaches to planning

The way in which an organization develops and implements its plans is inexorably linked to its structure and managerial culture. These two elements are therefore fundamental determinants of organizational efficiency and effectiveness.

In structural terms, an organization consists of two interrelated dimensions:

- The formal structure.
- The informal structure.

The formal structure or formal organization relates to the authority hierarchy, the division of labour and to job specifications. The informal organization, which is sometimes referred to as the oil that makes or allows the wheels to go round, is rather more concerned with the social dimensions and relationships within the business.

The informal organization has been shown on numerous occasions to be a powerful basis both for getting things done and for creating obstacles. Any planning process should therefore recognize not just the formal structures that exist, but also the informal structures so that the two can be harnessed for maximum effect.

Take a diagram of your organization's formal structure and superimpose on this your understanding of some of the informal relationships and organizations that exist. What appears to be the overall effect of the informal organization? Is it generally beneficial or obstructive?

Influences upon the formal structure

Formal structures are influenced by a variety of factors, the most obvious of which are:

- The size of the business.
- The location of its markets.
- The type of staff and their abilities and skills.
- The age of the organization.
- The type of technology that it is dealing with.
- Patterns of managerial thinking (one of the major moves in organizational thinking is the early 1990s was that management hierarchies should be flatter so that patterns of communication would be faster and levels of creativity increased).
- Managerial cultures.

Against this background we can identify the three principal approaches to organization structure; these are illustrated in Figure 1.11.

Organization by:	Advantages	Disadvantages

1 Function	Logical
	Allows for a clear
	    division of work
	    on the basis of
	    specialisms
		Poor communication
		Tends to inhibit
		    creativity
		Limits the
		    development of
		    cross-functional teams

2 Product/brand	Direct accountability
	    for the performance
	    of individual products
	    and brands
	Cross-functional
	    activities can be
	    integrated
	Levels of specialism
	    can be increased
		Costs tend to be
		    higher than for 1
		Levels of complexity
		    increase

3 Territory or
    market sector
	More focused market
	    decision making
	Better local knowledge
	Stronger links and
	    relationships with customers
		Higher overheads
		Possible duplication
		    of effort

Figure 1.11   The advantages and disadvantages of different organizational structures

Given the nature of these comments, it should be apparent that, whilst each of the three approaches has certain advantages, there is no one best method of organization. In an attempt to overcome this, many organizations have developed *matrix structures* which are designed so that staff work in a multi-disciplinary and task-focused way. The claimed advantages of this are that it makes a far better use of the resources from across the organization and encourages a higher degree of flexibility, a stronger and more obvious market focus, better teamwork, higher levels of motivation, and an emphasis upon creativity.

There are, however, disadvantages to a matrix structure, the most common of which are that the pattern of dual authority can lead to conflict; individuals may find it difficult to report to two or more managers; and that the possibly greater ambiguity of roles can create tensions.

The significance of managerial culture

Perhaps the most commonly used and workmanlike definition of management culture is that 'it is the way in which we do things around here'. Although organizational behaviourists are critical of the definition because of the way in which it fails to come to terms with the full richness of culture, it has a certain value because of the way in which it highlights the significance of the organizational philosophy, practice and methods of working.

The culture of an organization is likely to be influenced by a variety of factors, including:

- The attitudes of the chief executive and the senior management team. What, for example, are their priorities? Are they risk averse or risk takers? What are their backgrounds? What are their perceptions of competitors, customers and the workforce?
- The leadership styles that exist.
- The nature of the market and the bases and intensity of competition.
- Previous cultures and work practices.
- Organizational structures and the emphasis given to rigidity or flexibility, the adherence to long-standing practices, perceptions of the importance of work creativity, and so on.
- The type of business and the technologies it is working with.
- Economic factors including expectations of economic trends.
- Past performance levels and the degree of success achieved.

The outcome of this is that several distinct managerial cultures can be identified:

1 *Highly bureaucratic cultures* in which structures and formality predominate, levels of flexibility and responsiveness to the market are low, and creativity and innovation is not encouraged.
2 *Highly entrepreneurial and individualistic cultures* in which the emphasis is upon getting things done, being innovative and moving on to the next task. Outputs are expected to be high and job roles are sketchy.
3 *Task cultures* which again have an emphasis upon getting the job done through the development of multi-functional teams.
4 Cultures in which considerable emphasis is placed upon *personal relationships*.

Summary

Within this unit we have attempted to highlight the key elements of the introductory elements to the Planning and Control process and syllabus. As a check on your understanding of these key concepts, consider the following questions:

1   What types of marketing definition can be identified?
    On pages 2–4, we identify three categories of marketing definition:

    - Those that focus on marketing's functional elements and activities.
    - Those concerned with marketing as a process.
    - Those that reflect the view that marketing is essentially a philosophy of how to do business.

    Examples of each of these are given on pages 2 and 3.

2   What major changes in definition have emerged over the past few years? What are the principal causes of these changes?
    The major changes that have taken place are:

    - A greater emphasis upon marketing as a *process* rather than simply a set of functional activities and elements (refer to the AMA and CIM definitions on page 2).
    - Recognition of the need for *all* parts of the organization to be involved in the process of creating customer satisfaction (see page 2).
    - A heightened awareness of the importance of competitive position, and of aiming for and achieving higher levels of satisfaction than competitors (see page 2).
    - A greater emphasis upon the social consequences of marketing activity and the consequent need for marketing managers to take account of the social and ethical implications of their decisions (see pages 2–4).

3   Should marketing managers take account of the implications for society of their decisions? If so, why? What are the possible consequences of ignoring these implications? (see page 4).
    In thinking about this, you need to consider the general issue of the role that business should play within society and of the short- and long-term consequences of behaviour that is socially irresponsible. In doing this, try to identify some examples where organizations have behaved with little regard for the negative effects of their decisions. The consequences of behaving irresponsibly can be seen in terms of consumers buying unsafe products, being exposed to untruthful advertising messages, inadequate after-sales support, and so on. From the company's point of view, the consequences can be seen in terms of damage to its reputation and the possibility of being exposed to legal action (see pages 2–3).

4   In what circumstances might a marketing manager justify making a decision that is legal but unethical, or illegal but ethical? Give examples of these sorts of decisions (see page 4).
    Legal but unethical decisions include offering products which have not been banned from sale by legislation, but for which there is a body of evidence which illustrates the harm that they might cause; cigarettes are perhaps the most obvious example of this. Illegal but ethical patterns of behaviour would include the payment of bribes (incentives) in an overseas country in order to secure a contract. The US government has passed legislation that makes it illegal for US citizens to pay bribes overseas, but local customs may see such payments to be acceptable and ethical behaviour.

5   What is the relationship between marketing planning and strategic or corporate planning?
    The distinctions are highlighted on pages 4–6, and in particular in Greenley's suggestions (see p. 5).

6   What are the three levels of strategy?
    Strategic decisions are taken at three levels:

    - The corporate level.
    - The business unit or divisional level.
    - The functional level.

These are discussed on pages 5–7. Pay particular attention to the definitions by Cravens, Kerrin and Peterson, and McDonald which appear in the Definition box 1.2 (see page 7).

7 Define 'objectives', 'strategy' and 'tactics'.

These appear in Definition box 1.3 (see page 8).

8 What is a stakeholder? How do (or should) stakeholders' expectations influence marketing decisions?

Stakeholders are groups or individuals who have a stake in, or an expectation of, the organization's performance. They include employees, managers, shareholders, suppliers, customers and the community at large (see Definition box 1.4).

Their influence upon marketing decisions needs to be looked at in terms of their expectations of the organization, their proximity, their importance and the nature of the current or future relationship with the organization (see page 8).

9 What are the differences between efficiency and effectiveness? How might each be manifested in marketing?

This issue is discussed on page 9 (Definition box 1.5). In essence, however, efficiency is doing things right, effectiveness is doing the right things. In marketing terms, efficiency might be seen to involve moving a product speedily and at low cost through the distribution channel. Effectiveness would raise the question of whether the distribution channel reaches the correct market (see page 9).

10 Explain what is meant by scenario planning and contingency planning. What role should each play in the overall marketing planning process?

Scenario and contingency planning are both defined on page 10. With regard to their roles, both are designed to encourage or force managers to think about the various futures the organization might possibly be faced with and how the organization might respond. Given this, they should have the effect of making managers think about the unexpected and question the conventional wisdoms (see pages 10–11).

11 Draw a model of the planning and control cycle.

An example of this appears on page 13.

12 Is planning a worthwhile exercise? In what circumstances might it be seen to be a waste of time?

Done properly, planning has several benefits, which include:

- A greater understanding of the environment.
- A more detailed insight into organizational capability.
- A more precise statement of objectives.
- Detailed statements of how the objectives will be achieved.
- Motivation and control elements.

Recognizing this, planning is obviously a worthwhile exercise. However, some questions have been raised about its value, particularly when the environment is changing rapidly. However, in these circumstances, managers need to take a different and more flexible approach rather than dispensing with it (see pages 12–13).

13 What are the principal obstacles to effective planning?

These are listed on pages 13 and 14.

14 What is a marketing information system? What contribution to planning should it be capable of making?

A marketing information system consists of people, equipment and procedures to gather, sort, analyse, evaluate and distribute needed, timely and accurate information to marketing decision makers.

The contributions to planning that it is capable of making include:

- A better understanding of the market.
- A more precise evaluation of the nature and causes of market changes.
- A reduction in the likelihood of the organization being taken by surprise.
- Improved sharing of information.
- More informed decision making.
- Higher levels of performance.

(See pages 14–16.)

15 Draw a model of an MkIS.

A diagram illustrating an MkIS appears on page 15.

16 What sorts of information do marketing managers need?

Aguilar's analysis of what is needed appears on page 15.

17 What are the characteristics of good information systems?

Good (i.e. effective) information systems are those that help managers to make better, faster and more informed decisions. The ground rules are therefore provided by the answers to four questions:

- What do we need to know?
- How will the information be used?
- By whom?
- What is the preferred format?

(See page 16.)

18 What contribution to planning can marketing research make?

The contribution can be seen in terms of:

- Better market information (this includes general and specific trends, as well as customer and competitor information).
- More informed marketing mix decisions (see pages 17 and 18).

19 In what circumstances would you use:

(a) secondary data?
(b) primary data?

What are the pros and cons of each type?

Secondary data should be used in virtually any marketing research exercise, since it is capable of providing considerable background insight, often at low costs. Primary data would be used to answer specific questions and to fill in the gaps in the secondary data.

The principal pros and cons are:

	Pros	Cons
Secondary data	• Often low-cost • Widely available • Easily and quickly accessed	• Often provides only a broad background picture • Rarely answers specific questions
Primary data	• Highly specific	• Often costly • May be difficult to obtain • Time-consuming to set up, collect and analyse the data

(See page 19.)

20 What criteria would you use in selecting a research agency?

A variety of criteria should be used, including:

- The *type* of agency that is needed. Market research firms range from those that are capable of offering a wide range of services through to those that specialize by sector (e.g. industrial or consumer), type of market (e.g. foodstuffs, cars, drinks) and function (e.g. new product research, distribution research, advertising research). Equally, there are those that concentrate upon qualitative research and those that concentrate upon quantitative research. Others are international in their coverage, whilst some focus just upon the domestic market.
- The agency's size and the relative importance of the account to them.
- Their current and past client portfolio, since this will give an understanding not just of the breadth of their client range, but also the types of research work that they have undertaken in the past.
- Their understanding of the marketing problems faced, and their views of the ways in which a programme of research might possibly contribute to their resolution.
- Their reputation.

- The nature of their pitch and the extent to which it appears to reflect an understanding of the organization and its market.
- The costs that are likely to be incurred.

An additional and possibly very important factor which should be taken into account is the *degree of empathy* which exists between the agency and the client, since it is essential that a fruitful and profitable relationship is developed. Other factors to which consideration might possibly be given include any areas of specialist expertise and their financial stability.

21 What are the principal forms of organizational structure?

These are listed in Figure 1.11 (see page 20).

22 What influences:

(a) formal structures?

(b) informal structures?

(a) Formal structures are influenced by:

- The size of the business.
- The location of its markets.
- The typcs of staff and their abilities and skills.
- The age of the organization.
- The type of technology.
- Patterns of managerial thinking.

(b) Amongst the influences upon informal structures are:

- Working relationships.
- The nature of the task.
- Interdependencies between staff and departments.
- Worker/manager relationships.
- The length of time staff have worked together.
- Expectations.
- The complexity of the task.

(See pages 20–1.)

23 What is meant by managerial culture? Why is it typically seen to be so powerful an influence upon how an organization operates?

Management culture is loosely defined as 'the way in which we do things around here'.

It is a powerful influence because it affects patterns of behaviour and work, expectations, performance levels and relationships (see page 21).

EXTENDING YOUR KNOWLEDGE

Against the background of what has been said in this unit, you should look in detail at the trade and business press with a view to identifying how different organizations interpret the sorts of concepts that we have discussed here and how they operate. In particular, you should look at how effective their marketing appears to be *and why*.

Talk to the senior management within your organization, as well as to friends and contacts in other organizations, and get their views on some of the concepts that we have discussed. Think about how practices differ between one organization and another (and why) and what you might learn from this.

In terms of further reading, you should turn to:

Wilson and Gilligan with Pearson, (1992), *Strategic Marketing Management: Planning Implementation and Control* – Chapter 1.

Fifield, *Marketing Strategy* – Introduction and Chapters 1 and 2.

Activity debrief

Question 1.1 (i)   In answering this question, you are required to explain in detail what is meant by marketing strategy and corporate strategy (to help with this, consider the material that appears on pages 4–7). In doing this, you should give emphasis to the idea of a hierarchy, with corporate planning and strategy at the top and marketing planning and strategy below this (refer to Figure 1.4). Against this background, you should explain what sorts of activities are included in each of the two categories and how they interrelate. You should then arrive at a conclusion as to whether they are the same or different activities (the answer, of course, is that they are not one and the same, but that strong links exist).

Question 1.1 (ii)   You should begin by explaining what is meant by a strategic approach to marketing. Making use of examples, you should then go on to explain why a strategic approach is often difficult to achieve. There are several possible explanations for this, including the way in which relatively few managers are taught to think or act strategically and are instead measured very largely on the basis of short-term performance. Given this, there is an understandable temptation for managers to focus upon short-term and tactical issues rather than the longer-term strategic management of the marketing function. This temptation then tends to increase dramatically during periods of economic recession and when levels of competitive activity are particularly intense, and is reflected in an emphasis upon issues of *efficiency* rather than *effectiveness*.

In order to overcome short-term perspectives, managers need to be taught to look to the long term and then be given the freedom from achieving purely short-term results to work within larger time frames.

Question 1.2   Refer to the discussion on pages 10–11.

Question 1.3 (i)   You should begin by giving a definition of a marketing information system (see Definition 1.6) and, with the use of a diagram (see Figure 1.8), identify its four principal components (the internal records system, the marketing intelligence system, the marketing research system, and the decision support system (see pages 15–16). You should then identify the outputs from the MkIS, including:

- A better understanding of the market.
- A more precise evaluation of the nature and causes of market changes.
- A reduction in the likelihood of the organization being taken by surprise.
- Improved sharing of information.
- More informed decision making.
- Higher levels of performance.
- Better feedback and control of the plan.

The principal contribution needs therefore to be seen in terms of improvements to the implementation process by virtue of better analysis and improvements to the formulation of strategy and tactics.

Question 1.3 (ii)   You need to begin by explaining that in many organizations the sales force is the point of most immediate, direct and frequent contact with the market. Because of this it can be used to obtain general and specific feedback on product performance, levels of satisfaction, gaps and opportunities in the market, competitors' current and possible future behaviour, and distributors, as well as general trends in the marketplace. This information can be obtained most easily through structured feedback mechanisms and regular debriefs. However, it is essential that the sales force is fully briefed beforehand so that its members know what they are looking for. Equally, it is essential that the information obtained is evaluated and passed to the appropriate decision makers and that the sales force is kept aware of how the information is being used.

Question 1.4   The question requires you to identify a spectrum of the ways in which marketing research might possibly contribute to the marketing process. Included within this are the following areas:

- *Product research* (the identification of product opportunities; customers' perceptions of existing and proposed products; comparative perceptions of competing products; positioning studies; test marketing; and packaging studies).
- *Pricing research* (the effectiveness of the various elements of the promotions mix; image

studies; copy and media issues; sales effects; sales force studies; and comparative studies of competitors' promotional techniques).

- *Distribution research* (distributors' perceptions, attitudes and needs; and distribution alternatives).
- *Market studies* (short- and long-term market forecasts).
- *Corporate research* (consumers', competitors' and distributors' perceptions of the organization overall and others in the market).

Question 1.5 The question requires you to answer in briefing paper format. Amongst the criteria to which you should make reference are:

- The *type* of agency that is needed. Market research firms range from those that are capable of offering a wide range of services through to those that specialize by sector (e.g. industrial or consumer), type of market (e.g. foodstuffs, cars, drinks) and function (e.g. new product research, distribution research, advertising research). Equally, there are those that concentrate upon qualitative research and those that concentrate upon quantitative research. Others are international in their coverage, whilst some focus just upon the domestic market.
- The agency's size and the relative importance of the account to it.
- Its current and past client portfolio, since this will give an understanding not just of the breadth of its client range, but also the types of research work that it has undertaken in the past.
- Its understanding of the marketing problems faced and its views of the ways in which a programme of research might possibly contribute to their resolution.
- Its reputation.
- The nature of its pitch and the extent to which this appears to reflect an understanding of the organization and its market.
- The costs that are likely to be incurred.

An additional and possibly very important factor which should be taken into account is the *degree of empathy* which exists between the agency and the client, since it is essential that a fruitful and profitable relationship is developed. Other factors to which consideration might possibly be given include any areas of specialist expertise and its financial stability.

Assessing corporate capability

This unit focuses upon the nature and sources of an organization's strategic capability and the ways in which meaningful measures of capability can be arrived at. Subsequent units will examine how the measures can be used in the development of an effective, competitive marketing strategy.

In this unit you will:

- Examine the nine step process that managers need to go through in developing an overall picture of an organization's strategic capability.
- Understand the need to examine capability both in an absolute and a relative sense.
- Appreciate how an understanding of strategic capability should underpin the development of marketing strategy.

By the end of the unit you will be able to:

- Undertake an assessment of corporate capability.
- Identify the factors that heighten or inhibit organizational capability.

This unit provides the framework for a section of the syllabus accounting for about 10–15 per cent of the total. Although this might appear to be a relatively small element, particularly when compared with some of the later units, its importance should not be under-estimated, since any worthwhile marketing strategy must, of necessity, be based upon a clear and detailed understanding of what the organization is *really* capable of doing and achieving. Because of this, issues relating either directly or indirectly to the various dimensions of capability have been the basis of numerous examination questions in the past.

You should expect to spend about 6 hours working your way through the unit, although some of the activities could take considerably longer, depending upon the degree of co-operation that you are able to call upon. A number of the exercises, for example, require you to relate the material to your own organization and, in order to complete them fully, you will need to talk to people in a variety of functional areas. By the end of the unit you should have obtained a far clearer understanding of the sorts of factors that influence corporate capability and, in the case of your own organization, a greater insight to those elements which heighten or inhibit a manager's ability to achieve marketing objectives.

To help develop and broaden your understanding of the area, you should make a point of reading the quality and trade press with a view to identifying examples of good and bad practice in marketing – and the sorts of factors that contribute to this. You should also support your study of the area by reading Chapters 2, 3 and 17 of *Strategic Marketing Management: Planning Implementation and Control* by Wilson and Gilligan with Pearson, and Chapter 2 of *Marketing Strategy* by Fifield; both books are published by Butterworth-Heinemann.

The changing thinking on strategy

A considerable amount of thinking in the 1980s on corporate and marketing strategy focused upon the nature and structure of organizational environments and upon the ways in which the environment is – or should be – the principal influence upon strategy formulation. More recently, however, it has been argued that the significance of the environment has been over-emphasized and that a more appropriate focus for strategy formulation is the organization's resource base. By their very nature, resource-based strategies demand a clear understanding of the organization's strategic capability and it is this which provides the focus for this unit.

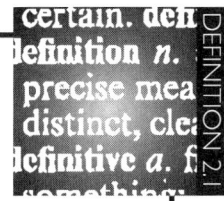

'A firm's *capabilities* relate to the distinctive competencies that it has developed to do something well and efficiently. A company is likely to enjoy a differential advantage in an area where its competencies outdo those of its potential competitors.'

Source: Dibb, Simkin, Pride and Ferrell (1994), *Marketing Concepts and Strategies*, (2nd European edition), Houghton Mifflin, page 538.

So what influences capability?

In coming to terms with strategic capability we need to examine the organization at various levels of detail. The starting point for this involves looking at the *broad issues of capability* which apply to the organization as a whole. In discussing this, Johnson and Scholes (1993, pages 115–116) comment that these:

> are largely concerned with the *overall balance* of resources and mix of activities. There are also assessments to be made of the quantity and quality of each *key resource area*, such as buildings, machines and people.

They go on to suggest that capability is 'fundamentally determined by the separate activities which it undertakes in designing, producing, marketing, delivering and supporting its products or services. It is an understanding of these various *value activities* and the *linkages* between them which is crucial when assessing strategic capability.'

It needs to be recognized, however, that in talking about capability we are not necessarily focusing only upon levels of *absolute* capability, but are instead, in many cases, rather more concerned with levels of *relative* capability. In other words, what do we do that is better (or worse) than our competitors? Equally, capability is not simply a function of an organization's internal resource base and how well or badly this is managed, but also of the way in which the organization interacts with the various parts of the chain that links it to its customers.

Looking at the industry or a market sector in which a part of your own organization operates, which competitors appear to be the most successful? What sorts of factors do you feel contribute to this? What dimensions of capability appear to be the most important?

There are therefore a number of elements which need to be examined when attempting to arrive at any realistic and worthwhile measure of corporate capability. These are illustrated in Figure 2.1 and include:

1 The nature and the quality of the internal and external resources that are available to the organization; these are most typically measured by means of a *resource audit*.
2 The *value chain* which is designed to highlight how the organization's resources are being used, controlled and linked together.
3 The way in which *resources are utilized*.
4 *Financial measures*.
5 *Comparative measures*, some of which may be *historical* (how has the organization's performance changed over time?), whilst others involve looking at *industry norms* (benchmarking) or *best practices* both within and outside the industry.
6 *Measures of balance* to ensure that the organization is not overly dependent upon particular geographic areas, parts of the product range, particular staff, particular processes, or specific customers.
7 The *performance-importance* grid.
8 A review of *marketing effectiveness*.
9 The identification of key issues in the form of a detailed *SWOT analysis* which summarizes the strategic insights gained from Stages 1–8.

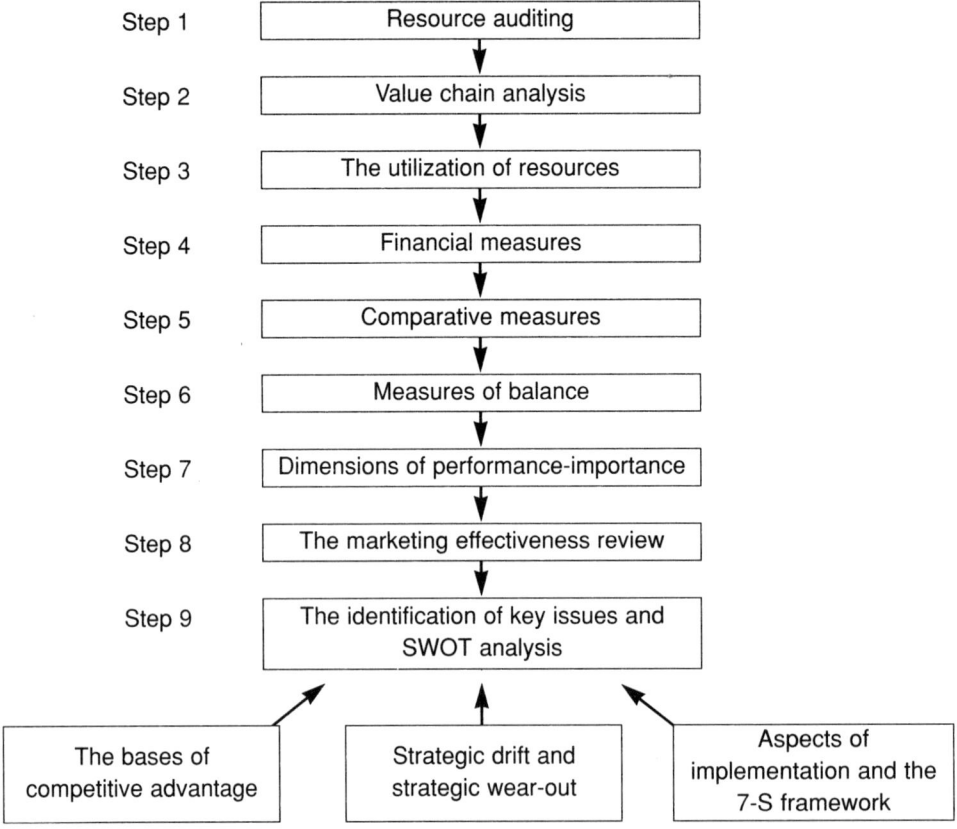

Figure 2.1 Assessing strategic capability

Many candidates, particularly in the mini and maxi case studies, make the mistake of making suggestions for action that would be far beyond the resource scope of the organization. In making suggestions, therefore, always think about issues of capability *and be realistic.*

Step one: the resource audit

The resource audit concentrates upon identifying and assessing the nature and strength of the internal and external resources that are available to the organization. These include:

- *Physical resources* such as the manufacturing capacity, the levels of production capability, retail outlets, and so on.
- *Human resources* including the appropriateness and mix of skills.
- *Financial resources* including the organization's capital base, its debtor/creditor ratio, and the sorts of relationships that it has with its shareholders and bankers.
- *Intangible resources* such as the image and reputation of the organization and the strength of its various brands.

In conducting the resource audit, several guidelines need to be borne in mind, one of the most significant of which is that resources and the resource base should be defined not just in terms of those that the organization owns in a legal sense, but also those to which the organization has access. Included within this will be distribution networks, political contacts, and individuals and organizations with which strategically useful relationships have been developed over the years.

> Try conducting a straightforward resource audit for your organization. Identify clearly the sorts of information that you would need if the exercise was to be done in detail, where this might come from and the sorts of problems that might be encountered in its collection.

ACTIVITY 2.2

Step two: the value chain

Having conducted the initial resource audit, you need to think about the ways in which these resources relate to the organization's performance. In other words, *how* are these resources used as a means of gaining and maintaining a competitive advantage? One of the ways in which this can be done is by means of the value chain.

Although value analysis has its origins in accountancy and was designed to identify the profitability of each stage in a manufacturing process, a considerable amount of work has been done in recent years in developing the concept and applying it to measures of competitive advantage. Much of this work has been conducted by Michael Porter who suggests that an organization's activities can be categorized in terms of whether they are *primary activities* or *support activities*; this is illustrated in Figure 2.2.

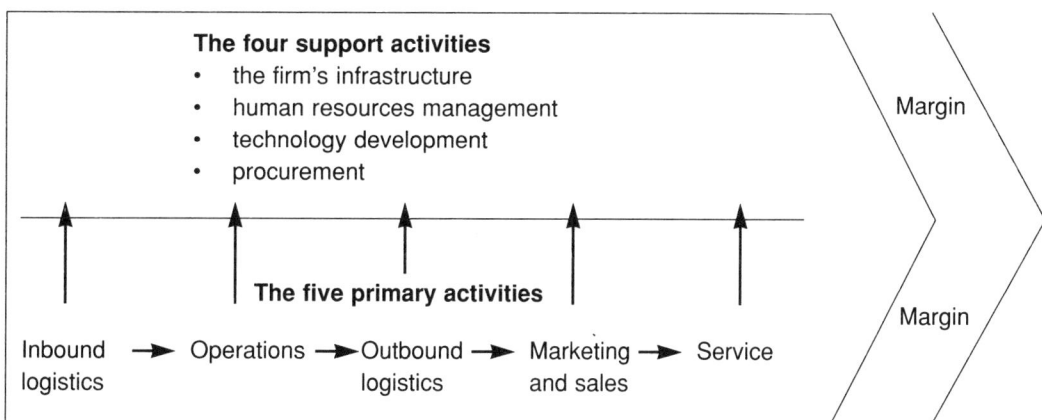

Figure 2.2 The value chain. (Adapted from M. E. Porter (1985), *Competitive Advantage*, Free Press)

The five primary activities that he identifies are:

1 *Inbound logistics* which are the activities that are concerned with the reception, storing and internal distribution of the raw materials or components for assembly.
2 *Operations* which turn these into the final product.
3 *Outbound logistics* which distribute the product or service to customers. In the case of a manufacturing operation, this would include warehousing, materials handling and

transportation. For a service this would involve the way in which customers are brought to the location in which the service is to be delivered.

4   *Marketing and sales*   which make sure the customers are aware of the product or service and are able to buy it.

5   *Service*   activities which include installation, repair and training.

Each of these primary activities is, in turn, linked to the support activities which are grouped under four headings:

1   The *procurement* of the various resource inputs.
2   *Technology development,* including research and development, process improvements and raw material improvements.
3   *Human resource management* including the recruitment, training, development and rewarding of staff.
4   *The firm's infrastructure* and the approach to organization including the systems, structures, managerial cultures and ways of doing business.

Porter suggests that competitive advantage is determined to a very large extent by how each of these elements is managed and the nature of the interactions between them. In the case of inbound logistics, for example, many organizations have developed just-in-time systems in order to avoid or minimize their stockholding costs. In this way, the value of the activity is increased and the firm's competitive advantage improved. Equally, in the case of operations, manufacturers are paying increasing attention to lean manufacturing processes as a means of improving levels of efficiency. Porter's message is therefore straightforward. Managers, he suggests, need to examine the nature and dimensions of each of the nine activities with a view to identifying how the value added component can best be increased.

ACTIVITY 2.3

Carry out a straightforward value chain analysis of your own organization and try to identify how each of the four primary and five secondary activities might be managed differently in order to create competitive advantage.

He goes on to argue that value chain analysis should not simply stop with the manager's own organization, but in the case of a manufacturer should also include the suppliers and distribution networks, since the value of much of what an organization does will be

QUESTION 2.1

How might an understanding of the value chain contribute to a manager's thinking on planning and control?

(Marketing Planning and Control, June 1994, Question 6.)

Step three: the utilization of resources

STUDY GUIDE

Refer back to page 9 of Unit 1 in order to refresh your memory of precisely what efficiency and effectiveness are and the sorts of factors that contribute to these.

influenced both by its *suppliers,* how they operate and the quality of their output, and the *distribution network* and how it interacts with the customer base, since this can either add or detract in a major way from the organization's marketing effort.

Because of the much higher levels of competition that the majority of organizations now face, the search for ever higher levels of efficiency and effectiveness is something that preoccupies many managers. In many cases this has led to a fundamental questioning of exactly how organizational resources are used and whether changes might possibly lead to competitive advantage. At its most extreme, this search can be seen to have been manifested in business process re-engineering in which possibly radical changes are made to the way in which the organization operates. However, as an intermediate step, managers need to ask – and answer – a series of questions, including:

1   How are resources allocated currently?
2   To what extent does each stage of the value chain process actually add value?
3   In what ways might these value added elements be increased?
4   What are the critical success factors in each of the organization's market sectors?
5   How do *customers* perceive value and what are the implications for how the organization operates?
6   Which elements of the marketing programme sustain any competitive advantage(s) that the organization has?
7   In what areas is the organization operating sub-optimally? Are the stock levels too high, for example? Would it be better to sub-contract the distribution function? Is the organization working sufficiently closely with the distribution intermediaries? Is there scope for re-assessing the advertising effort?
8   What scope exists for collaborating with other organizations in order to improve levels of efficiency and effectiveness?

Take the eight questions listed above and discuss them with a senior manager within your organization.

ACTIVITY 2.4

This search for greater efficiency and effectiveness can also be seen in terms of the need to focus on a regular basis upon a variety of other factors including:

● Supply costs.
● Economies of scale in marketing and distribution, as well as manufacturing.
● Levels of productivity.

These three elements are, of course, measures of *efficiency* and are therefore capable of providing only a partial insight into the organization. To broaden this picture, we need also to focus upon issues of *effectiveness,* since it is these which illustrate the *appropriateness* of what the organization is doing. At the heart of any measure of effectiveness is the degree of fit that exists between what the organization is offering and what the customer wants. The sorts of questions that therefore need to be asked include:

1   Is the product/service that is offered what the customer *really* wants?
2   Do the support services meet customers' expectations?
3   Are any unique features and added value elements that are offered actually seen by customers to be important?
4   Do the pre- and post-sales services that are offered add value that is then reflected in the prices that are charged?

Take one part of your organization and, by speaking to the managers responsible for this area, identify the sorts of factors that contribute to the levels both of efficiency and effectiveness. How do these appear to compare with those of your direct competitors? What are the competitive consequences of any levels of efficiency and effectiveness that are lower than those of your competitors? What would be needed in order to improve these levels?

Step four: financial measures

The link between an organization's financial standing and its strategic capability is a strong one, since it is the availability of financial resources that is one of the principal determinants of a manager's freedom of action. But although it is typically the case that organizations generate considerable amounts of financial information, much of this is largely operational in nature and tends not necessarily to be viewed in strategic terms. If, however, a manager's assessment of strategic capability is to be at all meaningful, it is essential that the sort of strengths and weaknesses analysis that we discuss at a later stage in this unit reflects a strong strategic perspective.

Although there are a variety of financial measures that can be used to assess financial performance and financial standing, it is relatively easy to identify the financial expectations of the four principal groups of stakeholders:

1   *The banks*   are most concerned with issues of risk and therefore focus upon the organization's capital structure, and especially the gearing ratio (that is, the ratio of debt to equity) since this is a measure of solvency.
2   *Suppliers and employees*   are typically concerned with liquidity, since this determines whether short-term financial commitments such as invoices and wages can be paid.
3   *Management*   tends to concentrate upon those measures which allow them to measure performance not just against the expectations of the shareholders, but also in relation to similar organizations (are we doing better or worse than our competitors?) and over time (are we doing better or worse than, say, twelve and twenty-four months ago?).
4   *Shareholders*   who concentrate upon the wisdom of their investment and whether the capital growth and/or income is increasing.

Given these comments, we can identify a series of financial measures that can be used to build a picture of performance. Included within these are:

1   Profit margins: the ratio of profit to sales.
2   Asset turnover: the ratio of sales to the capital employed.
3   The return on capital employed (ROCE): the profit as a percentage of the capital employed (this is sometimes referred to as the primary ratio).
4   Earnings per share.
5   Gearing: the ratio of debt to equity.
6   Stock turnover: the time between raw materials being purchased and used.
7   The debt collection period: the time taken for customers to pay after a sale.
8   The creditor collection period: the time between taking delivery of materials and paying the supplier.
9   The current ratio or working capital ratio: the difference between current assets and current liabilities.
10   The quick ratio or liquidity ratio: the difference between current assets less stock and current liabilities.

Numbers 6–8 are often referred to as *operational ratios,* since they refer to the way in which cash is managed on a short-term basis. Numbers 9 and 10 are *liquidity ratios* and refer to the organization's ability to turn assets into cash in order to meet all of its possible payment demands.

Although this is by no means an exhaustive list of the dimensions that can be taken into account in a financial analysis (indeed, we have deliberately ignored issues such as advertising ratios, share price, sales margins, and so on), it illustrates the sorts of factors that provide a measure of capability.

What are the key financial measures within your own organization?

What use can be made of ratios in monitoring the implementation of marketing plans?

(Marketing Planning and Control, June 1991, Question 10.)

Step five: comparative analysis

We made the comment at an earlier stage that, in many cases, measures of strategic capability are best looked at in *relative* rather than *absolute* terms. In other words, what is it that the organization is better or worse at than its competitors *in the eyes of the customers?* This can be answered in several ways including:

- Historical analysis in which comparisons are made with the organization's performance in previous years. By doing this, the nature and significance of any changes across a variety of measures of performance, such as the absolute level of sales, the rate of sales growth (or decline), the mix of sales, geographic coverage and financial ratios can be assessed.
- Comparisons with industry norms.
- The analysis of best practice by means of competitor profiling and benchmarking.

Although a *comparison with industry norms* is capable of providing a useful insight into the relative performance of the organization, the results need to be treated with a degree of caution. It may be the case, for example, that whilst it appears that the organization is performing well against its direct competitors in terms of, for example, sales, R&D spend, cost levels and so on, little or no account is being taken of other organizations which may be capable either currently or in the future of satisfying the same need. Equally, the comparison may fail to take account of the industry norms of similar companies in other countries.

For this reason, comparative analysis should also take account of both *competitors' profiles* and *benchmarks* as a means of gaining a greater understanding of *best practice.*

Competitor profiling, which is discussed in greater detail in Unit 3, involves building a detailed picture of each competitor with a view to understanding the depth and breadth of their strategic capability. In doing this, attention needs to be paid to their resource base, what they are good at, what they are bad at, what their priorities are, the level of commitment that they have to each market and their managerial cultures. Included within this is the analysis of their *marketing assets.*

'*Marketing assets* highlight the capabilities that managers and the marketplace view as beneficially strong. These capabilities can then be stressed to the company's advantage. Customer-based assets include brand image and reputation; distribution-based assets may involve density of dealers and geographic coverage; internal-marketing assets include skills, experience, economies of scale, technology and resources.'

(Source: Dibb, Simkin, Pride and Ferrell (1994) *Marketing: Concepts and Strategies* (2nd European ed), Houghton Mifflin, pages 538–539.)

The second dimension of best practice analysis involves *benchmarking* and the development of key performance targets for those activities which are seen to be crucial to success.

Benchmarking is an analytical process through which an enterprise's performance can be compared with that of its competitors. It is used to:

- Identify key performance measures for each business function
- Measure one's own performance as well as that of competitors
- Identify areas of competitive advantage (and disadvantage) by comparing performance levels
- Design and implement plans to improve one's own performance on key issues relative to competitors'

(Source: Wilson and Gilligan with Pearson (1992) *Strategic Marketing Management: Planning, Implementation and Control,* Butterworth-Heinemann, page 610.)

Although there are several ways of establishing benchmarks, the most common involves identifying the levels at which market leaders are operating and then attempting to achieve or improve upon these.

Although the idea of benchmarking has an apparent inherent logic, it has been subject to a certain amount of criticism in recent years. There are several reasons for this, although perhaps the most meaningful is that benchmarking is typically limited to the 'hard' factors of management; an example of this would be the productivity or wastage levels being achieved by a competitor. What is arguably more important in measuring yourself against competitors are the 'soft' factors and, in particular, the managerial cultures and levels of expertise that competitors possess, since it is these which ultimately determine how they behave and the levels of long-term performance that are likely to be achieved. Equally, much benchmarking can be criticized for the way in which comparisons are drawn between organizations within the industry rather than with *best practice* in similar, and also possibly very different, industry sectors. As an example of this, it is a relatively easy but ultimately limited exercise to benchmark and draw comparisons between the catering functions of different hospitals. What might be a more useful (additional) exercise, would be to bench-mark against different types of hotel or other catering suppliers.

Step six: issues of organizational balance

Having focused upon the individual elements of the organization and its resource base, attention needs then to shift to issues of organizational balance and the extent to which specific aspects of the resource base complement each other. In doing this, thought needs to be given to issues of flexibility and adaptability; the balance of skills that exists; and the extent to which the elements of the product/service portfolio are complementary.

In assessing *flexibility and adaptability,* the marketing planner is attempting to arrive at a measure of the organization's ability to cope with any changes that take place in the organization's environment. The most obvious – and straightforward – way of doing this simply involves listing those changes which can be foreseen, determining the organization's ability to cope with each of these, and then assessing the significance of any gaps that exist.

As part of this, thought needs also to be given to the demands that the environment is placing currently and will place in the future upon *managerial and workforce skills.* Is it the case, for example, that the sorts of individual and team skills that are increasingly being demanded by the environment actually exist within the organization to the depth and breadth that is needed?

What degree of flexibility and adaptability appears to exist within your own organization? What sorts of factors do you feel contribute to this? What would be needed for higher levels of flexibility and adaptability to emerge? How important do you think that these two dimensions will become in future years?

ACTIVITY 2.7

The third dimension of balance relates to the extent to which the various parts of the *product portfolio* balance each other. Although a variety of frameworks for portfolio analysis have been developed (these are discussed in greater detail in Unit 5), probably the most useful at this stage is the Boston Consulting Group's growth-share matrix. The matrix involves plotting the organization's portfolio of strategic business units (SBUs) against two dimensions: the market's annual growth rate and the SBUs' relative competitive position; the matrix is illustrated in Figure 2.3.

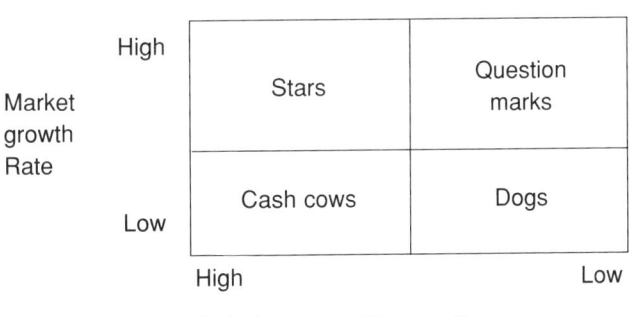

Figure 2.3 The Boston Consulting Group's growth-share matrix

The thinking that underpins the matrix is straightforward and based on the idea that SBUs should not be looked at in isolation but as parts of an interdependent portfolio. Thus, the cash generated by the cash cows should be used to fund the growth, and possibly the strengthening of the competitive position, of the stars, the question marks and, in certain circumstances, the dogs. In doing this, the marketing planner is aiming for an optimal balance between the nature, shape and health of today's portfolio and the nature, shape and health of tomorrow's portfolio.

You will undoubtedly have come across models of portfolio analysis such as the Boston Consulting Group's growth-share matrix in the past. Given this, what sorts of factors contribute to a healthy and an un-healthy portfolio?

QUESTION 2.3

Step seven: the performance–importance grid

Given the nature of our comments so far, it should be apparent that, although within this part of the workbook we are concerned principally with issues of *marketing* capability, only rarely can we look at elements of marketing capability in isolation. The reason for this is of course that, almost invariably, marketing issues – particularly at the strategic level – interact with a whole series of other elements within the organization and it is the interplay of these that influences or determines the organization's levels of capability. Because of this, any assessment of corporate capability needs to take account of at least four principal dimensions:

- Marketing specific factors.
- Financial elements.
- Manufacturing issues.
- Organizational factors such as managerial culture, organizational structures and staff capabilities.

These four areas can be brought together in one of a number of ways although one of the most useful tools for this is the performance–importance grid; an example of this appears in Figure 2.4. To use the grid you begin by giving a rating to your organization's performance ranging from a fundamental strength to a fundamental weakness for each of the forty-two dimensions running down the left-hand side of the grid. Having done this, you then give thought to the significance or importance of each of these elements. In the case of market share, for example, just how important or necessary is the possession of a high share in your industry? Equally, how important are product quality and the after-sales service? Having identified the importance of each of the elements you should have a far clearer *first* picture of capability. You can then expand upon this by going through the same exercise for each of your principal competitors. Having done this, you end up with a comparative picture which not only illustrates areas of absolute and relative strengths and weakness, but which also highlights those areas to which the greatest attention needs to be paid.

ACTIVITY 2.8

Using Figure 2.4, carry out a performance–importance analysis for your organization and its two principal competitors. Having done this, identify the areas of significant strength and weakness and consider the implications for marketing strategy.

The analysis can also be helped by identifying where in the matrix that is illustrated in Figure 2.5 each of the dimensions that is highlighted in Figure 2.4 lies. Those which fall into Cell 1 are, of course, the areas of highest priority, whilst those in Cell 4 are the areas to which perhaps too much (unnecessary) attention has been paid in the past.

Step eight: reviewing marketing effectiveness

Another way of assessing capability involves reviewing the organization's marketing effectiveness. Although there are several ways in which this can be done, including analysing sales and profit performance; market share levels and movements; levels of absolute and relative customer satisfaction; and new products success rates, the marketing effectiveness review (MER) typically concentrates upon arriving at a measure of the organization's performance or standing under five main headings:

1 The extent to which management practice reflects a customer-oriented philosophy.
2 Whether there is an integrated marketing organization.
3 The adequacy of the marketing information that exists.
4 The firm's strategic orientation.
5 The levels of operational efficiency.

	Performance					Importance		
	Major strength	Minor strength	Neutral	Minor weakness	Major weakness	High	Medium	Low
Marketing factors								
1 Market share	—	—	—	—	—	—	—	—
2 Image and reputation	—	—	—	—	—	—	—	—
3 Previous performance	—	—	—	—	—	—	—	—
4 Competitive stance	—	—	—	—	—	—	—	—
5 Customer base	—	—	—	—	—	—	—	—
6 Depth of customer loyalty	—	—	—	—	—	—	—	—
7 Breadth of product range	—	—	—	—	—	—	—	—
8 Depth of product range	—	—	—	—	—	—	—	—
9 Product quality	—	—	—	—	—	—	—	—
10 Programme of product modification	—	—	—	—	—	—	—	—
11 New product programme	—	—	—	—	—	—	—	—
12 Distribution costs	—	—	—	—	—	—	—	—
13 Size of dealer network	—	—	—	—	—	—	—	—
14 Dealer loyalty	—	—	—	—	—	—	—	—
15 Dealers' geographical coverage	—	—	—	—	—	—	—	—
16 Sales force, size and expertise	—	—	—	—	—	—	—	—
17 After sales service	—	—	—	—	—	—	—	—
18 Manufacturing costs	—	—	—	—	—	—	—	—
19 Manufacturing flexibility	—	—	—	—	—	—	—	—
20 Raw material advantages	—	—	—	—	—	—	—	—
21 Pricing	—	—	—	—	—	—	—	—
22 Advertising	—	—	—	—	—	—	—	—
23 Unique selling propositions	—	—	—	—	—	—	—	—
24 Structure and intensity of competition	—	—	—	—	—	—	—	—
Financial factors								
25 Cost of capital	—	—	—	—	—	—	—	—
26 Availability of capital	—	—	—	—	—	—	—	—
27 Profitability	—	—	—	—	—	—	—	—
28 Financial stability	—	—	—	—	—	—	—	—
29 Margins	—	—	—	—	—	—	—	—
Manufacturing factors								
30 Production facilities	—	—	—	—	—	—	—	—
31 Economies of scale	—	—	—	—	—	—	—	—
32 Flexibility	—	—	—	—	—	—	—	—
33 Workforce	—	—	—	—	—	—	—	—
34 Technical skill	—	—	—	—	—	—	—	—
35 Delivery capabilities	—	—	—	—	—	—	—	—
36 Supplier sourcing flexibility	—	—	—	—	—	—	—	—
Organizational factors								
37 Culture	—	—	—	—	—	—	—	—
38 Leadership	—	—	—	—	—	—	—	—
39 Managerial capabilities	—	—	—	—	—	—	—	—
40 Workforce	—	—	—	—	—	—	—	—
41 Flexibility	—	—	—	—	—	—	—	—
42 Adaptability	—	—	—	—	—	—	—	—

Figure 2.4 The performance–importance grid. (Source: adapted from Kotler, 1988, page 53)

Performance

	Low	High
High (Importance)	The focus for greater managerial effort in order to improve performance 1	Continue with the current effort to ensure that performance does not decline 3
Low (Importance)	Areas of low priority 2	Re-think the current effort. Is it worth spending in these areas? 4

Importance

Figure 2.5 The performance–importance matrix

A detailed framework for reviewing marketing effectiveness appears on pages 30–32 of *Strategic Marketing Management* and you might usefully refer to this. However, in the absence of this, identify the sorts of questions that would help you to gain an insight into each of the five dimensions of marketing effectiveness that are referred to on page 38.

Step nine: the identification of key issues by means of SWOT analysis

Although SWOT analysis is a particularly well-known and a frequently used management tool, evidence suggest that far too many managers carry out SWOT analyses which are generally too bland to be of real value. There are several reasons for this, the most common of which is that managers simply list strengths and weaknesses and then the opportunities and threats without paying any or sufficient attention to their real significance. The result is what is sometimes called 'a balance sheet approach,' with managers taking comfort from the way in which the organization's strengths seemingly outweigh the weaknesses, but failing to recognize that one or more of the weaknesses may well cancel out all or most of the strengths; an example of this would be an impending cash flow crisis which undermines any strengths and limits managerial action.

The second major failing of many analyses of strengths and weaknesses is that they are carried out internally without sufficient attention being paid to market perceptions. In assessing an organization's strengths and weaknesses, detailed attention *must* be paid to the organization's strengths and weaknesses *as perceived by customers and competitors*. To illustrate this Nigel Piercy (1991, page 261) makes reference to two of the most commonly identified strengths:

- We are an old established firm.
- We are a large supplier.

Whilst it may well be the case that the organization is large and long established, these may not necessarily be seen as strengths in the marketplace. Instead, Piercy suggests, they may be seen by customers as indicators of an organization that is inflexible, old fashioned, lacking in innovation and overly bureaucratic. The lesson therefore is always to look at the strengths and weaknesses from the market's point of view.

A third failing of many SWOTs is that they are not sufficiently focused, the obvious consequence of which is that they end up as bland generalizations. Recognizing this, any SWOT analysis needs to be based on a clear and detailed definition of the area that is being evaluated. This can be done by focusing upon specific areas such as:

- Products and markets.
- Customer segments within a given market.
- Distribution systems for particular customer groups.
- Promotional activities within specific market sectors that are targeted at different customer groups and decision-making units.
- Pricing policies in specific markets.
- Product policies in given markets.
- Named competitors or groups of competitors.

The fourth limitation of many SWOT analyses is that, having conducted the exercise, managers do not then go on to examine in sufficient detail the implications of the analysis for future strategies. To help with this, Figure 2.6 illustrates the ways in which action should be taken to convert weaknesses into strengths, threats into opportunities, and how strengths are only meaningful when used to capitalize upon opportunities.

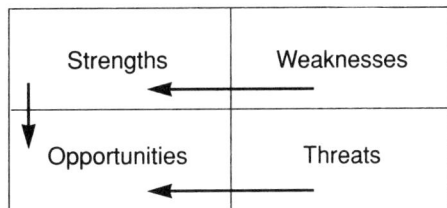

Figure 2.6 The SWOT framework

Conduct a *detailed* SWOT analysis for one of your organization's pro-ducts or services. What implications for future strategy emerge from the analysis?

Against the background of these comments it should be apparent that SWOT analysis is not necessarily quite as straightforward as it often appears or indeed is often made out to be. Before going on to conduct a SWOT, there are several points that might usefully be borne in mind, including in the case of any opportunities and threats that are identified that:

> they can never be viewed as 'absolutes'. What might appear at first sight to be an opportunity may not be so when examined against the organization's resources, its culture, the expectations of its stakeholders, the strategies available, or the feasibility of implementing the strategy. At the risk of oversimplification, however, the purpose of strategy formulation is to develop a strategy which will take advantage of the opportunities and overcome or circumvent the threats.
>
> (Johnson and Scholes, 1988, page 77)

Turn to Unit 9 of the Workbook and read the New Directions case study.
  This case, which focuses upon a retail organization, was used as the mini case study for the Marketing Planning and Control examination in December 1992 and required candidates to conduct two SWOT analyses – one for the period before a takeover and one for the period following the takeover – as a prelude to examining the implications for planning and control. Using the knowledge that you have gained from the unit so far, conduct the SWOT analyses and then compare the results with the outline answer that appears on page 215.

(i) What practical contribution is SWOT analysis capable of making to the marketing planning and control processes? (Marketing Planning and Control, June 1993, Question 10.)

(ii) What problems might be encountered in carrying out a worthwhile SWOT analysis?

Strategic capability and the bases of competitive advantage

A considerable amount of marketing thinking is based on the identification, pursuit and exploitation of competitive advantage. A competitive advantage can be gained in a variety of ways, although the three principal categories of advantage can be seen to be:

1 Organizationally-related advantages (e.g. economies of scale, issues of flexibility, size, financial strengths, image, reputation and managerial cultures).

2 Departmental and functional advantages (e.g. strengths in marketing, R&D, production and personnel).

3 Advantages that are based on relationships with external bodies (e.g. customers, distributors, politicians, competitors and suppliers).

These are illustrated in Figure 2.7.

In assessing and coming to terms with an organization's strategic capability, you should therefore take each of these in turn with a view to identifying, firstly, its significance within a particular market and then, secondly, the extent to which the advantage either exists currently or might possibly be developed in the future.

Strategic drift and strategic wear-out

We have made the comment at several stages that, for a variety of reasons, corporate capability should be viewed in relative rather than absolute terms. By the same token, managers need to recognize that a high level of strategic capability often proves to be a transitory phenomenon. There are two inter-related reasons for this: the first is illustrated by the notion of *strategic drift,* the second being *strategic wear-out.*

The idea of strategic drift is straightforward and is a reflection of the way in which as the environment changes, so strategies need to be modified to take account of the newly emerging opportunities and threats. All too often, however, strategic reviews take place too infrequently or too superficially and the growing gap between what the market wants and what the organization is offering only then becomes apparent at a late stage (see Figure 2.8).

These problems are then compounded by the *wear-out* or tiredness that almost inevitably eventually affects how an organization operates. In commenting on this Wilson et al (1992, page 271) suggest:

> The need for change often becomes apparent only at a later stage when the gap between what the company is doing and what it should be doing increases to a point at which performance and prospects begin to suffer in an obvious way. It is by this stage that an observant and astute competitor will have taken advantage of the company's increased vulnerability. The argument in favour of regular environmental and strategic reviews is therefore unassailable. Specifically, the sorts of factors which contribute to strategic wear-out include:
>
> - Changes in market structure as competitors enter or exit.
> - Changes in competitors' stances.
> - Competitive innovations.
> - Changes in consumers' expectations.
> - Economic changes.
> - Legislative changes.
> - Technological changes; these include in some instances, the emergence of a new technology which at first sight is unrelated or only indirectly related to the company's existing sphere of operations.

The sources of a sustainable competitive advantage can be categorized as:

1 Organizational advantages

- Economies of scope and scale.
- Levels of flexibility.
- The appropriateness and proactivity of the competitive stance.
- The size and power of the organization.
- The ability to identify and exploit opportunities.
- Past performance and size of the resource base.
- Financial strengths.
- Patterns of ownership and influence.
- Image and reputation.
- Managerial cultures.

2 Departmental and functional advantages

Marketing
- The size and loyalty of the customer base.
- Detailed knowledge of customers.
- New product skills.
- Pricing strategies.
- Communication and advertising.
- Distribution strategies.
- Sales force.
- Services support.
- Reputation.
- Detailed knowledge of competitors.

Research and Development
- Product technology.
- Patents.

Production
- Technology.
- Process efficiency.
- Economies of scale.
- Experience.
- Product quality.
- Manufacturing flexibility.

Personnel
- Management-worker relations.
- Workforce flexibility.

3 Advantages based on relationships with external bodies

- Customer loyalty.
- Channel control.
- Preferential political and legislative treatment.
- Government assistance.
- Beneficial tariff and non-tariff trade barriers.
- Cartels.
- Intra-organizational relationships.
- Access to preferential and flexible financial resources.

Figure 2.7 Competitive advantage
(Adapted from Wilson and Gilligan with Pearson, 1992, *Strategic Marketing Management: Planning, Implementation and Control*, Butterworth-Heinemann, page 34.)

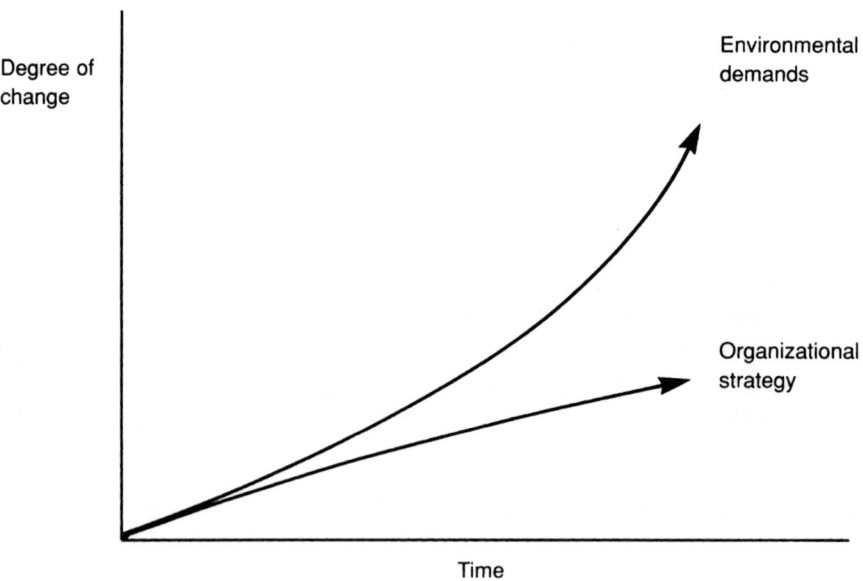

Figure 2.8   Strategic drift

- Distribution changes.
- Supplier changes.
- A lack of internal investment.
- Poor control of company costs.
- A tired and uncertain managerial philosophy.

ACTIVITY 2.12

Take three separate industries or market sectors and identify examples – and the consequences – of strategic wear-out. To what extent do you think that this wear-out might have been avoided?

QUESTION 2.5

Evidence suggests that many marketing programmes continue to be pursued long after their effectiveness has diminished. Explain why this is so and suggest how the strategic and tactical wear-out of a marketing programme might possibly be identified and avoided. (Strategic Marketing Management: Planning and Control, December 1994, Question 4.)

Corporate capability and issues of implementation

One of the biggest and most frequently recurring problems faced by managers is not that of planning but rather that of implementation. All too often, plans that seemed in the early stages to promise a great deal prove to be disappointing in that they fail to deliver what was hoped for. In many cases this is due to too little attention having been paid to the implementation phase, with the cost, time or resource implications having been underestimated. It is because of this that the issue of exactly *how* an organization implements its plans can be a major influence upon corporate capability. With this in mind, we can categorize the dimensions of planning and implementation in terms of a simple matrix; this is illustrated in Figure 2.9.

Marketing Planning

		Bad (inappropriate)	Good (appropriate)
Marketing Implementation	Bad (ineffective)	**1 Failure** The marketing programme fails to exploit environmental opportunities and build upon the resource base	**2 Trouble** The answer lies in focusing upon issues of implementation
	Good (effective)	**3 Trouble** The plan is flawed and any attempt at implementation is therefore of little value	**4 Success** The marketing programme achieves its objectives

Figure 2.9 The planning and implementation matrix. (Adapted from Bonoma, T, 1985, *The Marketing Edge: Making Strategies Work*, Free Press.)

Looking at your own organization, where in Figure 2.8 would you place it? Assuming that it is not in Cell 4, what appear to be the principal problems? What would be needed in order to overcome these?

ACTIVITY 2.13

'Marketing planning is generally a straightforward exercise; the marketer's real problems are those of effective implementation.' (Anonymous)

Identify the nature of the barriers to effective implementation that marketers typically encounter and suggest how, if at all, these barriers might be reduced. (Marketing Planning and Control, December 1992, Question 7.)

QUESTION 2.6

It has long been recognized that effective marketing is based upon the identification and exploitation of meaningful competitive advantage(s). Making reference to the possible bases of competitive advantage, explain why so many marketing campaigns fail to do this and reflect instead a 'me too' approach.

(Strategic Marketing Management: Planning and Control, June 1995, Question 8.)

QUESTION 2.7

Corporate capability and the 7-S framework

Even when an organization has developed a clear – and appropriate – strategy that is supported both by the necessary systems and managerial structures, it may still fail to achieve its objectives. The sorts of problems that can cause this were touched upon in the previous section but are taken a step further in the McKinsey 7-S framework. The model, which was developed initially by Peters and Waterman as the result of their study of excellently managed and high performing companies, illustrates that capability is influenced not just by the three traditional 'hard' areas of management – strategy, structure and systems – but also, and in some cases more significantly, by the four 'soft' elements of *style* (the employees' style of behaving and thinking); *skills* (those needed to carry out the company's strategy); *staffing* (the extent to which staff have been trained well and assigned to the tasks which best match their talents); and *shared values* (the employees' understanding of and commitment to the same guiding values and missions). Refer also to pages 146–7.

ACTIVITY 2.14

Looking at your own organization, to what extent does there appear to be a conscious and well thought out process for managing the soft elements of the 7-S framework?

Summary

Within this unit we have attempted to identify the principal dimensions of corporate capability and highlight the range of factors that influence it. As a check on your understanding of the material, consider the following questions:

1   In what ways is thinking on strategy changing?
    The principal changes can be seen to be:

  - A greater emphasis upon the organization's resource base and, in particular, its areas of distinctive competence as determinants of strategy.
  - The need to be more flexible in thinking in order to reflect the faster pace of environmental change and greater degree of uncertainty.

    (See page 29.)

2   What is meant by 'capability'?
    A firm's capabilities refer to the distinctive competencies that it has developed to do something well and efficiently. A company is likely to enjoy a differential advantage in an area where its competencies outdo those of its competitors (see pages 29–30).

3   What are the principal influences upon capability?
    Capability is influenced by:

  - The firm's resources.
  - The value chain.
  - The way in which resources are used.
  - Financial factors.
  - Strengths relative to competitors.
  - The degree of balance within the organization.
  - Managerial ability.
  - The understanding of the market.
  - Access to the market.
  - The management culture.

    (See pages 29–30.)

4   What is involved in conducting a resource audit?
    The resource audit involves focusing upon:

  - Physical resources.
  - Human resources.
  - Financial resources.
  - Intangible resources.
  - Resources external to the organization, but to which it has access.

    (See pages 30–2.)

5   Explain what is meant by the value chain and how it can contribute to planning and control.

The concept of the value chain was developed by Michael Porter and involves focusing upon five primary activities and four support activities (see pages 31–2). He argues that its performance and competitive advantage is determined to a very large extent by how each of these elements is managed and the nature of the inter-relationships between them. The value chain therefore contributes to planning and control by highlighting these interrelationships and the ways in which they can be managed more effectively.

6   What is meant by 'efficiency' and 'effectiveness'? Which, if either, is the more important of the two concepts?

Efficiency and effectiveness were defined on page 9 and are elaborated upon on page 33. Organizations need, quite obviously, to be both efficient and effective, although of the two it is the latter (doing the right thing) which is arguably the more important.

7   Why is a comparative analysis of capability so important?

Comparative analysis helps the planner by demanding an external rather than a purely internal focus. It does this by requiring measures of capability to be looked at not in an absolute sense, but relative to competition. This, in turn, provides a far greater insight into the areas in which improvement is needed and/or possible.

8   What is 'benchmarking'?

This is defined in Definition box 2.3.

9   What are the possible limits of benchmarking as it has traditionally been practised?

The two principal limitations are the emphasis upon 'hard' (i.e. the easily meas-ured factors) rather than 'soft' (e.g. areas such as management culture) elements, and a tendency to benchmark within the industry rather than looking at best practice in an absolute or rather broader sense (see page 36).

10   Explain what is meant by organizational flexibility and adaptability.

Flexibility and adaptability are a measure of the organization's ability to cope with any changes that take place in the environment (see page 37).

11   How might portfolio analysis be used to arrive at a measure of organizational balance?

Models of portfolio analysis, such as the Boston Consulting Group framework, provide a framework for examining the nature, shape and health of an organiza-tion's portfolio currently and how this is likely to change in the future. With this information it is possible to determine the balance between the cash-generating and cash-using parts of the business (see page 37).

12   What are the key dimensions of the performance importance matrix?

The matrix is illustrated on page 39.

13   What financial measures should be used to arrive at a measure of capability?

Ten principal measures exist:

1   Profit margins.
2   Asset turnover.
3   The return on capital employed (ROCE).
4   Earnings per share.
5   Gearing.
6   Stock turnover.
7   The debt collection period.
8   The creditor collection period.
9   The current or working capital ratio.
10   The quick or liquidity ratio.

(See page 34.)

14   What is meant by an 'opportunity' and a 'threat'?

An *opportunity* is any sector of the market in which the organization would enjoy a competitive advantage.

A *threat* is a challenge posed by an unfavourable trend or development in the environment which, in the absence of a distinct organizational response, will lead to an erosion of the company's market position.

(See pages 40–1.)

15 What are the principal bases of competitive advantage?

These are listed in Figure 2.7 on page 43.

16 What are the causes of strategic drift and strategic wear-out?

- Changes in market structure as competitors enter or exit.
- Changes in competitors' stances.
- Competitive innovations.
- Changes in consumers' expectations.
- Economic changes.
- Legislative changes.
- Technological changes; these include, in some instances, the emergence of a new technology which at first sight is unrelated or only indirectly related to the company's existing sphere of operations.
- Distribution changes.
- Supplier changes.
- A lack of internal investment.
- Poor control of company costs.
- A tired and uncertain managerial philosophy.

17 Why is implementation so frequently a problem for organizations?

There are several causes, the most obvious of which are:

- The failure to think through in detail what would be involved if the objectives that have been set are to be achieved.
- Inadequate financing.
- A short-term management focus.
- Unexpected environmental changes.
- A flawed plan.
- Unrealistic objectives.

(See pages 44–5.)

18 What contribution is the 7-S framework capable of making to our understanding of the determinants of good and bad implementation?

The framework highlights the importance of understanding not only the three 'hard' factors of strategy, structure and systems, but also the four 'soft' elements of style, skills, staff and shared values. It is the failure to recognize the significance of the interrelationships between these and insufficient attention to the soft factors that all too often creates difficulties.

EXTENDING YOUR KNOWLEDGE

Because an understanding of capability is so fundamental to the development of an effective strategy, it is essential that you come to terms with the sorts of factors that encourage – and inhibit – *true* capability. Although we have already made reference in the study guide at the beginning of the unit to the need to read Chapters 2, 3 and 17 of *Strategic Marketing Management* and Chapter 2 of *Marketing Strategy*, it is perhaps worth emphasizing the importance of these yet again. You should also extend your knowledge by spending time with your senior managers and asking how they perceive areas of strength and weakness within the organization, and hence organizational capability.

Activity debrief

Question 2.1 You should begin by explaining the value chain (**Hint**: make use of a diagram such as the one on page 31) and the sort of thinking that underpins its use. In doing this, you need to highlight Porter's suggestion that competitive advantage is determined to a very large extent by how each of the five primary and four support activities is managed and the nature of the interactions between them. Against this background, you should then go on to discuss how this needs to be reflected in the approach to planning and control. This part of the answer offers scope for considerable detail, and so here we will make reference to just one of the nine dimensions, that of service.

In planning the service element, what objectives and standards are you intending to achieve? How might these be developed to give you a competitive advantage? In measuring your performance at a later stage, what are the implications for the future? (see pages 31–2).

Question 2.2 You should begin by identifying and explaining (briefly) the ten ratios that are most commonly used (these are listed on page 34). You should then go on to discuss how they provide a measure of performance from one time period to another (and hence provide a measure of effectiveness) and how they can be used to provide a measure of performance (and hence effectiveness) relative to one or more competitors (see pages 35–6).

Question 2.3 Several factors contribute to healthy and unhealthy product portfolios. Indications of health include the existence of cash cows which appear to have a long life; a number of up and coming stars; question marks which are moving towards the star cell; and few, if any, dogs.

Question 2.4 (i) You should begin by explaining what is meant by SWOT analysis. Having done this, you should then discuss how an understanding of strengths and weaknesses provides the planner with a measure of organizational capability. Following on from this, you need to show how an analysis of opportunities and threats highlights gaps in the market and any possible dangers for the organization. Armed with this information, plans can then be developed which are both organizationally and environmentally realistic.

Question 2.4 (ii) The potential problems of SWOT analysis include:

- An over-bland approach.
- A 'balance sheet' approach.
- The failure to examine strengths and weaknesses in terms of customers' perceptions and competitors' abilities.
- An insufficiently tight focus.
- The failure to consider the implications of the analysis for future strategies.

(See pages 40–1.)

Question 2.5 You should begin by explaining what is meant by strategic drift and strategic wear-out (this is discussed in some detail on pages 42 and 43). Having done this, move on to consider how the problems might possibly be avoided. In doing this, you should give emphasis to the need for:

- Managerial awareness of the potential problems and causes.
- Fighting complacency.
- A proactive stance.
- A regular review of internal processes and attitudes.
- A regular review of environmental shifts and the consequent opportunities and threats.

Question 2.6 You should begin by highlighting the implementation problems that are most commonly encountered (these are discussed on pages 44–5). Having done this, you should discuss the ways in which these barriers might be overcome. These include:

- A proactive stance.
- Detailed thinking during the planning stage about what will be involved during implementation.
- Regular feedback on performance.
- Well-developed control measures.
- A culture of responsibility and accountability.

Question 2.7 You should begin by defining or explaining competitive advantage (e.g. something which an organization is able to perform more efficiently or effectively than its competitors and which, *very importantly*, is meaningful to customers) and the need for the advantage to be sustainable. Having done this, explain the three principal bases of competitive advantage (see Figure 2.7) and, making use of Figure 5.5, the consequences of *not* having an advantage. You should then go on to suggest that despite the obvious importance of and need for a competitive advantage that gives customers a reason to buy, many organizations fall into the trap of being 'me too' companies (in other words, they simply do the same as everyone else). There are several possible explanations for this, the most obvious of which are:

- Managerial complacency and an adherence to old and increasingly tired marketing programmes.
- A failure to allocate the responsibility for marketing sufficiently clearly.
- A lack of managerial focus.
- A lack of understanding of market dynamics.
- A failure to invest sufficiently in the possible bases of differentiation.
- A desire to avoid confrontation, with this being reflected in an attitude of mind that leads to the copying of competitors' strategy.
- A belief that existing customers will remain loyal, even in the absence of a meaningful selling proposition.

Environmental analysis

In this unit you will examine the nature and structure of the marketing environment. As a result of this you will understand:

- Why a regular analysis of the environment is strategically and tactically important.
- How managers go about analysing and interpreting the environment.
- The principal environmental changes that have taken and are taking place.
- The key elements of an environmental scanning system and marketing information system.
- The key dimensions of competitor and customer analysis.

By the end of this unit you will:

- Appreciate how the environment influences and needs to be reflected in an organization's marketing strategy.
- Be aware of the interrelationships that exist between an organization and its environment.
- Be capable of analysing competitors and customers.
- Understand the principal dimensions of an environmental monitoring system.

This unit covers a selection of material from Stages 2 and 3 of the Planning and Control syllabus. As such it accounts for approximately 25 per cent of the syllabus and, together with the supporting reading, should take you about 9 hours. The additional activities may, of course, increase this significantly, depending upon the help that you are able to call upon.

Because the marketing environment is the ultimate determinant of an organization's performance, it is essential that a marketing manager has a clear and detailed understanding of its constituents, the nature of the interrelationships that exist, and of the ways in which the environment is changing currently and how these patterns of change are likely to develop in the future. It is therefore essential that in your study programme you make sure that you relate the course material to market developments. One way of doing this is to acquire the habit of scanning both the quality press and the trade press for up-to-date articles, surveys and reviews that relate businesses to their environments. You should, in turn, supplement this by listening to and watching business programmes on the radio and television. As you will see from the exam tip that appears later, many of the questions require you to apply your knowledge and to give examples.

Because of the pivotal importance of the environment to the marketing planner, particular elements of the environment are introduced and discussed in all four modules of the Diploma. You should therefore make a conscious effort to explore the ways in which these dimensions combine to paint a complete picture of the environment within which marketing managers have to operate. Given this, it is perhaps understandable that the area has in the past proved to be a fertile ground for exam questions. In some instances these questions have required candidates to focus upon particular elements of the environment (approaches to customer or competitor analysis would be an obvious example) whilst others have been rather more general in their nature and relate to the ways in which environmental factors might possibly influence the development of a marketing strategy (this would typically emerge in the mini and maxi case studies).

As with the other units in this workbook, we have concentrated upon identifying the principal elements that you should focus upon against a background of a more detailed programme of reading. Included within this should be:

Wilson and Gilligan with Pearson (1992) *Strategic Marketing Management: Planning, Implementation and Control*, Butterworth-Heinemann, Chapters 4, 5 and 7. Fifield (1992), *Marketing Strategy*, Butterworth-Heinemann, Chapter 3.

The marketing environment

In discussing the nature and significance of the marketing environment Wilson et al (1992, page 163) have commented that:

> Strategic marketing is . . . an essentially iterative process. It is iterative for a number of reasons, the most significant of which is that as the company's external environment changes so opportunities and threats emerge and disappear only to re-emerge perhaps in a modified form at a later stage. Because of this, the marketing strategist needs to recognize the fundamental necessity both for an environmental monitoring process that is capable of identifying in advance any possible opportunities and threats, and for a planning system and organizational structure that is capable of quite possibly radical changes to reflect the environment so that the effects of threats are minimized and that opportunities are seized.

This comment goes some way towards highlighting the significance of the environment and illustrates the need for marketing planners to understand its various dimensions and interrelationships in some detail. Without this knowledge, marketing decisions will be made in something of a vacuum and almost inevitably will fail to achieve the expected or hoped for impact. It follows from this that there is a need for managers to adopt a strong external focus in which detailed consideration is given to analysing and interpreting what is happening in the environment currently and to forecasting what changes are likely to occur in the future. One way of doing this involves developing an environmental monitoring system. However, before we discuss the nature and structure of the environment and how an environmental monitoring system might best be developed, complete the following activity.

Given our comments above, identify two examples of organizations which have failed to monitor the environment sufficiently and which, as a consequence, have been taken by surprise by changing market structures (this might include the emergence of new competitors, a different market approach by the firm's current competitors, new customer demands, and so on).

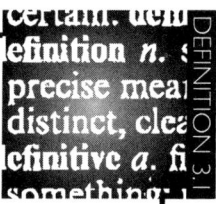

Kotler (1991, page 129) defines a company's marketing environment as being

'made up of the actors and forces that affect the company's ability to develop and maintain successful transactions and relationships with its target customers.'

This environment, which is illustrated in Figure 3.1, consists of two distinct components:

- The macro environment.
- The micro environment.

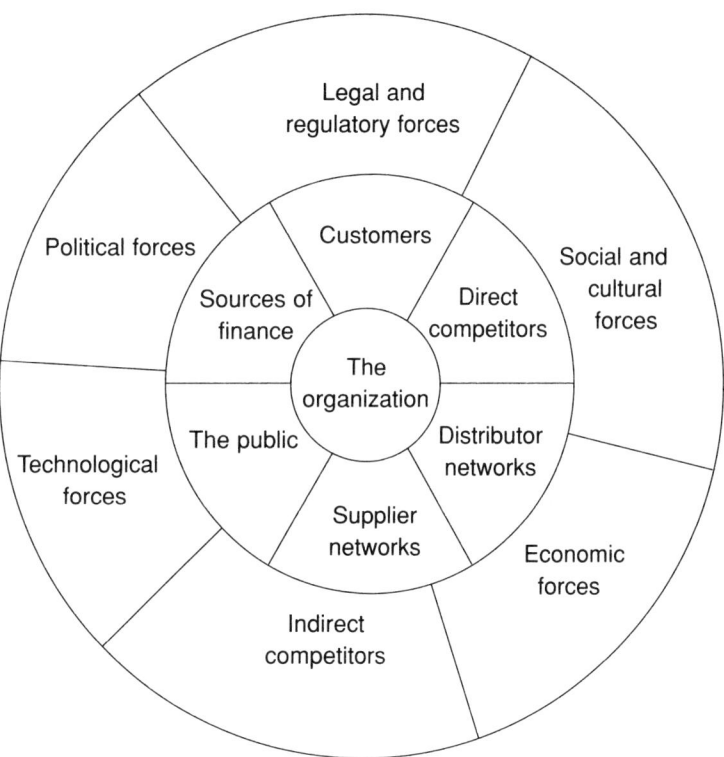

Figure 3.1   The marketing environment

The *micro* environment is the closer of the two to the organization. It is that part of the environment with which the organization interacts most immediately. Included within this are suppliers, customers, competitors, the public at large and the distribution network.

The *macro* environment consists of the rather broader set of forces that surround the organization including political, economic, social, cultural, demographic, technological and legal factors. These elements make up what are often referred to as the non-controllable elements of marketing and represent the framework within which most marketing decisions are made; this is illustrated in Figure 3.2. Although the elements on the left-hand side of the diagram are generally labelled as non-controllable, in practice it is often the case that at least some control can be exerted over several of the elements in the medium to long term. In the case of competitors, for example, strategic alliances might be developed, mergers might take place, and cartels – although often illegal – might be established, all of which have the effect of allowing for a degree of control to emerge. Equally, in the case of the legal environment, an organization's trade association might lobby Government in an attempt to have legislation passed that will be of benefit to member organizations; the immensely powerful tobacco

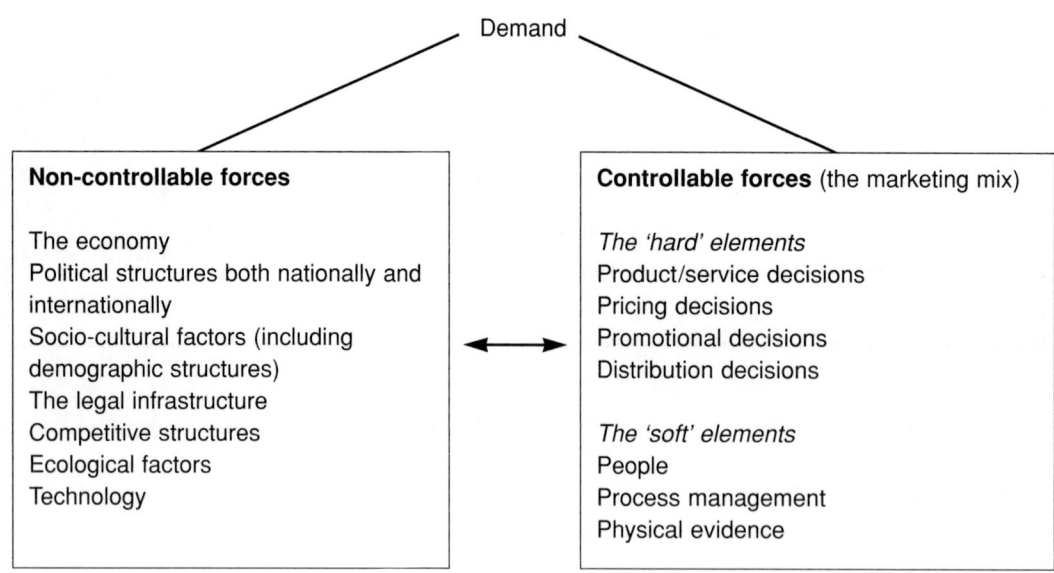

Figure 3.2 The marketing framework

lobby in Japan which has managed to limit severely the volume of western tobacco and cigarettes that can be imported into the country is an example of this. In the case of the political and economic dimensions, although the influence that can be exerted is perhaps less obvious, an organization – particularly a multinational – is likely to direct its investment patterns and marketing actions towards those parts of the world in which inflation rates are low, levels of political stability are high, and levels of consumer and organizational spending are buoyant. It is in this way that non-controllable factors become at least partially controllable.

Select two market sectors and identify the principal non-controllable elements in the macro environment. Having done this, identify how firms try to 'manage' these non-controllable elements in an attempt to reduce their impact or unpredictability. What success do they appear to have had?

The purpose of environmental analysis

The essential purpose of environmental analysis is to provide managers with a clear and detailed understanding of their current and future environments. Given this knowledge, managers should then be in a far stronger position to match the demands of the environment with the sorts of organizational capabilities that we referred to in Unit 2. However, while this might appear at first sight to be a relatively straightforward exercise, there are potentially a series of difficulties in doing this. This is partly because of the complexity of most environments, but also because there is often a degree of uncertainty as to how the environment *really* influences the organization. There are therefore two questions which the marketing planner needs to consider:

1 To what extent does or should the environment affect an organization's corporate strategy?
2 In what ways might organizational strengths and capabilities then best be related to the demands of the environment?

Because an understanding of the environment is so fundamental a part of any marketing strategy, always think in detail about the sort of environment that the organizations that feature in the mini and maxi case studies are faced with. Think also about the implications of this environment for management, the key forces and how well (or badly) the management team appear to have come to terms with these.

Environmental types

A number of writers have proposed methods for categorizing environments. Among the best known of these is the framework developed by Miles (1980) who advocates an approach based on the answers to six questions:

1　What degree of complexity exists in the environment?
2　How standardized or routinized are the organization's interactions with the environment?
3　What interconnections exist between the various dimensions of the environment?
4　What degree of dynamism and unpredictability exists in the environment?
5　To what extent is management receptive to the ways in which environmental pressures affect the organization's input and output processes?
6　What degree of flexibility does the organization possess in responding to the environment?

It is the answers to these questions which enables us to categorize environments as being:

- Simple/static.
- Dynamic.
- Complex.

Depending upon the type of environment faced by the organization, so the implications for approaches to environmental analysis – and subsequently the management of the organization – will vary. Remember, though, that particular problems emerge when an environment that previously has been relatively stable suddenly becomes far more volatile and complex.

Identify examples of each of the three environmental types referred to above. What are the marketing implications of each type for how an organization might operate?

In thinking about environmental types and the implications for management, Figure 3.3 should be of some help. In this, we move from the three forms referred to by Miles to four.

The first two of these – stability and incremental change – are both relatively straightforward, although stability is an environmental form which few organizations today experience. However, in both stages any changes that do take place are likely to be predictable and easy to manage. Rather bigger problems begin to emerge in Stage Three where the nature and magnitude of the changes increases, possibly fairly dramatically. For the marketing strategist there are two principal difficulties associated with this: firstly, that of forecasting what is likely to happen in the future, and then secondly, developing and implementing plans that are able to cope with these higher rates of change. These difficulties are then magnified further in Stage Four which we have labelled 'crazy days,' a phrase which

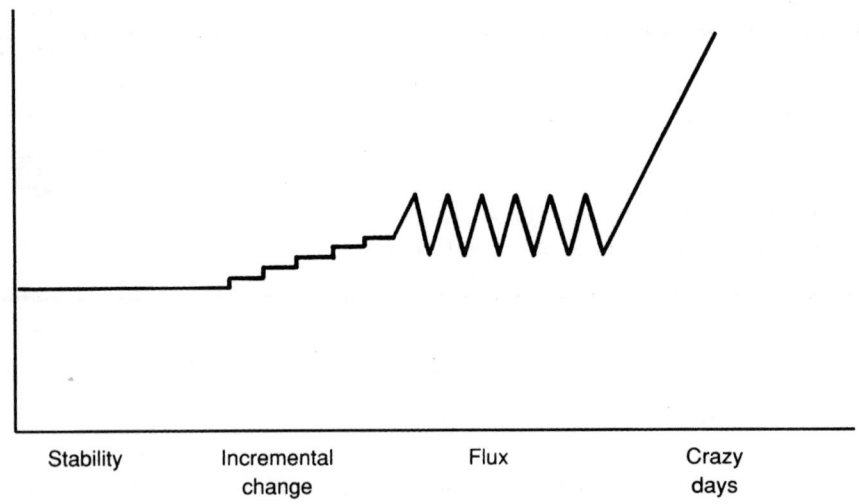

Figure 3.3 Patterns of environmental change

is taken from Tom Peters' book *Liberation Management*. In this, Peters argues that in the mid to late 1990s environmental uncertainty is the only certainty. Recognition of this and of the crazy days in which environmental structures change dramatically – and possibly increasingly malevolently – demands, he suggests, the far more innovative responses that he labels 'crazy ways'.

Look at the environment in which your organization operates and compare it with the sort of environment that existed ten years ago. In what ways has it changed? What problems have been experienced by the organization and its managers in coming to terms with the new environment? In what ways does it seem that the environment will change over the next few years? To what extent do you think that the organization's existing strategies, structures, systems and people will be able to cope with this?

(i) Identify the principal strategic challenges that marketers are likely to face over the next decade and comment upon their implications for approaches to marketing planning.

(Planning and Control, December 1992, Question 3.)

(ii) How would you assess the attractiveness of a proposed new market?

(Strategic Marketing Management: Planning and Control, June 1995, Question 6.)

Environmental change and the corporate response

For many organizations, the marketing environment of the late 1980s and early 1990s changed dramatically. Although one of the most obvious changes from the viewpoint of many consumers was the general slowdown and stagnation of western economies, there were in fact many other changes that were taking place at the same time. The implications for virtually all organizations were significant, and led to a series of often dramatic changes and responses, including a substantial amount of corporate restructuring; a summary of some of the ways in which the environment changed, and the organizational responses that emerged as a result of this, appears in Figure 3.4.

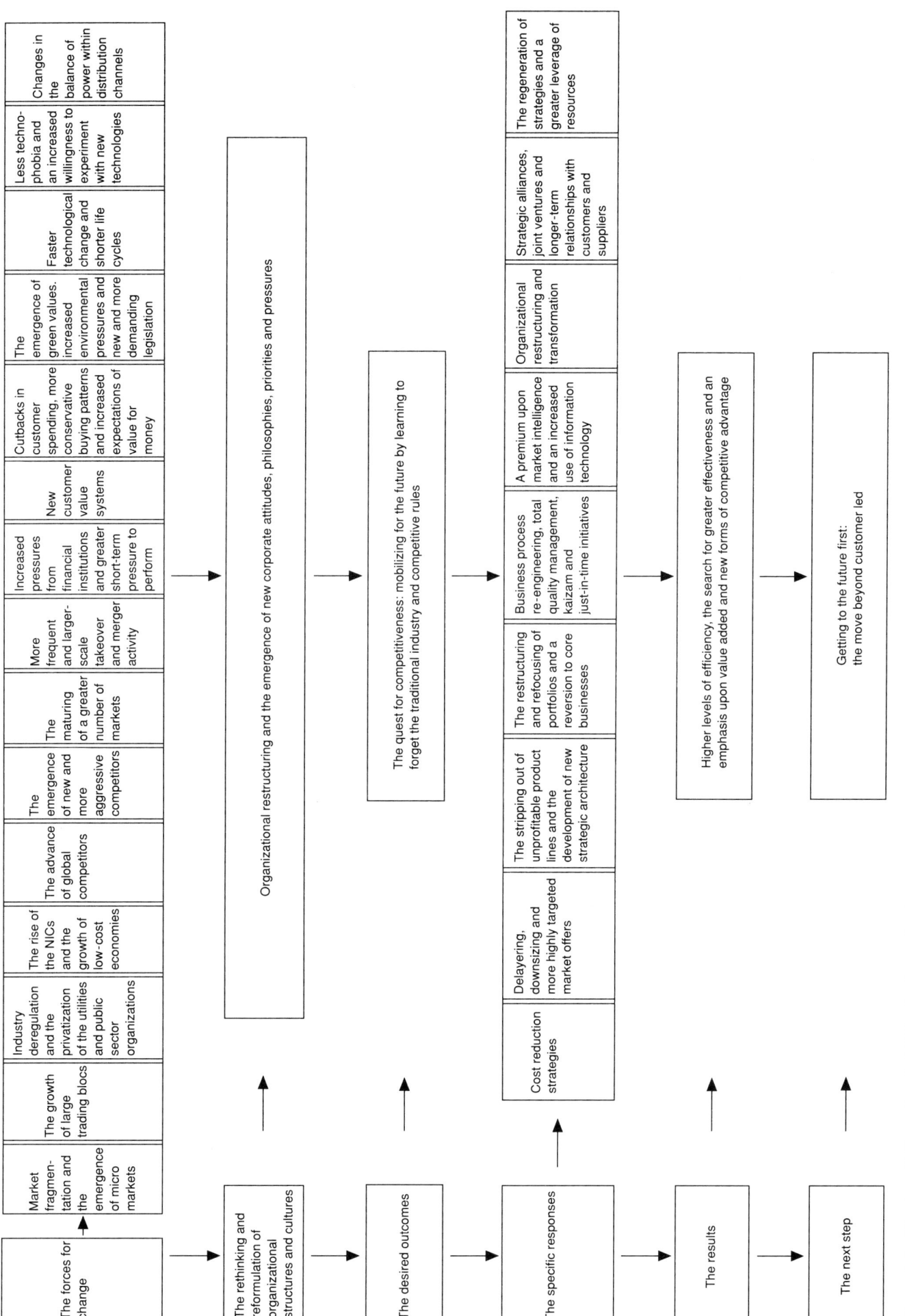

Figure 3.4 The late 1980s and early 1990s: the forces leading to corporate restructuring

The six stages of environmental analysis

Any analysis of the environment needs to be structured and detailed. It is therefore essential not only that environmental analysis takes place on a regular basis, but that it also has a clear focus and the results are then fully analysed, distributed to the appropriate people in the organization, and used subsequently in the development of strategies and tactics. Although a variety of approaches to environmental analysis exist, the most common involves a series of increasingly focused steps of the sort illustrated in Figure 3.4. The sequence, which was proposed by Johnson and Scholes (1993, page 76), is designed to provide the marketing planner with a clear understanding not just of the current state of the environment, but also how it is most likely to develop. In this way a picture of the principal opportunities and threats can be built up and a series of decisions then made about the strategic stance that the organization should adopt.

Making use of Figure 3.5, use Stages 1–3 to analyse your organization's environment. What picture emerges from this?

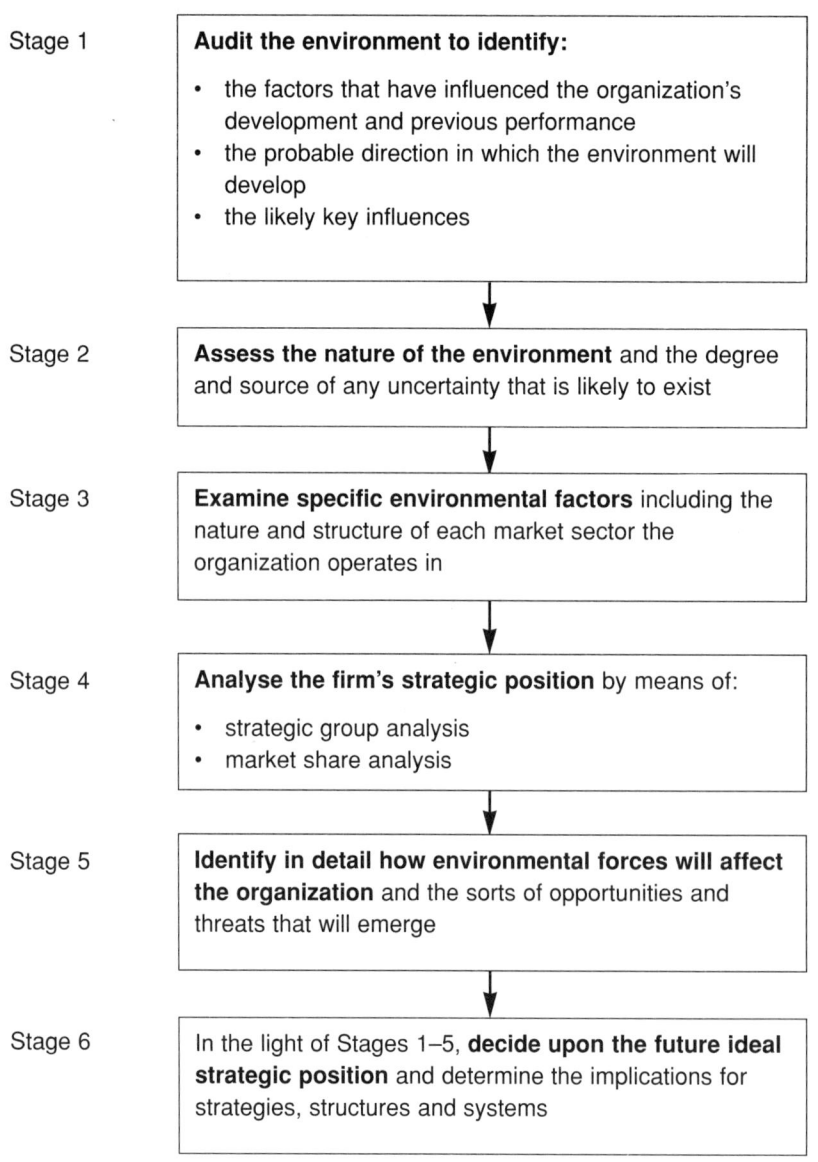

Stage 1	**Audit the environment to identify:**
	• the factors that have influenced the organization's development and previous performance
	• the probable direction in which the environment will develop
	• the likely key influences

| Stage 2 | **Assess the nature of the environment** and the degree and source of any uncertainty that is likely to exist |

| Stage 3 | **Examine specific environmental factors** including the nature and structure of each market sector the organization operates in |

Stage 4	**Analyse the firm's strategic position** by means of:
	• strategic group analysis
	• market share analysis

| Stage 5 | **Identify in detail how environmental forces will affect the organization** and the sorts of opportunities and threats that will emerge |

| Stage 6 | In the light of Stages 1–5, **decide upon the future ideal strategic position** and determine the implications for strategies, structures and systems |

Figure 3.5 The six stages of environmental analysis

(Adapted from Johnson and Scholes, 1993, *Exploring Corporate Strategy*, 3rd ed, page 76.)

The PEST framework

The general audit of environmental influences (Stage 1) represents the first stage of any environmental analysis and is designed to provide the strategist with an understanding of what is happening in each of the four principal dimensions of the environment: the political, economic, social and technological arenas. This analysis is typically referred to as PEST analysis and is illustrated in Figure 3.6.

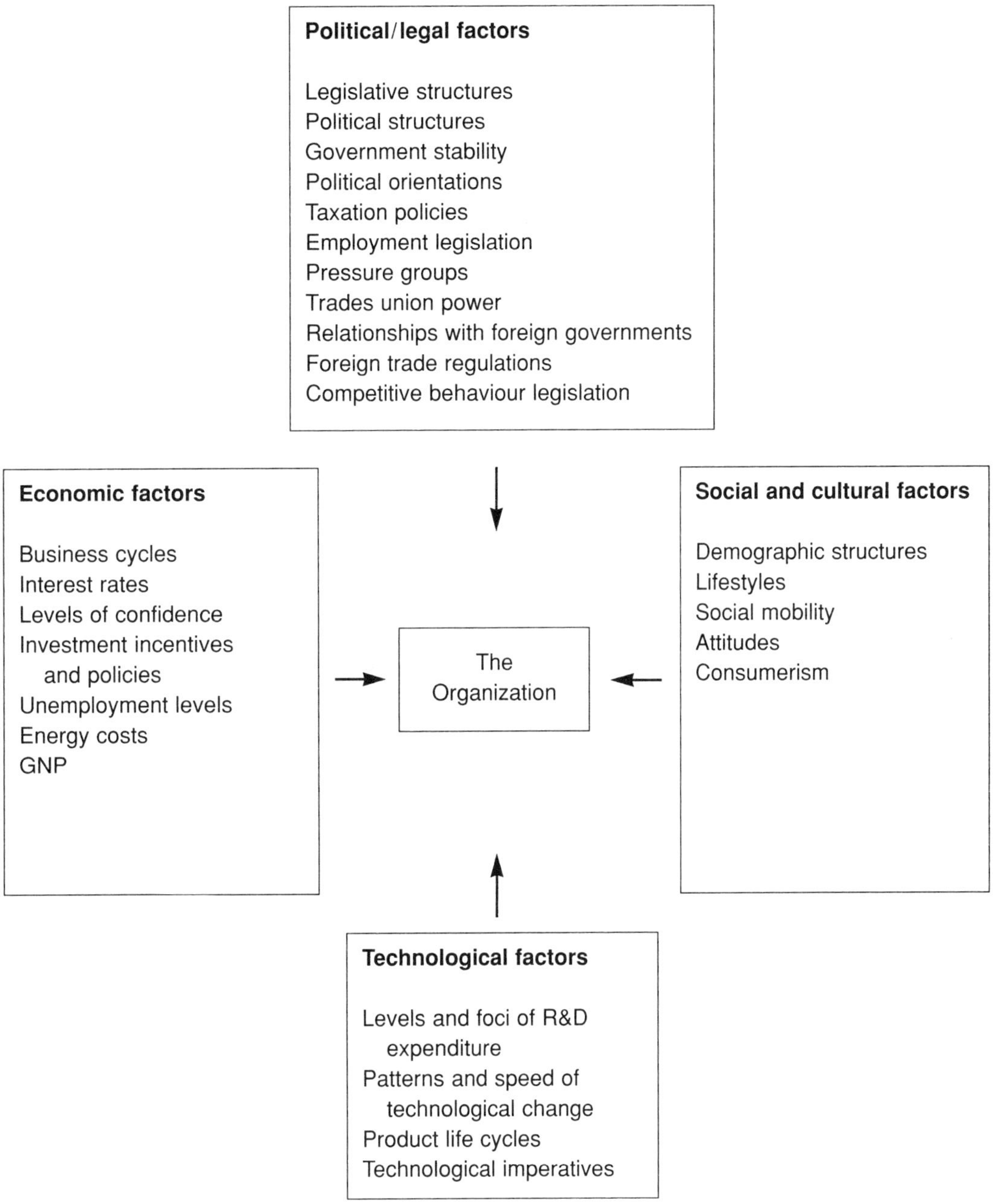

Political/legal factors

Legislative structures
Political structures
Government stability
Political orientations
Taxation policies
Employment legislation
Pressure groups
Trades union power
Relationships with foreign governments
Foreign trade regulations
Competitive behaviour legislation

Economic factors

Business cycles
Interest rates
Levels of confidence
Investment incentives
    and policies
Unemployment levels
Energy costs
GNP

The Organization

Social and cultural factors

Demographic structures
Lifestyles
Social mobility
Attitudes
Consumerism

Technological factors

Levels and foci of R&D
    expenditure
Patterns and speed of
    technological change
Product life cycles
Technological imperatives

Figure 3.6 The PEST framework

Take two market sectors and identify the principal environmental forces currently and how they appear to be reflected in the marketing strategies that firms are pursuing. In what ways do you think these pressures might change over the next few years? What are the implications of this for approaches to marketing planning and control?

ACTIVITY 3.6

Developing an environmental monitoring system

Evidence suggests that the majority of firms have only poorly developed environmental monitoring systems, something which is reflected in a comment by Wilson et al (1992, page 170):

> Recognition of the potential significance of environmental change highlights the need for a certain type of organizational structure and culture which is then reflected in both a balanced portfolio of products and in an adaptive management style supported by a well-developed intelligence and information monitoring system. Without this, the likelihood of the firm being taken unawares by environmental changes of one sort or another increases dramatically. Against the background of these comments, the need for environmental analysis would appear self-evident. All too often, however, firms appear to pay only lip service to such a need.

However, when organizations do recognize the need for a structured approach to environmental analysis, it appears that they move through a three-stage process in developing an environmental monitoring system:

1. *An appreciation stage* in which there is a general recognition within the company of the need to monitor the environment.
2. *An analysis stage* in which these approaches are formalized, the search for information is widened and greater attention is paid to the evaluation of information.
3. *An application stage* in which the process is formalized yet further with information evaluations being incorporated within strategies and plans.

QUESTION 3.2

What types of information should be collected as part of an environmental monitoring system? Is there a danger of collecting too much information with the result that managers are overwhelmed by the sheer volume of information available? Assuming that this is the case, how might you develop a truly user-friendly system?

The changing PEST environment

Perhaps the most obvious characteristic of the majority of today's markets is the degree of change that is taking place. Included within these changes are:

The political and legal environments

- A growing body of legislation that is designed to protect consumers from organizations abusing their power; legislation designed to limit large companies harming smaller ones; and legislation that protects society at large.
- The greater degree of influence that is being exerted by bodies such as the European Union.
- An upsurge in environmental and ecological issues.

The economic and competitive environments

- Possibly higher levels of economic uncertainty.
- A shift in economic and competitive power from Europe and the United States to Japan, the Pacific Rim and the industrializing nations.
- More intensely competitive markets with a greater emphasis upon new forms of competition.

The socio-cultural environments

- Changing demographic structures.
- Changing family structures.

- Shifting values.
- Major lifestyle changes.
- A greater willingness to accept technology.
- A greater emphasis upon value for money.
- Changing family roles.

The technological environment

- A seemingly ever-faster rate of technological change.
- Shorter product life cycles.

Quite obviously, the points that we have identified here do little more than simply scratch the surface. You should therefore think in detail about how each of these four elements is likely to change over the next few years and the probable implications for how organizations are likely to have to operate.

The June 1994 Planning and Control mini case study focused upon a firm of pump manufacturers who had been severely affected by a series of changes in their market. Question 1 put candidates in the position of the company's newly-appointed market analyst who had been given the responsibility for developing an environmental monitoring system. You might therefore find it useful at this stage to turn to the Unit 9, read the Watergate Pumps case study and attempt Question 1.

For a detailed discussion of approaches to market and environmental analysis, turn to Chapter 7 of *Strategic Marketing Management* by Wilson and Gilligan with Pearson, and to Chapter 3 of *Marketing Strategy* by Fifield.

Approaches to competitor analysis

In discussing issues of competition and approaches to competitor analysis, Wilson et al (1992, page 78) comment:

> Although the vast majority of marketing strategists acknowledge the importance of competitive analysis, it has long been recognized that less effort is typically put into detailed and formal analysis of competitors than, for example, of customers and their buying patterns. In many cases this is seemingly because marketing managers feel that they know enough about their competitors simply as the result of competing against them on a day-to-day basis. In other cases there is almost a sense of resignation with managers believing that it is rarely possible to understand competitors in detail and that as long as the company's performance is acceptable there is little reason to spend time collecting information. In yet others, there is only a general understanding of who it is that the company is competing against. The reality, however, is that competitors represent a major determinant of corporate success and any failure to take detailed account of their strengths, weaknesses, strategies and areas of vulnerability is likely to lead not just to a less than optimal performance, but also to an unnecessarily greater exposure to aggressive and unexpected competitive moves. Other probable consequences of failing to monitor competition include an increased likelihood of the company being taken by surprise, its relegation to being a follower rather than a leader, and to a focus on the short term rather than on more fundamental long-term issues.

Given the significance of this comment, they then went on to suggest that there is a need for marketing managers to pose five questions:

1 Who is it that we are competing against?
2 What are their objectives?
3 What strategies are they pursuing and how successful are they?
4 What strengths and weaknesses do they possess?
5 How are they likely to behave and, in particular, how are they likely to react to offensive moves?

It is the answers to these questions that enable the marketing planner to gain a greater understanding of the competitive environment (see Figure 3.7) and, ultimately, a far clearer idea of each competitor's probable response profile (see Figure 3.8).

Using your own organization or one with which you are familiar, complete Figure 3.7.

Your organization's products/services	The principal competitors	Your organization's market position	The intensity and bases of competition	The likelihood of new entrants to the sector	Your core marketing strategy
1					
2					
3					
4					

Figure 3.7 Coming to terms with the competitive environment

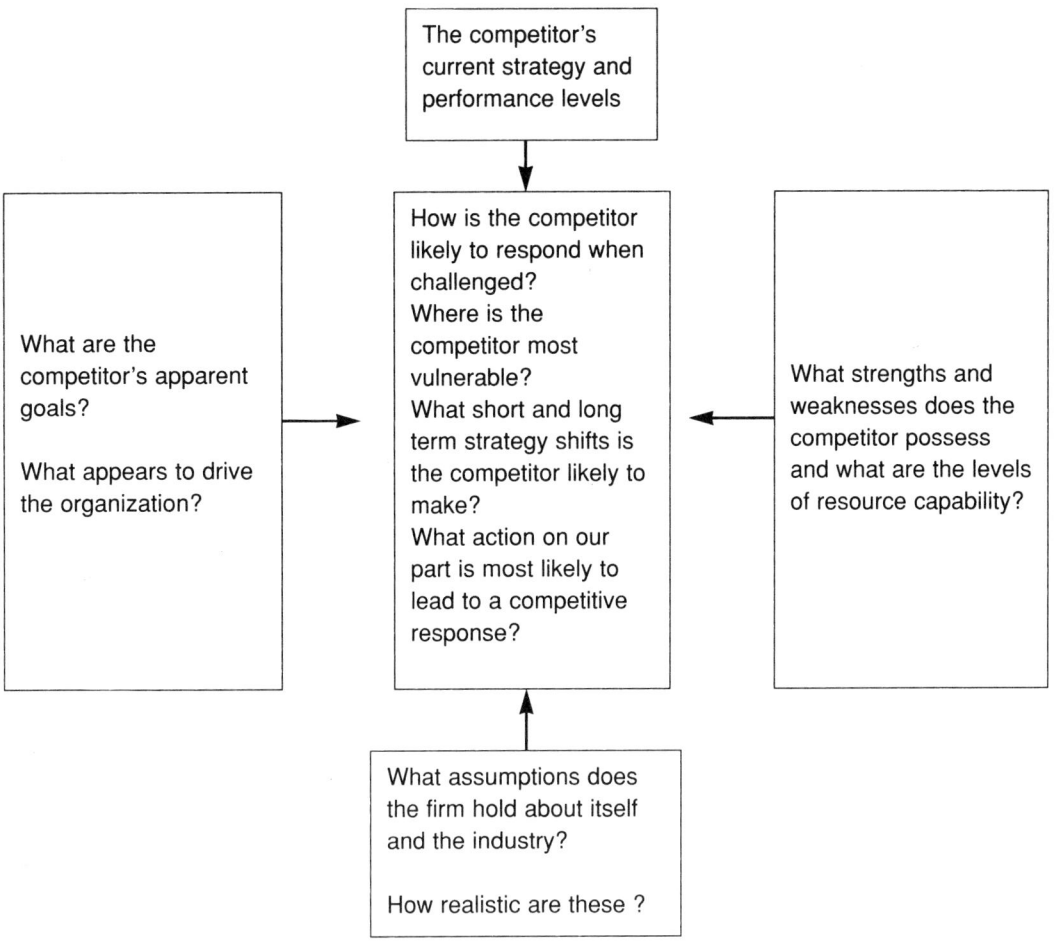

Figure 3.8 Identifying a competitor's response profile

One of the most significant contributions over the past few years to our understanding of competitive structures and of how competitive environments influence strategy has been made by Michael Porter.

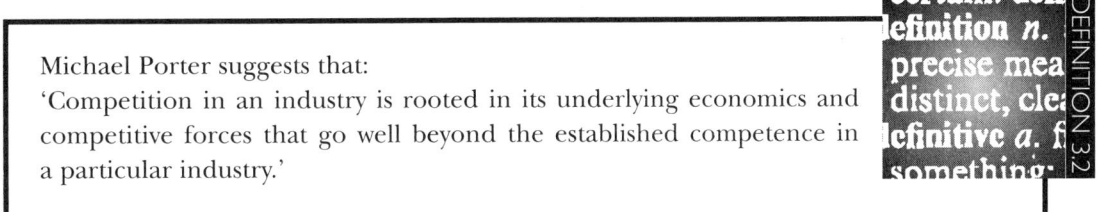

Michael Porter suggests that:
'Competition in an industry is rooted in its underlying economics and competitive forces that go well beyond the established competence in a particular industry.'

Coming to terms with existing and new competitors

If business history teaches us anything at all, it has to be the extent to which many organizations have failed to identify or recognize the significance of the competitive threats posed. All too frequently, managers either underestimate what an existing competitor is capable of doing, fail to react to competitive moves until considerable damage has been done, or are taken by surprise by a new entrant to the market. In many cases the reasons for this can be traced to the unnecessarily narrow ways in which managers define and perceive their competition. One of the first to comment upon this in detail was Theodore Levitt who in his now classic article 'Marketing Myopia' highlighted the almost inevitable consequences of adopting what is now usually referred to as 'an industry perspective of competition'. This perspective tends to lead to competitors being viewed in terms of those organizations which offer a broadly similar product or service. Because of this, the products are seen to be close substitutes for one another and the cross-elasticity of demand is therefore high; one of the most obvious and commonly cited examples of this is the market for butter. When the price of butter rises and/or a series of health concerns emerge about the fat content of butter, consumers switch to margarine.

The alternative to this involves adopting a far broader perspective of competition and, at its most extreme, defining it in terms of any product or service that might possibly attract consumers' spending power (this is referred to as 'the market perspective of competition'). In practice, of course, this extreme view is of little real value and so something more manageable is needed. In discussing this, Levitt refers to several examples, including the American railways system whose operators for many years made immense profits. Subsequently, however, the system has contracted enormously as 'new' competitors emerged in the form of airlines, transport companies, long-distance bus services and, of course, far higher levels of car ownership. Faced with this, the railways at first failed to recognize the threat but then underestimated its significance until it was too late to respond in any meaningful way. The result has been the virtual collapse of the industry.

The question that this raises is whether managers within the industry might possibly have identified the nature and significance of the threat at an early enough stage and then responded in such a way that the impact upon the railway companies might have been avoided altogether or, perhaps more realistically, minimized. The answer to this *has* to be that if the threat had been recognized as it emerged and grew, then a series of moves might have been made which would very largely have avoided the sorts of problems that the industry ultimately faced.

QUESTION 3.3

In the light of the comments above, what strategies might the railway companies have pursued that would have helped them come to terms with the growing competition?

In thinking about this question, you need to identify the alternatives that were open to the railway companies. Included within these were ignoring or failing to recognize the growing threat (this is broadly what they did); adopting the 'bunker mentality' by battening down the hatches in the hope that the threat would eventually go away; improving their levels of service (this is likely to be of only short-term value); and coming to terms with the threat by developing alliances with the new competition.

The fourth of these four alternatives involves recognizing several essential truths about competition:

- Competitive threats and challenges can come from unexpected as well as expected sources.
- New competitive threats can change market structures in a number of significant and far-reaching ways.
- In responding to competitors, a series of unorthodox, and often unpalatable, changes might be needed.
- Competitive arrogance is one of the most common reasons for organizations suffering a decline in their market position.

ACTIVITY 3.9

Look at your own organization and consider the following questions:

- Which competitive perspective – the industry perspective or the market perspective – predominates?
- What sorts of competitive changes are occurring in each of your major markets?
- Are these changes being led by your own organization or by another firm?
- To what extent does it appear that the full significance of any threats is recognized?

Against the background of our comments so far, turn to the activity below.

Using Figure 3.8, develop a response profile for one of your principal competitors. What picture emerges from this and what are the implications for the way in which you should try to 'manage' the competition?

The need to have a clear understanding of who exactly your competitors are and the nature of their strengths and weaknesses is also illustrated in Figure 3.9. In this, we list some of the alternatives to aluminium. Although not all of the materials listed in Column One are alternatives in each and every situation in which aluminium is used, the table goes some way towards illustrating how an overly narrow competitive perspective could well lead to an organization being taken by suprise as customers switch to the alternatives.

Material	*Advantages*	*Drawbacks*
Mild steel	Very cheap Widely available	Weight Rusts easily
Low chrome ferritic stainless steel	Similar price Widely available	Weight Rusts in sea water
Titanium	Strength (especially at temperature) Corrosion resistance	Cost Processing (not easily extrudable)
Magnesium	Very light weight	Vulnerable to fire
Polystyrene unplasticated PVC	Light weight Reasonably cheap	Low strength No temperature/fire resistance
ABS, nylon engineering plastics	Light weight Strong	Cost
Wood	Cheap Widely available	Variable quality Rots
Composites		
Aluminium MMC's	Stiffer Stronger Harder	Extra cost Processing difficulties
Fibre reinforced plastics	Lighter for quality stiffness/strength	Can lack toughness Extra cost

Figure 3.9 Substitutes for aluminium

Competitive relationships

In trying to understand how firms compete, there is a need to consider four questions:

1 What is each organization's existing strategy?
2 What performance levels are they achieving currently?

3 What strengths and weaknesses do they possess?

4 What might we expect of each competitor in the future?

?

(i) What information might a marketing manager need in order to understand a competitor? Where might this information come from? What problems might be encountered in collating this information?

(ii) What factors should be taken into account in conducting a detailed analysis of your competitors? What models or frameworks might be useful in this exercise?

(Strategic Marketing Management: Planning and Control, June 1995, Question 5.)

A variety of approaches can be used to examine competitive relationships, including the idea of strategic groups; an example of this appears in Figure 3.10. The thinking behind strategic grouping is straightforward and based on the idea that in the majority of industries competitors can be categorized on the basis of the similarities and differences that exist in the type of strategy being pursued; in Figure 3.10 this is done on the basis of the breadth of each firm's geographic coverage of the market and the extent to which the product range is broad or narrow. Having plotted the market's strategic groupings, the marketing planner needs then to focus upon each firm's strengths and weaknesses, its market position (leader, challenger, follower or me-too), and its probable response to market changes. The question of how to go about analysing strengths and weaknesses was discussed in Unit 2 and it may be worth referring back to this in order to refresh your memory.

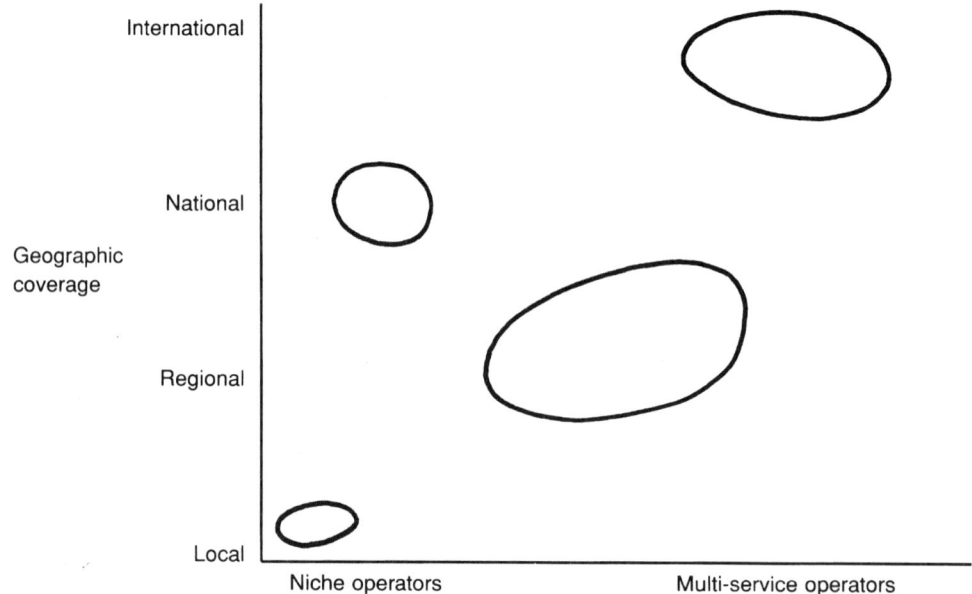

Figure 3.10 Strategic groups

With regard to the issue of market position, several frameworks have been developed. Two of the most useful involve categorizing firms on the basis of their relative position *within* a strategic group (is it the case for example that the firm's position is dominant, strong, favourable, tenable, weak or non-viable?); and focusing upon each organization's competitive status along the lines of the example in Figure 3.11.

Level	Competitive Status	Examples
1	One or a number of significant competitive advantages exist and are fully exploited	
2	A number of relatively small advantages exist that together give the organization a significant advantage	
3	Meaningful advantages either do not exist or are not recognized or exploited by the management team	
4	No real advantages exist	
5	Competitive disadvantages exist	

Figure 3.11 The five levels of competitive status (Adapted from Davidson, 1987, page 160.)

Look at Figure 3.11 and identify examples for each of the five levels of competitive status. Where within this would you put your own organization?

ACTIVITY 3.11

So what do you need to know about your competitors?

Marketing strategy must, of necessity, be based upon a clear and detailed understanding of each competitor's strengths and weaknesses. As a first step, therefore, the marketing planner needs to collect information under a number of headings as a prelude to a full comparative assessment of the principal competitors. In discussing this, Wilson et al (1992, page 92) suggest that the information that is typically needed includes:

- Sales.
- Market shares.
- Cost and profit levels and how they appear to be changing over time.
- Cash flows.
- Return on investment.
- Investment patterns.
- Production processes.
- Levels of capacity utilization.
- Organizational culture.
- Products and the product portfolio.
- Product quality.
- The size and pattern of the customer base.
- The levels of brand loyalty.
- Dealer and distribution channels.
- Marketing and selling capabilities.
- Operations and physical distribution.
- Financial capabilities.
- Management capabilities and attitudes to risk.
- Human resources, their capability and flexibility.
- Previous patterns of response.
- Ownership patterns and, in the case of divisionalized organizations, the expectations of corporate management.

Quite obviously, collecting such a depth and breadth of information on any single competitor is likely to prove difficult, time-consuming and expensive. For multiple competitors, the problems are of course confounded. It is for this reason that the majority of firms adopt a generally pragmatic approach by focusing upon those organizations which they perceive to be their most immediate or significant competitors and which, therefore, appear to pose the most obvious threat, and then collecting information under a rather more limited number of headings than appears in the list above.

ACTIVITY 3.12

Who are your organization's three principal competitors? How much detailed information exists on each of these? What other information would be of value?

However, even when large amounts of competitive information are readily available, managers still face the problem of making use of this in an effective way. Only rarely is competitive information available in the form that managers really want and so they are often faced with the task of interpreting and coming to terms with ambiguity and having to second guess the implications of the sorts of pictures that emerge. Because of this, there are major benefits to be gained from developing a *structured* information system that, on a regular basis, pulls together the information that managers see as being the most strategically and tactically useful and significant.

The potential sources of this information are discussed in rather greater detail in the next section, but would generally include customers, distributors, the trade press, trade shows, and the company's own staff.

The interpretation and assessment of information is a problem that many managers face and it is for this reason that it is often worth developing comparative profiles that take account of customers' principal buying factors. One of the ways in which this can be done is by means of the sort of framework that appears in Figure 3.12 and, returning for a moment to Unit 2, Figure 2.4 on page 39.

ACTIVITY 3.13

Using Figure 3.12, prepare a comparative assessment of your organization's performance against its three principal competitors (the guidelines for how the figure should be completed appear at the bottom of the figure).

The sources of competitive information

Information on competitors is typically available from a large number of sources. The task faced by the planner can therefore be seen in terms of identifying in detail what sorts of competitive information would be the most valuable and then developing the systems that will ensure that this information is collected in a regular and systematic way.

QUESTION 3.5

It has been suggested that the sales force is a potentially valuable but frequently under-utilized source of marketing information. Given this, explain how a sales force might be used as a structured source of information. What types of information might they be expected to generate? (Planning and Control, December 1993, Question 3.)

Customers' buying factors	Our organization	Performance of competitors		
		1	2	3
Products				
Design				
Quality				
Performance				
Value for money				
Add-ons				
Running costs				
Reliability				
Breadth of the product range				
Depth of the product range				
Prices				
Price levels				
Volume discounts				
Promotion				
Levels of advertising				
Apparent effectiveness				
Product literature				
Performance at exhibitions and trade shows				
Sponsorship				
Selling and distribution				
Sales force calibre				
Experience				
Geographic coverage				
Sales force – customer relations				
Service				
Servicing costs				
Flexibility				
Speed				
Service levels				
Overall product performance				
Performance against promise				

Notes: In completing this, you should rate each dimension for each organization as Excellent, Good, Equal, Fair or Poor. In doing this you should not rely upon preconceived (and possibly misconceived) notions, but instead make use of marketing intelligence studies of current and potential customers, suppliers and distributors.

Figure 3.12 The comparative assessment of firms
(Adapted from Wilson and Gilligan with Pearson, 1992, *Strategic Marketing Management*, page 93.)

There are, in essence, three major sources of competitive data:

1 *Recorded data* such as primary market research; secondary sources such as the Mintel reports, the trade press, government reports, public documents, the daily press and technical journals; and company annual reports.
2 *Observable data* including competitors' price levels and shifts, their advertising campaigns, sales-force feedback, and product comparisons.
3 *Opportunistic data* such as that which emerges from trade shows, discussions with raw material suppliers, distributors, sub-contractors, packaging suppliers, company newsletters, conferences, new recruits, and a competitor's disgruntled employees.

Together, these are – or should be – capable of providing an increasingly detailed picture of competitors, although ultimately, of course, their value depends upon the interpretations that are put upon them (that is, the way in which the raw data are turned into useable information) and, subsequently, how the information is used. All too often, for example, information comes into an organization and is not then either evaluated properly or channelled to the most appropriate people.

The different types of competitor

In Figure 3.8 we outlined how competitors' response profiles might possibly be developed. With this information, competitors can be categorized in various ways. Kotler (1988, page 247), for example, identified four types:

1 *Laid back competitors* who only rarely react quickly or aggressively.
2 *Selective competitors* who respond to certain types of initiative such as a price cut, but not to others such as an increase in advertising levels.
3 *Tiger competitors* who respond quickly and aggressively, irrespective of the type of competitive move.
4 *Stochastic competitors* who exhibit unpredictable reaction patterns. In some cases these firms will respond aggressively to a competitor's move whilst on other occasions they will ignore broadly similar moves.

As an alternative to Kotler's approach, you might also think about Michael Porter's classification of firms as 'good' or 'bad' competitors. A 'good' competitor, he suggests, sticks to the industry's unwritten rules, avoids upsetting the status quo, avoids aggressive price changes, and generally works towards maintaining the balance of a healthy industry. 'Bad' competitors, by contrast, typically pursue unnecessarily aggressive moves, slash prices and, by virtue of their actions, force others in the industry to take high risks.

What makes a competitor vulnerable?

Any analysis of competitors needs to identify their areas of vulnerability. There are various factors that contribute to organizational vulnerability, including:

Financial factors
- A shortage of cash.
- Low margins.
- High operating costs.
- Inflexible cost structures.

Market factors
- An over-dependence upon one market.
- An over-dependence upon one account.
- A low market share.
- A high market share which leads to organizational complacency.
- Premium pricing.
- A dependence upon low-growth markets.
- A predictable strategy and response pattern.
- A poorly defined competitive stance.

Product factors
- Poor product quality.
- High servicing costs.
- Product obsolescence.

Organizational factors
- Bureaucratic structures.
- Complacent managerial attitudes.
- Low levels of staff skills.
- Poor training.
- A short-term focus.
- A lack of planning and foresight.
- Poor labour relations.
- Organizational myopia.
- Competitive arrogance and a belief that the organization's current position can not be eroded.
- Organizational inertia.

What is the underlying cause of organizational vulnerability? (In thinking about this, recognize that the factors that we have listed are the result of something more fundamental within an organization.)

QUESTION 3.7

Setting up a competitive information system (CIS)

It should be obvious from our discussion so far that the benefits of a competitive monitoring, intelligence and information system are potentially significant. Equally, it should be apparent that the consequences of *not* having such a system are likely to be reflected in the organization being taken by surprise and being forced ever more frequently into a reactive posture. Given this, we can identify several straightforward guidelines for establishing a CIS:

- Deciding in detail what information is needed.
- Collecting the data.
- Analysing and evaluating the data.
- Disseminating the information to the appropriate managers throughout the organization.
- Developing strategies based upon the information.
- Feeding back the results in order to monitor and improve the system.

These ideas have been discussed by Davidson (1987, page 34) who, in commenting on the mechanics of a CIS, highlights the need for the following:

- A focus upon three or four key competitors.
- Selecting and briefing data collectors in each department.
- Allocating the responsibility for chasing, co-ordinating and evaluating the data that emerge to a single person and ensuring that this is seen as an integral and important part of that person's job.
- Ensuring that the data collectors also know that it is an integral part of their job rather than an additional and dispensable activity, and that they provide regular and detailed data flows.
- The publication of regular tactical and strategic reports.

To this we can add the need for the reports to be presented in a way that the users find meaningful and that the system is driven by a member of the senior management team who is fully committed to it. Without this, it is likely that the system will be seen to be of little real value. (Again, you might find it useful to refer to Unit 9 and the Watergate Pumps mini case and suggested solution.)

For a detailed discussion of approaches to competitor analysis, turn to Chapter 4 of *Strategic Marketing Management* by Wilson and Gilligan with Pearson, and to pages 57, 64–6 and 82 of *Marketing Strategy* by Fifield.

Understanding customers

In discussing approaches to customer analysis, Wilson et al (1992, page 101) have suggested that:

> It has long been recognized that marketing planning is ultimately driven by the marketing strategist's perception of how and why customers behave as they do and how they are likely to respond to the various elements of the marketing mix.

> In the majority of markets however, buyers differ enormously in terms of their buying dynamics. The task faced by the marketing strategist in coming to terms with these differences is consequently complex. In consumer markets, for example, not only do buyers typically differ in terms of their age, income, educational levels and geographic location, but more fundamentally in terms of their personality, their lifestyles and their expectations. In the case of organizational and industrial markets, differences are often exhibited in the goals being pursued, the criteria employed by those involved in the buying process, the formality of purchasing policies, and the constraints that exist in the form of delivery dates and expected performance levels.

> Despite these complexities, it is imperative that the marketing strategist understands in detail the dynamics of the buying process since the costs and competitive implications of failing to do so are likely to be significant.

Understanding buyer behaviour – the first step

The first step in any analysis of consumer or organizational buyer behaviour involves posing – and answering – seven questions:

1. Who is in the market and what degree of power do they have?
2. What do they buy?
3. Why do they buy?
4. Who is involved in the buying process?
5. How do they buy?
6. When do they buy?
7. Where do they buy?

Because an understanding of buyers and their motives is so fundamental a part of the marketing process, a considerable amount of time and effort has been directed towards the development of frameworks and models that will help in this. The first and most basic of these takes the form of what is referred to as a black box model, an example of this is illustrated in Figure 3.13. Although within a black box model we understand the inputs and the outputs, we do not understand exactly *how* the buyer evaluates and processes the inputs and arrives at a decision. Because of this, a considerable amount of research work in recent years has concentrated upon trying to improve our understanding of the evaluation process.

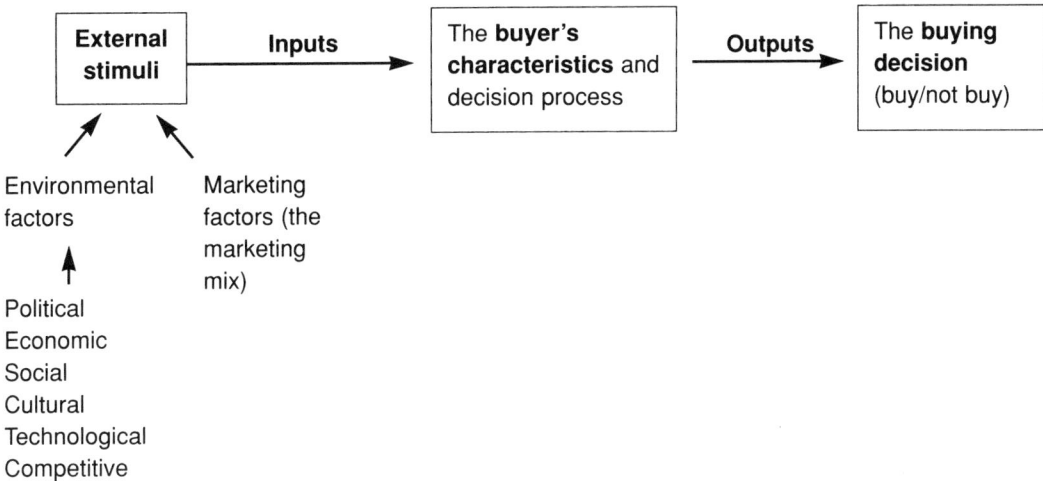

Figure 3.13 A black box model of the buying process

The differences between customers and consumers

Before going any further, we need to make a distinction between customers and consumers. The customer is the buyer of the product or service but may not necessarily also be the user. Instead, it is the user of the product who is the consumer. In the case of industrial products, for example, the customer may be the purchasing department which is operating to a series of distinct and written purchasing guidelines. The consumer or user might be a secretary or a machine operator. In the case of consumer goods, a parent might be the customer in that he or she buys the product, whilst the product is then consumed, or used, by the child. In both instances we need to recognize the possible different expectations of the customer (value for money, reliability, credit terms, and so on) and the consumer (image, range of features, immediate availability, and so on) and subsequently how these need to be reconciled and reflected in the marketing campaign.

The four types of buyer behaviour

Because products vary considerably in terms of their complexity, their prices and what we expect of them, we need to think about how they can be categorized so that approaches to analysing buyers reflect these differences. One way of doing this involves focusing upon two principal dimensions:

- The degree of involvement that the customer has with the product.
- The extent to which the buyer sees differences between the product or brand alternatives to be significant.

Using these two dimensions enables us to develop a simple matrix of the sort in Figure 3.14.

The customer's degree of involvement
with the product

	Low	High
Low	Repetitive buying behaviour	Behaviour designed to reduce buyer dissonance
High	A search for variety	Complex buying behaviour

The degree and significance of differences between the brand alternatives

Figure 3.14   The four types of buying behaviour (Source: adapted from Assael, 1987, page 87.)

ACTIVITY 3.15

Using Figure 3.14, find examples of the four types of buyer behaviour and consider the implications for marketing behaviour.

Influences on consumer behaviour

It is generally acknowledged that there are four main influences upon consumers:

1   *Cultural factors* such as:

- The culture of the society in which the individual grows up.
- Sub-cultures including nationality groups, religious groups, racial groups and geographical areas, all of which exhibit degrees of difference in ethnic taste, cultural preferences, taboos, attitudes and lifestyle.
- Social stratification and, in particular, social class.

2   These cultural factors are then influenced by a series of *social factors* including:

- Reference groups.
- The family.
- Social role.
- Status.

3   The third category consists of *personal influences* on behaviour such as:

- Age and life cycle stage.
- The person's occupation.
- Economic circumstances.
- Lifestyle.
- Personality.

4   The final set of influences are *psychological* and include:

- Motivation.
- Perception.
- Learning and beliefs.
- Attitudes.

These are illustrated in Figure 3.15 and highlight the typically broad or general influence exerted by cultural factors and the increasingly specific influence of the other three dimensions as you move through the model towards the buyer.

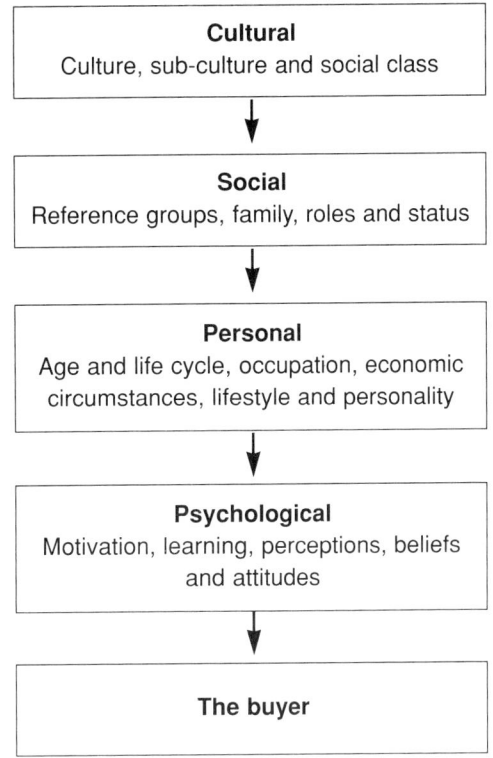

Cultural
Culture, sub-culture and social class

Social
Reference groups, family, roles and status

Personal
Age and life cycle, occupation, economic circumstances, lifestyle and personality

Psychological
Motivation, learning, perceptions, beliefs and attitudes

The buyer

Figure 3.15 Influences upon consumer behaviour

How might the model that is illustrated in Figure 3.15 be used to increase our understanding of consumer buying patterns for:

- Foodstuffs?
- Cigarettes?
- Brands of alcohol?
- Cars?

Which are the seemingly most important influences upon consumer choice in each case? What are the implications for the marketing planner?

QUESTION 3.8

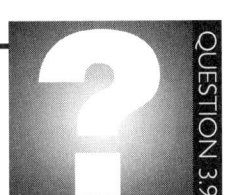

(i) Making reference to a product or organization of your choice, identify the principal socio-cultural characteristics that appear to influence buyer behaviour. What are their implications for marketing planning?

(Marketing Planning and Control, June 1993, Question 4.)

(ii) Making reference to examples, identify the principal influences upon the consumer buying process. What are the implications of these for the marketing planning process?

(Strategic Marketing Management: Planning and Control, December 1995, Question 5.)

QUESTION 3.9

The buying decision process

With an understanding of the factors which influence behaviour, the marketing planner needs then to turn to the buying process. In doing this there is a need to focus upon:

- The types of buyer behaviour.
- The various buying roles within the decision making unit.
- The decision process.

We have already made a brief reference to the first of these three areas and it may therefore be worth returning for a moment to Figure 3.14 and the accompanying activity.

With regard to *buying roles*, we can distinguish between those circumstances in which identifying the buyer is a relatively easy exercise and those in which a number of people are involved. In the case of the family holiday or a car, for example, there are five clear roles:

1 The *initiator* who initially suggests buying the product or service.
2 The *influencer* or *influencers* who are capable of affecting the decision that ultimately is made.
3 The *decider* who makes the buying decision.
4 The *buyer* who physically makes the purchase.
5 The *user* or *users* who consume the product.

ACTIVITY 3.16

Taking the example of a family holiday, identify who might play each of the five buying roles and how the decision might be arrived at. What, if any, trade-offs might occur within the process? In what ways might a holiday company influence the decision and at whom should the message(s) be aimed?

It should be apparent from this that there is a very real need to understand the buying decision process in considerable detail, since it is this understanding which allows the marketing effort to be focused at the appropriate individual and the message tailored to fit their information needs. To help in this, it is useful to think about the stages which people typically go through in arriving at a decision; these are illustrated in Figure 3.16.

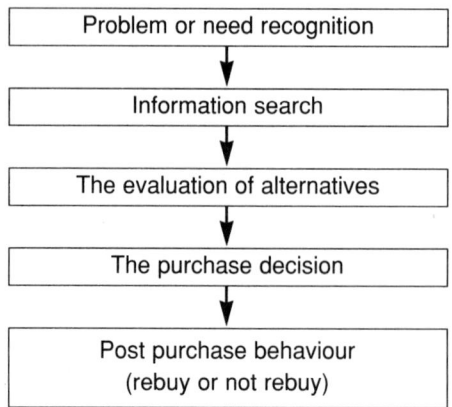

Figure 3.16   The five stages of the buying process

Although sequential models of this type have been heavily criticized for their rather simplistic nature and failure to take account both of the richness and complexity of the decision process, they have a useful role in highlighting the principal stages through which buyers move either explicitly or implicitly.

It can be seen from Figure 3.16 that the process begins with the *recognition of a problem or need*. This can be sparked off in one of several ways including an advertisement, a friend or colleague's comment, the increasing unreliability of a car (and therefore the need for a new model), or changing food tastes.

The second stage involves the *search for information* and can range from the casual reading of an advertisement through to the detailed analysis of brochures, the specialist press, discussions with experts, and so on. The outcome of this is that the consumer's awareness, knowledge and understanding of the brand alternatives is increased dramatically and leads to an *evaluation of the alternatives* and a reduction in the number of brands that are seen to be serious candidates for purchase; this filtration of brands is illustrated in Figure 3.17.

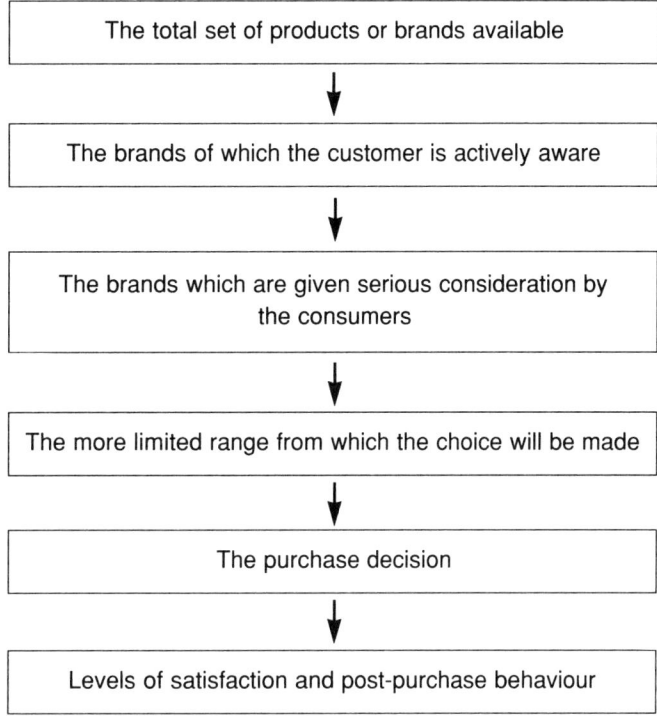

Figure 3.17   The consumer filtration process

The criteria which will be used in the ultimate choice will, of course, vary from one product to another and one consumer to another. It has been suggested, for example, that consumers can be categorized in terms of whether they are *deliberate* buyers in that they search actively for considerable amounts of information which they then carefully process, or whether they are *compulsive* buyers. Equally, consumers differ enormously in terms of their susceptibility to particular dimensions of the marketing programme such as price, advertising appeals, the type of distribution outlet, packaging, special offers and even country of origin. However, underpinning this is one simple fact that marketing planners should never lose sight of. It is that:

Customers do not buy products, they buy the benefits that the product or service delivers.

This has been discussed in some detail by Malcolm McDonald who argues for the 'which means that' test in order to link a product's features with the benefits that these features deliver. Amongst the examples that he gives to illustrate this is 'Maintenance times have been reduced from 4 to 3 hours *which means that* most costs are reduced by . . .'

Think about a product or service offered by your organization and list the various benefits that it offers and then apply McDonalds '*which means that*' test. To what extent does the marketing programme really give em-phasis to these? What benefits do competitors offer and stress? What benefits do customers really want?

So how does the consumer buying process work?

In coming to terms with buyer behaviour, marketing managers need to understand not just the sorts of factors that influence behaviour, but also how these influences are then reflected in the buying process. Is it the case, for example, that buyers consistently exhibit high degrees of brand loyalty and almost irrespective of what other organizations offer would not be swayed, or is it the case that in buying terms they exhibit a high degree of brand promiscuity? Amongst the other sorts of questions that therefore need to be answered are:

- How important is price?
- What role does advertising play?
- How much information do customers need?
- How significant is the product's country of origin?
- Do customers need the help of store assistants?

Knowing in detail *how* customers buy is therefore an important dimension of the marketing process. Because of this, researchers have proposed a variety of models in an attempt to understand more fully the buying process and hence how customers' behaviour patterns might most readily be influenced.

The earliest of these was proposed by Marshall, an economist, who developed the idea of 'economic man'. 'Economic man', he suggested, acts in a wholly rational manner and attempts to maximize the utility of any purchase. Although the model provides a potentially useful conceptual underpinning for any analysis of buyer behaviour, it is quite obviously a far from accurate reflection of how people behave in practice. Because of this, a number of models that gave a greater and more explicit recognition to the consumer's psychological state before, during and after the purchase began to be developed in the 1960s. The best known of these models were developed by Nicosia (1966), Engal, Kollat and Blackwell (1968), and Sheth (1969). Labelled the 'comprehensive models of consumer behaviour', they attempted to illustrate the breadth of the inputs to the decision process, the complexity of the information processing, and the ways in which the outputs need to be seen not just in terms of the purchase decision, but also in terms of the implications for perception and learning.

EXTENDING YOUR KNOWLEDGE

For a discussion of the structure of these models, refer to page 117 of *Strategic Marketing Management* by Wilson and Gilligan with Pearson.

Although these – and other – models have undoubtedly helped in our understanding of how buyers' behaviour patterns are influenced, they have been subjected to considerable criticism in recent years. Foxall (1987, page 128), for example, has suggested that:

1 The models assume an unrealistic degree of consumer rationality.
2 Observed behaviour often differs significantly from what is described.
3 The implied decision process is too simplistic and sequential.
4 Insufficient recognition is given to the relative importance of different types of decisions – each decision is treated by comprehensive models as significant and of high involvement, but the reality is very different and by far the vast majority of decisions made by consumers are relatively insignificant and of low involvement.
5 The models assume consumers have a seemingly infinite capacity for receiving and ordering information – in practice, consumers ignore, forget, distort, misunderstand or make far less use than this of the information with which they are presented.
6 Attitudes towards low involvement products are often very weak and only emerge after the purchase and not before as comprehensive models suggest.
7 Many purchases seem not to be preceded by a decision process.
8 Strong brand attitudes often fail to emerge even when products have been bought on a number of occasions.

9   Consumers often drastically limit their search for information, even for consumer durables.

10 When brands are similar in terms of their basic attributes, consumers seemingly do not discriminate between them but instead select from a repertoire of brands.

ACTIVITY 3.18

Take two different types of purchase that you make (e.g. a low cost and frequent purchase and a much higher cost and less frequent purchase) and attempt to construct a model that not only explains the thinking processes that you go through but which would also enable someone else to predict how you are likely to behave in the future.

Organizational buying behaviour

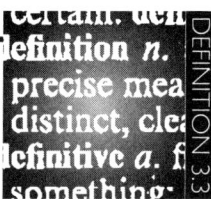

Webster and Wind (1972, page 2) define organizational buying as 'the decision-making process by which formal organizations establish the need for purchased products and services, and identify, evaluate and choose among alternative brands and suppliers.'

Although organizational and consumer buying processes have numerous points of similarity, there are also many areas in which they differ. In discussing this, Kotler (1988, page 208) highlights the way in which:

- Organizations buy goods and services to satisfy a variety of goals: making profits, reducing costs, meeting employee needs, and meeting social and legal obligations.
- More persons typically participate in organizational buying decisions than in consumer buying decisions, especially in procuring major items. The decision participants usually have different organizational responsibilities and apply different criteria to the purchase decision.
- The buyers must heed formal purchasing policies, constraints, and requirements established by their organizations.
- The buying instruments, such as requests for quotations, proposals, and purchase contracts, add another dimension not typically found in consumer buying.

The strategic importance of organizational buying has been referred to by a growing number of writers in recent years, all of whom have emphasized the sort of comment made by Turnbull (1987, page 147) when talking about the telecommunications market:

Some telecommunications equipment manufacturers now buy in items accounting for up to 80 per cent of total cost. Thus even a 2 per cent procurement saving can have a marked effect on profitability or give the company a significant price advantage in the marketplace.

ACTIVITY 3.19

Look at the purchasing process within your organization and think about the following questions:

- How is the purchasing process organized?
- How influential within the organization is the person who has overall responsibility for purchasing?
- How often are suppliers reviewed?
- What sort of criteria are used for this?
- What evidence is there that purchasing is viewed *strategically* and as a potential source of competitive advantage?

The differences between consumer and organizational markets

We have already made the comment that organizational and consumer markets have a number of points both of similarity and difference. These differences have been summarized by Wilson et al (1992, pages 118–119) as:

1 The existence of a smaller number of buyers each of whom typically buys in larger quantities than is the case in consumer markets.
2 A (high) degree of buyer concentration, with a limited number of buyers often accounting for the bulk of purchasing within the industry.
3 Geographical concentration.
4 Close relationships between suppliers and customers, with products often being modified to fit the specific needs of the customer.
5 Inelastic demand, particularly in the short term.
6 Demand is generally derived, with the result that the strategist needs to examine the secondary markets which influence the demand for the primary products.
7 Professional purchasing which is performed by buyers who often work as part of a buying team and who, in attempting to satisfy particular performance of quality criteria, employ a greater degree of overtly rational thinking than is generally the case in consumer markets.
8 Reciprocal trading patterns often exist, making it difficult for new suppliers to break the market.

EXAM TIP

Exam questions sometimes require you to focus specifically upon either a consumer or an organizational market. Never forget that the two sectors can be very different and that the implications for your answer can be significant. Far too many candidates make the mistake of treating them in the same way.

However, despite these differences, the process for coming to terms with organizational markets is broadly the same as for consumer markets, with the strategist needing answers to several key questions:

- *Who* makes up the market?
- What *buying decisions* are made?
- *Who is involved* in the buying process?
- What are *the key influences* upon the buyer?
- What *organizational buying policies* and priorities exist?
- What *procedures are followed* in arriving at a buying decision?

The different types of buying decision

In 1967, three American researchers, Robinson, Faris and Wind, put forward a framework for categorizing buying situations, each of which demands a particular form of behaviour on the part of the supplier. These situations or buy classes are:

- The straight rebuy.
- The modified rebuy.
- The new task.

These terms are for the most part self-explanatory and their significance needs therefore to be seen in terms of the buyer's familiarity or unfamiliarity with the situation and how he or she tries to come to terms with this by searching for information in order to minimize risk.

Identify examples of each of the three types of buying situations within your organization. What sort of criteria are employed in each case when purchasing decisions are taken? Who is involved at each stage?

Who is involved in the buying process?

The majority of organizational buying decisions are taken by a group of individuals working to a pre-determined set of purchasing criteria. This group is known both as the buying centre and the decision-making unit (DMU).

The DMU is 'those individuals and groups who participate in the purchasing decision-making process, who share some common goals and the risks arising from the decision.' (Webster and Wind, 1972, page 6.)

There are typically six roles in this buying process:

1   *The users* of the product who possibly initiate the buying process and who in some circumstances may be involved in defining the specification of the product or service.
2   *The influencers* who make an input into the process of evaluating the alternatives available.
3   *The deciders* who decide upon the final product specification and the supplier(s).
4   *The approver(s)* who authorize the purchase proposal.
5   *The buyer(s)* who negotiate the purchase terms.
6   *The gatekeeper(s)* who in one way or another are able to stop or inhibit sellers from reaching individuals in the DMU. Included within these are secretaries, receptionists and purchasing agents.

What sort of buyers do you have in your organization?

In their book *Strategic Marketing Management*, Wilson et al (1992, page 121) make reference to a piece of research conducted in the US in 1967 by Dickinson in which seven types of buyer were identified:

1   *Loyal buyers* who remain loyal to a source for considerable periods.
2   *Opportunistic buyers* who choose between sellers on the basis of who will best further his long-term interests.
3   *Best deal buyers* who concentrate on the best deal available at the time.
4   *Creative buyers* who tell the seller precisely what they want in terms of the product, service and price.
5   *Advertising buyers* who demand advertising support as part of the deal.
6   *Chisellers* who constantly demand extra discounts.
7   *Nuts and bolts* buyers who select products on the basis of the quality of their construction.

Speak to those people within your organization who have responsibility for purchasing and try to identify what sort of buyer(s) they are.

Influences upon the organizational buying process

Much of the thinking that underpinned the earliest research on organizational buying reflected the idea that industrial buyers are wholly rational in their behaviour patterns. More recently, however, a considerable amount of research has highlighted the naivety of this and illustrated that a variety of other factors need to be taken into account. Harding (1966, page 76), for example, has suggested that:

> Corporate decision-makers remain human after they enter the office. They respond to 'image'; they buy from companies to which they feel 'close'; they favour suppliers who show them respect and personal consideration, and who do extra things 'for them'; they 'over-react' to real or imagined slights, tending to reject companies which fail to respond or delay in submitting requested bids.

The significance of this is also apparent in Figure 3.18 below, which shows the four types of influence upon the ways in which buyers behave.

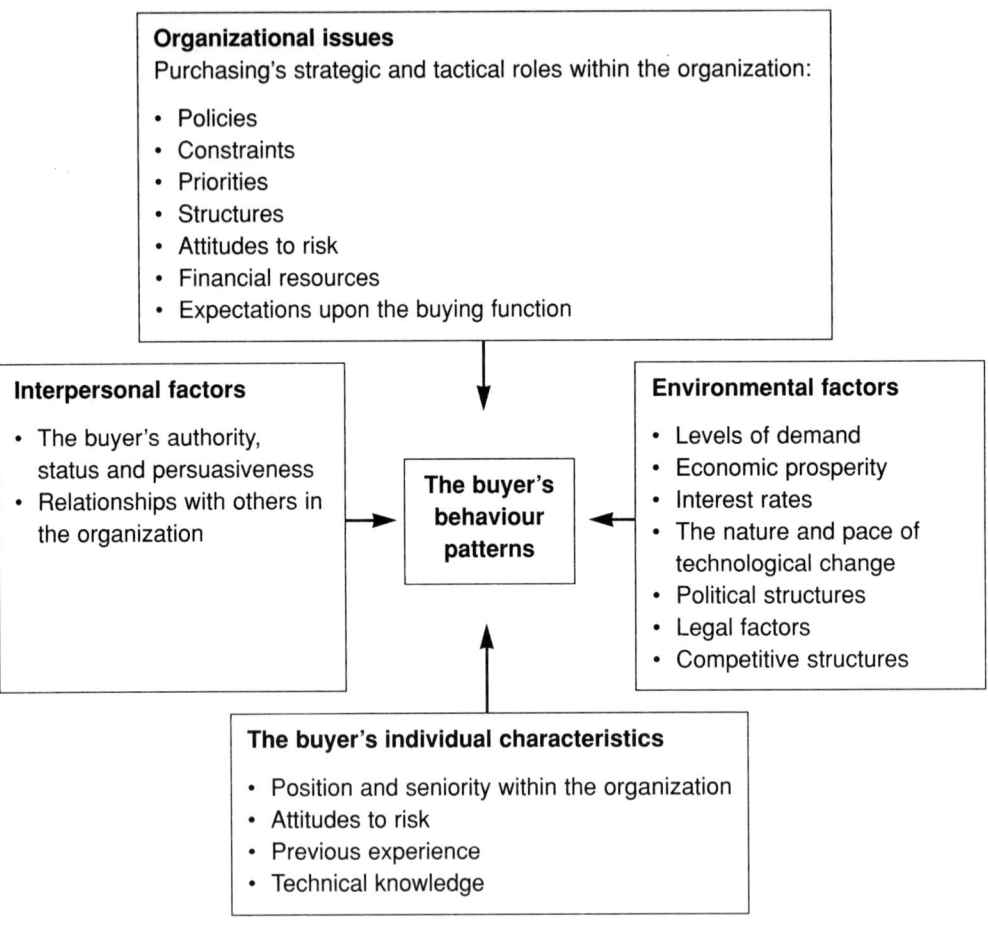

Figure 3.18 Influences upon the organizational buyer

Arriving at a buying decision

In discussing consumer buying behaviour at an earlier stage in the unit, we suggested that buyers move through a five-stage process, beginning with the recognition of a problem and culminating in post-purchase behaviour; this was illustrated in Figure 3.16 on page 76. In the case of organizational buying, the pattern of thought is generally very similar, although Robinson, Faris and Wind extend the thinking slightly by identifying a further three steps. They then linked these to the three types of buying decision to form what is referred to as the *buy-grid framework*; this is illustrated in Figure 3.19 opposite.

Product selection criteria

As you might expect, the sorts of criteria that buyers use to choose between possible suppliers varies enormously depending upon the type of purchase that is being made. These have been summarized by Lehmann and O'Shaugnessy (1974) in terms of:

Buy phases	Buy classes		
	Straight rebuy	Modified rebuy	New task
1 The recognition of the problem	N	Possibly	Y
2 The determination of the general need	N	Possibly	Y
3 The specific description of the required product	Y	Y	Y
4 The search for potential suppliers	N	Possibly	Y
5 The detailed evaluation of suppliers	N	Possibly	Y
6 The selection of a supplier	N	Possibly	Y
7 The establishment of an order routine	N	Possibly	Y
8 Performance review and feedback	Y	Y	Y

Figure 3.19   The Buy-grid matrix (Source: adapted from Robinson, et al, 1967.)

- *Routine orders* (straight rebuy)   delivery, price, reputation and reliability.
- *Procedural-problem products*   such as office equipment: technical service, flexibility and product reliability.
- *Political-problem products*   which might lead to arguments within the organization about their suitability: price, supplier regulation, product and service reliability, and supplier flexibility.

Identify two examples of each of the three types of purchase within your own organization and compare the buying criteria that are used with those identified by Lehmann and O'Shaugnessy.

ACTIVITY 3.22

Models of organizational buying behaviour

For a more detailed discussion of organizational buying models, turn to pages 123 and 130 of *Strategic Marketing Management* by Wilson and Gilligan with Pearson.

EXTENDING YOUR KNOWLEDGE

There are, in essence, four types of organizational buying behaviour models:

1   *Task-related models*   which are similar in concept to the idea discussed earlier, of Marshallian economic man, in that the rationality of the purchasing behaviour and process is emphasized.
2   *Non-task related models*   which give explicit recognition to the personal dimensions and interests of the decision maker. Included within these are issues such as the desire to avoid risk, develop relationships inside and outside the organization, and personal advancement.
3   *Complex and multi-disciplinary models*   which incorporate a spectrum of social, cultural, psychological and economic factors.
4   *Interactive models*   which emphasize the nature of the buying process and the relationships which develop within and between the buying and selling organizations.

The interactive approach has been the foundation of the work conducted by Hakansson and the IMP (International Marketing and Purchasing of Industrial Goods) group and has led to a far greater recognition of the way in which industrial buying and selling is typically concerned with the development and management of relationships. This has, in turn, led to the idea of relationship marketing.

The growth of relationship marketing

It has long been recognized that the costs of gaining a new customer, particularly in mature and slowly declining markets, are often high. Given this, it is argued, the marketing planner needs to ensure that the existing customer base is managed as effectively as possible. One way of doing this is to move away from the traditional, and now largely outmoded, idea of marketing and selling as a series of activities concerned with transactions, and to think instead of them being concerned with the management of long(er) term relationships; this is illustrated in Figure 3.20, below.

Transaction marketing	Relationship marketing
Focus on single sales	Focus on customer retention and building customers loyalty
Emphasis upon product features	Emphasis upon product benefits that are meaningful to the customer
Short timescales	Long timescales recognizing that short-term costs may be higher, but so will long term profits
Little emphasis on customer retention	Emphasis upon higher levels of service that are possibly tailored to the individual customer
Limited customer commitment	High customer commitment
Moderate customer contact	High customer contact with each contact being used to gain information and build the relationship
Quality is essentially the concern of production and no one else	Quality is the concern of all and it is the failure to recognize this that creates minor mistakes that lead to major problems

Figure 3.20 Transaction v relationship marketing
(Adapted from Christopher, Payne and Ballantyne, 1994, *Relationship Marketing*, page 9.)

ACTIVITY 3.23

What approach to marketing does your organization reflect – a transactional approach or a relationship approach?

The potential benefits of this are considerable and can be seen not just in terms of the higher returns from repeat sales, but also in terms of the opportunities for cross-selling, strategic partnerships and alliances. In developing a relationship marketing programme, there are several important steps:

- Identify the key customers, since it is these, particularly in the early stages, that the most profitable long term relationships can be developed.
- Examine in detail the expectations of both sides.
- Identify how the two organizations can work more closely.
- Think about how operating processes on both sides might need to be changed so that co-operation might be made easier.

- Appoint a relationship manager in each of the two organizations so that there is a natural focal point.
- Go for a series of small wins in the first instance and then gradually strengthen the relationship.
- Recognize from the outset that different customers have very different expectations and that these need to be reflected in the way in which the relationship is developed.

QUESTION 3.10

Your managing director has returned from a seminar at which reference was made to 'relationship marketing'. Prepare a briefing paper explaining what relationship marketing entails and what the implications for marketing planning might be. (Strategic Marketing Management: Planning and Control, December 1994, Question 5.)

Summary

Within this unit, we have discussed in some detail the various dimensions of the environment and how an analysis of the environment, including competitors and customers, might be conducted. As a check on your understanding of the material, consider the following questions:

1 Why is a detailed understanding of the environment so necessary for marketing planners?

   In the absence of a detailed environmental understanding, it is almost inevitable that the planner will fail to identify emerging market opportunities and be taken by surprise by changes in the marketplace. The consequences of this are likely to be seen in terms of a less than optimal performance and the more astute competitors gaining advantage (see pages 54–7).

2 What makes up the micro and macro marketing environments?

   The micro environment includes suppliers, customers, competitors, the distribution network, and the public at large.

   The macro environment includes political, economic, social, cultural, demographic, legal and technological factors.

   (See page 53.)

3 Identify the three environmental types outlined by Miles.

   - Single/static.
   - Dynamic.
   - Complex.

4 What do we mean by 'crazy days, crazy ways'?

   This phrase was coined by Tom Peters and is used to refer to the much greater levels of environmental turbulence, uncertainty and malevolence that now exist. Faced with infinitely high levels of environmental unpredictability, Peters argues that the old response formulae do not work. Because of this, he suggests that completely new and radically different responses are needed (see pages 55–6).

5 What are the six stages of environmental analysis?

   1 An audit of the environment.
   2 An assessment of the nature of the environment.
   3 An examination of specific environmental factors.
   4 An analysis of the firm's strategic position.
   5 The identification will be affected by environmental forces singly and jointly.
   6 In the light of 1–5, decide upon the ideal strategic position.

   (See page 58.)

6 What specific factors would you include within a PEST analysis?

   This is illustrated in Figure 3.6 on page 59.

7   What are the three stages that organizations generally move through in developing an environmental monitoring system?

1   An appreciation stage.
2   An analysis stage.
3   An application stage.

(See page 60.)

8   What do you see to be the major changes that are likely to take place over the next few years in each of the four dimensions of PEST analysis?

Quite obviously, the changes are difficult to forecast. However, some of the changes that are taking place currently, and which seem likely to become even more significant over the next few years, are listed under the heading of 'The changing PEST environment' on pages 60–1.

9   What five questions should managers pose when analysing competitors?

1   Who are we competing against?
2   What are their objectives?
3   What strategies are they pursuing and how successful are they?
4   What strengths and weaknesses do they possess?
5   How are they likely to behave and, in particular, how are they likely to respond to offensive moves?

(See pages 61–2.)

10   What do we mean by a competitor's response profile?

The response profile is a measure of a competitor's vulnerability, its likely strategy shifts, and the reactions that are likely to occur as the result of competitive moves on our part (see page 63).

11   What was the essential message of Levitt's 'Marketing Myopia'?

Levitt argued that far too many managers adopt an overly narrow approach and, as a consequence, fail to recognize threats posed by those outside the immediate industry or competitive forum. The consequences of this, he suggested, can be catastrophic, and highlight the need for a market rather than an industry perspective of competition.

(See pages 63–4.)

12   What are the four essential truths about competition?

1   Competitive threats can come from unexpected as well as expected sources.
2   New competitive threats can change market structures in far-reaching ways.
3   Responding to competitors often requires unorthodox approaches.
4   Competitive arrogance can have major implications for an organization's position (see page 64).

13   Distinguish between the industry and market perspectives of competition.

The industry perspective sees competitors in terms of those offering a broadly similar product or service. The market perspective defines competition in terms of any product or service that might attract consumers' spending power (see pages 63–4).

14   How would you go about developing a strategic grouping for an industry?

The methodology for this is discussed on page 66.

15   What are the five levels of competitive status?

1   One or more significant competitive advantages exist and are exploited.
2   A number of relatively small advantages exist, which together give the organization a significant competitive advantage.
3   Advantages either do not exist or are not recognized or exploited.
4   No real advantages exist.
5   Competitive disadvantages exist.

(See page 67.)

16   What information do you need to know about your competitors?

A list of the sorts of headings under which you need information appears on page 67.

17 What are the principal sources of competitive information?

1   Recorded data, such as primary and secondary data.
2   Observable data.
3   Opportunistic data.

(See page 69.)

18 Identify the four types of competitor.

1   Laid-back competitors.
2   Selective competitors.
3   Tighter competitors.
4   Stochastic competitors.

(See page 70.)

19 What does Porter mean by 'good' and 'bad' competitors?

A good competitor sticks to the industry rules, avoids upsetting the status quo, avoids aggressive price changes, and tries to maintain the balance of a healthy industry. Bad competitors typically pursue unnecessarily aggressive money, slash prices, and force competitors to take risks (see page 70).

20 What makes a competitor vulnerable?

A list of the potential sources of vulnerability appears on pages 70–1.

21 What seven questions is any understanding of buyer behaviour based upon?

1   Who is in the market and what is their power?
2   What do they buy?
3   Why do they buy?
4   Who is involved in the buying process?
5   How do they buy?
6   When do they buy?
7   Where do they buy?

(See page 72.)

22 Distinguish between customers and consumers.

The customer is the buyer but not necessarily the user. The consumer is the user but not always the buyer (see page 73).

23 What are the four types of buying behaviour?

1   Repetitive buying behaviour.
2   The search for variety.
3   Buying that is designed to reduce dissonance.
4   Complex buying behaviour.

(See page 74.)

24 What factors influence consumer behaviour?

1   Cultural factors.
2   Social factors.
3   Personal influences.
4   Psychological influences.

(See pages 74–5.)

25 What five roles need to be played in the consumer buying process?

1   The initiator.
2   The influencer.
3   The decider.
4   The buyer.
5   The user(s).

(See page 76.)

26 What is the difference between and significance of features and benefits?

A *feature* is a tangile dimension of a product. The *benefit* is what it delivers to the buyer in terms of advantages. The significance of this distinction needs to be seen in terms of the fact that customers do not buy products, they buy the benefits that these deliver (see page 77).

27 What is meant by 'economic man'?

The term was coined by Marshall and refers to wholly rational buying behaviour which attempts to maximize the ability of any purchase (see page 78).

28 What are the principal differences between consumer and organizational markets?

The eight principal differences are listed on page 78.

29 What are the three types of organizational buying decision?

1 The straight rebuy.
2 The modified rebuy.
3 The new task.

(See page 80.)

30 What roles are played in organizational buying?

1 The users.
2 The influencers.
3 The deciders.
4 The approvers.
5 The buyer(s).
6 The gatekeeper(s).

(See page 81.)

31 What sorts of factors influence the organizational buying process?

These are illustrated diagrammatically on page 82 (refer to Figure 3.18).

32 What is the buy-grid framework?

The framework, which was developed by Robinson *et al*, is illustrated on page 83 (refer to Figure 3.19).

33 Identify the four types of model of organizational buying behaviour.

1 Task-related models.
2 Non-task-related models.
3 Complex and multidisciplinary models.
4 Interactive models.

(See page 83.)

34 What is relationship marketing and why is it becoming more important?

The differences between transaction marketing and relationship marketing are illustrated in Figure 3.20 on page 84. The reasons for the growth in its importance include the greater complexity and competitiveness of markets, the high costs of attracting new customers and of losing existing ones, and the potential for selling additional products/services to a customer once a relationship of trust exists.

EXTENDING YOUR KNOWLEDGE

Against the background of what has been said in this unit, think in detail about how much – or how little – your organization appears to know about its environment generally and its competitors and customers specifically. Find examples of organizations that exhibit the principles of good practice in these areas and try to identify how and why they have a detailed knowledge of their environment. Think about the lessons that might be learned from how they operate. Having done this, turn to Chapters 4, 5 and 7 in *Strategic Marketing Management* and Chapter 3 in *Marketing Strategy*.

Activity debrief

Question 3.1(i) Experience has shown that managers' perceptions both of the future and of the opportunities and threats that are likely to emerge are capable of varying considerably. There is not therefore a single 'right' answer to this question. Instead, the examiners were looking for evidence that candidates had an understanding of how the environment is *likely* to develop and what the implications might be. There was also the expectation that suggestions of how the environment might change would be put into a structured framework; the PEST framework is perhaps the most obvious of these. With regard to how the environment might change, a number of possibilities are listed under the heading of 'The changing PEST environment' on pages 59–61.

Question 3.1(ii) You should explain that, in principle at least, the attractiveness of a market is influenced by a series of factors, including its size, market trends, the nature and levels of competition, governmental and legislative regulations, and so on (you might find it useful at this stage to turn to the outline answer for Question 5.3, since reference is made within this to the issues of industry attractiveness). You should then explain that in practice, however, the attractiveness of a market needs to be looked at not just in absolute terms, but also from the viewpoint of the company, since it is the organization's capabilities which will determine the extent to which it is able to operate with any degree of effectiveness within the market. Within your answer, you might also make reference to issues such as the type of environment (see page 55) and to the PEST framework (see pages 59–61).

Question 3.2 You should begin by explaining what is meant by an environmental monitoring system (EMS) and how such a system might be structured; this is discussed on page 60. The sorts of headings under which information might be collected include the PEST framework, which is discussed on pages 60–1. The question of whether it is possible to overwhelm managers with too much information is very realistic, and highlights the need for systems to reflect managers' needs and their experience/ability to use market information. The consequences of being faced with too much information or information that is inappropriately presented are that much of it will be misinterpreted or ignored. The development of a user-friendly system is therefore based on a clear understanding of users' needs, their experiences in handling market data/information, and how the information will be used.

In developing an EMS, organizations typically go through three stages (an appreciation stage, an analysis stage, and an application stage; these are discussed on page 60), and reference should be made to these in discussing how a user-friendly system might be developed.

Question 3.3 This question is concerned with Levitt's ideas of marketing myopia and the lessons that emerge from this. The answer therefore hinges upon what is said on pages 63–4 under the heading of 'Coming to terms with existing and new competitors'. However, in presenting the strategic alternatives open to the railway companies, you should distinguish between the short-term strategic responses (e.g. improving the delivery element of the service) and their longer-term development (e.g. alliances and diversification).

Question 3.4(i) You should begin by distinguishing between direct and indirect competitors and/or the industry versus the market perspectives of competition. By doing this, you are more easily able to identify *who* it is that you are competing against. You should then make reference to the four questions that are posed on pages 65–6 under the heading 'Competitive relationships'. Following on from this, you should discuss and present the competitive response profile framework (see Figure 3.8) and the list of points that appear on pages 67–8 under the heading 'So what do you need to know about your competitors?'

The sources of this information include recorded data, observable data and opportunistic data (see page 69). The problems of collection are discussed on page 70.

Questions 3.4(ii) You should begin by explaining why an understanding of competitors and competitive relationships is so important; the quote from Wilson *et al* on page 61 will help you with this. You should then distinguish between direct and indirect competition (this is the issue of an industry versus a market perspective of competition, which is discussed on pages 63–4.

Against this background, you then need to identify and discuss the spectrum of factors that should be taken into account in analysing competitors. Included with this is the nature and structure of the market, as well as the points identified on pages 67–8 under the heading 'So what do you need to know about your competitors?'

With regard to the models that might be of value, you might usefully refer to Figures 3.8 (Identifying a competitor's response profile) and 3.10 (Strategic groups). You might also discuss issues such as the five levels of competitive status (Figure 3.11) and how to come to terms with the competitive environment (Figure 3.7).

Question 3.5   You should begin by explaining that for many organizations the sales force is the point of most immediate, direct and frequent contact with the market. Used properly, it can therefore provide a considerable amount of valuable information. However, all too often the sales force is not used in this way. To overcome this, you need to identify what information the company needs and the extent to which the sales force is capable of collecting it. You then need to put in place the sales force briefing mechanisms, the incentives to collect, the feedback mechanisms, and the collection, evaluation and dissemination processes. You should also demonstrate to the sales force that their information is being used, and how.

With regard to the types of information they can collect, this most obviously includes general and specific market trends, and customer, competitor and distribution information. It needs to be recognized, of course, that the primary purpose of the sales force is to sell, and that their information collection role should not conflict with this.

Question 3.6   It needs to be recognized that a competitive monitoring system (CMS) is essentially a sub-set of the broader environmental monitoring system.

To establish an effective CMS (the guidelines for this are outlined on pages 71–2), you need to begin by identifying which competitors you intend or need to focus upon (refer back to the discussion for Question 3.4). Having done this, you need to think about how the information will be used. Against this background, you can then begin to put in place the components of the system (refer here to the section on pages 67–8, 'So what do you need to know about your competitors?'; and Figures 3.8 and 3.12). You should then discuss the possible sources of the data; this is discussed on page 69.

Question 3.7   The causes of organizational vulnerability are listed on pages 71–2.

Question 3.8   In answering this, you need to begin by discussing generally how the various elements of the model interact and influence buying processes. Against this background, you then need to consider how these ideas apply to the four product categories. In doing this, you need to pay particular attention to the importance of the social, personal and psychological elements.

Question 3.9(i)   The direction of your answers will depend to a large extent upon your choice of product. Having selected a product, you need to identify the spectrum of socio-cultural factors and how these interact with the personal and psychological dimensions of the model in Figure 3.14. In doing this, you need to pay particular attention to the role of reference groups, sub-cultures, social class and the family, and then give emphasis to the ways in which these are, in turn, influenced by factors such as age, life cycle, lifestyle, personality, and so on.

Question 3.9(ii)   You should begin by explaining (briefly) the differences between customers and consumers (see page 73). Against this background, you should then outline the consumer buying process (this is illustrated on page 75). Having done this, go through each of the stages of the model (cultural influences, social influences, and so on) and, making reference to examples, discuss how they influence buyers in their patterns of buying behaviour e.g. the impact of reference groups on the choice of brands). From here, you should move on to explain that it is essential that marketing managers have a detailed understanding of the buying process, since it is this which provides a basis for making decisions on market entry, segmentation, targeting and positioning, and the nature of the marketing mix.

Question 3.10   You should begin by explaining what is meant by relationship marketing and how it differs from the more traditional transaction marketing (see Figure 3.20). Against this background, you should explain why relationship marketing is becoming so much more important. In doing this, you should refer to the higher levels of competition that now predominate, market stagnation, the costs and difficulties of recruiting new customers, the greater cost-effectiveness of working with existing customers, the scope for cross-selling, and so on. You should then turn to the implications for marketing planning. These are listed on page 84.

Market segmentation, targeting and positioning

Segmentation, targeting and positioning are key strategic issues. They enable you to understand the nature of the organization's marketplace and to select the marketing programmes that will be profitable for the organization.

In this unit you will:

- Understand how to segment markets.
- Decide what makes a robust market segment.
- Explore ways of marketing to these segments.
- Consider how to position a company in its marketplace.

By the end of this unit you will be able to:

- Appreciate the characteristics and planning needs of organizations in a variety of sectors so that the marketing mix can be tailored to meet the needs/wants of identified market segments.
- Understand how positioning the organization has a powerful effect upon the development of the marketing mix.
- Differentiate between those segments of the market that an organization should target and those which should be avoided.

This unit is critical to Marketing Strategy. Although it only represents a small part of the syllabus, decisions taken on segmentation, targeting and positioning can be the key to a pass mark in the major case study.

Segmentation will often be a key factor to understanding the different market needs so being able to identify the opportunities open to the organization. Many of the past Planning and Control papers have included a question on segmentation and it accounted for 30 per cent of the marks on the ATC case study in the Analysis and Decision paper (December, 1994).

Company positioning, once correctly identified, will point the way for deciding the marketing mix which forms the basis of the marketing plans. Positioning formed the basis of Question 1 on the Analysis and Decision paper for December 1995 and carried 20 per cent of the marks for that paper.

As you work through this unit remember that good strategy must be thought out carefully. The market, as always, must be the inspiration for good marketing. The better you know and understand the market and its needs, the better quality your marketing will be.

After you have completed this unit, review the press adverts in your usual papers. Can you identify what segments the advertisers are aiming their offerings at?

From a review of TV or trade press, can you find examples of good and bad practice.

What can you see of good and bad:

- Targeting?
- Positioning?

What are the consequences of bad decisions in these two areas?

What is segmentation?

Segmentation was first described as a concept in the 1950s, but only really came to the fore in the 1980s and looks set to be of critical importance to marketing strategy and strategists in the 1990s. There are two principal reasons for this increased interest in market segmentation. First, after so many years of recession, many companies have simply run out of cost savings that they can make and are now starting to look harder at how they can improve the effectiveness of their marketing spend.

Secondly, the interest in segmentation is directly related to the evolution of most western markets. If the 1960s and 1970s were typified by mass production and volume sales, the 1990s will be typified by people's search for a greater sense of individualism and for identity. People today are much more demanding and discriminating and much less ready to settle for a mass-produced standard item, be it a consumer or industrial product or service. Today's search is for something special, something different, something which reinforces the buyer's own sense of identity as a person, as an individual, as someone separate from the herd. The 1990s product offer stands witness to this ever-growing demand for wider and wider choice.

The net result for most organizations in most markets (except those still artificially regulated or protected) is that segmentation is no longer an option – it is a requirement. Customized marketing is re-emerging as the way to make money in the nineties.

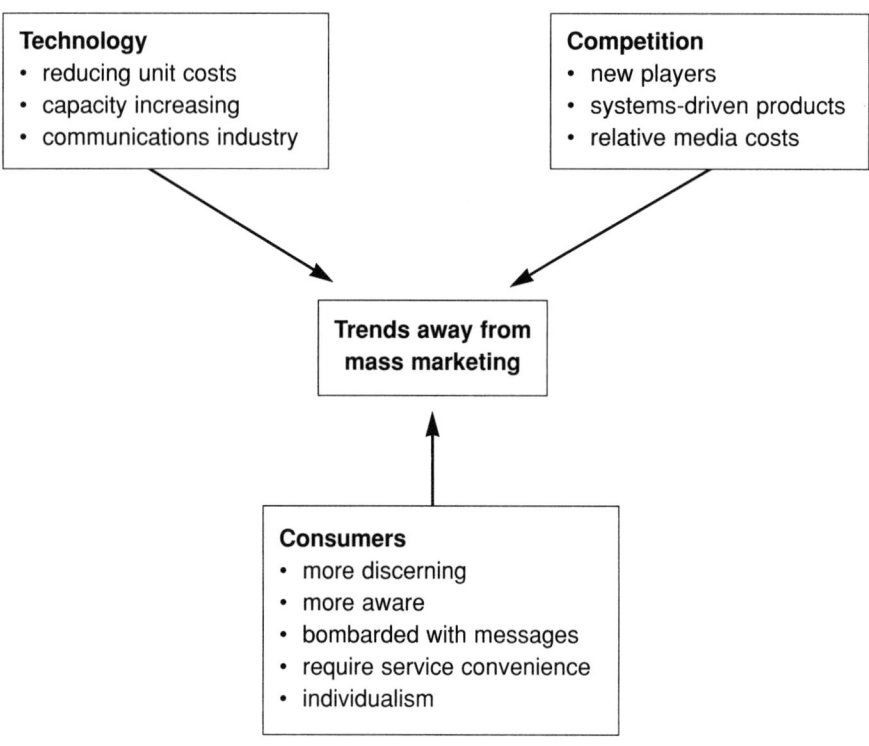

Figure 4.1

In some markets, such as luxury cars or bespoke tailoring, the providers can deal with each and every buyer as an individual and tailor the product accordingly – they can afford to pay for it. In other markets this is not possible – at least not at a price the market is happy to pay. So we have to look for a profitable compromise between the standardized product and the individually tailored. Enter the market segment.

Making reference to examples, discuss how lifestyle and geodemographic approaches to market segmentation might be used by a marketing manager to develop a detailed understanding of a market.

December 1994

(**See** Activity debrief at the end of this unit.)

Unfortunately, for a term that is so frequently used, market segmentation is one of the least understood of all marketing terms. However, used correctly it can be the source of significant competitive advantage.

Market segmentation is the sub-dividing of a market into homogeneous sub-sets of customers, where any sub-set may conceivably be selected as a market target to be reached with a distinct marketing mix.

(Kotler)

From this quite precise definition we can see that market segmentation is all about the identification of 'homogeneous sub-sets of customers', that is, customers who are alike in some way or other. Where any one of these groups 'may conceivably be selected as a market target' in other words we can go for one or all of these groups but we can treat them as a stand alone market target. The final implication, 'a distinct marketing mix', is that the segments, once identified, may each actually demand something different from us as a producer; in other words, the marketing mix is likely to be different from segment to segment. Such a breaking up of our marketing into a number of different mixes is obviously more costly in terms of marketing investment and control. The argument goes that with a more appropriate mix you should improve your penetration of a given market segment and the increased volume in sales would more than pay for the additional costs incurred.

Segmentation needs to be clearly integrated into the strategic process. The steps the marketer might follow are:

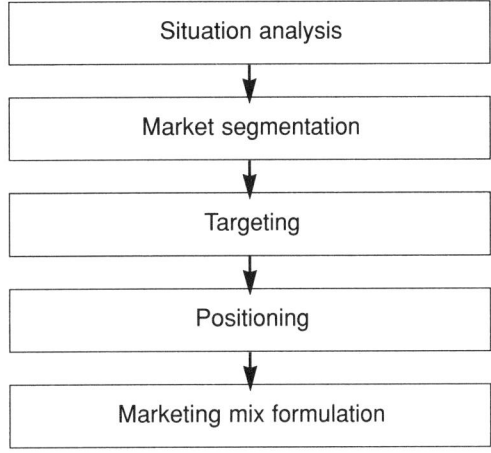

Figure 4.2

Take the example of Johnny Walker. A review of the marketplace obviously showed potential for more than just one type of Scotch whisky. In some duty free shops you can now find up to seven different brands of Johnny Walker – from 'Red Label' at £9 per bottle to 'Honour' at £130 per bottle. Johnny Walker Honour is targeted at the Japanese market and has been positioned as a prestige gift product rather than just an alcoholic drink.

Segmentation bases

How can markets be segmented? Historically, the list is practically endless. Think of a segmentation base and someone somewhere has tried it and probably someone else will swear that it is the only possible way to segment their particular marketplace. Markets are normally broken up by:

- *Geography*   national, international markets, regions, county, town, even by street and house.
- *Demographics and socioeconomics*   by age, sex, family life stage, income, occupation, or education.
- *Psychographics*   social class, lifestyle and personality.
- *Behavioural*   product usage, benefits sought, store usage, usage rate, price sensitivity, user status, loyalty status and critical events.

These and other bases are covered in greater depth in Wilson and Gilligan with Pearson, pages 200–15.

Probably one of the most useful bases for segmentation is that of benefits sought. Benefit segmentation is not new – as a concept it has been around for almost thirty years, nevertheless it still forms the basis for most segmentation, certainly in consumer markets. The past four years have seen a number of developments in the area of segmentation. Much work has been carried out in the area of demographic and geodemographic segmentation. One operation (MOSAIC) is soon to incorporate the VALS typology into its surveys. These developments are in response to organizations' needs to understand more fully their customers' needs, wants and behaviour. Both the Planning and Control and Analysis and Decision papers are asking questions more frequently in the area of segmentation and students need to have a good grasp of the variables involved in strategic segmentation decisions.

One of the most powerful aspects of benefit segmentation is that, by focusing on purchase motivation, it forces the marketer to understand a fundamental truth about market segmentation. The marketplace segments itself. The terminology used in segmentation (both in the literature and company practice) always seems to imply that the organization or the marketer is actually doing something to the marketplace. This is a dangerous misconception. People, by their actions, fit themselves into particular market segments – and out of others. The concept of marketers forcing their customers into pre-determined groups for administrative convenience is seriously outdated. The job for marketers today is simple: identify how the market has divided itself up and package and present the marketing mix(es) accordingly.

Caution

Remember, you are looking for the best way of segmenting your particular marketplace. You are looking for *a* base, not *any* base.

A recently privatized utility company audited its segmentation methods and counted 37 different methods of customer categorization used by different parts of the business. Assuming an average of six types under each category, this produced a total number of potential 'segments' (6^{37}) that surpassed the number of customers by several magnitudes!

QUESTION 4.2

Many marketing managers acknowledge that lifestyle approaches to segmentation become increasingly necessary as individuals progress through the hierarchy of needs. By reference to examples, identify the extent to which lifestyle segmentation might be used to improve our understanding of consumers.

June 1991

(**See** Activity debrief at the end of this unit.)

So, the question really becomes 'How can we identify relevant segments in our market-place?'

ACTIVITY 4.3

- How does your organization segment its markets?
- Can you count more than one approach?
- How well does your organization use its segmentation approach to improve customer satisfaction?
- How do your competitors segment the market?
- Is segmentation used as a strategic tool?

Segmenting industrial markets

Although most of the work in recent years on segmentation has been applied to consumer markets, segmentation is becoming more and more important in the industrial and business-to-business markets too. Industrial buyers, like consumers, rarely buy on price alone and are constantly seeking value added for themselves and their organizations when they make their 'rational' purchases.

Typical segmentation bases which have been used for industrial markets include:

- *Demographic*   classification by industry, by type and size of company, by location.
- *Operating variables*   by principal form of technology which the customers use, user status (high, medium, low user), customer capabilities (broad or narrow range of needs).
- *Purchasing approaches*   buying criteria (quality, service or price), buying policies (purchase, lease, lowest bid), current relationships (new or existing customers).
- *Situational factors*   urgency (speed of delivery), size of order (large or small), applications (general or specific).
- *Personal characteristics*   loyalty, attitude to risk, organizational culture, status of the buyer in the organization.

QUESTION 4.3

Evaluate the proposition that our knowledge of how to segment industrial markets effectively now lags a considerable way behind how this might be done in consumer markets.

December 1992

(**See** Activity debrief at the end of this unit.)

It has been the trend over recent years for many industrial businesses to organize their markets in terms of 'vertical markets' and thereby divide their markets into commercial types such as banking, transportation, manufacturing, financial services etc. As long as this mode of classification produces groups of customers and prospects have more in common than, say, a collection of 'risk averse' organizations from different industries then the organization has a segment.

Tests of segmentation

There are a number of ways in which we can test potential market segments. Taking the best from the theorists, the questions you should be asking yourself are:

- *Is the segment homogeneous?* The most important question, will all the members of the segment act in a uniform manner and respond in the same way to the marketing input that they receive? If not, then you probably have a 'classification' but not a segment.
- *Is the segment measurable?* Do we know where it is, how big it is, and exactly how it differs from the market at large and other segments in particular?
- *Is the segment accessible?* There could be a perfect segment in the marketplace but if we can't get to it with our communication, or our delivery channels then that segment remains of purely hypothetical value.
- *Is the segment substantial?* Is it big enough for us to make profit out of? We must bear in mind the extra expense incurred in managing more than one marketing mix into our market segments and of course people's willingness to pay a premium price.
- *Is the segment exclusive?* Maybe a little purist, but will the segment understand and relate to messages directed at it and be turned off by messages originally aimed at another segment?
- *Is the segment recognized by the customers themselves?* If they don't identify with the segment, not only will they not understand or identify with the promotion or communication aimed at them, they may actually reject this enforced membership and wreak their vengeance upon your product offering.
- *Is the segment recognized by the intermediaries in the channel?* If they don't, they are unlikely to co-operate in the marketing activity making it unlikely that you and your organization will be able to satisfy properly the segment's needs.
- *Will the products or services be premium priced?* If not, why are you doing this? It is difficult for an offering to be seen as really different if you charge a standard price.
- *Will the segment offer above-average returns?* Not just desirable, but mandatory. You will be looking for profit from a smaller overall market – it must offer good returns.

These commonsense questions need to be answered if you are to be sure of having a potentially profitable segment on your hands.

Problems with segmentation

The key problems with segmentation as currently implemented in many organizations can be summed up from the following diagram.

Past Correlation Description	Future Causality Motivation

Most organizations talk about segmentation in terms that relate to the words in the left-hand column rather than the words on the right.

- *Past and future*   When asked how they segment and what they are doing in the area, invariably people will start to describe their past experiences with customers; how people reacted; what they did and even an analysis of where the last three years' sales have come from. As we all know, the future is unlikely to be a straight-line extrapolation from the past, much as we would like it to be so.

  As marketers trying to put together a marketing strategy which will deliver what the business needs, our concerns must be for the future. Our attention must centre on where we should invest our marketing spend and our energy for both short and long-term returns from the marketplace. The past has gone. There is some value to be gained from understanding the lessons of the past but only if they can improve our future activity.

- *Correlation and causality*   The second problem is that when you press people to explain the rationale behind their segments you are often presented with a whole series of correlations. What we need to uncover is some degree of causality. There may be some relationships which an in-depth study of our existing customers could expose, however it is dangerous to build a strategy on relationships which lack an identifiable cause. In other words, is there an underlying motivational reason why people act in a certain way that we can understand from their circumstances?

- *Description and motivation*   Finally, there is a general misunderstanding between description and motivation. An in-depth description of our existing customer base and our existing 'segments' in terms of age profiles, sex, income, occupation, education, family life stage or even socio-economic grouping is only really valid if we believe that these characteristics are motivational. Descriptors tend to come from the past. 'This is how last year's customers looked.' Only very rarely will a customer group described in these terms surprise us by acting in a way unique from the rest of the market.

  The only thing we know for sure about the future is that our ideas and predictions will be wrong; but it is still worthwhile working to reduce the margin of error. It is our job to ensure that we make the best possible return on the money which the organization invests in its markets. Returns are based upon informed judgement of how a segment will respond to our offer and what will motivate it to buy.

Once proper behavioural segments have been identified in the marketplace, the next important job is to describe these segments in such a way that practical operational marketing can be brought to bear on them. This is the point at which terms such as demographics, lifestyles, usage patterns and socio-economic groupings can properly be brought into play as targeting methods. As long as we remember that these are descriptive terms and not the reason why people will buy the product or service offered, they can be a useful shorthand way of enhancing general understanding of the segments.

Making reference to examples, discuss the extent to which developments in approaches to market segmentation over the past decade have advanced our understanding of consumer markets.

December 1991

(**See** Activity debrief at the end of this unit.)

Market targeting

Marketing is not only about satisfied customers today. It is about the longer term. It is about profits. It is about matching the organization's resources to market needs – it is about planning. If we have segmented our markets properly we will have identified different areas of need. We will also know where these groups are, how big they are and what it is they want from us.

This section will look at the key decisions that the marketer must take now. What is the future for the identified segments? Which segments should we approach and which should we leave? How do we market to the selected segments?

Market segmentation is – or ought to be – about improving the organization's return on its marketing investment. Segmentation will normally appeal more to the longer-term thinker than the 'quick buck' marketer because it involves an initial outlay in costs to adapt our marketing offer to the precise need(s) of the identified segment(s). If we are interested in tomorrow's returns on today's investments, then we need to have some idea about where the segments are going.

- *Is the segment growing or declining?* Here we are interested in two broad aspects of growth and decline. What is the projected future of the segment in terms of volume sales and profitability? Despite much argument to the contrary there need not be a link between volume sales and profit. Declining volumes in certain market segments can still be extremely profitable for the organizations which service them. It's often more a question of how the segment is managed rather than what the segment is doing.

Looking at your organization and its markets, can you identify emerging segments – the segments where tomorrow's money will be made?

- *Is the segment changing?* There are three aspects to this question of change. First, we need to try and get a feel for how the structure and make-up of the segment is likely to change over time. Is the segment starting to attract new and slightly different members to its centre? What effect will this have on the segment's needs?

    The second aspect of change relates to the nature of the products and services which we would expect this segment to be demanding in the future. In other words, do we see any significant change in the way in which the members of the segment are likely to translate their needs into buying behaviour? Will they want different products or services in three years time?

    The third area of segment change must consider the movements of the segments over time. For example, do we see the overall array of segments changing? There are two ways in which this structural change can occur. Segments may merge and combine to create larger more 'shallow' segments. Larger segments may fragment over time into smaller more precise market targets for the organization to approach.

Which segments should we enter?

Just because they are there doesn't mean that you have to be competing actively in each and every segment.

- *What does our strategy tell us?* This is the point at which you must touch base with your organization's business objectives and corporate positioning. Market segments ought to be selected according to the broader strategic decisions taken by the company. For example, the organization aiming for a 'differentiated' position in the marketplace will need to retain a certain degree of flexibility which will allow it to operate in a number of related market segments while still retaining its differentiated market position. The 'focused' organization on the other hand will necessarily have to get much, much closer to its fewer market segments, and will have to predict fragmentation and merging long before this phenomenon arises. It must be prepared and be able to continue to service changing segment needs as they arise. Failure to do this by the focused organization will leave it very vulnerable to competitive attack in its core markets.

- *And what about our resources and capability?* As well as identifying those segments which 'fit' our broader strategic aspirations, we ought to consider how well we are able to meet the identified needs of the various segments. It is wise to concentrate on those segments where your organization has the capability and resources to satisfy customer needs.

Ordering the segments

Now that we have identified the market segments and the likely evolutions of those segments over the next few years, we need to decide what to do with this information. Again, this doesn't mean hitting everything that moves, it means being selective. There are two reasons why selectivity should be considered.

First, marketing and business resources are necessarily limited, therefore we must choose where to invest our resources for the right level of returns. The second reason why selectivity is important concerns customer perceptions. In the 1960s and 1970s the large conglomerates could lay claim to being in a variety of different businesses. Their size was a major factor in this argument and customers accepted the claim that an adequate product and service could come from a large, non-specialist organization. The 1980s and the 1990s are seeing this claim being less readily acceptable in the marketplace. Quality, it is perceived, is more likely to come from specialization. The organization should then select market segments which will reinforce this image in the marketplace.

Unfortunately, marketing resources are normally limited so we have to consider approaching market segments in some ordered fashion. We can do this by looking at a number of quite clearly defined criteria as shown in Figure 4.3.

Criteria	Weight	Segments				
		1	*2*	*3*	*4*	*5*
1 Long-term volume growth 2 Long-term profit growth 3 Short-term volume growth 4 Short-term profit growth 5 Organizational image 6 Offensive strategic reasons 7 Defensive strategic reasons 8 Internal resource/capability 9 Relative competitive strength 10 Other . . . 11 12						
Total						
Priority						

(Ratings 1–10, 10 = highly attractive)

Figure 4.3

The order depicted here need not necessarily be the one that you should follow; the order will largely depend upon the circumstances depicted in the examination case or question. There will also be additional criteria to be included that are specific to the market situation described in the paper.

A simple and convenient (although not mathematically precise) analysis of market/segment attractiveness can be carried out with the diagram shown. After listing all the relevant criteria and the market segments in question, you can attempt to rate – using points out of 10 – each segment against each criteria.

1   *Long-term volume growth potential*   These are typically the growing market segments which will generate large amounts of tomorrow's volume.

2   *Long-term profit growth*   Profit growth and volume growth need not necessarily be contained in the same segment. Long-term profit growth could come from a declining segment where competition is vacating the segment and leaving more profit opportunities for our organization.

3   *Short-term volume growth*   As we all know, long-term vision and strategy is essential for the survival of the organization. Nevertheless, it is important that the organization lives long enough to realize the potential coming from its future markets. In other words, we have to generate volume sales today if for no other reason than to make sure we are around tomorrow.

4   *Short-term profit growth*   Short-term profits are as important as long-term profits. It is short term profits which allow us to invest in the future. These segments should be identified and should be carefully nurtured. They should not, however, be the only segments that we attack.

5   *Organizational image*   There are things in life other than profit, at least more important than directly attributable profit. In the same way that the men's wet shaver business has used the concept of selling razors at a low price and making the margin on the blades, so we can extend this idea into strategic terms. There may be segments within which the organization must be a major or at least an active player if its strategic market position is to be credible in the marketplace. It may be that these segments produce no profit of their own but by being in this segment we are allowed to be in another segment where profit is generated. Combined segment profitability must be positive over the long term but individual segment losses need to be watched very carefully indeed.

6   *Offensive strategic reasons*   The organization's business strategy may involve the development of new segments or the creation of bridgehead segments which in themselves hold no intrinsic value for the organization, but which will allow the achievement of the organization's business objective over the longer term.

7   *Defensive strategic reasons*   These are segments which may appear to be much less attractive to the organization in terms of volume or in terms of profits or maybe even in terms of image and company positioning. However, falling out of the initial research in competitor analysis and competitive opportunities, it may become apparent that our competitors' strategies might take them into certain market areas which could, in the long term, prove quite dangerous for our organization's position.

8   *Internal resource/capability reasons*   There will always be segments which we could tap purely because we happen to be good at producing the products and services that the segment demands; however, just because we have the internal ability and maybe the short-term profit looks attractive, this does not necessarily mean that we should be attacking these segments.

9   *Relative competitive strength*   As above, there will also be segments where your organization has definite competitive strength and advantage over the competition. Again, it may or may not be a wise decision to attack these segments. Always look to the long term and the strategic rather than the tactical issues involved.

10   *Other*   The industry or organization depicted in the examination question will probably have its own special criteria for what makes an attractive segment. But before you add extra measures make sure that you are not just dealing with conventional wisdom or industry 'myth' (see also Unit 2).

Once you have rated and weighted for various segments you can see what order of priority the segments are in. You should consider whether those lowest on the list need to be approached at all.

Look at your organization. Can you apply these tests to the segments that you have identified? What does this imply for the way that you organize your marketing to the various segments?

After having considered segmentation in one part of your answer (especially the major case study) use the conclusions of your work when answering further questions. For example, show how different mixes and marketing approaches can better target different segments.

Marketing to the segments

Having discovered now that your market is made up of a number of different segments, each with their own needs, doesn't automatically mean that you have instantly to modify all your marketing activities for each segment. You have three choices.

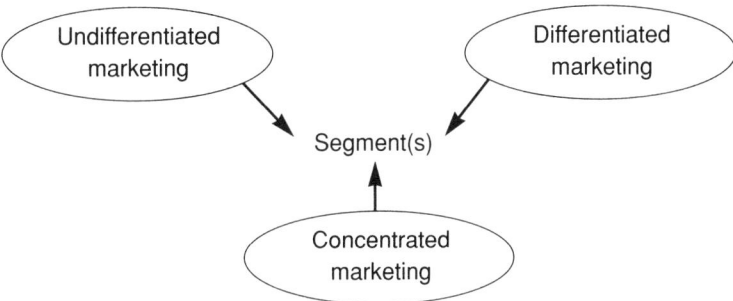

Figure 4.4

1 *Undifferentiated marketing* Your know your market is made up of a number of different segments but you decide not to differentiate your marketing approach by segment. Maybe your competition is not particularly strong, or the needs among the segments are not particularly different. In any event you must keep a close eye on the segments and their development over time. Supporting more than one marketing platform can be expensive and the returns from the market need to justify this. Also, if there is no pressure from competition to segment your marketing why rush?

2 *Differentiated marketing* You have identified the segments that make up your market and decide to offer a range of marketing offers to match the different needs. Under this scenario, you have decided to differentiate your marketing to better match the segments' needs. How far you move from a single, undifferentiated offer is, of course, up to you.

   You should bear in mind though that your branding policy is important too. Differentiated offers under the same brand can be confusing for customers and can dilute recognition of what the brand stands for. Multi-brand strategies avoid this problem but are quite expensive to maintain. See discussion on branding policy in *Marketing Communications Strategy 1997–98* by Tony Yeshin (1997), Butterworth-Heinemann.

   Lastly, there is the management aspect. Keeping control of different marketing propositions so that each is clear and credible to the target market is not an easy task. Managing the propositions, especially where this 'overlap' occurs, takes time and effort – make sure that the market response makes this extra effort worthwhile.

3 *Concentrated marketing* You have decided to concentrate your marketing effort on one or more of the segments that you have identified – and specifically not to market to others. The concentration and specialist nature of your marketing should be clear for everyone to see. If you are going to profit from this approach, typically we would

expect to see a more tailored offer than other companies, better targeted than other companies, greater choice (within the target market) than other companies and higher prices than other companies.

ACTIVITY 4.7

Which of these three approaches is used by your organization?

Strategic positioning

Most readers will be well aware of Porter's work in the area of competitive strategy and his description of the three generic competitive strategies, cost leadership, differentiation and focus (see also Unit 5). Leaving aside discussion on the cost leadership strategy which is discussed in another section, focus and differentiation strategies both depend upon a successful positioning strategy by the organization to be successful. Porter's work in this area should always be read alongside the important article by Levitt – 'Differentiation – of anything' (*Harvard Business Review*, January/February 1980).

Both Porter and Levitt assert that in today's highly competitive marketplaces an organization (and its products or services) need to be seen by the marketplace and their customers as offering something different or unique from every other organization. This way lies profits. In deciding the organization's market position, the marketer will be stating to customers what the company stands for and how its products differ from current and potentially competing products.

Positioning is therefore the process of designing an image and value so that customers within the target segment or segments understand what the company or brand stands for in relation to its competitors. It should be readily apparent from this that company positioning is a fundamental element of marketing strategy, since any decision on positioning has direct and immediate implications for the whole of the marketing mix. In essence, therefore, the marketing mix can be seen as the tactical details of an organization's positioning strategy.

This being the case, it is then the marketing strategist's job to decide, in detail, the basis of the differentiation which it will hold in its own competitive arena. In other words the organization must identify and build a collection of competitive advantages that will appeal to the target market and then communicate these effectively.

EXTENDING YOUR KNOWLEDGE

Essential reading for any would-be strategist is the mould-breaking article 'Marketing Myopia' by Levitt (*Harvard Business Review*, 1960). Positioning the organization, in customer terms, will be essential for good grade passes in the major case study.

The process of positioning

The process of strategically positioning an organization can be described in a number of sequential steps:

1 Identify the total target marketplace and the manner in which the marketplace segments itself (see above).
2 Assess the organization's resources and capabilities and identify the possible alternative competitive advantages which the organization may decide to capitalize on in its target marketplaces (see Unit 2).
3 Comparing 1 and 2, identify possible matches of competitive advantage to target market needs.
4 Select a particular emphasis (strategic market position) for the organization to pursue over the longer term planning period. The selection must be made from those positions seen as credible by the organization's customers.

5   Implement the positioning strategy in market terms. This process will require a careful analysis of which market segments to target (see above), which products and product ranges need to be developed and marketed to support the agreed market position in the marketplace, and the branding policy which is required to support the positioning strategy.

6   Communicate the identified position to the target marketplace in such a way that the customers understand how the organization and its product or service offering is different from the competition and the nature of the additional value they will gain from purchasing from the organization.

'Market niching' is the term used to describe those organizations, usually small firms, who prosper by specializing in parts of the market which are too limited in size and potential to be of real interest to larger firms. By concentrating their efforts in this way 'nichers' are able to build specialist market knowledge and often avoid head-on competition with larger organizations.

Making use of examples, identify the criteria for effective market niching and discuss whether it is a strategy suited only to small organizations.

December 1992

(**See** Activity debrief at the end of this unit.)

Positioning problems

If the organization or the strategist fails on any of the steps involved in positioning strategy this is likely to lead to one of three common problems:

1   *Confused positioning*   This happens when buyers are unsure of what the organization stands for and do not clearly see how it is different from the competitive companies and products in the choice presented. British banks continue to suffer from this.

2   *Over positioning*   This occurs where customers perceive the organization's range of products and/or services as being simply expensive. The implication here is that the organization has either mis-identified or badly communicated the additional benefits inherent in the range. This is the area of the glittering but brief product appearances. Examples can be found from the Ford Edsel to many of today's glossy magazines that are launched and fold within months.

3   *Under positioning*   A common problem, it happens where the message is simply too vague and customers have little real idea of what the organization stands for and exactly how it is different from the competition. Middle market tabloid newspapers suffer from this problem. The Daily Mail and the Daily Express fight constantly for the same market.

These three positioning problems are always evident in examination answers to case study questions. Look at your past exam attempts and identify where you have fallen into these traps. What could you have done to avoid them?

Remember, bad positioning can only lead to bad marketing mix answers!

Summary

In this section we have seen that market segmentation, targeting and positioning are essential ingredients to a modern practical marketing strategy. The mass market is an outdated concept in the vast majority of business areas and segmentation is an essential ingredient for any business which needs to understand customer needs in order to make profits. In the area of market segmentation we have seen:

- Segmentation is about improving the effectiveness of marketing activity.
- Segmentation is about better market penetration and better profits.
- Organizations don't segment markets, markets segment themselves.
- Segments must be based on motivation not description.
- Segments need to be tested.

Segmenting the market is only the first step. Once you have identified the segments that make up your marketplace you must:

- Plot where the segments are going.
- Decide which segments you are going to attack.
- Decide how you are going to market it to them.

Once decisions have been made on the structure of the market (in its segments and the ideal targets that the organization should focus upon) the marketing strategist needs to consider how best to position the organization, product range and brands within the marketplace. Positioning and identity are key strategic factors which will enable the organization to stand out in an ever more competitive marketplace. Segmentation and positioning, like marketing itself, are as much an art as a science; feel your way carefully. Do not go faster than others in your organization can understand and therefore can implement. Do not go faster than the market can understand, it also prefers evolution to revolution.

As a check on your understanding of what has been covered in this unit, consider the following questions:

1 What is meant by market segmentation?
2 Why is market segmentation becoming an ever more important part of marketing?
3 In what ways might you segment:
   - consumer markets
   - industrial markets
   What are the pros and cons of each method?
4 What are the nine tests of segmentation?
5 What problems are typically encountered when segmenting markets?
6 What is meant by market targeting?
7 What factors should be taken into account when targeting?
8 How might you decide upon which segments to enter?
9 Explain what is meant by undifferentiated marketing, differentiated marketing and concentrated marketing.
10 Why is positioning strategically significant?
11 How might you go about positioning?
12 What problems are often experienced in attempts to position? Can you give examples of companies that have made these mistakes?

EXTENDING YOUR KNOWLEDGE

Having read this unit, look in detail at how a variety of organizations segment, target and position. What lessons might be learned from them? Look then at organizations which seemingly have little understanding of how to segment or the benefits that can emerge. What appear to be the competitive consequences of this?

To supplement your understanding of the subject you should also read: Wilson and Gilligan with Pearson (1992), *Strategic Marketing Management*, Chapter 8, and Fifield (1992), *Marketing Strategy*, pages 122–134.

Activity debrief

Question 4.1 December 1994 Market segmentation is a key method of developing a detailed understanding of any organization's markets. It helps the marketing manager identify the range of different needs that exist in the market and the reasons (motivation) for the existence of those needs. The beginning of a successful marketing plan. A good answer to this question would begin by explaining (briefly) the strategic importance of segmentation in making sense of a particular market. It would then go on to explain (again briefly) what is typically meant by geodemographic segmentation and lifestyle segmentation.

You are asked specifically to use examples in your answer, so failure to do so will probably result in failure. Given the two segmentation methods cited in the question, examples should be drawn from consumer markets, although you could choose examples from fmcg markets (e.g. food) or services (e.g. restaurants) or consumer durables (cars), and all would be acceptable.

Using the examples chosen, your answer needs to show how segmentation can help a marketing manager to develop a detailed understanding of a market. You might, for example, look at the lifestyle approach to motor cars and show how an understanding of the various life stages (dependent–pre-family–family–late) can help the marketer understand a buyer's needs when considering car purchase.

Bonus marks can be obtained by commenting on the current criticisms of these (and other) bases of segmentation. Critics maintain that customer behaviour today is too complicated to be explained by the use of any *one* model, and a combination of models should be used.

Question 4.2 June 1991 A good answer to this question will follow a clear and logical structure. You are asked to cite examples to illustrate your answer and the main points that you make, and you must be sure that you do this. Given the nature of the question, your examples will come from consumer markets, fmcg, services or consumer durables; all will be acceptable.

You might begin your answer by briefly describing the hierarchy of needs (by Maslow) and then showing how lifestyle approaches interact with this model – for example, how a person moving from, say, pre-family to family life stage will have his or her hierarchy of needs modified by the move. The arrival of the first child will affect the person's needs for sustenance and safety.

The second part of the question asks you to explain (again with examples) the extent to which lifestyle segmentation might be used to improve our understanding of consumers. A good answer here might take the main lifestyle stages and, using an example for each, demonstrate how the marketer's understanding of consumers is improved.

Question 4.3 December 1992 This question clearly asks you to 'evaluate the proposition' that our 'knowledge' of how to segment industrial markets lags behind how this might be done in consumer markets. When asked to evaluate a proposition, you should assess both sides of the argument and then come to a clear decision that you are prepared to justify.

The nature of this question really means that there is no 'right' answer. You could argue the case and decide either for or against the proposition. In both events, good marks can be obtained.

In fact, most candidates argued that our knowledge of how to segment industrial markets does not lag behind our knowledge of how to segment consumer markets – but fewer industrial organizations do segment. You might then consider the reasons for this; they may include:

- Less competition.
- Fewer customers.
- Customers are 'known'.

Question 4.4 December 1991 Whenever examples are asked for in the question, you must cite them in order to gain marks. The question also specifically asks about developments in consumer markets, so examples drawn from industrial or business-to-business markets will not be relevant!

The word 'segmentation' was first used in the marketing literature in the 1950s and seized upon by organizations operating in the competitive fmcg markets. Since then the concept has been developed, and is now defined as a process which divides a varied and differing group of buyers or prospects into smaller groups within which broadly similar patterns of buyers' need's exist.

By better understanding the different buyer needs and motivations, marketers can begin to build up a more complete picture of the nature and forces for change within the market-place. They can then direct their strategy accordingly.

The past ten years have seen a degree of change in consumer behaviour unprecedented in previous periods. Many segmentation bases and approaches designed in the 1960s and 1970s have proved unable to explain many of today's behaviours, and newer methods have risen to take their place. Socio-economic and demographic bases do not explain behaviour as they once did. Methods such as geodemographic, psychological lifestyles, critical event segmentation and values-based segmentation methods are now better at explaining contemporary consumer behaviour.

Your answer should, where possible, use examples to highlight how these methods are used.

Question 4.5 December 1992   Your answer must cite examples. You should also begin by explaining what is meant by 'market niching'.

Market nichers are companies who survive and prosper by choosing to specialize in parts of the market which are too limited in size and potential to be of real interest to other firms.

The criteria for effective market niching might include:

- Identification of a real segment in a market.
- That segment's needs are not being well met by major players in the market.
- The target segment is big enough to make profits from.
- The target segment is small enough that its loss will not hurt the major players.
- The target segment has growth potential.
- The firm has the skills required to meet the target segment's needs.

Examples of market nichers might include Compaq, Toshiba, Sock Shop, Tie Rack, Avon Tyres and many others.

Secondly, you are asked to discuss whether niching is only a valid strategy for smaller organizations. Again, there is no 'right' answer, and you can decide either way – as long as you argue convincingly, arrive at a decision and justify your decision.

Formulating the marketing strategy

OBJECTIVES

In this unit you will examine the various dimensions of marketing strategy and the ways in which an appropriate strategy might possibly be formulated. As a result of this, you will understand:

- What is meant by a strategic perspective and why a strategic perspective is important.
- The rationale for portfolio analysis.
- The various models of portfolio analysis.
- Porter's three generic strategies.
- How market position influences and needs to be reflected in strategy.

By the end of this unit you will:

- Be able to analyse a product portfolio.
- Appreciate the need for a clear competitive strategy.
- Understand how market forces influence strategy.
- Be capable of formulating a marketing strategy.

STUDY GUIDE

Within this unit we focus upon an important element of Stage 3 of the Planning and Control syllabus and one which feeds in very obviously to the Analysis and Decision case study. Given that the Diploma has become far more strategic in its orientation over the past few years, it is essential that you understand the sort of frameworks within which strategic marketing decisions are made and the sorts of models that can be used.

To support the content of this unit, you should read the specialist marketing press with a view to identifying, as clearly as possible, the sorts of strategies that firms are using.

Although this unit covers only about 12–15 per cent of the syllabus, its importance cannot be over-stated. You should therefore spend 4–5 hours on this unit, but supplement this with as much reading as possible, and discussions with managers to find out how they go about developing their strategies. You should also spend time reading the maxi case studies for the Analysis and Decision examination with a view to identifying the linkages between the material covered here and the maxi case.

The growth of strategic perspectives

The widespread growth of corporate and marketing strategic planning can be traced back to the early 1970s when managers, faced with the consequences of a series of major environmental changes and upsets, began searching for stronger and more analytical frameworks that would help them to identify opportunities and threats more readily and manage their businesses more effectively. This new planning process, which became known as portfolio analysis, was based on three main ideas:

1   An organization should be managed along the same lines as an investment portfolio with the interdependencies and interrelationships between different parts of the business being recognized and decisions on their development or deletion being made on this basis.
2   Detailed attention should be paid to each element's short and long-term profit potential.
3   A *strategic* approach to the management of the business should be adopted with emphasis being paid to such issues as the industry structure, business opportunities, organizational resources and levels of capability.

However, if such an approach is to be adopted, managers need to recognize – in detail – the nature of the interrelationships that exist between different parts and levels of the organization. In the majority of organizations there are three principal levels that need to be considered. In commenting on this Wilson et al (1992, page 224) suggest:

> At the *corporate level* the decisions made are concerned principally with the corporate strategic plan and how best to develop the long term profile of the business. This, in turn, involves a series of decisions on the levels of resource allocation to individual business units, be it a division or a subsidiary, and on which new potential businesses should be supported. Following on from this, each *business unit* should, within the resources allocated by corporate headquarters, then develop its own strategic plan. Finally, marketing plans need to be developed at the *product level*. Plans at all three levels need then to be implemented, the results monitored and evaluated and, where necessary, corrective action taken.

This is illustrated in Figure 5.1.

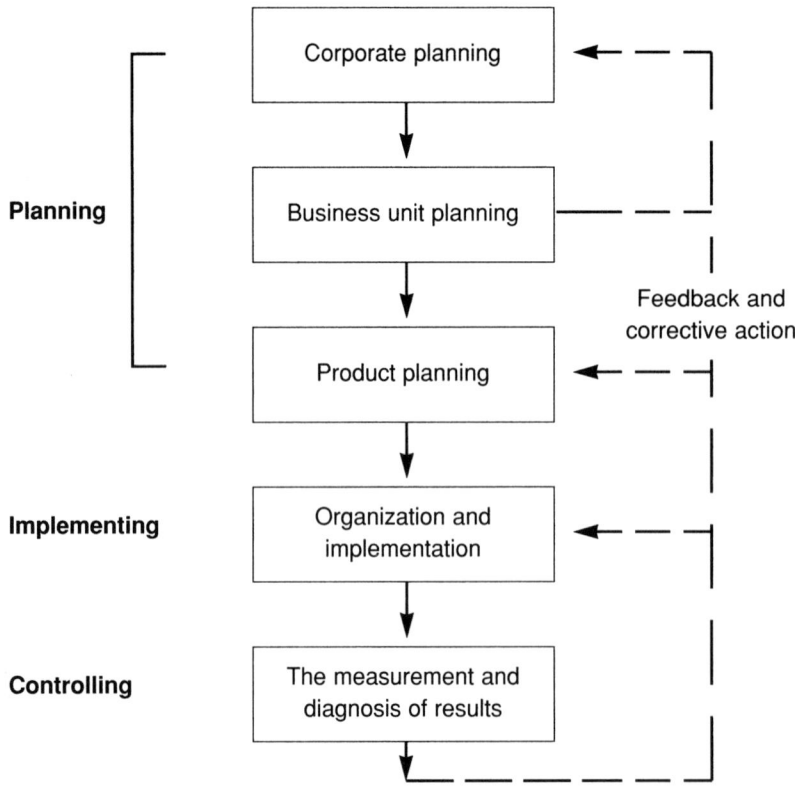

Figure 5.1   The cycle of planning, implementation and control

Approaches to planning

There are, in essence, three principal approaches to planning:

1   *Bottom-up planning* in which individual business units are given considerable freedom to develop their own objectives and strategies, with corporate management requiring only that the targets set are then achieved.

2   *Top-down planning* in which corporate management sets the objectives and maintains a close involvement with both the development and the implementation of strategy and tactics.

3   *Goals down/plans up* planning in which corporate management establishes the broad planning parameters in terms of targets and then allows the business units to decide how these will be achieved.

QUESTION 5.1

What do you think are the major advantages and disadvantages of each of these three approaches to planning? Which approach predominates in your own organization?

Regardless, however, of which approach is used, corporate management has the responsibility for the four principal dimensions of the planning process:

1   Defining the business mission.
2   Establishing the organization's strategic business units.
3   Conducting an evaluation of the existing portfolio.
4   Identifying areas for development.

EXAM TIP

It is often very apparent both in the Planning and Control and the Analysis and Decision examinations that candidates have only a hazy idea of the sorts of factors that should influence marketing strategy. You should therefore make sure that you understand the sorts of models that can be used and how market position is capable of exerting a powerful influence on strategy.

The role of strategic business units (SBUs)

Planning on the basis of strategic business units (SBUs) was first developed in the 1960s and was designed to give explicit recognition to the way in which the vast majority of organizations operate across a variety of market sectors with a variety of products or services. Because of this, any approach to planning needs to reflect the significance of each market sector and the very different opportunities and threats that exist. Without this, it is likely that managers will fail to appreciate the complete picture and concentrate instead upon particular parts of the portfolio at the longer term expense of the others.

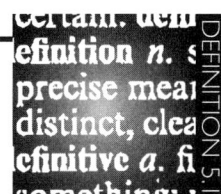

DEFINITION 5.1

A strategic business unit (SBU) is:

- A single business or a collection of related businesses which offer scope for independent planning which might feasibly stand alone from the rest of the organization.
- Has its own set of competitors.
- Has a manager who has responsibility for strategic planning and profit performance and who has control of profit influencing factors.

Source: Wilson and Gilligan with Pearson, *Strategic Marketing Management*, page 226.

We said earlier that portfolio analysis involves taking account of the interrelationships and inter-dependencies that exist between the organization's various SBUs. An important aspect of this is concerned with identifying the scope for development and the profit potential of each SBU and where, therefore, investment should be directed. A variety of frameworks to help with this have been developed, one of the earliest of which was proposed by Peter Drucker in 1963 who suggested labelling products as follows:

- Tomorrow's breadwinners.
- Today's breadwinners.
- Products that are capable of making a contribution assuming drastic remedial action is taken.
- Yesterday's breadwinners.
- The also rans.
- The failures.

ACTIVITY 5.1

Using Drucker's framework, conduct an initial analysis of your organization's SBUs. What picture emerges? Is it one that senior management can be happy with?

Although it has been argued that Drucker's classification of products in this way is too simplistic, it is potentially useful as a starting point for portfolio analysis in that it highlights the sorts of interrelationships that exist between the different parts or SBUs of an organization and the patterns of cash generation and cash usage that are likely to exist. Without this sort of understanding, it is likely that decisions on SBUs will be made with at least a degree of insularity with the result that the net long-term outcome will be rather less than it might otherwise be.

Using this sort of framework as a base, a number of rather more detailed and specific models, which collectively are labelled models of portfolio analysis (PA), have been developed.

Models of portfolio analysis

One of the earliest and best known approaches to portfolio analysis was put forward by the Boston Consulting Group (BCG). This model involves SBUs being plotted on a matrix according to:

- The rate of market growth.
- Their market share relative to that of the largest competitor.

The thinking behind the model is straightforward and based on the idea that, in making investment and marketing decisions, managers need to give specific thought to the market's future potential (the annual growth rate) and to the SBU's competitive position (relative market share); this is illustrated in Figure 5.2.

The undoubted success of the BCG's growth-share matrix and the way in which it has subsequently been the forerunner for a number of other models of portfolio analysis can be attributed to several factors, including the apparent ease with which the model can be applied and the prescriptive strategies that were seemingly associated with each of the four cells. In the case of cash cows, for example, it was suggested that they should be milked or managed for their large positive cash flow. Dogs, it is argued, should either be phased out (shot) or, if they have a modest positive cash flow, managed to maximize this. Stars need the support of a well-formulated investment policy, whilst question marks need either substantial investment in order to strengthen their position or, if they offer little real long term potential, phased out.

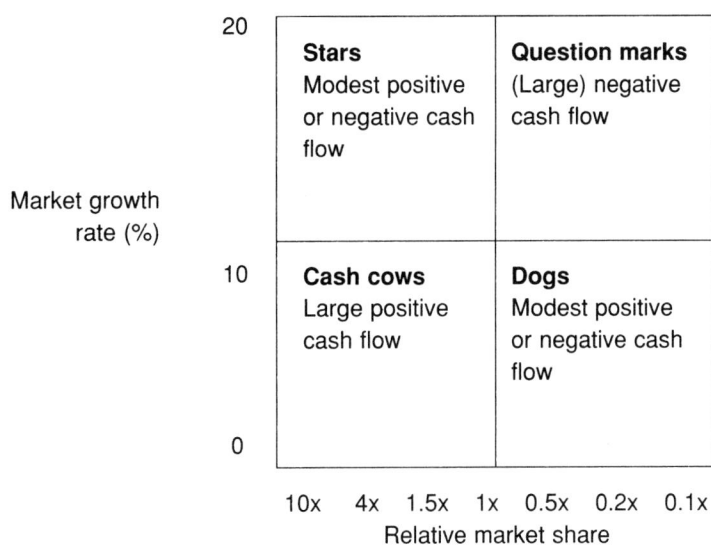

Figure 5.2   The Boston Consulting Group's growth-share matrix

An apparent attraction of the BCG matrix is the way in which it provides the strategist with an initial picture of the shape, health and balance of the organization's portfolio. Having this enables the strategist to make a series of decisions relating to the objectives, strategy and budget for each SBU. Typically, this then leads to a choice of one of four broad strategies involving:

1   Building market share in order to strengthen the SBU's position.
2   Holding the share at the current level to ensure that the maximum amounts of cash are generated.
3   Harvesting as much cash as possible in the short term, even if it weakens the SBU's long-term future.
4   Divesting by getting rid of the SBU so that it no longer acts as a drain on resources.

Using the BCG growth-share matrix, plot the position of your organization's SBUs. What sort of picture regarding the balance and health of the portfolio emerges? To what extent can you identify *explicit* strategies for each of the SBUs? In what ways do they correspond with the four strategies identified above? (Examiner's tip: in plotting the position of the SBUs, always start with the market growth rate. In the case of Figure 5.2, this goes from 1–20 per cent, although you may have to change this to reflect the specifics of your market; the key issue is that you distinguish between low and high growth. Turn then to the horizontal axis which focuses upon relative competitive position. This is measured logarithmically against the market share of the firm's largest competitor. If you have half the share of this firm, your relative position is 0.5x. If you are joint leader you have 1.0x. If you have the biggest SBU and your next biggest competitor has half the share that you have, you would position yourself at 2.0x.

In evaluating the shape of any portfolio, several factors need to be taken into account. In essence, a balanced portfolio exhibits certain characteristics including a mixture of cash cows and stars. By contrast, an unbalanced and potentially dangerous portfolio would have too many dogs or question marks and too few stars and cash cows, since this would lead to insufficient cash being generated on a day-to-day basis to fund or support the development of other SBUs.

The mini case study for the December 1994 Planning and Control examination was based upon an organization called RTJ Engineering Ltd. The case study included details of five SBUs. Candidates were required to comment upon the apparent state of the firm's portfolio and recommend how it should be developed. You should therefore turn to this mini case in Unit 9 and try to answer the question posed; the solution appears at a later stage in the unit (see pages 202–4, 230–4).

The limitations of portfolio analysis

Although models such as the BCG matrix are capable of providing the strategist with a picture of an organization's overall portfolio, the reader needs to recognize this is simply a snapshot at one particular point. In order to arrive at a clearer and more strategically useful picture, the strategist needs to think about how the portfolio is likely to develop over the next few years and what the implications of this probable shape are for the future of the organization. One way of doing this is to plot the portfolio not just for the current time period but also for, say, three and/or five years ahead. In doing this, you do of course have to make a series of assumptions, one of which might be that the current product/market mix will stay broadly the same. A second assumption might be that competitors will not make any major changes to their strategies. Given this, it should then be possible to identify the sort of strategic action that is needed in terms of decision on new products, marketing support, and possibly product deletion. The picture can then be made richer still if portfolio analyses are conducted for each of the firm's major competitors both for t0 and t+3 (t0 is today whilst t+3 is three years ahead), since this will provide the strategist with a greater understanding of each competitor's current and probable future portfolio strengths and weaknesses, as well as any portfolio gaps that might emerge.

What characterizes:

- A balanced portfolio?
- An unbalanced portfolio?

Although the Boston Consulting Group matrix has proved to be enormously useful in helping many managers to think far more strategically about the nature of their portfolio and the decisions that need to be made, it needs to be recognized that the real value of portfolio analysis is influenced very firmly not just by the quality of the basic data inputs, many of which have proved to be difficult to find and measure, but also by the broader environment within which decisions are made. It was very largely in an attempt to overcome these sorts of problems and to give recognition to a greater number of factors that a variety of other approaches to portfolio analysis have been developed. Included within these are the General Electric multi-factor matrix, the Shell directional policy matrix, the Arthur D Little strategic condition matrix, and Abell and Hammond's 3 × 3 investment opportunity chart.

In the case of the General Electric multi-factor model the thinking is based on the idea that it is often too limiting to set objectives and develop strategies simply on the basis of the BCG's market growth rate and relative competitive position. Instead, it is argued, success (and hence the basis on which decisions should be made) is determined by the *attractiveness of the SBU's markets* and the degree to which the SBU possesses the sorts of *business strengths* needed to operate and succeed in each of these markets; the GE matrix is illustrated in Figure 5.3.

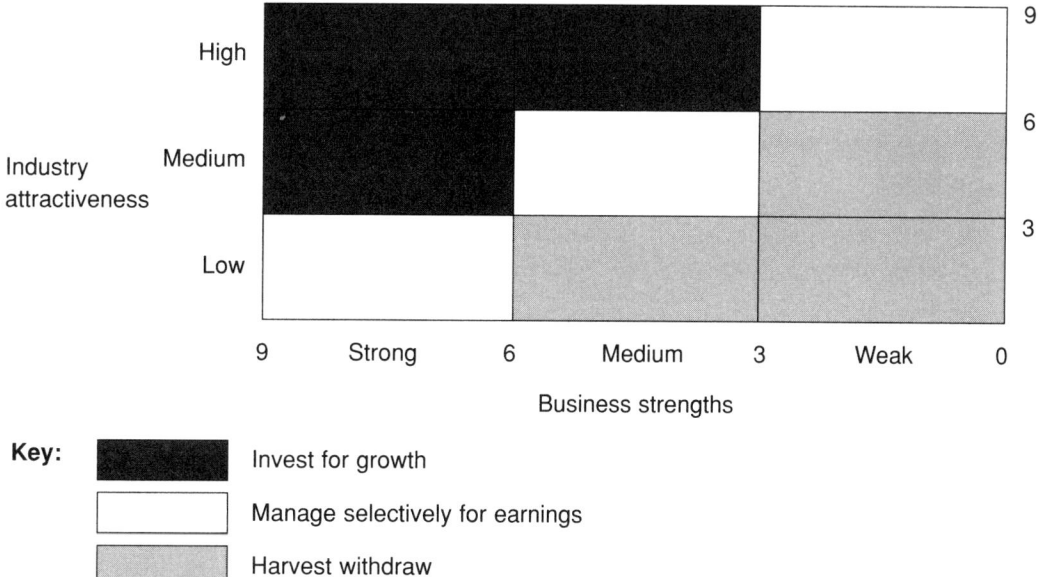

Figure 5.3 The General Electric multi-factor portfolio model

QUESTION 5.3

What sorts of factors do you feel contribute to:

- industry attractiveness?
- business strength?

Although the titles of the axes of other portfolio models such as Shell's directional policy matrix and Abell and Hammonds 3 × 3 matrix differ slightly from those used in the General Electric model, the thinking in each case is broadly similar.

EXTENDING YOUR KNOWLEDGE

Very deliberately, we have focused upon just two portfolio models. For a far more detailed discussion of portfolio analysis, the variety of models that have been proposed, and an examination of their areas of strength and weakness, refer to pages 233–236 of *Strategic Marketing Management* by Wilson and Gilligan with Pearson.

The current status of portfolio analysis

Although it is generally recognised that portfolio analysis (PA) has been useful in helping managers to think more strategically about their businesses, a variety of criticisms of PA have emerged over the past few years. Amongst the critics has been Douglas Brownlie who has argued that portfolio analysis:

- Is over-simplified.
- Often offers a misleading representation of strategy options.
- Makes use of inappropriate and overly general measures.
- Rests on an assumption that market leadership invariably offers benefits.
- Ignores the real potential and the benefits of marketing niching.
- Ignores a series of important and strategic factors in the competitive environment.

Others have suggested that far too many managers have failed to recognize that, if portfolio analysis is to be carried out meaningfully, the data inputs are often considerable, the exercise time-consuming, and the implications for strategy far more subtle than is often suggested by the almost knee-jerk idea of milking cash cows, shooting dogs, and so on.

(i) Although a considerable amount of attention has been paid to the development of techniques of portfolio analysis, it is increasingly being recognized that managers still make only limited use of them. Comment upon the possible explanations for this and discuss how portfolio analysis might be applied more widely.

(Planning and Control, June 1994, Question 8.)

(ii) How would you evaluate an organization's product portfolio?

(Strategic Marketing Management: Planning and Control, December 1995, Question 6.)

Porter's three generic competitive strategies

One of the major contributors over the past few years to the ways in which we think about competitive strategy has been Michael Porter who has argued that there are, in essence, only three generic types of strategy:

- Overall cost leadership.
- Focus.
- Differentiation.

He suggests that in order to compete effectively, strategists need to select a particular strategy and then pursue it consistently. In practice, of course, there is no one 'best' strategy, even within a particular industry. The choice therefore needs to be made so that the firm maximizes its relative competitive strengths, something which can only be done against the background of a clear understanding of five factors:

1 The bargaining power of suppliers (in other words, how strong relative to you are your suppliers and to what extent are they capable of influencing or determining your strategy?)
2 The bargaining power of customers (are you, for example, dealing with a whole series of small customers who individually have little bargaining power, or are you dealing with a small number of large, powerful and individually influential customers?)
3 The threat of new entrants to the industry.
4 The threat of substitute products.
5 The rivalry amongst current competitors.

It is the combination of these factors which determines the nature, level and intensity of competition within an industry and which, Porter argues, should influence or determine the choice of strategy.

Cost leadership: the achievement of the lowest cost base within the industry. Although this would typically then be reflected in a low price strategy, this is not always the case and the firm may opt instead for higher levels of investment in areas such as R&D, manufacturing, or marketing.

Focus: the concentration of the marketing effort upon one or more narrow market segments.

Differentiation: an emphasis upon the one or more elements of the marketing mix which are perceived by customers to be important and which, if performed particularly well and distinctively, offer scope for distancing the organization from its competitors and creating a competitive advantage.

A summary of the ways in which each of the three strategies might be achieved, together with the benefits and possible problems that are associated with each of the three strategies, appear in Figure 5.4.

Type of strategy	Ways to achieve the strategy	Benefits	Possible problems
Cost leadership	• Size and economies of scale • Globalization of operations • Relocating to low cost parts of the world • Modification/simplification of designs • Greater labour effectiveness • Greater operating effectiveness • Strategic alliances • New sources of supply	The ability to: • Out-perform rivals • Erect barriers to entry • Resist the five forces	• Vulnerability to even lower cost operators • Possible price wars • The difficulty of sustaining it in the long term
Focus	• Concentration upon one or a small number of segments • The creation of a strong specialist reputation	• A more detailed understanding of particular segments • The creation of barriers to entry • A reputation for specialization • The ability to concentrate efforts	• Limited opportunities for sector growth • The possibility of out-growing the market • The decline of the sector • A reputation for specialization which ultimately inhibits growth and development into other sectors
Differentiation	• The creation of strong brand identities • The consistent pursuit of those factors which customers perceive to be important • High performance in one or more of a spectrum of activities	• A distancing from others in the market • The creation of a major competitive advantage • Flexibility	• The difficulties of sustaining the bases for differentiation • Possibly higher costs • The difficulty of achieving true and meaningful differentiation

Figure 5.4   Porter's three generic strategies

Although Porter argues very firmly that success comes from identifying and pursuing the generic strategy that is most suited to an organization's capabilities and position within a particular market sector, many strategists either fail to recognize this or fail to achieve what they set out to do. The result of this is that the organization has no particular strategy and instead drifts into what can loosely be termed the strategic abyss or wilderness which is typically known as being 'stuck in the middle'. This is illustrated in Figure 5.5 and is a reflection of the organization not having a clear, distinctive or appropriate strategy.

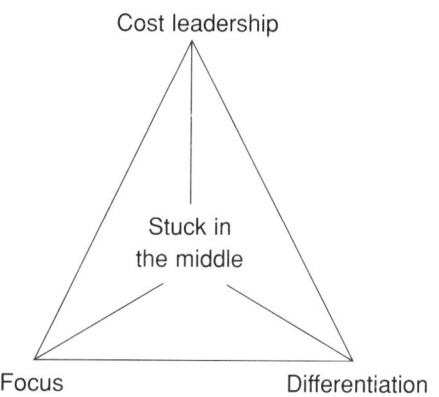

Figure 5.5   The three generic strategies (and the strategic wilderness)

In Porter's terms, which of the three generic strategies is being pursued by each of your organization's SBUs? Which strategies are your competitors' SBUs pursuing? Is there any evidence in your own organization of a 'middle of the road' or a 'stuck in the middle' strategy?

Making reference to examples, discuss how Michael Porter's ideas of generic competitive strategies can be used by the marketing planner.

(Marketing Planning and Control, December 1992, Question 5.)

Issues of competitive advantage

The development, pursuit and exploitation of competitive advantage is at the very heart of marketing strategy and was first discussed on pages 42–3; you might therefore briefly return to these.

Competitive advantage is achieved whenever you do something better than competitors. If that something is important to consumers, or if a number of small advantages can be combined, you have an exploitable competitive advantage. One or more competitive advantages are usually necessary in order to develop a winning strategy and this, in turn, should enable a company to achieve above-average growth and profits.

Source: Hugh Davidson (1987), *Offensive Marketing*, Penguin, page 153.

Davidson, the author of the definition above, has identified what he sees to be the eight most significant potential bases of competitive advantage as being:

1 *Superior product benefits.*
2 Advantages in the product or brand that, by virtue of the brand's advertising, its country of origin, and so on, are *perceived by customers* to be important.
3 *Low cost operations* which offer scope for aggressive pricing.
4 *Legal advantages* such as patents and copyright.
5 *Superior and influential contacts* with those within the industry or government.
6 *Greater knowledge* as the result of market research, experience or information systems.
7 *Economies of scale.*
8 *Competitively offensive attitudes* and a determination to succeed.

Which of Davidson's eight bases of competitive advantage does your organization appear to have? To what extent are these exploited? Which competitive advantages does each of your competitors have?

Market position and strategy

EXAM TIP

In discussing marketing strategy, candidates often treat all organizations as broadly the same; they are not. You should make sure therefore that your answer reflects the size and market position of the organization.

Marketing strategy is typically influenced by a spectrum of factors including:

- The organization's relative size.
- The existence of competitive advantages.
- What the organization has done in the past and the types of strategy that it has pursued.
- Previous levels of performance.
- Perceptions of risk.
- Stakeholders' expectations.
- Managerial objectives.
- Perceptions of market opportunities and threats.
- Competitors.
- Market, product and brand life cycles.

In addition, of course, strategy is also influenced – often to a very high degree – by the organization's market position. Is the firm, for example, a market leader, a market challenger, a market follower, or a market nicher?

Market leaders typically, but not invariably, have the largest market share and, by virtue of their position, are able to determine the nature, bases and intensity of competition.

Market challengers have a rather smaller share of the market and adopt an aggressive position by attacking the market leader or others in the industry in an attempt to strengthen their position and perhaps gain the leadership position.

Market followers pursue less aggressive strategies, avoid direct confrontation and are generally willing to accept current market structures and the status quo.

Market nichers concentrate their efforts upon small and often specialized parts of the market and in this way avoid head-on fights and develop a detailed but specific market knowledge.

DEFINITION 5.4

Select a market sector and identify the position that each firm *appears* to occupy. What type of strategy is each of these firms pursuing? To what extent can you find evidence of a challenger's strategy? How successful does it appear to be?

ACTIVITY 5.6

Strategies for market leaders

It has been recognized that market leadership has a number of significant attractions, not the least of which is the competitive power that it gives a firm. At the same time, however, leaders are an attractive and a natural target for others in the industry and often therefore find themselves subject both to direct and indirect attacks. It follows from this that if a market leader is to remain a market leader it needs to follow a distinct and often proactive strategy. Without this it is likely that the firm will see its share of the market being eroded. The guidelines for the marketing strategist in these circumstances are therefore straightforward and involve focusing upon three areas:

1 The various ways in which the total market might possibly be expanded.
2 Ensuring that the firm's current market share is protected.
3 Identifying how, if at all, the firm's market share might possibly be increased.

These are illustrated in Figure 5.6

Market leadership

Expansion of the overall market	Guarding the existing market share	Expansion of the current market share
• Targeting groups that currently are non-users • Identifying new uses for the product/service • Increasing usage rates	• Strong market positioning • The development and refinement of meaningful competitive advantage • Continuous product process innovation • A generally proactive stance • Heavy advertising • Strong customer relations • Strong distributor relations	• Heavy advertising • Improved distribution • Price incentives • New product development • Mergers • Takeovers • Geographic expansion • Distributor expansion

Figure 5.6 Strategies for market leaders

The first of the three dimensions – *the expansion of the overall market* – can generally be achieved in one of several ways, including:

● Finding new users for the product or service.
● Finding new uses.
● Finding ways in which current and potential users of the product might use it more frequently and/or in greater quantities.

The second major need for market leaders involves ensuring that the firm's *existing share of the market is guarded* as effectively as possible. Given our earlier comment that leaders are often an attractive target for other firms, it follows that leaders need to be constantly vigilant so that any areas of vulnerability are minimized as far as possible. In practice, of course, this can be a difficult exercise, since it involves strength across a series of geographic, market and product sector fronts. Insofar as it is possible to identify how this might best be done, it is in terms of continuous innovation and the development of ever stronger competitive advantages and stronger selling propositions.

The third major dimension of a leadership strategy involves trying *to build market share* yet further. However, in doing this the issue of monopoly power needs to be considered and how the monopoly legislation which exists in the majority of the developed countries can prove to be a constraint.

Strategies for market challengers

Organizations which currently are not market leaders have a straightforward strategic choice: either they try to build share in an attempt to become leaders themselves (market challengers), or they adopt a less proactive and offensive approach by accepting the general status quo (market followers).

For those organizations which decide to challenge for leadership, there are several ways in which a challenge can be mounted, including:

- A direct attack on the current market leader.
- An attack upon firms of similar size to itself but which for a variety of possible reasons such as a lack of finance or a weak management team are vulnerable.
- An attack upon smaller firms.

The wisdom of a direct attack on an established market leader will depend very largely upon the sort of market in which the organization is operating and, very obviously, the sort of firm in the leadership position. When the leader shows signs of being over-stretched and vulnerable, a direct attack may well work. More frequently, however, a direct attack is likely to prove costly, time-consuming and, ultimately, self-defeating. There are several reasons for this, the most obvious of which is that, by virtue of being market leader, the firm under attack will generally – but certainly not invariably – have the advantages of size, economies of scale and greater financial resources. It is because of this that many astute challengers opt for a different approach and try to build their position by attacking firms of a similar size to themselves or a series of smaller firms.

Insofar as it is possible to identify a series of lessons which have emerged from the activities of successful – and unsuccessful – market challengers over the past few years, it has to be that the challenger must have a sustainable and meaningful competitive advantage; without this, any attack, regardless of whether it is upon a market leader or simply another player in the market, is likely to prove of little real value.

With regard to the specific ways in which an attack can be launched, Wilson et al (1992, page 264) have identified ten possible strategies:

1. Price discounting.
2. A different price-quality combination.
3. Product innovation.
4. Improved service levels.
5. Distribution innovation.
6. Intensive advertising.
7. Market development.
8. A more prestigious image.
9. Product proliferation.
10. Cost reduction.

Identify examples of market challengers for each of the ten bases of a challenge that are listed above. How successful does each one appear to have been?

ACTIVITY 5.8

Market leaders have often proved to be a natural target for ambitious, growth-oriented companies. Identify the marketing strategies that experience has shown to be the most effective in challenging market leaders, and discuss how market leaders might fight off such a challenge.

(Strategic Marketing Management: Planning and Control, June 1995, Question 3.)

Strategies for market followers

As an alternative to challenging for leadership, many organizations opt for a rather quieter life by remaining as market followers. For those who do so, there are three distinct positions:

1 *Following the leader or challenger closely* by offering a similar market mix and operating in broadly similar market segments, but taking care not to pose any real threat or challenge to the leader.
2 *Following at a distance* so that whilst there are obvious similarities, there are also areas of difference.
3 *Following selectively* so that in some instances, there is little to choose between the leader and the follower, whilst in others there is a major gap.

Executed carefully, a market following strategy can prove to be highly profitable, since it is likely to mean that virtually all of the costs and risks of product and market development are borne by the market leader or challenger, with the follower then learning from their experiences. It is also a strategy which in mature markets in particular makes a great deal of sense. In such a market, organizations are often faced with what is referred to as a zero-sum game. Because there is little scope for overall market growth, an individual company can only increase its sales at someone else's expense. Given this, it often makes sense to recognize that higher, longer term profits are most likely to be made by avoiding challenging the market leader.

At the same time, of course, followers can prove vulnerable, particularly if market challengers see the basis for their challenge to be that of taking over the smaller and seemingly less aggressive firms in the industry. Recognizing this highlights that, if a follower is to succeed, it requires a distinct strategy on their part reflecting:

- Careful market segmentation.
- The efficient use of (limited) R&D budgets.
- An emphasis upon profitability rather than sales growth or market share expansion.
- A willingness to challenge conventional wisdoms.
- A distinct competitive strategy rather than a set of largely implicit actions.

In what circumstances would you recommend that an organization pursues a market follower strategy?

Strategies for market nichers

As an alternative to leadership, challenging or following, some organizations pursue a market niching strategy. Although often associated with smaller organizations, niching – if performed well – can often prove to be an attractive and profitable strategy for divisions or SBUs of far larger businesses. The principal attraction of niching is that it enables the organization to concentrate its efforts upon a particular segment of the market and in this way avoid concentration and competition. The criteria for niching are straightforward and have been identified by Kotler (1988, page 342) as being:

- The niche must be sufficiently large to be profitable.
- It must have growth potential.
- It must be of little interest to larger competitors.
- The firm must have the skills needed to serve the niche effectively.
- The firm must be able to defend itself, at least initially, against competitive inroads.

There are, of course, problems with niching, not the least of which is that the firm may outgrow the niche and ultimately find it to be too small. Equally, organizations can find themselves in a vulnerable position if for one reason or another the niche contracts or if a major competitor decides that the niche offers sufficient long-term potential to justify an attack. It is for these sorts of reasons that it is often strategically far more sensible to operate in several niches simultaneously in order to spread the risk.

With regard to the bases for niching, we can identify seven principal ways. These involve niching or specializing:

1 Geographically.
2 By the type of end user.
3 By product or product line.
4 On a quality/price spectrum.
5 Service.
6 Type of customer.
7 Product feature.

Identify an example for each of the seven bases for niching.

ACTIVITY 5.9

(i) Making use of examples, identify the criteria for effective market niching and discuss whether it is a strategy suited only to small organizations.

(Marketing Planning and Control, December 1992, Question 10.)

(ii) Explain, with examples, the possible benefits of a market niching strategy and the circumstances in which niching is most likely to prove worthwhile.

(Strategic Marketing Management: Planning and Control, December 1995, Question 9.)

QUESTION 5.8

For a detailed treatment of how market position influences strategy turn to Chapter 10 of Wilson and Gilligan with Pearson (1992) *Strategic Marketing Management*. The chapter also discusses how thinking on business strategy has been influenced by military strategy.

EXTENDING YOUR KNOWLEDGE

Summary

Within this unit we have focused upon a variety of the factors that need to be taken into account in developing a marketing strategy. As a check on your understanding of this, consider the following questions:

1   Why did an increasing number of managers begin to develop strategic perspectives from the 1970s onwards?

This was very largely a legacy of a series of major changes and environmental upsets in the early 1970s. In an attempt to impose a degree of order on the planning process which, it was hoped, would help with the identification of opportunities and threats and the more effective management of their businesses, managers began searching for stronger and more analytical frameworks (see pages 107–8).

2   What is meant by portfolio analysis?

Portfolio analysis involves looking at the product range as a whole, with a view to identifying interrelationships. Given an understanding of these, the totality of the range can then be managed far more effectively than by looking at each product in isolation (see pages 110–14).

3   What are the three levels of planning?

Planning takes place at three levels:

- The corporate level.
- The business unit level.
- The product level.

(See page 108.)

4   Draw a model of the cycle of planning, implementation, control and feedback.

The model is illustrated on page 108 (Figure 5.1).

5   What are the three main approaches to planning?

- Bottom-up planning.
- Top-down planning.
- Goals down/plans up.

6   What is an SBU?

A definition of an SBU appears on pages 109–10 (see Definition 5.1).

7   What purpose do skills play in the planning process?

Skills provide a focus for analysis which allows managers to identify not just their current and probable future performances, but also their cash needs and cash-generating potential. This, in turn, allows for a holistic view of the range and the more effective management of the range as a whole (see pages 109–10).

8   What are Drucker's six categories of product?

1   Tomorrow's breadwinners.
2   Today's breadwinners.
3   Products that are capable of making a contribution if drastic remedial action is taken.
4   Yesterday's breadwinners.
5   The also-rans.
6   The failures.

(See page 110.)

9   Draw the BCG framework.

This is illustrated in Figure 5.2 on page 111.

10   What are the apparent attractions of the BCG framework?

- The apparent ease with which the model can be applied.
- The apparent clarity of the picture of the shape, health and balance of the portfolio that it provides.
- The prescriptive strategies associated with each of the four cells.

(See pages 110–11.)

11   What strategic alternatives does the BCG framework lead to?

1   Build share.
2   Hold share.
3   Harvest.
4   Divest.

(See page 111.)

12   What are the limitations of portfolio analysis (PA)?

- The simplicity of many of the models.
- The least partially questionable relevance/appropriateness of the axes that are used.
- The overly prescriptive nature of the strategies associated with each of the cells.
- The difficulties of achieving a detailed analysis and the tendency for managers to take an overly simplistic approach.
- The difficulties of forecasting the future shape and implications of the portfolio.
- The difficulties of allowing for unexpected environmental changes, including competitive moves.

(See pages 112–14.)

13   Identify models of PA other than the BCG framework.

- The General Electric multi-factor portfolio model (see Figure 5.3, page 113).
- Abell & Hammond's 3×3 matrix.
- The Shell directional policy matrix.

(See pages 112–13.)

14   What is the current status of PA?
      This is discussed on page 113.

15   What are Porter's three generic strategies?

1   Overall cost leadership.
2   Focus.
3   Differentiation.

(See pages 114–16.)

16   In what circumstances is each of these strategies appropriate?
      This is discussed in Figure 5.4 on page 115.

17   What are Davidson's eight bases of competitive advantage?

1   Superior product benefits.
2   Customers' positive perceptions.
3   Low-cost operations.
4   Legal advantages.
5   Superior and influential contacts.
6   Greater knowledge.
7   Economies of scale.
8   Competitively offensive attitudes.

(See page 116.)

18   What factors should influence marketing strategy?
      Numerous factors are capable of influencing the strategy, the most significant of which are listed on page 117.

19   Define market leaders, market followers, market challengers and market nichers.
      A definition of each of these appears on page 117 (Definition 5.4).

20   Identify the key elements of the strategies appropriate to each market position.
      The strategies are illustrated in Figure 5.6 on page 118.

Activity debrief

Question 5.1 You should begin by identifying and outlining each of the three approaches (bottom up, top down and goals down/plans up). You should then identify, in as much detail as possible, the pros and cons of each type. In doing this, you should make reference to issues such as the planner's proximity to (or distance from) the market, levels of market knowledge, time frames, and aspects of implementation and control, as well as the probable motivational elements.

Question 5.2 You should explain initially what is meant by portfolio analysis and what it is designed to achieve (refer to pages 110–12). You should then explain what is meant by an unbalanced portfolio (too many dogs or question marks and too few cash cows and stars) and a balanced portfolio (a mixture of cash cows and stars). You should then make reference to the implications of an unbalanced portfolio.

Question 5.3 Industry attractiveness is determined by market size, rates of growth, the degree of competition, the pace of technological change, the sorts of profit margins that historically have been achieved, and the extent to which the industry is constrained by government or legislative regulations.

Business strength is determined by factors such as market share, product quality, the brand's reputation, the distribution network, production capacity, production effectiveness, financial and human resources, access to markets, new technologies, and so on.

Question 5.4(i) Portfolio analysis has a number of limitations, and it is these which seemingly have led to lower levels of usage than had previously been thought. You should therefore highlight some of the limitations (these are identified on page 113 and in the answer to Question 12 above). You should then discuss how some of the problems might be overcome (e.g. more rigorous analysis, rather subtler strategic recommendations, better training of managers, a stronger future perspective, and so on).

Question 5.4(ii) You should begin by saying that a portfolio can be evaluated in a variety of ways, although the most obvious involves making use of the sorts of models of portfolio analysis (PA) that have been developed by, amongst others, the Boston Consulting Group, General Electric, Shell, and Abell & Hammond. You should then explain how one or more of these might be used, and the sorts of problems that are typically encountered (see pages 110–14). You should then go on to suggest that other factors also need to be taken into account, including product and market life cycles, the management team's expectations and the extent to which the portfolio is capable of satisfying these, the managerial ability to exploit the portfolio's potential, the portfolio's investment needs, and so on.

Question 5.5 You should begin by identifying and explaining Porter's three generic strategies (cost leadership, differentiation and niching). The circumstances and ways in which the strategies might be used are discussed in Figure 5.4, and it is this which should then provide the basis for your answer.

Question 5.6 You should begin by explaining what is meant by market leadership, why leadership is often seen to be an attractive market position (size, power, the greater returns, and so on), and hence why leaders are so often attacked by ambitious and growth-oriented companies. You should then identify the strategies that challengers often use. These include direct attacks on the leader, attacks on firms of equal size, and attacks on smaller firms. In doing this, make reference to approaches such as price discounting, innovation, intensive advertising, and so on (a full list appears on page 119).

In fighting off challengers, leaders need to guard their current markets, work to expand their current share, and attempt to expand the market as a whole. The detail of the ways in which this might be done appears in Figure 5.6.

Question 5.7 Begin by explaining what is meant by market following and the three manifestations of this:

1 Following close.
2 Following at a distance.
3 Following selectively.

(This is discussed on page 120.) The circumstances in which market following is appropriate include:

- When there is limited scope for market growth, and so any offensive move would lead to an aggressive response and little, if any, gain.
- There are few/insufficient financial resources to do anything other than follow.
- Expansion would demand high levels of investment.
- The profit returns of growth would be low.
- Management is content with the current position.

Question 5.8(i) Explain what is meant by market niching and then turn to the criteria for market niching. These include:

- The niche must be sufficiently large to be profitable.
- It must have growth potential.

- It must be of little interest to competitors.
- The firm must have the skills needed to serve the niche.
- The firm must be able to defend itself against competitors, at least in the short term.

As a strategy, niching is not limited just to small firms (although it is an attractive option for them), but is relevant to all types and sizes of organization, assuming that there is scope for specialization and profit opportunities exist.

Question 5.8(ii) You should begin by explaining what is meant by a market niching or focus strategy and what it involves (in doing this, you might usefully make reference to Porter's idea of generic competitive strategies; these are discussed on pages 114–16). The benefits are spelled out in Figure 5.4. The circumstances in which it is likely to prove worthwhile have been identified by Kotler, and are listed on pages 120–1.

Managing the marketing mix

In this unit you will examine the vehicle through which managers' ideas on marketing strategy are translated into a series of strategic and tactical moves. As a result of this, you will understand:

- The principal dimensions of the marketing mix.
- How an effective marketing mix can be developed.

By the end of this unit you will:

- Understand how the various elements of the mix can be managed strategically and tactically.

Within this unit we focus upon an important element of Stage 4 of the Planning and Control syllabus and, as with Unit 5, one which has obvious applications within the Analysis and Decision case study. To support the content of this unit, you should read the specialist marketing press with a view to identifying as clearly as possible how managers are making – and implementing – decisions concerning not just the individual elements of the marketing mix, but also how the overall mix is being managed, and to what effect.

The unit accounts for about 15–20 per cent of the Planning and Control syllabus, although in a number of ways its importance is far greater than this. Without a clear understanding of the mix and how it can be managed, it is unlikely that you will score anything other than the very minimum of marks in either of the Strategic Marketing Management examinations. Having worked your way through this unit, you should therefore look at a number of the mini and maxi case studies with a view to identifying how your knowledge might be applied.

Managing the marketing mix

The idea of the marketing mix and the 4Ps (Product, Price, Place and Promotion) was first discussed by McCarthy several decades ago. More recently, however, it has been recognized that there are several other elements that need to be taken into account in marketing mix planning and within this section we will therefore focus upon the 7Ps; these were first introduced in Unit 3 (page 54) and are illustrated again in Figure 6.1.

Given the pivotal importance of the marketing mix, it is not surprising that it has been the focus for a large number of questions in the Planning and Control examinations over the past few years.

Although the left-hand box in Figure 6.1 is labelled 'uncontrollable factors', remember that we said in Unit 3 that in practice many of these can be controlled or managed, particularly by large firms, if not in the short term, certainly in the medium to long term. The economy, for example, can be 'managed' by focusing upon areas of the world in which the economy is buoyant. Equally, competitors can be 'managed' by takeovers and alliances whilst political factors can be 'managed' by means of lobbying.

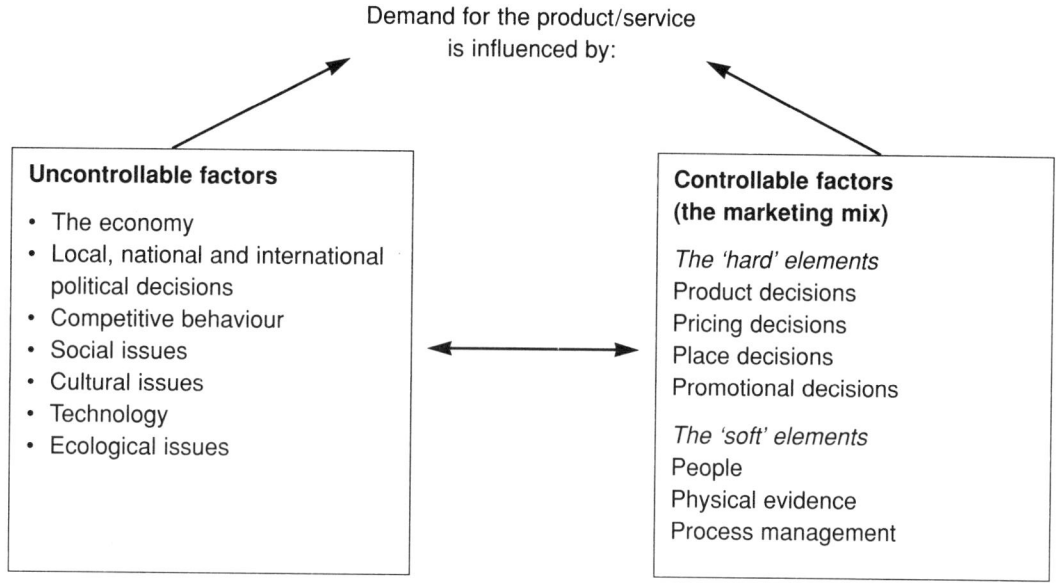

Figure 6.1 Demand influencing factors

What other factors should be added to the list of uncontrollable elements? Taking each point in turn, identify how it might be 'managed' through a marketing strategy.

Product decisions

The normal starting point for any discussion of the marketing mix is the product or service, since the majority of other mix decisions are directly influenced by what is offered. The product – and here we use the term to refer both to a physical product and to a service – is made up of three main elements:

1 *The product attributes* including its features, styling, brand name, quality, packaging, and the size and colour variations offered.
2 *The product benefits* that stem from its performance and image and which contribute to the 'bundle of satisfactions' that it delivers.
3 *The marketing support services* that are provided in addition to the product itself. These might include elements such as pre-sales services, delivery, installation, and after-sales support.

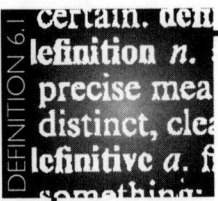

The *product mix* is the group of products sold by the organization. An example of this would be Ford with cars, vans, trucks, buses and tractors.

The *product line* is a group of broadly similar products targeted at a similar group of customers.

Select one of the products (services) offered by your organization and identify the three levels referred to above. In what areas do you appear particularly strong or weak?

Product management is based very largely upon the application of two major concepts:

- The product life cycle.
- Portfolio analysis.

Portfolio analysis was discussed in Unit 5 and you might therefore refer back to this unit to make sure that you fully understand the concept and how it can be applied.

The product life cycle (PLC) has been referred to as 'possibly the best known but least understood concept in marketing' (see *Strategic Marketing Management*, page 273). The reason for this comment is that only rarely does a marketing manager claim ignorance of the life cycle, but only a very small minority understand how, if at all, it might be used for marketing planning.

The thinking behind the PLC is straightforward and based on the idea that products have a finite life and that during this life they pass through a number of distinct stages, each of which demands a particular type of strategy. There are, however, several problems that are associated with using the PLC as a management tool, the majority of which stem from the difficulties of identifying the nature, length and precise shape that the life cycle will take. However, most discussions of the life cycle make use of a simple diagram of the sort illustrated in Figure 6.2.

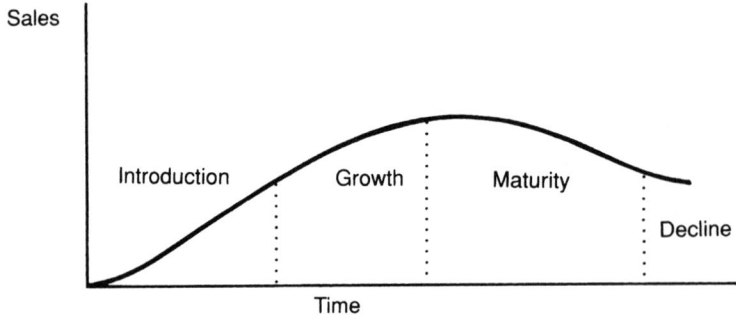

Figure 6.2   The product life cycle

In practice, of course, the length and shape of a life cycle is capable of varying enormously, since it is influenced by a whole series of factors, some of which are within the control of the marketing staff whilst others are not. The net effect of this is that numerous PLC shapes other than the simple S curve that is shown above have been identified. These include the four that appear in Figure 6.3, although to these we could add a further thirteen that have been identified by Swan and Rink.

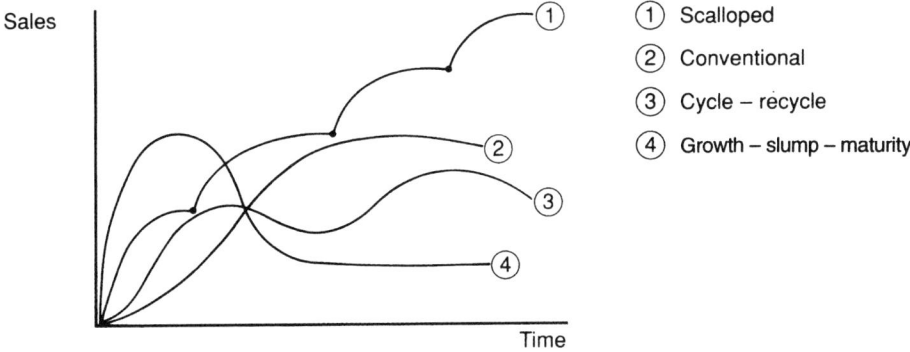

Figure 6.3 Four typical life cycle curves

It follows from this that using the life cycle in the neat and easy way that is often suggested in textbooks is only rarely possible and that the concept needs to be treated with a degree of care; it is certainly not, for example, the predictive framework that many have claimed it to be. However, it does have a value in that:

- It highlights the need for marketing strategy to change over time.
- It identifies the broad strategic issues that need to be considered at each stage.
- It can be used as a control tool in that comparisons can be drawn with broadly similar products in the past.

These points are examined in Figure 6.4.

Marketing mix strategies	Introduction	Growth	Maturity	Decline
Product	Basic product, limited range	Develop product extensions and service levels	Modify and differentiate Develop next generation	Phase out weak brands Consider leaving market
Price	Low price strategy	Penetration strategy	Price to meet or beat competitors	Reduce
Distribution	Selective Build dealer relations	Intensive. Limited trade discounts	Intensive. Heavy trade discounts	Selective. Phase out weak outlets
Advertising	Heavy spending to build awareness and encourage trial among early adopters and distributors	Moderate to build awareness and interest in the mass market. Greater word of mouth	Emphasize brand differentiation and special offers	Reduce to a level that maintains hard core loyalty. Emphasize low prices to reduce stock
Sales promotion	Extensive to encourage trial	Reduce to a moderate level	Increase to encourage brand switching	Reduce or stop completely
Planning time frame	Short to medium	Long range	Medium range	Short

Figure 6.4 The management of the product life cycle. (Adapted from Wilson and Gilligan with Pearson, 1992, *Strategic Marketing Management,* page 276.)

(i) The majority of products spend much of their life cycle in the mature phase of the product life cycle. To what extent does current thinking and research on the product life cycle provide marketing managers with worthwhile guidelines on how best to manage products during this phase?

(Marketing Planning and Control, December 1991, Question 5.)

(ii) To what extent does the product life cycle provide the marketing planner with worthwhile guidelines on how to manage products in the *introductory* and *decline* stages?

(Marketing Planning and Control, December 1992, Question 6.)

(iii) It is generally recognized that product life cycles are shortening. What are the implications of this for the marketing planning and control processes?

(Marketing Planning and Control, December 1993, Question 9.)

(iv) What problems would you be likely to experience in attempting to forecast the nature and shape of the product life cycle for an innovatory product aimed at a rapidly changing consumer goods market? How, if at all, might these problems possibly be overcome?

(Marketing Planning and Control, June 1994, Question 4.)

(v) What criteria should be taken into account when deciding whether to rejuvenate a product or service that is in the mature phase of its life cycle?

    Assuming that rejuvenation was felt to be worthwhile, what strategies might achieve rejuvenation?

(Strategic Marketing Management: Planning and Control, December 1995, Question 4.)

Managing the brand

An integral part of any product policy is the question of how the organization's brands are managed. In essence there are four types of brand strategy which can be pursued:

1 *Corporate umbrella branding* where the company's name is used to cover the complete spectrum of products and services offered (e.g. Heinz).
2 *Family umbrella names* to cover a range of products in a variety of markets (e.g. Marks & Spencer's use of its St Michael brand).
3 *Range brand names* which link products within a specific market sector (e.g. Mars with Mars bars, a Mars drink and Mars ice cream).
4 *Individual brand names* which are used for one type of product in one or more markets (e.g. Lucozade).

In managing brands, several factors need to be considered:

- What values are associated with the brand name?
- How can the brand be developed?
- How far can the name be stretched (in other words, to what extent does it lend itself to being moved into related or possibly new market sectors)?
- How much is it worth?

Valuing brands

The question of how to value brands has grown in importance in recent years as managers have come to recognize the significance of brand names as assets and how they might possibly contribute to the balance sheet. Although there is no one agreed method of brand valuation, there are several guidelines (see Wilson et al, 1992, pages 300–1). Included within these are:

1 The brand's market position (leaders are worth more than followers).
2 The age and stability of the brand.
3 The nature of the market (brands in market sectors such as food and drinks are less prone to fashion and have less unpredictable and fast-changing life cycles than, say, fashion or computers).
4 Geographic spread.
5 Sales trends in the market.
6 The trade marks or patents that give a form of protection.
7 The levels of advertising and the patterns of expenditure over the past few years.

Your company, which markets a range of biscuits and confectionery, is the target of an aggressive and unwanted takeover bid. As the company's marketing manager, you are required to prepare a report for the marketing director discussing how the firm's brands might be valued.

(Strategic Marketing: Planning and Control, December 1994, Question 2.)

Developing new products

An important element of any product strategy is the modification of existing products and the development of new ones. There are two ways in which new products can be added to the range:

- Internal new product development.
- Going outside and acquiring them from other organizations.

In the case of acquisition, this can include buying other firms, buying licenses or franchises, and buying patents. In the case of internal new product development, the process involves generating ideas, evaluating these ideas, disposing of those which seemingly offer little potential, and launching those which seem to offer the greatest promise.

But although NPD is an important dimension of strategy, almost inevitably it proves to be risky, time consuming and expensive. In an attempt to come to terms with this, a considerable amount of research on the causes of NPD success and failure has been con-ducted. The outcome of this research suggests that failure is typically associated with:

- Managers overestimating the size of the market.
- The product under-performing.
- Competitors being too firmly entrenched.
- The product being poorly positioned.
- Distributors lacking real commitment to the product.
- The product idea having been pushed through the NPD process by a senior manager, even though evidence exists to suggest that the product is likely to fail.

Why is NPD typically an expensive and risky activity? In what ways might these be avoided or minimized?

Although we tend to use the term *new product* in a rather general way, there are several specific manifestations that need to be thought about, including:

- Products that are new to the world and which then go on to create a completely new market.
- Products that help the company to enter a new market.
- Additions to existing lines.
- Improvements to existing products.
- Repositionings which allow the organization to target new markets.
- Minor product modifications.

Why is NPD important?

NPD, if conducted effectively, is capable of performing several distinct roles, including:

- Ensuring that product obsolescence is avoided.
- Helping to ensure that the organization can compete in new and growing market segments.
- Reducing the dependence upon one or more (declining) market sectors.
- Matching or beating competitors.
- Helping to achieve long-term growth.

The NPD process

The starting point for any discussion of the NPD process is the work in the 1960s of the American consultancy firm Booz, Allen and Hamilton. Faced with clients who were experiencing high new product development failure rates, they developed a logical, analytical and sequential approach to NPD which was designed to ensure that managers did not miss out certain key stages; this is illustrated in Figure 6.5.

QUESTION 6.4

(i) What guidelines has research in recent years provided on how the new product development process might most effectively be organized?

(Marketing Planning and Control, December 1992, Question 8.)

(ii) Good practice in new product development has long been seen by many writers to be a linear process. Explain why, in today's environment, this is over-simplistic and inappropriate, and comment upon the nature of the approaches that might more effectively be used.

(Marketing Planning and Control, June 1994, Question 10.)

Although it has long been recognized that NPD is a potentially difficult, expensive, time-consuming and risky but, for many organizations, very necessary activity, these problems have in recent years been magnified as the result of seemingly ever faster changing market environments – something which is reflected in the second of the two examination questions above. To cope with this, managers have needed to become far more environmentally aware and have needed to respond far faster and in far more innovatory ways as opportunities emerge, possibly for a far shorter time than in the past.

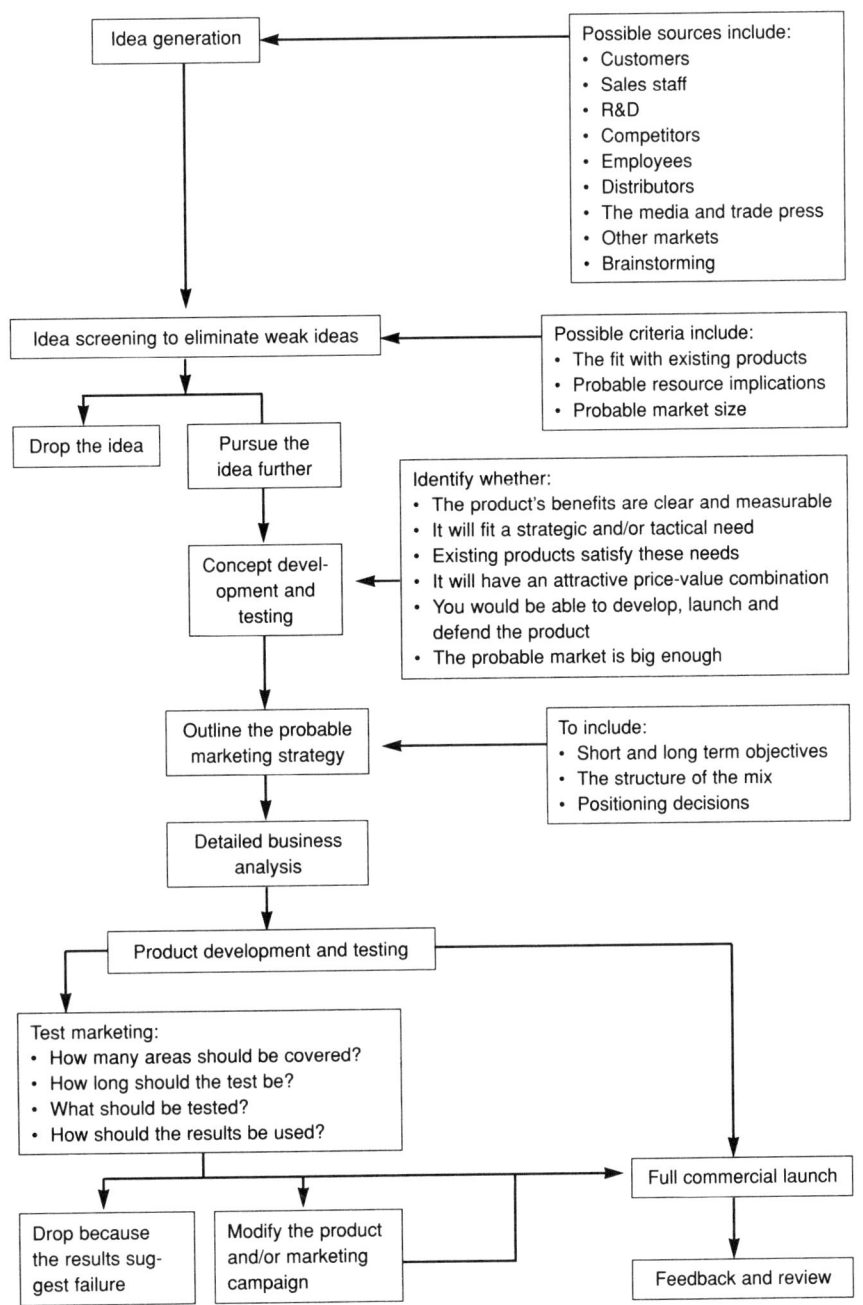

Figure 6.5 The new product development sequence

The problems with test marketing

Although test marketing is often seen to be an integral part of the NPD sequence, many firms now avoid this stage, preferring instead to go straight from the detailed business analysis and product development/testing stages to the full launch. There are several reasons for this, including:

- The dangers of the test market alerting competitors.
- The problems of finding representative test areas.
- The time needed to identify repurchase rates.
- Distributors being reluctant to become involved in test marketing costs.
- The difficulties of interpreting what is often an ambiguous results pattern.

These, together with the far faster pace of many markets, has led managers to argue that, if they are truly confident in the product, they should go ahead as fast as possible.

(i) Identify the types of information that might emerge from test marketing and discuss how this information might be used.

(Marketing Planning and Control, June 1992, Question 9.)

(ii) A succession of studies have shown that a majority of products which have generated encouraging test marketing results and which subsequently have been launched nationally, ultimately fail. Explain how this might be caused and how it might be overcome.

(Marketing Planning and Control, December 1993, Question 7.)

(iii) Identify the criteria that should be used in deciding whether to test market a new product and explain why so many test market results prove to be ambiguous.

(Strategic Marketing: Planning and Control, December 1994, Question 5.)

Pricing decisions

Organizations are essentially either *price takers* or *price makers*. In other words, either they have only a limited ability – or willingness – to control the prices they charge and therefore follow the lead set by others in the market, or because of their size, power or strong competitive advantages, are able to determine the prices which others then follow.

Looking at your own organization, identify whether a price taking or price making approach is adopted. To what extent is there evidence of a *strategic* approach to pricing?

Although prices are often influenced by a whole series of factors, the five most significant can be seen to be:

- The firm's corporate objectives and what it is trying to achieve in each sector of the market.
- The nature, structure and intensity of competition.
- The stage reached on the product life cycle.
- Consumers' response patterns.
- Cost structures.

Looking again at your own organization, what other factors appear to influence the prices charged? What about, for example:

- Distributors' expectations.
- Managerial fears about sparking off a price war.
- The cost and marketing interrelationships between different parts of the product mix.
- Price dumping by an overseas competitor.
- Collusion between firms in the form of cartels (whilst often illegal, implicit cartels exist in many markets).
- Prices that have been set in the past and a lack of willingness on the part of management to sit down with a clean sheet of paper and pose a series of fundamental questions about precisely what the price strategy is designed to achieve.

> Speak to one or more financial managers in the organization and identify how detailed an understanding exists of cost structures for:
>
> 1 Each product.
> 2 Each market sector that you operate in.

The sorts of factors that we have identified as influences upon price can be seen to act as the general framework within which specific pricing decisions are taken. In taking these decisions, the first major step involves setting in detail the pricing objectives. Although in practice the organization may well have a variety of objectives, the most common include:

- Survival: when the organization is faced with a particularly difficult market and cash flow is poor, prices can be slashed simply to increase the flow and maintain a base of working capital.
- Setting out to achieve a predetermined return on investment.
- Stabilization of the market.
- Attempting to gain market share.
- Minimizing competitive conflict by setting prices at the same level as competitors.
- Skimming the market by means of a high price strategy initially and then gradually lowering prices to attract new segments.
- Penetrating the market with a low price in order to capture as many sales as quickly as possible.
- Early cash recovery.
- Pricing to stop other firms entering the market.

> Price is potentially an enormously valuable strategic and tactical weapon, although many managers try to avoid price competition by taking price out of the competitive equation. In preparing both for the Planning and Control and Analysis and Decision exams, think about the sorts of factors that influence price, how you might set a price, and the implications for pricing of more volatile and competitive market structures.

Having set the objectives, the marketing strategist can then go on to the question of *how* to set the price, something which involves a choice between cost-oriented and market-oriented techniques.

Cost-oriented techniques are, as the title suggests, based firmly upon a clear understanding of cost structures and include:

- Mark-up pricing (identify the costs associated with the product and add a previously determined mark-up).
- Target return on investment pricing (decide upon the ROI required and then price to achieve this).
- Early cash recovery pricing.

By contrast, market-oriented techniques involve focusing in far greater detail upon the market and, in particular, customers' response patterns, competitors, and opportunities. The techniques include:

- Perceived value pricing (what value does the market put upon the product?).
- Going rate pricing (what are the pricing norms in the industry?).

(i)   What factors should be taken into account when deciding upon the price of a new product? In what ways might the relative importance of these factors be influenced by the type of industry in which the company is operating?

(Marketing Planning and Control, June 1991, Question 7.)

(ii) It has been suggested that pricing is the most difficult single marketing decision since so many variables are involved. Evaluate this contention making reference to the factors likely to influence the pricing of a new and innovatory machine tool.

(Marketing Planning and Control, June 1992, Question 6.)

(iii) What information would you require in order to set a price for an innovatory new product aimed at a consumer durable market? What particular problems might be experienced in obtaining this information and how, if at all, might they be overcome?

(Marketing Planning and Control, December 1992, Question 9.)

(iv) How would you attempt to predict the effects of a change in the price of a service in a competitive consumer market?

(Marketing Planning and Control, December 1993, Question 10.)

Any worthwhile pricing strategy must, of course, take explicit account of competitors, their costs and their probable patterns of behaviour. Without this, it is likely that sooner or later the firm will be taken by surprise by a competitor's moves.

What competitive information would you need when setting prices?

Hint: refer to pages 336–7 of Wilson and Gilligan with Pearson (1992) *Strategic Marketing Management.*

Promotional decisions

In developing a promotional strategy, the marketing strategist needs to begin by focusing upon the corporate and marketing objectives with a view to identifying precisely how promotional activity can contribute to their achievement. In doing this, you need to think about the complete spectrum of promotional activities; these are brought together in the idea of the promotions mix and its four principal dimensions:

- Advertising.
- Personal selling.
- Publicity.
- Sales promotion.

Advertising: any paid form of non-personal presentation and promotion of ideas, goods, or services by an identified sponsor.

Personal selling: an oral presentation in conversation with one or more prospective purchasers for the purpose of making sales.

Publicity: the non-personal stimulation of demand for a product, service or business unit by planting commercially significant news about it in a published medium or obtaining favourable presentation of it upon radio, television or stage that is not paid for by the sponsor.

Sales promotion: those marketing activities, other than personal selling, advertising and publicity, that stimulate consumer purchases, such as displays, shows and exhibitions, demonstrations, and various non-recurrent selling efforts not in the ordinary routine.

In thinking about promotional strategy, seven questions need to be considered:

- What are we trying to achieve?
- How might we achieve it?
- How much will we need to spend?
- Where will we need to spend it?
- When will we need to spend it?
- What creative appeal is most likely to work?
- How can we best measure the results, feed these back into the decision-making process, and improve the strategy?

QUESTION 6.8

Identify the principal decisions that have to be taken in the development of an advertising campaign and discuss the contribution to these that marketing research might possibly make.

(Marketing Planning and Control, June 1993, Question 6.)

Because the CIM's Diploma includes a syllabus and examination paper dealing with Marketing Communication Strategy, it is not our intention within this workbook to look at the area in detail, but instead simply to highlight the main areas that you need to concentrate upon. The first of these is the question of objectives.

Promotional objectives can be categorized most obviously in terms of those that are sales related and those that are communication related. Thus, a sales-related objective would be designed to:

- Increase sales from A to B.
- Strengthen the competitive position.
- Generate N enquiries/coupon responses.
- Reduce the sales impact of a competitor's advertising.

A communication-related objective would be designed to:

- Improve the image.
- Help in repositioning.
- Raise levels of awareness.
- Change perceptions.

Having developed the objectives, attention needs then to turn to the question of the *promotional budget.* Given our earlier comments, the question of budgeting should be relatively straightforward: what are we trying to achieve and how much will this cost? In practice, however, the majority of organizations resort to one of a variety of other approaches, including:

- Affordable (how much can we afford to spend on promotion? In taking this approach, little account is taken of opportunities, objectives or indeed competitive threats).
- Competitive parity (how much are competitors spending? Having identified this, you spend broadly in line with their levels and in so doing avoid upsetting the status quo).
- Percentage of sales (setting the budget on the basis of a predetermined percentage of last year's or the forthcoming year's sales).

As an alternative to these techniques, all of which are inward looking, the budget setter can return to the idea outlined above which involves identifying your specific objectives, identifying in detail what will be needed in order to achieve them, and then calculating the costs. This approach, which is referred to as the objective and task method has an inherent logic but largely because of the amount of detailed information that is needed is often ignored in favour of a simpler approach.

QUESTION 6.9

Why, despite pressure upon costs and calls for an ever greater degree of accountability within marketing, do rule of thumb methods of advertising budgeting appear still to predominate?

(Marketing Planning and Control, December 1991, Question 7.)

Having set the budget, the planner needs then to think about *how the budget can best be allocated.* In doing this there is, of course, an element of iteration in that in setting the objectives and the budget thought should have been given to the contribution that each of the elements is capable of making to the achievement of these objectives and the costs that will be incurred. Nevertheless, within the constraints of the budget that has been agreed, the *detailed* allocation represents the next step. The *criteria for allocation* are, in one sense at least, straightforward: what is each of the alternative media and promotional vehicles capable of delivering?

QUESTION 6.10

In the light of the wide range of promotional vehicles and media that are now available, explain how you would plan the allocation of a promotional budget and how you might evaluate the success of this allocation.

(Marketing Planning and Control, December 1993, Question 6.)

Having made the allocation, the next question is concerned with *timing.* In other words, when will the money be spent? In deciding upon this, the planner has a choice between:

- Burst advertising which involves highly concentrated periods of heavy promotion.
- Drip promotion which involves spreading the campaign over a far longer period.

The issue of *where to spend the money* involves choosing between the variety of media available. What, therefore, are the benefits of the national press relative to the trade press or special internet magazines? What about posters or television?

EXAM TIP

Refer to the work that you are doing for Marketing Communications Strategy and identify the pros and cons of each of the major media.

The issue of the sort of *creative appeal* that is to be used needs to be considered against the background of a clear understanding of the image that the organization is attempting to create and its general positioning strategy. In essence, however, there is a choice between:

- The brand image approach which involves finding out what the brand means to the consumer and then emphasizing the product as a means of self-fulfilment.
- The unique selling proposition approach which focuses upon a highly specific and tangible benefit that the product is capable of delivering (buy this product, get this specific benefit).

The final stage is concerned with the measurement of results and here we have to go back to the objectives. What exactly has the campaign achieved and to what exent have the objectives been met? Given that we started this section by categorizing objectives as communication-related objectives and sales-related objectives, any measurement process needs to reflect this categorization. Thus, there are measures of:

- Awareness levels.
- Attitudes towards the product.
- The extent to which repositioning has been achieved.
- Image measures.

and

- Sales levels.
- Enquiry levels.
- Market share.

For many organizations, measuring the sales effect of a campaign is often difficult, largely because sales are typically affected by a spectrum of factors quite apart from advertising. Nevertheless, given the amounts of money that are spent on promotion, managers need to arrive at at least a broad measure of its impact.

In addition to post-testing, campaigns can also be pre-tested so that their probable effect can be gauged before the campaign is run and any necessary changes made. Amongst the pre-testing techniques available are:

- Direct rating tests whereby potential customers rate alternative appeals.
- Portfolio tests which involve customers listening or viewing a range of advertisements and then being asked to recall their content either on an aided or unaided basis.
- Laboratory tests which measure physiological responses to alternative ads.

Explain how an advertising campaign targeted at industrial markets might possibly be pre- and post-tested and how the test results might subsequently be used in the promotional planning process.

(Marketing Planning and Control, December 1994, Question 9.)

QUESTION 6.11

Although we have talked here about the various issues that are associated with the development of a promotional campaign, many of the decisions that need to be taken are taken in conjunction with an advertising agency. The question of the sorts of criteria that should be used in the selection of an advertising agency were the focus of the second of the two questions on the mini case study in the December 1993 Marketing Planning and Control examination. You should, therefore, attempt the question on the next page.

What criteria should be taken into account in the appointment of an advertising agency?

Distribution and salesforce decisions

Distribution is the fourth of the 'hard' elements of the marketing mix and, it has been argued, amongst the most critical of the decisions faced by management. There are several reasons for this, although the two most significant stem from the way in which distribution decisions typically involve a series of long-term commitments to other firms and that the choice of channel affects all other marketing decisions.

DEFINITION 6.4

Marketing channels can be viewed as sets of interdependent organizations involved in the process of making a product or service available for use or consumption.

(Source: Kotler (1991) *Marketing Management: Analysis, Planning, Implementation and Control*, Prentice Hall, page 508.)

Choosing the distribution channels

For many organizations there is often little real choice in terms of how the product is to be distributed and the type of distribution channel that is to be used. Instead, it is simply a case of plugging into an already well-developed – and often efficient – system that has been operating for some time; an obvious example of this would be the distribution system for foodstuffs. However, for other organizations there may well be a far greater degree of freedom, with the choice being between what is generally referred to as a 'short' or zero level channel (the producer sells direct to the user) or a 'long' and multi-level channel (the producer sells to a wholesaler network which in turn sells to a retail network which then sells to the consumer).

The role of the distribution network

Managed effectively, a distribution network is capable of performing several functions, including:

- The *collection of information* on customers, competitors, and the sorts of developments that are taking place within the market.
- The *promotion* of the product.
- The *financing* of inventories.
- The *delivery and physical transfer* of the product to the customer.
- A degree of *risk sharing*.
- An *ordering* function.

Infuences upon the channel decision

We said earlier that distribution channels can be categorized very broadly in terms of their length, that is the number of intermediaries that are used. In choosing between channel alternatives, there are several factors that typically influence the decision, including:

- *The product's characteristics:* Is it, for example, perishable? Is it of a particularly high value and does it need specialist installation and after-sales support?

- *The characteristics of the intermediaries* that might possibly be used. What particular skills and levels of sales expertise do they have? What geographic coverage are they able to offer and what particularly valuable sales contacts do they have? How important would the product be to them and what level of effort would they put into the sales exercise? What profit margin would they expect and what level of pro-motional support would be needed?
- *Competitive characteristics:* How are the organization's direct competitors distributing *their* products? Do we want or need to adopt broadly the same approach so that potential customers are always faced with a choice between the alternatives, or is there scope for doing something completely different that would give us a competitive advantage?
- *Company characteristics:* What have we done in the past and what sorts of relationships have we developed with possible intermediaries? What level of resources do we have and what flexibility might this give us? What are the organization's long-term objectives and how might these influence the choice of network?
- *Environmental factors:* Are there any legal issues that might need to be taken into account? Is the economy generally buoyant or depressed and what are the implications of this for the costs, margins and prices?

Against the general background of these sorts of issues, the marketing planner can then begin to make a series of decisions, including whether to opt for *intensive, selective* or *exclusive distribution*.

Intensive distribution involves selling the product through as many types of distribution outlet as possible in order to maximize market coverage; examples of organizations which pursue this approach include cigarette and confectionery manufacturers.

Selective distribution involves choosing between the various types of outlet which would be willing to stock and sell the product and focusing the marketing effort upon those which it believes will offer the greatest potential and produce the highest long-term return.

Exclusive distribution involves the use of a very limited number of intermediaries in order to achieve a greater degree of control over how the product is sold and the sort of sales support that is given. Many exclusive distribution arrangements also go hand-in-hand with an obligation upon the distributor not to sell competing products; an obvious example of organizations which use this approach are the manufacturers of luxury cars.

Evaluating the channel alternatives

Having identified the channel alternatives that are open to the organization, the marketing planner needs to evaluate each of these against three criteria: *cost, control* and *flexibility*.

In the case of relatively low-priced items or where the scope for differentiation and competitive advantage is low, the *cost* or *economic* criterion is the most obvious and significant influence upon the decision. In taking this into account, the planner needs to identify the costs and sales that are likely to be associated with each of the channel alternatives and to weigh these against issues such as the segmentation and positioning strategy and the organization's long-term objectives.

Having done this, the planner needs then to take account of the implications for *control*. The company's own salesforce, for example, can be controlled in a direct way with the focus of their sales effort being channelled in order to reflect short- and long-term opportunities and priorites. By contrast, sales agents and intermediaries who are carrying large numbers of products, of which ours is just one small part, offer much less scope for being managed in a highly directed fashion. The planner may therefore be faced with what is often a classic trade-off between the levels of cost and control.

The third criterion that needs to be taken into account is concerned with *flexibility*. We made the comment earlier that distribution decisions often involve long-term commitments. Because of this, the degree of flexibility that exists is typically low; once decisions have been made, they offer little real scope for changes to be made, particularly in the short term. Given this, the planner needs to think at the outset about the ways in which environmental conditions might change, what the implications for the company's approaches to distribution might be, and how levels of potential flexibility might possibly be maximized.

ACTIVITY 6.5

Take a market sector and, in the light of what has been said so far, identify the *length* of the channels that are being used, the sorts of factors which appear to have *influenced* the choice and development of channels, the *role* played by the various channel members, and the apparent *efficiency* and *effectiveness* of the channel.

Managing the channel

Managing distribution channels involves four principal activities:

1   The *selection* of the appropriate channel members.
2   Their *motivation*.
3   Their *evaluation*.
4   When appropriate, the dropping of those channel members who are failing to achieve what is expected of them and their replacement with others.

The sorts of issues that influence the first of these has been the underlying theme of much of what we have said in our discussion so far and you might therefore try listing the factors that need to be taken into account.

Motivating the channel

Distribution channels can be motivated in a variety of positive *and* negative ways. Amongst the *positive* incentives are:

*   The overall sales and profit potential that the product or product range offers.
*   The extent to which sales support in the form of advertising and sales leads can be provided.
*   Giving the distributor geographic sales exclusivity.
*   The development of long-term co-operative relationships.
*   A programme of sales incentives (the most obvious way in which this might be done would involve linking higher profit margins to certain levels of sales).
*   Short term sales contests.

Included within the *negative* incentives are:

*   A reduction in margins.
*   A slowing down of deliveries.
*   The threat to reduce or stop supplies altogether.

(i) By what criteria might you measure the efficiency of a distribution channel? Illustrate your answer with appropriate examples.

(Marketing Planning and Control, June 1993, Question 8.)

(ii) What financial and non-financial criteria should be taken into account in evaluating current and potential distribution channels?

(Strategic Marketing Management: Planning and Control, June 1995, Question 2.)

(iii) What factors should be taken into account in the development or modification of distribution channels?

(Strategic Marketing Management: Planning and Control, December 1995, Question 3.)

Evaluating the channel

At its most basic, the evaluation of channel members comes down to the simple question of whether each of the intermediaries is doing what is expected of it and achieving the performance levels that are required. If they are, the planner might possibly think about how these levels might be improved yet further. If, however, the expected levels of performance are not being achieved, thought needs then to be given to the reasons for this and how, if at all, the intermediaries might be supported and motivated so that their levels of performance are improved. If, however, the planner concludes that there is little real scope for their development and improvement, the decision needs then to be taken either to accept that the full potential of the market is not and will not be realized or that *modifications to the channel* will have to be made.

Channel dynamics

Only rarely do distribution channels remain unchanged for long periods. Instead, they typically evolve gradually over time as the responsibilities and performance levels of channel members fluctuate. Amongst the consequences of this is that the balance of power that exists within the channel also change; an obvious example of this in grocery retailing in most highly developed markets is the emergence of small numbers of large and powerful retail chains which are to a large extent able to dictate terms to the food producers.

Occasionally, however, we see the emergence of what is referred to as a 'category buster' which changes the entire industry and how the distribution task is carried out; an example of this would be the the the entry into the market of an organization such as *Toys Я Us* which, by virtue of its size, scale of operations, the siting of its enormous stores and its general way of doing business, has radically altered how toys are sold.

ACTIVITY 6.6

Identify two examples of industries in which the approach to distribution has changed dramatically over the past few years or is currently going through a series of major changes. What has been driving these changes and what are the marketing implications for the suppliers within the industry?

Because the costs of distribution often represent a significant proportion of the final selling price of a product (anything between 20–80 per cent), the potential for making major savings – and gaining a competitive advantage – if the distribution process is managed more efficiently and effectively, are significant. Given this, the dynamic nature of many channels with the increasing development of vertical and horizontal marketing systems can frequently be seen to be a search for competitive advantage.

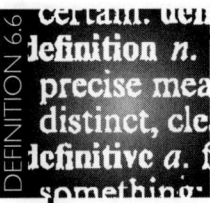

DEFINITION 6.6

certain. def
definition *n.*
precise mea
distinct, cle
definitive *a.* f
something:

A *vertical marketing system* involves the producer(s), wholesaler(s) and retailer(s) acting together in a unified way so that levels of conflict are reduced, and the operating economies and market impact are maximized. In this way, the profits of each of the members are increased.

A *horizontal marketing system* involves unrelated companies putting together the resources that are needed in order to exploit emerging market opportunities which, separately, neither would be able to capitalize upon.

Managing the salesforce

Managing the sales force involves a series of decisions that are concerned with its objectives, the way in which it is to be structured, and how the individual members are to be selected and motivated.

Managed effectively, the sales force is a powerful and highly visible part of the organization which is capable of performing a series of roles in addition to that of selling on a day-to-day basis. These include:

- *Prospecting* for new customers and markets.
- *Communicating* with customers and distributors.
- *Providing technical advice* and servicing distributors and customers.
- *Gathering market information.*

The *type* of salesforce that a firm uses is influenced by a variety of factors, including the nature of its products and their technical complexity, the types of customer that exist and their needs, the geographic location of its markets, the numbers of customers and their relative importance, the breadth of the product range, the scope for cross-selling, and so on. The implications of these factors are then reflected in the choice that needs to be made between:

- *Territorial structures* in which each member of the sales force is allocated an exclusive territory and expected to represent the company's full product line. The advantages of this approach, which is best suited to a relatively straightforward sales task, include its simplicity and the lack of ambiguity in reporting lines and issues of responsibilities. Insofar as problems with this approach are encountered, they stem from the question of the size and shape of the territories that should be used so that workloads and market potentials are allocated fairly.
- *Product-structured salesforces* in which individual members of the salesforce are given responsibility for a particular product or product line which they then sell across a far wider geographic area. Such an approach is best suited to markets in which the product is technically rather more complex and the buyers' needs more specialized. Although the costs of a product-structured salesforce tend to be rather higher than those of one structured around territories, the benefits are seen to be those of a more specialized and knowlegeable salesforce.
- *Market-structured salesforces* in which the sales staff concentrate upon specific types of end user. It might therefore be the case that there are various types of customer for what is broadly the same product, but that their application needs differ. Recognizing this, the salesforce would be divided up on this basis; an example of this would be the computer firms which struture their salesforces along the lines of those who sell to the banks, those who sell to manufacturing industry, and so on.

Approaches to salesforce motivation

The question of how best to motivate the sales force is one that preoccupies many managers. If they are paid too much, costs rise unneccessarily. If they are paid too little it is likely that morale and performance will be low. Achieving the right balance is therefore important not just in terms of motivation, but also for the recruitment and retention of the best people.

However, motivation should not be seen just in financial terms, since sales staff – in common with most employees – are motivated by a variety of other factors, including the potential for personal development, recognition by senior management of what they are achieving, opportunities for promotion, ego, drive, fringe benefits, and being part of a winning team.

In practice, these sorts of points translate into a choice between three main approaches to remuneration:

1   *Straight salary* in which each member of the salesforce is paid a fixed amount, irrespective of performance levels. The advantages of this are essentially that management can realistically expect members of the sales team to focus upon aspects of the business which will produce a return only in the long term, since this will not affect their immediate salary. However, if the sales team is guaranteed a certain level of income irrespective of their sales performance, their motivation to push harder, it is argued, will be reduced.

2   *Straight commission* in which the earnings of each of the sales staff are linked directly to their individual sales performance. Although this is an approach which can work well, it almost inevitably leads to a focus upon the very short term, with little attention being paid to longer term issues such as market development. Sales teams that are paid on this basis also tend to suffer from a high turnover of staff, since if the sales levels drop, individuals are perhaps understandably tempted to go eleswhere.

3   *Salary plus commission* in which sales staff are paid a basic salary which is then supplemented by a commission which is related to the individual's or the sales team's performance during a given period. Of the three approaches discussed here, it is this which tends to be seen as the fairest and most useful, since not only do the individual members of the team have a degree of security from their guaranteed income, but there is also a potentially powerful incentive to achieve high levels of sales performance.

QUESTION 6.14

(i)   To what extent has research in recent years improved our understanding of how field sales staff can most effectively be motivated and controlled?

(Marketing Planning and Control, June 1992, Question 8.)

(ii)   Making reference to examples, discuss the factors that should be taken into account when deciding how best to motivate and control a sales force and explain why so many firms experience problems in this area.

(Strategic Marketing Management: Planning and Control, December 1994, Question 10.)

Evaluating the salesforce

There are several ways in which the performance of sales staff individually and the sales-force overall can be evaluated, including:

- The levels of sales that are achieved and how they compare with the targets that were set and agreed at the beginning of the period.
- The number of new accounts opened.
- Sales calls per day.
- The average time per sales call.
- The average cost per sales call.
- The cost per sale.
- The number of lost customers.
- Sales person to sales person comparisons.
- Comparisons with previous time periods.
- Customer feedback and evaluations.

ACTIVITY 6.7

Speak to your sales director and discuss the sorts of issues raised within this section of the workbook. Ask about the sorts of problems that the company faces in managing its sales force and how it attempts to overcome these.

The 'soft' elements of the marketing mix

Our discussion so far has focused upon the traditional idea of the marketing mix and the 4Ps. Over the past few years, however, it has been argued that marketing management is concerned not just with product, price, place and promotion, but also with a series of rather 'softer' elements. The three most significant of these are, it is suggested:

- People.
- Process management.
- Physical evidence.

The *people* dimension is concerned with the types and skills of your staff, their ability to get things done, and – very importantly – how they interact with customers and suppliers.

The second 'soft' dimension – *process management* – is concerned with the ways in which customers are dealt with from the moment of the initial contact right through to the sales follow-up and the after sales service, whilst *physical evidence* relates to the surroundings in which the other elements are delivered and the sorts of messages they send to the customer.

ACTIVITY 6.8

Look at your own organization and assess the strengths and weaknesses of each of the 'soft' elements of the mix. To what extent does there appear to be a conscious effort to manage them? How does each of your competitors perform on these dimensions?

It follows from this that the marketing planner needs to think not just about the obvious dimensions of marketing (the 4Ps), but also the less tangible aspects, since for many organizations it is these which can play a powerful role in determining how the rest of the marketing programme is perceived. Their importance can also be understood by recognizing that, as market expectations of customer service levels increase, so the differentiating point between one organization and another will shift towards the 'softer' elements that are associated with the delivery of the product or service.

EXAM TIP

When analysing the major case study in the Analysis and Decision paper, make a conscious effort to identify how the 'soft' elements might contribute to the more effective performance of the organization.

Internal marketing

In 1982, Peters and Waterman published their book *In Search of Excellence* in which they focused upon high performing organizations and attempted to identify the sorts of characteristics which contributed to above average and excellent performance. Included within their findings was the way in which high performing organizations recognized the real value of their staff and made a conscious and sustained effort both to maximize and make full use of their potential. In doing this, it appeared that managers placed emphasis upon issues such as the careful selection of staff, the development of their skills, the pursuit of a clear and appropriate management style and – perhaps most importantly – the creation of shared values.

These ideas have, in turn, led to the idea of internal marketing.

Internal marketing refers to 'any form of marketing within an organization which focuses attention on the internal activities that need to be changed in order that marketing plans may be implemented.'

(Source: Christopher A., Payne A., and Ballantyne D., 1991, *Relationship Marketing*, page 79, Butterworth-Heinemann.)

Internal marketing is therefore concerned with creating the sort of culture and climate within an organization in which there is a far clearer understanding amongst all staff of the objectives, the key values and the sorts of implementation issues that need to be addressed. It follows from this that you should recognize that there is a need to focus not just on external customers, but also on a series of internal customers:

> The approach aims first to get a better understanding of the importance and performance of various activities within a particular work area which might be contributing to an internal quality group. The department then identifies by working with its internal customers and internal suppliers the key opportunities for improvement. Small problems are best tackled first to build mutual confidence through results.
>
> Source: Christopher et al, page 80.

Explain what is meant by 'internal marketing' and why it has been the subject of increased attention over the past few years. What factors should be taken into account when developing a programme of internal marketing for an organization?

(Marketing Planning and Control, June 1994, Question 5.)

Summary

Within this unit we have examined the various dimensions of the marketing mix. As a check on your understanding of this material, consider the following questions:

1   What are the 7Ps of the marketing mix?

Product	)	
Price	)	The 'hard' elements
Promotion	)	
Place	)	
People	)	
Physical evidence	)	The 'soft' elements
Process management	)	

(See pages 126–7, 146.)

2   How might the so-called 'uncontrollable' elements of the mix be managed?

These elements, which include the economy, legislation, demographics, political decisions, socio-cultural issues, technological developments, ecological issues, and competitors, are outside the direct or day-to-day control of management, but are capable of having a significant effect upon demand. Because of this, although it may be difficult or impossible to control them, it is necessary to manage them as far as possible. This can be done in a variety of ways:

(i)	The economy	Redirect the marketing effort to more attractive geographic markets
(ii)	Legislation	Lobby government and trade associations
(iii)	Demographics	See (i) above
(iv)	Political decisions	See (ii) above
(v)	Socio-cultural factors	See (i) above
(vi)	Technology	Invest more in R&D, work with outside agencies, develop alliances with technological leaders
(vii)	Ecological issues	Lobby government
(viii)	Competitors	Develop alliances, buy them out, or come to an agreement with them (this may be illegal under competition laws)

(See page 127.)

3 What are the three elements of the product?

- The product attributes.
- The product benefits.
- The marketing support services.

(See page 127.)

4 Define 'product mix' and 'product line'.

The *product mix* is the group of products sold by the organization (e.g. Ford with cars, buses, trucks and tractors).

The *product line* is a group of broadly similar products targeted at a similar group of customers.

(See page 128.)

5 Of what value is the PLC?

Although the PLC has been criticized for its overly general nature and the problems of forecasting its length and shape, it has a value in that it provides a broad framework for thinking about how sales might develop and how marketing strategies need both to manage and reflect the length and shape. It is not, however, a precise forecasting tool as has been claimed in the past.

(See pages 128–9.)

6 How should marketing strategy change over the life cycle of the product?

This is illustrated in Figure 6.4 on page 129.

7 Identify the four types of broad strategy:

(a) Corporate umbrella branding.
(b) Family umbrella names.
(c) Range brand names.
(d) Individual brand names.

These are discussed in greater detail on page 130.

8 How would you value a brand?

This has been the subject of considerable discussion and controversy. However, one approach involves taking account of:

- The brand's market position (leader, follower, challenger, nicher).
- The age and stability of the brand.
- The nature of the market.
- Geographic spread.
- Sales trends.
- The existence of trade marks or patents.
- Advertising levels and patterns.

(See pages 130–1.)

9 Why is NPD important?

NPD is a major contributor to the fortunes and future of the organization. In particular, it:

- Ensures that obsolescence is avoided.
- Helps to ensure that the organization can compete in new and growing markets.
- Reduces the dependence upon declining market sectors.
- Contributes to long-term growth.
- Helps in the fight against competition.

(See page 132.)

10   What problems are typically associated with NPD?

The major problems are those of cost, time, the failure rate, high levels of risk, the difficulties of determining the areas in which NPD activity should take place, the faster pace of change that now demands much more of organizations, and the shorter life cycles which allow for shorter periods for achieving a positive return. (See pages 131–2.)

11   Draw a model of the NPD process.

A model is illustrated in Figure 6.5 on page 133.

12   What problems are associated with test marketing?

The five principal problems are:

- The danger of alerting competitors.
- The problems of finding representative test areas.
- The time needed to identify repurchase rates.
- The difficulties of achieving representative distribution profiles.
- The difficulties of interpreting what are often ambiguous results.

(See pages 133–4.)

13   What is a price taker and a price maker?

By virtue of market structures, the small size of the organization and/or the lack of distinctive product or service features, a price taker has no control over the price charged in the marketplace. A price maker, by contrast, is able to determine the prices which others then have to follow (see page 134).

14   Identify nine possible pricing objectives.

These are listed on page 135.

15   How would you set a price?

The is done very largely on the basis either of *cost-related factors* (mark-up pricing, target return on investment pricing, or early cash recovery) or *market-related factors* (perceived value and going rate pricing).
(See pages 135–6.)

16   What is the promotions mix?

The promotions mix consists of the spectrum of promotional activities that a firm might use. The four principal tools are advertising, personal selling, publicity, and sales promotion. To these, however, you can also add exhibitions sponsorship, point of sale, direct marketing, and packaging.
(See page 136.)

17   Define each of the four principal elements of the mix.

A definition of these appears on pages 136–7 in Definition 6.3.

18   Distinguish between sales-related and communication-related promotional objectives.

Sales-related objectives might include increasing sales from A to B, strengthening the organization's position, generating a specific number of coupon enquiries, and minimizing/reducing the impact of a competitor's advertising.

Communication-related objectives might include raising levels of awareness, re-positioning, changing perceptions, and altering the image (see page 137).

19   How would you set the promotions budget?

Four principal methods exist:

- The affordable approach.
- Competitive parity.
- Percentage of sales.
- The affordable and task technique.

These are discussed on page 138.

20 How would you measure the effects of a promotional campaign?

This can be done by measuring and comparing across time:

- Awareness levels.
- Attitudes.
- The extent to which repositioning has been achieved.
- Images.
- Enquiry levels.
- Sales levels.
- Market share.

(See page 139.)

21 Why are distribution decisions so important?

There are six principal reasons:

- Distribution decisions have a knock-on effect to all other marketing decisions.
- They tend to involve long-term commitments.
- Distribution decisions determine the nature and breadth of contact with the market.
- The intermediaries frequently demand a significant margin which has an effect upon the selling price.
- It is through the distributors that much of the final selling effort is made.
- Much of the post-sales support is provided by distributors.

It is for these reasons that if distributors are chosen and managed badly, much of the other marketing effort is wasted.
(See page 140.)

22 Distinguish between intensive, selective and exclusive distribution.

These are defined on page 141 in Definition 6.5.

23 What should be taken into account in measuring distribution efficiency?

Distribution efficiency is concerned very largely with the speed, costs and levels of stock loss/breakage.
(See pages 141–3.)

24 What is meant by internal marketing?

Internal marketing is concerned with creating the sort of culture and climate within an organization in which there is a far clearer understanding amongst all staff of the objectives, the key values and the sorts of implementation issues that need to be addressed.
(See pages 146–7.)

Very deliberately, within this unit we have highlighted the key issues associated with the management of the marketing mix. For a more detailed discussion of each of these elements turn to Chapters 11–14 of *Strategic Marketing Management* by Wilson and Gilligan with Pearson.

Activity debrief

Question 6.1 (i)–(v)

Over the past few years, a variety of questions on the product life cycle have appeared on the exam papers. Many candidates perform badly on these, very largely because they have a tendency to put down everything they know about the PLC rather than addressing the *specifics* of the question.

In each of the questions posed here, you should begin with a brief (one or two sentences) explanation of the life cycle (it is a model of product and market evolution which highlights the need for and way in which strategies should change over time). Having done this, you should focus upon the detail of what is being asked of you. Typically this will be an evaluation of the life cycle (see pages 128–9); recommendations of how strategies should vary from one stage to another (see Figure 6.4); or the implications for managing the life cycle in the face of environmental change (see pages 128–9).

Question 6.2   Brand evaluation is an important but difficult area, with a variety of views on how exactly this should be done. You should therefore begin by outlining the nature of the debate and then move on to suggest how this might be done; one possible approach appears on pages 130–1.

Question 6.3   You should begin by explaining briefly what is meant by NPD (see Definition 6.2) and then turn to the reasons why it is so frequently an expensive and risky activity. The principal cause of this is the high failure rate; the six factors that contribute to this are listed on page 131 under the heading 'Developing new products'. You should then explain how the failure rate might be reduced. Included within this would be a greater environmental awareness; improvements to the ideas and product screening/evaluation processes (see Figure 6.5); better test marketing; more careful launch processes; fewer 'me too' products and more products which offer the customer a significant benefit.

Question 6.4   Questions on the new product development process often focus upon failure rates and how they might be reduced by making changes to the development process; these might include better search and evaluative stages, a speeding up of the process as a whole, and so on. In the case of the two questions here, you should begin by outlining the nature of the NPD problems that are typically encountered, and how in (i) these might be overcome by structuring the process more effectively (see Figure 6.5); and in (ii) conducting as many activities as possible simultaneously rather than sequentially.

Question 6.5 (i)–(iii)

In answering each of these questions, you should begin by explaining briefly what is meant by test marketing (TM) and what it is designed to achieve. You should then concentrate upon the specific issues, including:

(i)   Customers', competitors' and distributors' responses to the new product; the effectiveness of the various elements of the marketing mix; repurchase rates; and further market opportunities.

(ii)   A poor choice of test area; competitive action which spoils the results; insufficient or too many resources allocated to the TM; too short a TM period; difficulties in analysing/interpreting the results; and a changed environment by the time the product is launched.

(iii)   Cost; time; competitive action; the degree of newness of the product; the availability of representative TM areas; the amount of detailed market analysis that has been conducted at an earlier stage; experience in this or similar markets; and management confidence in the new product.

Question 6.6 (i)   The five principal factors influencing price are referred to under the heading of 'Pricing decisions' (see page 134). Other influences are listed in Activity 6.4.

Question 6.6 (ii)   You should begin by explaining why pricing decisions are so difficult (e.g. the implications for revenues, the problems of price wars, the market's price awareness/sensitivity, the issue of costs, product range interdependencies, and so on). You should then discuss their implications for the machine tool. Given that it is innovatory, what are the pricing implications? Think about issues of positioning, the likelihood of others copying the product and then undercutting you (this might be an argument for a low initial price), the levels of demand you need, and so on).

Question 6.6 (iii)   The sort of information needed would include the probable patterns of customer response at each level of price, the scope for market growth/development, competitors' probable behaviour, distributors' expectations, internal expectations of the product, and so on. The problems of getting this information are essentially the normal problems of researching markets.

Question 6.6 (iv)   Look at your or other companies' experiences in similar markets elsewhere, with a view to identifying general lessons; speak to industry experts and experienced managers; and try a small-scale experiment in a representative market area.

Question 6.7 Ideally, you would have information on:

- Each firm's competitive posture and probable patterns of response.
- Their cost levels.
- The relative importance to them of each of their products and markets and their commitment to each of these.
- The potential returns from cutting prices.
- Their past pricing history (offensive or defensive).
- The distinctiveness of each of their products.
- The probable response of distributors.

Question 6.8 Your answer should be based around the seven decision areas. These include:

- The objectives (what are we trying to achieve)?
- How might this be done?
- How much is to be spent?
- Where will the budget be spent?
- When will it be spent?
- What sort of creative appeal should be used?
- How might the results by measured?

Research can contribute at virtually all stages by providing a better picture of the market, and hence identifying what is possible; giving an insight to competitors' spending patterns; evaluating possible creative appeals; identifying the most profitable/receptive target markets; evaluating the results, and so on.

Question 6.9 You should begin by explaining briefly why there is a greater budget accountability today. Outline (again briefly) the approaches to advertising budget (affordable, competitive parity, and percentage of sales), highlighting their attractions (e.g. their simplicity and, in some cases, their apparent logic). Turn then to the more complex models (e.g. objective and task, and the decision models), and discuss the difficulties associated with their use. Conclude by stating that because of the difficulties of obtaining the information needed for the more complex approaches, managers revert to those that are easily used.

Question 6.10 Begin by identifying some of the new promotional vehicles and media (e.g. cable and satellite television, more exhibitions, a greater use of sponsorship, and so on). You should then examine the sorts of factors that should influence the allocation of the budget. These will include the ability of each of the alternatives to reach the target market, competitors' use of the media, the costs, the credibility of each of the alternatives, and so on. The success would then be measured in terms of the extent to which each of the sales-related and communication-related objectives (see page 137) has been achieved.

Question 6.11 You should begin by outlining the various ways in which advertising campaigns can be pre- and post-tested.

These involve measuring:

- Awareness levels, and how these change before and after the campaign.
- Attitudes, and, again, how these change.
- The extent to which repositioning is achieved.
- Image changes.
- Sales levels.
- Enquiry levels.
- Market share moves.

The results can then be fed back in a relatively straightforward manner, in that depending upon how successful a campaign is proving to be, so it influences what is done next.

Question 6.12 The criteria that should be used for selecting an advertising agency are broadly similar to those for a market research agency; these are outlined on page 19. In addition, however, you would want to take account of their creative skills and, possibly, the in-house production facilities.

Question 6.13 (i) You should begin by outlining (briefly) the channel alternatives open to an organization. You should then state that, depending upon the type of channel (short or long), so the evaluative criteria will vary. In general terms, however, evaluation would take account of:

- *Economic factors*: costs, margins, stock levels, losses, and so on.
- *Control factors*: the extent to which the distributors can be managed proactively.
- *The flexibility of the channel*: to what extent can the channel be modified to match changing markets?

Question 6.13 (ii)   A variety of criteria need to be taken into account in evaluating current and potential channels, including the scope they offer for competitive advantage, the costs and any investment needed, the margins that might be achieved and the levels of profitability, their length and the number of intermediaries, the degree of flexibility, the marketing support they will need, the need for training, their speed and reliability, levels of control and risk, competitors' presence, the access they give to related markets, levels of security, the degree of price flexibility, stock levels, payment terms, any exit costs, and the length of any commitment to the channel. Quite obviously, the importance of these will vary from one company to another.

Question 6.13 (iii)   In developing or modifying a channel, the sorts of issues that need to be taken into account include product-specific factors (bulk, perishability, unit value and the need for pre- and post-sales support); the characteristics of potential intermediaries; competitors; company characteristics (current approaches to distribution, the need/desire for control, resources, the product mix, long-term objectives, and so on); and general environmental characteristics (legal regulations, etc.). Other factors that need to be taken into account include the implications of each of the alternatives for *costs, control* and *flexibility*.

Question 6.14 (i) and (ii)

In both cases you should make brief reference to the role of the sales force and how these can differ significantly depending upon the type of product (low-tech, high-tech), the type of market (size, location) and the type of customer (consumer or business-to-business, levels of knowledge, and so on). Having done this, you should refer to the different approaches to motivation and control that are typically used (straight salary, straight commission, salary plus commission). You can then go on to discuss the limitations of each of these and the need for what, in Maslow's terms, would be an emphasis upon satisfying the higher level needs.

The problems of motivation and control typically came from an overly mechanistic approach to management and a failure to recognize the need for the 'softer' issues of motivation.

Question 6.15   You should begin by explaining what is meant by internal marketing (this is discussed on page 146 and defined in Definition 6.7), and then move on to discuss why it has become more important in recent years (e.g. to achieve a greater unity of purpose, better communication and co-ordination, a tighter focus, a better staff understanding of values and priorities, a stronger commitment, and so on).

Strategic evaluation and appraisal

Evaluation and appraisal are key issues in strategic marketing. Nothing the manager does can remove risk completely from business decisions but proper evaluation and appraisal can reduce these risks to levels more acceptable in highly competitive situations.

In this unit you will learn how to evaluate and appraise strategy and to choose among strategic options available. You will see:

- What criteria are available and how to choose between them.
- How to choose between options.
- What constitutes a 'good marketing' company.

By the end of this unit you will be able to:

- Initiate appraisal systems for marketing planning.
- Apply financial and non-financial criteria to choice evaluation.
- Identify the resource implications of mix decisions.
- Conduct feasibility studies and risk evaluation.

There are strong links between this unit and Unit 6 which focuses on the management of the mix and the development of marketing strategy.

This unit is primarily concerned with choice. It is an essential step between the previous stage of analysis and the following stage of decision.

In the major case study, especially, decision plays an important role and marks can be lost in the examination if clear recommendations for decision and action are not given.

This unit accounts for approximately 10–15 per cent of the syllabus content on both Planning and Control and Analysis and Decision papers. This unit should take up to 5 hours of study (workbook and recommended texts).

In this section you should work carefully to master the various tests and approaches so that you are able to see easily the advantages and disadvantages of the strategic options that analysis reveals.

The primary consideration in this unit is the evaluation of alternative strategic options open to the organization. Previous units have considered the options and methodologies open to strategic marketers and have shown the number of different routes that the strategist might consider in his or her planning. In previous units of this workbook you will have considered and understood the implications of:

- Controllable and uncontrollable environmental factors
- Competition
- Customers and their needs
- Market segmentation and targeting
- Positioning
- Strategic models
  - Portfolio analysis
  - Porter
  - Competitive advantage

- Strategy formulation
- Marketing mix
  - Product decisions
  - Pricing decisions
  - Promotion decisions
  - Distribution decisions
  - Sales-force decisions

In short, you have analysed and considered the options open to an organization. Once you have uncovered all the options, how do you decide which is the best way to go?

Most candidates seem to encounter problems when it comes to moving from analysis to decision. The effective marketer will only produce profits for the organization when the ideas are implemented. There is no way of guaranteeing success in a dynamic marketplace. There is, however, a way of guaranteeing failure – analyse everything and do nothing!

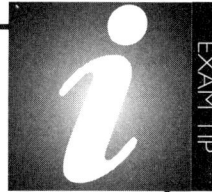

Many questions require an explicit or implicit understanding of choice criteria, be they marketing specific or financial.

Considering both broad business and marketing strategies as well as more detailed marketing programmes, the marketer is faced with two separate but related problems:

1. What choice criteria should be used?
2. How can we appraise and evaluate alternative options that appear to be open to the organization in question?

Short versus long term

Before considering the best way to evaluate and appraise marketing strategy, it is probably wise to stop at this point and consider just what we mean by strategy. Since strategy is about marshalling the gross resource of the organization to match the needs of the marketplace and achieve the business objective, this cannot be a short-term activity. Every organization is complex and any change takes time to accomplish. Strategic decisions, like the General choosing his battleground, will have long-term implications. Strategic decisions, such as which business area to enter, cannot be reversed at a moment's notice – momentum has to be built up over a planned period of time.

Neither is strategy just yet another word for important tactics. Tactics can be likened to manoeuvres on the field of battle and can be changed as often as required in response to the changing situation faced by the organization in its markets. No matter how important or critical the tactic under review, this does not make it strategy. For the want of a nail the horseshoe, the horse, the knight, the battle and the war were lost – agreed, but once a thousand soldiers have found a nail each they should all know the reason why they were there was to win the war.

The laws of physics apply to all activities. Short-term returns above the average often have to be paid for in the long term. You might recognize the following UK companies who regularly produced profits at a level three times higher than their international counterparts during the 1980s.

- Coloroll
- Polly Peck
- Maxwell Corporation
- Mountleigh Properties
- Ratners
- Burton
- BCCI

You might well ask 'Where are they now?'

The choice of evaluation and appraisal methods are critical because very quickly they become the main reasons for the organization's activities. One of the main reasons for organizational under-performance has been management's confusion between 'purpose' and 'measures of success' (see below). We have to be careful that the evaluation and appraisal methods are aimed at assessing how well the war was won not how many nails were collected!

Marketing strategy is about the long-term success of the organization. Its success or failure must be measured by control systems which take into account this long-term view. A practical evaluation and appraisal system should note any short-term set-backs in the plan – but more importantly – should be capable of setting these within a long-term context.

Financial versus non-financial measurement

In marketing and business texts generally there is surprisingly little discussion over the difference between those measures which assess efficiency and those which assess effectiveness. Efficiency is defined as 'doing things right' and effectiveness is defined as 'doing the right things'. Efficiency and effectiveness were discussed in Unit 1. You might like to return there for a moment to refresh your memory.

Looking at your work, how much of your time each day is spent on activities which are primarily aimed at improving 'efficiency'? 70 per cent, 80 per cent, more?

How much of your work, as a marketer, is spent on 'effectiveness' activities – that add direct value to your customers? How might you improve this balance for the good of the business?

Efficiency measures are by far and away the most common in business generally and tend to evaluate, often on an ongoing basis, the efficiency or precision with which actions are carried out by the organization – mostly internal. When we look at effectiveness measures

– and these are much less common in most organizations – we will be looking at how well the organization is doing the right things. In other words, how well the organization is meeting its external customers' needs.

Figure 1.6 (page 9) showed just how important the differentiation of these measures can be. For the rare organizations who manage to be both effective and efficient, that is they are efficient in their operations and also are delivering what their customers want, the future looks very rosy. For those organizations who are neither effective nor efficient then it is just a matter of time. In the middle, however, the situation is quite interesting. It is clear that organizations can become more and more efficient, leaner and leaner in their operations, but if they still fail to supply to the market what the market wants and needs it is only a matter of time before they are supplanted by eager competition. On the other hand, as long as an organization continues to supply what the market wants, the demand remains rather buoyant. They may not be very efficient in their operations and the way they supply the marketplace, but they are likely to survive.

More worryingly for organizations, however, is that the majority of measures which are used to evaluate and appraise strategy tend to be of the efficiency rather than the effectiveness nature. The majority of financial and accountant-driven measures also fall into this category. While, of course, there must be a point of inefficiency beyond which no organization can survive, efficiency of itself is no guarantee of the organization's long-term survival. Unless the organization delivers what the market wants it will die – albeit slowly.

Strategy is always about balance. In this case, balance between efficiency and effectiveness measures. Ensure that your answers to questions and cases deal with and show this balanced thinking.

By what criteria might you measure the efficiency of a distribution channel? Illustrate your answer with appropriate examples.

June 1993

(**See** Activity debrief at the end of this unit.)

The answer, as in most strategic issues, is one of striking the elusive balance between these two apparently opposing forces. An organization's survival over the long term depends upon it being both effective and efficient. We should be searching out the evaluation and appraisal measures which allow us to pursue both these goals simultaneously. The problem is further compounded when we look in a little more detail at what effectiveness probably means. If we simplify the model of the firm down to its absolute basics we can see that the task of management is to satisfy the opposing needs of its two major publics:

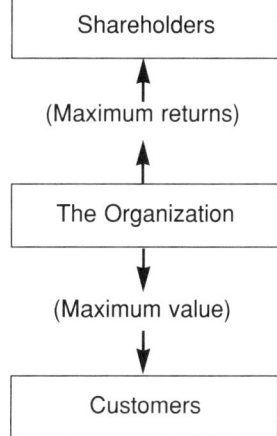

Figure 7.1

The organization's most important two publics are its shareholders – who provide the finance and capital that the organization needs to continue, and its customers – who supply the revenue which pays for the product and produces the returns for the shareholders. We can see that these two publics require quite different things from the organization. Whatever the problems, it is the management's job to ensure that it satisfies both of these key publics if it is to survive over the longer term. How then can we evaluate our strategy within this context?

ACTIVITY 7.2

The financial requirements, and so the demands on marketing, can be strongly affected by an organization's stakeholders and what they require from their investment.

Can you identify the most important stakeholders in your organization? What do they require from your organization? What are the financial implications? What are the marketing implications?

QUESTION 7.2

Identify the areas to which you would need to pay attention in conducting a review of marketing effectiveness. How might the results be used to improve methods of planning and control?

December 1993

(**See** Activity debrief at the end of this unit.)

Financial measures

The more usual measures of evaluation under this heading will include:

- Profit.
- Profitability.
- Shareholder return.
- Cash flow/liquidity.
- Share price.
- Earnings per share.
- Return on net assets.
- Return on sales.

These were defined in more detail in Unit 2.

The interrelationships and working of these various measures can be seen in the extremely simplified diagram below.

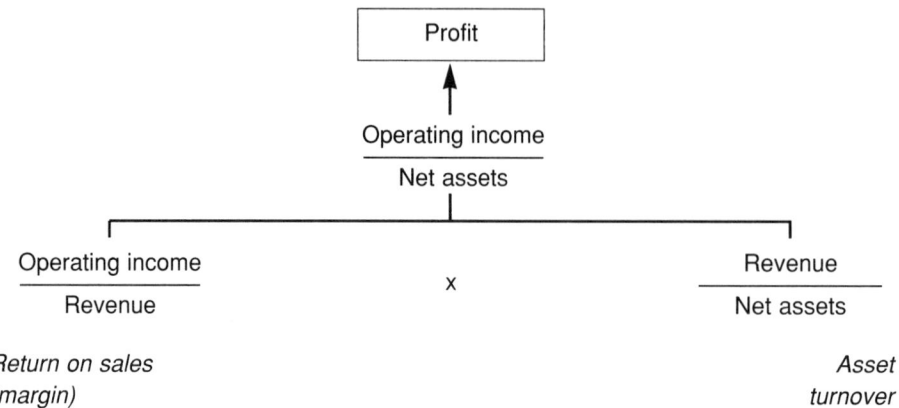

Figure 7.2

Most of these traditional measures concentrate on profit and it goes without saying that profit is essential to the long-term survival of any business no matter what size or shape. However, as Levitt said 'profit is a requisite not a purpose of business'. Profit is essential to any business but is not the only reason why we are here. More importantly, evaluation and appraisal processes which rely exclusively on profitability can overshadow the fact that the only way we make profits is by satisfying customers!

Also important, if somewhat shorter term, liquidity/cash flow evaluation is essential. Lack of long-term profitability is not a major reason for the demise of businesses but cash flow problems can even eliminate companies with a rising order book. Despite everything we have said about strategy being longer term, the one thing we have to bear in mind is short-term cash flow. Without this there is no longer term.

What forms of financial control can most usefully be employed in marketing?

June 1994

(**See** Activity debrief at the end of this unit.)

QUESTION 7.3

Non-financial measures

The non-financial measures of performance tend to measure the effectiveness rather than the efficiency side of the equation, although not exclusively so. Non-financial measures may include:

- Market share.
- Growth.
- Competitive advantage.
- Competitive position.
- Sales volume.
- Market penetration levels.
- New product development.
- Customer satisfaction.
- Customer franchise.
- Market image and awareness levels.

The major case study often includes appendices with financial data. Be sure you also look at the non-financial data for measures of performance too.

EXAM TIP

Two things should be readily apparent from a review of the above list. Firstly, that any one of these measures taken in isolation is unlikely to be sufficient to guarantee the long-term survival and development of the organization. Secondly, implicit (although more often than not unstated) is that growth is always a good thing. The growth aspect to strategy is very much a development of the heydays of the 1970s and remains largely unquestioned in most texts.

There are times when a rapidly rising order book can be dangerous to the financial stability of a company. 'Overtrading' is a major cause of business failure – especially after a recession.

Do you understand what overtrading means?

Talk to a manager from the finance section of your company and find out what 'selling too much' can mean.

Certainly the organization must develop if it is to continue to adapt and remain in touch with its marketplace. But growth? Growth of what? Growth can be a good and healthy influence but if pursued for its own sake can lead to problems. Sales maximization and volume growth can often lead to serious declines in profitability, especially in static or highly competitive marketplaces. Directed and controlled growth based on a qualified and detailed analysis of the marketplace and potential business opportunities can lead to a flourishing organization. However, as Ed Abbey has noted, 'growth for the sake of growth is the ideology of the cancer cell.'

Making reference to examples, discuss the factors that should be taken into account when deciding how best to motivate and control a sales-force and explain why so many organizations experience difficulties in this area.

December 1994

(**See** Activity debrief at the end of this unit.)

Growth is just one example but there are a number of examples of marketing ideas that are just accepted as 'good things'. At Diploma level, examiners are looking for evidence of students being able to think for themselves, not just for regurgitated theory straight out of the textbooks. Before you answer a question, do you understand why you are recommending a given course of action? Or is it just conventional wisdom again?

Multiple criteria

In almost every situation the dependence upon a single criterion for evaluating and appraising strategy is likely to be dangerous. As Wilson, Gilligan and Pearson note there are two extremely good reasons why we should consider using more than one criterion in our evaluation of strategy. This is because:

- Organizations behave ineffectively from some points of view if a single criterion is used.
- Organizations fulfil multiple functions and have multiple goals, some of which may be in conflict. It would be inappropriate to assess strategies purely on the basis of any one criterion.

Many questions require an explicit or an implicit understanding of evaluative criteria. You should therefore be aware of them and the circumstances in which they can be applied.

The major case study requires a clear demonstration of an evaluation among strategic options and a clear decision based upon this analysis.

Organizations and their strategies can best be regarded as living entities. If they follow their markets they will also need to be dynamic and evolving entities just to be able to survive, let alone flourish. Time, if no other reason, will always act to make certain measures redundant and other measures important in new situations.

We have also seen from the discussions above that conflicts naturally arise in the management of any organization. These require that different performance measures need to be traded off in different situations, for example:

- Customers' need for value versus shareholders need for return.
- Cost of achieving market share versus need for profitability.
- Organizations' need for efficiency versus customers' need for service.
- Production efficiency requirement for long runs versus the market's need for choice.
- The organization's drive to standardization versus the consumer's need for individualism.

The choice of the most appropriate measures for evaluation and appraisal will depend entirely on the organization's situation and the strategist's ability to balance internal and external needs.

In the Diploma examinations, questions and cases have been prepared carefully to give you a context within which to propose a *practical* marketing solution – don't ignore it.

Always make sure your solution fits the question.

Choosing the right criterion

How then can we make sure that we are choosing the right criterion against which to evaluate our longer term marketing strategy? Although there are no hard and fast rules for this selection the application of simple common sense can take us a long way forward. The judicious use of some selective models could also shed light on this problem. For example, if we consider the well-known product life cycle as a concept it is worthwhile trying to plot our organization's position on this cycle. Whether we consider this cycle applicable for the organization, the industry, the product or service category or even the particular brand, it will help us to select those criteria which are of most relevance to the situation at hand.

From the example above it can be seen clearly that an organization which plots its position at point 'A' (see Figure 7.3) and still decides to evaluate its long-term strategy according to either market share growth or maintenance, is only likely to be able to do this at the expense of profitability. Looking beyond the product life-cycle model to another popular model, the Boston Matrix, we can see that the same form of guidance is also available for those who wish to look.

Although there is much debate about the continuing validity of the BCG matrix, and much care must be taken in its use, it can still be useful for conceptually placing products or businesses in the overall organization's portfolio. Figure 7.4 shows that different forms of evaluation need to take place depending on the market and business situation of the product or the business considered. For example, 'dog' products or businesses need to be measured according to the net free cash flow which they generate. On the other hand 'question marks'

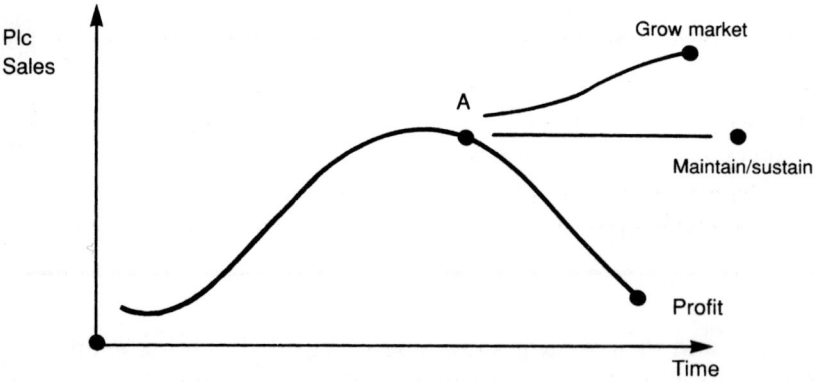

Figure 7.3

Figure 7.4   BCG Matrix

are best evaluated by the sales volume and revenue which they are able to generate in their particular market situation. 'Stars' are best evaluated by an assessment of net present value while the all important 'cash cows' need to be assessed, evaluated and managed to generate the maximum return on investment.

GEC matrices and other models can also be used, with a little common sense, to ensure that we are using the right measures for the market situations that we face.

> It has been argued that one of the main reasons for the demise of the British motorcycle industry was their dependence on one key measure of performance – gross margin. As the Japanese advanced they retreated from one sector after another as margins were squeezed. The rest, as they say, is history.

Critical success factors

Much has been written about critical success factors (CSFs) although not all of it is in agreement. CSFs can be a useful way of focusing the attention of the organization onto those things, amid the wild array of important daily activities, that are really important. CSFs are not the same thing as performance measures and are not the same thing, strictly, as methods of evaluation and appraisal of long-term strategy.

CSFs need to be capable of measurement – obviously. This, however, can lead to organizations choosing 'quantities' rather than 'qualities' although the latter are no less important than the former. Also CSFs should not be based on variables that have only short-term importance. Nor should they be based only on internal variables. A study conducted in 1990 showed that companies which concentrated on achieving CSFs that were related to the external environment (e.g. customer needs, demand growth) were markedly more successful than those companies where CSFs were related to aspects of the internal environment.

Ideally CSFs are a short and pithy list of the key activities which, if the organization concentrates on and achieves, will go a long way towards achieving the long-term strategic aims of the business. CSFs are often a derivative of evaluation criteria and should always be causally linked to them. Examples of CSFs will tend to be very specific to the organization in hand and may even vary between organizations in the same industry depending upon their competitive situation.

CSFs can relate to, amongst other things:

- The speed of introduction of new products.
- Product and market profitability.
- Improving customer service.
- The development of creativity in management activities.
- Identification of new product opportunities.
- The achievement of critical mass in production or distribution channel throughput.
- Achievement in product or market leadership.
- Achieving a position of good corporate citizen.

ACTIVITY 7.4

What are (or should be) the six most important CSFs used in your organization?

How does your marketing activity relate to these CSFs?

The good marketing company

Considering the area of evaluation and appraisal of marketing strategy, the question always arises, 'so what would one of Britain's best marketing organizations be doing?' Always a difficult question to answer since much depends upon the environment, the industry and the prevailing competitive situation of any particular organization.

However, as far as it is possible to answer such a general question, recent research carried out by the CIM and Cranfield School of Management have identified the following factors as those evidenced by the successful marketing company:

1 Start at the top.
2 Involve everyone in the organization in the marketing philosophy.
3 Be prepared for structural change.
4 Use the new structure to feed a 'customer facing strategy'.
5 Review marketing tactics (4Ps), do they work from the customer's point of view?
6 Accept that change is a way of life.
7 Understand the difference between 'quality systems' and quality products and services.
8 Focus on the customer, not the competition.
9 Look 'end-to-end' not piecemeal, customers expect seamless service.
10 Keep the end user in sight, don't be distracted by the middleman.
11 Measure the success of the marketing approach and be able to demonstrate the link between customer focus and profit.

This review gives good guidance to the types of evaluation criteria that can/should be used to drive practical marketing strategy.

How well does your organization measure up against these points? What changes would you propose?

Tomorrow's company

Major research carried out by the RSA in 1993 also showed the danger inherent in using the wrong measures of success.

The study shows that for tomorrow's company, success will depend on the organization's ability to meet the needs of five different groups (see Figure 7.5):

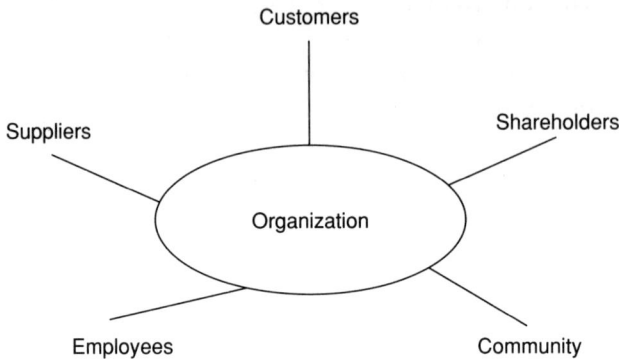

Figure 7.5 Tomorrow's company (RSA)

The study also identified the key forces for change:

- Globalization.
- Technology developments.
- New employment patterns.
- New organizational structures.
- Environmental issues.
- Death of deference – employees, customers, communities.
- Need to maintain public confidence in company operations and business conduct.
- Need to maintain 'licence to operate'.

Finally, it also identified the four key barriers to change in UK companies:

- Continuing adversarial approach to supplier relationships.
- Complacency and ignorance of world standards
  - 70 per cent thought they were achieved
  - 2.3 per cent actually were world class.
- Over-reliance on financial measures.
- Misunderstanding of directors duties.

Further information can be obtained from the Royal Society for the Encouragement of Arts, Manufacture & Commerce, 8 John Adam Street, London WC2N 6EZ.

Summary

In this unit we have looked at how you should evaluate and appraise alternative strategic options that may be open to the organization. This unit is not easy to understand in a single reading, but is critical for success at Diploma level. Are you sure that you really understand the concepts and exactly how you will apply them in the mini and major case study exams? If the unit is not absolutely clear, do not move on, but read again, and wider. The activity ideas will help you discover how organizations do/should evaluate strategic options.

We considered the pressures upon the organization that must be considered before attempting any evaluation, including the time period, outside factors, market conditions and internal factors. We also looked at what is thought to be required in order to be a successful organization in tomorrow's market conditions. The two studies covered are just a sample of current research, as organizations begin to come to grips with the business realities of the 1990s. Do you understand how to take account of these pressures in the evaluation of strategy?

The unit compared financial and non-financial measures and the case for using multiple criteria. The examination cases are rarely clear cut and will normally be dependent upon the questions posed in the exam or the nature of the company described in the case study. Financial measures, although used too often by business, are still a critical area of study. Too often the key 'black hole' for marketers. You need to understand financial controls and how they operate. You cannot simply ignore this area of the syllabus.

Finally, we considered how to choose the right criteria and the particular role of CSFs. The unit concluded by looking at what constitutes a 'good marketing company' and the types of evaluation criteria that can be used to achieve this position.

Having completed this unit, consider the following questions as a check on your understanding.

1   How might the timescale (short versus long term) influence your choice of evaluative criteria?
2   Distinguish between efficiency and effectiveness.
3   Why should financial and non-financial measures be taken into account in deciding between alternatives and evaluating performance?
4   Identify the common financial measures of evaluation and performance.
5   Identify the common non-financial measures of evaluation and performance.
6   Why should multiple evaluative criteria be used? What problems are associated with this?
7   How might you go about selecting the 'right' criteria.
8   What are 'critical success factors'?
9   What is meant by 'a good marketing company'?
10 What are the implications of the 'Tomorrow's company' research results on strategy evaluation?

For a more detailed treatment of the sort of criteria that can be used in choosing between alternative strategies and evaluating performance, read:

Strategic Marketing Management, Wilson and Gilligan with Pearson, Chapters 15 and 16.

Marketing Strategy, Fifield, pages 27–38 and 174–89.

Activity debrief

Question 7.1 June 1993   To obtain maximum marks on this question your answer must be well constructed and clearly presented. Distribution channels can be considered for industrial, consumer or services – all will be taken as valid examples. Examples of all must be cited to pass.

The question specifically asks you to explain the criteria you would employ – not to solve any particular distribution problems. The question also asks you to assess the 'efficiency' of a distribution channel. You can explain the difference between efficiency and effectiveness, but this is bonus mark work!

Your answer might consider defining efficiency as output divided by input, but you should also stress that distribution needs to be considered from a cost-benefit analysis point of view. Simple cost assessments are not enough – an organization needs to assess what benefits it received too.

Criteria you might consider are, of course, up to you. The list might include:

- Cost per unit
- Speed to market   (e.g. fresh food)
- Stock in the system   (e.g. book publishing)
- Customer satisfaction   (e.g. BMW)
- Value added by the distribution system   (e.g. computer software)
- Bargaining power of the system   (e.g. supermarkets)
- Image added to the product/service   (e.g. Direct Line)

A way of using examples might be to show an organization for whom a particular criterion is especially important.

Question 7.2   December 1993   You would be advised to start this question by showing that you understand the difference between 'efficiency' (doing things right) and 'effectiveness' (doing the right things). The question asks you specifically to address the latter and not the former.

In any review or audit, a number of items and measures are assessed. Typically efficiency is measured internally and effectiveness is measured by what the organization does right – outside the organization, in the marketplace. Therefore the areas that you need to identify are those external to the firm. The marketing audit areas that you might consider will be included under the headings:

- Macro environment
- Task environment   – Markets
                      – Competition
                      – Distributors
                      – Suppliers

The second part of the question asks you to explain how the 'results' of such a review might be used to improve 'methods' of 'planning' and of 'control'. Better answers here will contain a distinct structure. A logical sequence might be:

- Identify key planning methods.
- Show how results of effectiveness review could improve methodology.
- Identify key control methods.
- Show how results of effectiveness review could improve methodology.
- Conclusions.

Question 7.3   June 1994   This is a very straightforward question. However, a note of caution. The Diploma examinations are a test of a candidates ability to apply strategic marketing knowledge. It is not a test of your ability to commit data to memory. When you see a question such as this, you should remember that application always gains more marks. Look for where you can apply knowledge, even if such application is not apparently asked for in the question.

This question specifically asks for an explanation of 'financial control'. You can mention non-financial controls as the other half of the control tool kit, but do not spend pages describing what non-financial controls are – you will gain no marks for this.

Your answer should begin with an explanation of financial controls:

- Profit
- Profitability
- Shareholder return
- Share price
- Earnings per share
- Return on net assets
- Return on sales
- Liquidity
- Cash flow
- Other ratios

and financial control processes:

- Costing
- Budgeting
- Variance analysis.

A good structure is essential for this question. One way of approaching the answer would be:

- Introduction (brief)
- Financial control 1   – explain control
                         – explain how it can be employed in marketing
- Financial control 2
- Financial control 'n'
- Conclusion.

Question 7.4   December 1994   As well as testing your knowledge and ability to apply theory in the area of sales force activity, this question also tests your ability to select and apply relevant control mechanisms. Your answer must use examples.

A good answer to this question would begin by positioning the sales force as part of the organization's promotional activity and would explain why it is important that sales force activity is consistent with:

- Other elements of the promotional mix   – advertising
                                          – public relations
                                          – sales promotion/publicity
- Other elements of the marketing mix   – product policy
                                          – pricing policy
                                          – distribution policy
                                          – people/physical evidence/process policy

Once you have highlighted the main reasons why the sales force activity needs to be controlled, you can begin to explain how it may be done. The key aspects in controlling a sales force are the same as controlling any activity:

- Standard setting (objectives).
- Performance measurement (what is happening?).
- Performance diagnosis (why is it happening?).
- Taking corrective action (if required).

You should consider the best blend of financial and non-financial measures that could be used to create an effective control system. Use examples to illustrate.

Part two of the question asks you to discuss why so many organizations experience difficulty in this area. In a discussion question of this nature there is no 'right' answer. You must consider the alternatives and come to a justified decision. Your answer might consider the following points (among others):

- What gets measured gets done – do we always measure the most important aspects or the easiest to measure?
- Should organizations target and motivate on sales turnover or profitability?
- Should organizations use more non-financial controls in sales?
- What conflict can be created between sales motivation and customer satisfaction?
- How can sales forces be motivated/controlled to produce the right 'quality' of sales rather than (indiscriminate) quantity?
- Do most organizations concentrate on short-term sales motivation? Does this conflict with long-term marketing objectives?

Strategic implementation and control

In this unit you will consider the practical implementation of marketing strategy. Before strategy can be turned into reality you will need to understand:

- The barriers to strategic implementation.
- The drivers for strategic implementation.
- Control systems.

By the end of this unit you will:

1 Have an understanding of the issues associated with effective implementation and control of marketing plans.
2 Understand the principal barriers to implementation.
3 Be capable of showing how these barriers might be overcome.

This unit covers Section 5 of the Planning and Control syllabus and part of Sections 4 and 6 of the Analysis and Decision syllabus. This unit covers approximately 10 per cent of the syllabus and should take you up to 5 hours of study (workbook and recommended texts).

It is important that, no matter how good, elegant or sophisticated the marketing strategy which you have developed is, unless it is executed in an equally sophisticated manner it remains just a document which will gather dust. Much has been written in the literature about marketing tactics and the methods by which implementation of strategy is to be achieved, but far less attention has been paid to the barriers which stand in the way of successful implementation.

Implementation and control systems are now key features on both strategic marketing management papers and you are urged to prepare this section fully and be able to explain or propose appropriate measures in the exam.

One way of find out what happens in practice is to discover what happens in your own organization. Many barriers will be present and control systems in place. How many can you identify?

Previous units have considered the environment, customer needs, strategic alternatives and evaluation as well as managing the marketing mix.

Implementation is the final and possibly most important part of the process.

This workbook is titled *Strategic Marketing Management*. We have spoken at length about the first two words in the title; now let us talk about the third. Strategic implementation needs to be 'managed' through the organization to the marketplace.

Management can be defined as 'Getting things done through people'.

The word 'management' is key. If you are doing it yourself you are not managing. If you are not getting things done you are not managing.

Implementing marketing strategy means making things happen through other people. As you might imagine, there is more to this than just designing the plan and working out what ought to happen.

We will consider the implementation process and begin by analysing the barriers to successful implementation of the marketing strategy.

Barriers to implementation

There are many barriers that stand in the way of successful implementation of marketing strategy, some evident, some not so. The barriers fall broadly into three separate categories; external pressures on the organization, internal pressures on the marketing function and pressures within the marketing function itself. We will consider these three forms of pressure independently.

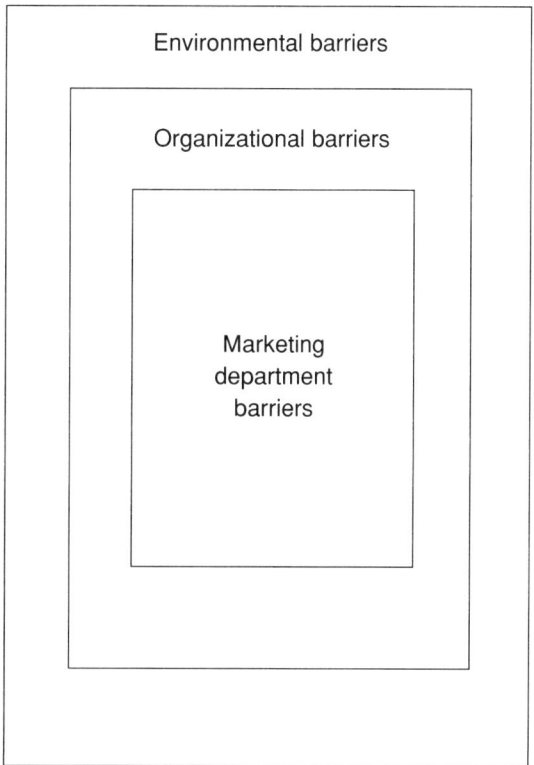

Figure 8.1 Barriers to implementation

Many candidates make recommendations both in the mini and the maxi cases that lack realism. Far too often they simply ignore the realities of organizational life and fail to take account of the implications of their suggestions.

You should think in detail about the implications for implementation of any suggestions or recommendations you make.

External barriers

To consider the external pressures on the organization first, these are best described under the traditional PEST or SLEPT headings to describe the environment. (These are described in more detail in Unit 3.)

Social factors Changing demographic and social patterns such as an ageing relation, fewer school leavers, and the shift in emphasis from manual to white collar skills will have a major impact on any strategic plans which require implementation over the next 5 to 10 years. British society is also undergoing some level of fundamental change and trends such as ecology, class structure and individualism need to be accounted for in your plans. Customers and consumers are also part of the social element of the environment but these will be considered in more detail under the heading 'drivers for strategic implementation' on page 176.

Legal There are an increasing number of laws which are affecting business activity on a wider and wider scale. Laws now cover employment, pay and price policies, health and safety as well as specific acts to control particular industries such as financial services and telecommunications. Also, as time progresses we can expect more impact on British activity from European based laws.

Economic factors The past 10 years have witnessed an unparalleled level of change in the British economy. Not only is this change expected to accelerate but other economies are starting to show signs of following the British example. Strategic implementation of plans needs to take into account the changes which are likely to occur in the marketplace and you should consider aspects such as changes in your own marketplace such as mergers, joint ventures, share price movement and investment as well as any trade union activities. Suppliers' actions and changes to include vertical integration and disintermediation (the decline of intermediaries in the process). Distribution channels are also undergoing a radical change in a number of industries and successful implementation will depend upon a good forecasting of likely change in areas such as distribution infrastructure as well as in transportation and channel management and control. Internationalization is a major factor in all economic situations and is likely to affect your customers' perceptions of your offer, and the whole nature of competition. Competition itself is one of the most important factors to forecast in strategic implementation since no marketing strategy ever operates in a vacuum. You should be attempting to analyse not only the direct (own industry) competition but also the important, and often more difficult to predict, indirect competition from outside your traditional industry base. Competition is expected to increase in all sectors over the next 10 years, driven primarily by the internationalization of business and the fragmentation of so many markets.

The previous unit looked at recent research on 'Tomorrow's company'. There are other examples of such views of the future to be found.

It has been suggested that one of the most fundamental challenges likely to be faced over the next few years by manufacturers of consumer goods will stem from the seemingly inexorable increase in levels of retail concentration. Citing examples, comment upon the implications of this trend both for retailers and manufacturers, and suggest how branded manufacturers, intent on retaining the strength of a brand franchise, might possibly respond.

June 1991

(**See** Activity debrief at the end of this unit.)

Political factors   There is a general trend in most western markets for Government to take an increasingly active role in business. Political activities include taxation, lobbying, as well as the ability to pass laws which affect not only your organization's ability to act in a free market, but also affects customers' ability to buy your products or services. In all markets political activities are often aimed at influencing competitive activity. Whatever the intention behind political actions, the result is always some form of restriction over the organization's activities in a marketplace. These restrictions need to be forecasted and attempts made to modify implementation of the strategic plan within this emerging framework.

Technological factors   Technology generally has had a massive effect over the past 10 years and we can expect this influence to continue if not to accelerate. Technology has made radical changes in manufacturing technology possible and has perhaps been a major catalyst in the recent proliferation of new products and services. A major factor in the development of technology has been its ability to reduce, if not sometimes eliminate, barriers to market entry. The application of modern technology has enabled small and medium-sized organizations to operate at cost levels previously the exclusive preserve of much larger organizations. Economies of scale are no longer the barriers they used to be.

Carry out a PEST analysis on your organization.

- What are the three most significant items under each heading that might block the implementation of marketing strategy?
- What can be done to avoid or reduce the effect of these factors?
- What is currently being done?

Identify the principal strategic challenges that marketers are likely to face over the next decade and comment upon their implications for approaches to marketing planning.

December 1992

(**See** Activity debrief at the end of this unit.)

Internal pressures on the marketing function

As well as external pressures acting upon the organization that will affect the successful implementation of marketing strategy, there are a number of factors which are internal to the organization which will also affect its ability to implement its strategic plans successfully. All of these factors act as significant potential blockages to implementing marketing strategy and unless these blockages can be overcome inside the organization the marketer has little choice but to amend the goals and strategy to those which the organization is able to implement. To look at some of these factors in more detail:

Leadership   There is little doubt that the ultimate success and implementation of any strategic plan will depend upon the degree to which top management buys into the process. This is especially evident where the strategic thrust of the plan involves any form of significant change. The organization's leadership may be opposed to the objectives of the plan for any number of reasons. For example, they may be from non-marketing disciplines, may feel that the need for change is not yet apparent or simply be more comfortable with 'steady state' management style. Whatever the reasons, unless the leadership has bought into the plans completely and feels that it owns these plans, little progress is likely to be made.

A recent survey (1995) by the British Institute of Management (BIM) among its members asked two interesting questions:

1   What are the main benefits of improved customer focus?

Base: 789 respondents	%
Retention of existing customers	68
Enhanced reputation of organization	58
Competitive advantage in the marketplace	53
Attraction of new customers	43
Increased profitability	28
Improved staff morale and loyalty	25
Cost efficiency	11
Better productivity	10
Other	2

2   What are the main barriers to improving customer focus?

Base: 787 respondents	%
Emphasis on short-term goals only	58
Lack of commitment from top management	53
Lack of training	47
Lack of resources	34
Lack of commitment from employees	32
Lack of commitment from line management	31
Cost restraints	24
Effects of the recession	12
Other	4

Organizational culture   There are many forms of organizational culture and, in truth, few of these are customer or market focused. In the organization with a non-market oriented culture, chances of successfully implementing a truly customer-focused strategic marketing plan must be severely limited. Marketing in this type of organization tends to be all about marketing services, often linked or even subservient to the important sales function. In the product or production-oriented organization the marketer's role is to provide sales materials, product information and market analysis to support the sales and production functions of the organization. The market or customer-oriented organization is the only one which sees the marketer's role as that of catalyst and change agent to focus the rest of the organization's activities on the one activity that really matters – the customer. Changing the culture of an organization is never a short-term task. However, as today's markets become more and more competitive the option is becoming clearer – change the culture or the organization may not survive beyond the medium term. If the culture will not change in the short to medium term then goals and strategies will need to be amended to something which the organizational culture can assimilate.

It has been argued that achieving customer focus depends on two key activities: senior management customer focus and staff involvement (see Figure 8.2).

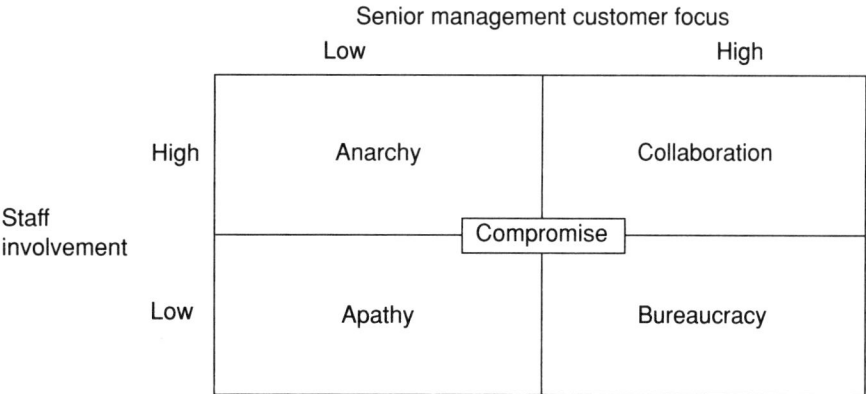

Figure 8.2 Achieving customer focus

Organization design In many organizations the existing organization structure is simply not designed to be able to deliver the proposed marketing strategy as is intended. Too many organizations are designed for the convenience and administrative ease of those who work in them rather than being designed to deliver satisfaction to customers. It is simply unrealistic to design a customer-focused marketing strategy without spending some time looking at the organization's ability to deliver on the promises which you may be making to your customers. If organizations are so rigid that they cannot be redesigned, then your marketing strategy may need to be modified accordingly. 'Re-engineering' or 'Business Process Redesign' initiatives may be successful in this regard but only if they are directed at redesigning the organization in customer terms and not simply aimed at restyling the IT processes.

When dealing with organizations (culture and design) it is important to consider the 'soft' elements such as style, skills, staffing and shared values as well as the traditional 'hard' values. Remember, an organization is nothing without the people who work inside it. The 7-S Framework places these elements together (see Figure 8.3).

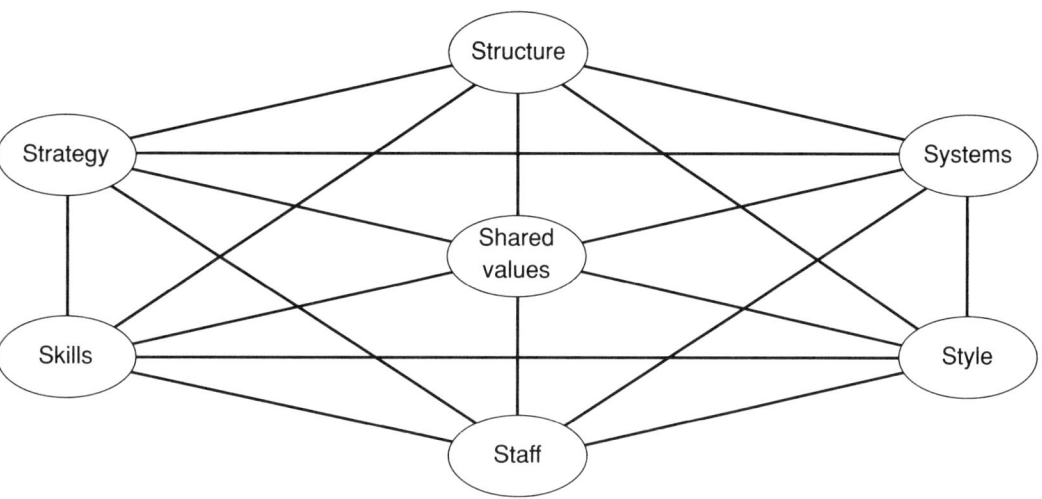

Figure 8.3 McKinsey 7-S framework

Functional policies A subset of organization structure, most functions in an organization (finance, operations, human resources . . . and marketing!) tend to grow up and produce a number of functional policies and procedures which determine how their part of the organization and their staff manage the day-to-day business. The intended marketing strategy may fall foul of these procedural processes and will encounter a blockage on the path to implementation.

Resources The proposed marketing strategy may require that either significant additional resources be allocated to certain functions or even the reappropriation of resources into different areas of the organization. Successful implementation will depend upon either these resources being available for implementation of the plan or making the appropriate resources available so that the plan can be implemented fully. The potential blockage here is likely to be either in the resources simply not being available or that senior management considers that other causes are more deserving. In any case this could provide a significant blockage to implementation.

Evaluation and control procedures The lack of appropriate monitoring and evaluation procedures in an organization will be a significant block to the successful implementation of any strategy. This potential blockage can be less of a problem than those outlined above in that you are not necessarily faced with overcoming perception or resource problems. As long as the proper control measures are installed there need be no problems in implementation. Control measures will be considered in more depth later in the unit.

ACTIVITY 8.2

Critically review your organization (or one that you are familiar with) for internal blockages.

- What blockages to marketing implementation can you identify?
- Why are these blockages present?
- How might they be overcome?

Given the scale and complexity of the blockages and pressures upon the marketing function from inside its own organization, the importance of internal marketing starts to become apparent. An integral part of successful strategic implementation, internal marketing involves all the processes necessary to carry the message of the strategic marketing plan inside to the various audiences that comprise the organization. We can see from the list of possible blockages which exist in the organization above, that success or failure of strategic marketing strategy can depend upon people and functions inside the organization not only believing the message but putting their weight behind the effort too. Internal marketing means more than just promotions, it means the same as it does in the external environment, the application of the full marketing mix to achieve some predetermined behaviour change. Internal marketing, like external marketing, to be successful requires a good understanding of the needs and motivations of the target audiences. The above review should start to give the marketer a reasonable understanding of where people in the internal organization currently stand and the measures needed to gain their full and willing support for the proposed marketing strategy (see also Unit 6, page 146).

QUESTION 8.3

What factors should be taken into account in the development of a marketing feedback and control systems? In what ways might the information generated possibly be used?

December 1995

(**See** Activity debrief at the end of this unit.)

Pressures within the marketing function

Not only are there a number of issues internal to the organization which can act as blockages to developing and implementing quality marketing strategy, there are a number of aspects of the marketing department or function which can also act as potential blockages to the development and implementation of your plans.

Marketing's interface with other functions Delivering satisfactions to customers may be the responsibility of the marketing function but it is not a job that marketers can carry out on their own. In order to deliver customer satisfaction and thereby improve the organization's position against competition, the entire organization needs to operate as an effective partnership and deliver seamlessly. In order to do this marketing needs to interact positively with other functions within the organization, such as production, purchasing, personnel and finance. Unfortunately some of these functions may consider that they have competing responsibilities and may not fix the priorities in exactly the same way as marketing. Once again the solution is not in 'telling' other functions what to do, but in involving them in the process. The marketing manager must find means of securing better co-ordination amongst the various functional sub-systems that are not directly under his or her control. This may be achieved by improving communications and inter-organizational understandings about what is in the interests of the organization as a whole.

The role of marketing/marketer The role of the marketer will depend largely upon the organization culture and structure. In the non-market-oriented organization marketing tends to be synonymous with 'advertising and promotion'. The marketing manager is often taken on as a necessary (and expensive) evil because the competition seems to be making inroads into the organization's markets by advertising. Other managers in the organization often have little understanding of the marketing concept and don't realize their role in satisfying customers. The role of the marketer in the production or product-oriented organization is two fold – to give his or her internal customers what they want and, secondly, to act as a catalyst for change toward a more customer-oriented position. In the case of a customer or market-oriented organization the role of the marketer and the marketing function is quite different. Rather than concentrating on advertising and promotion, the marketer's function is to identify, anticipate and satisfy customer needs profitably. To do this needs much more than a depth knowledge of advertising and promotional methodology and techniques. In this type of organization the marketer's key area of responsibility is to understand the organization's customers and to feed this information back into the organization and other functions so that people may act upon it profitably.

Marketing feedback How effective a marketer is in his or her job and how well the strategic marketing plan is implemented will depend, to a great extent, on how much, how relevant and how good his or her information is and how well it is interpreted and acted upon. Information is critical. Information and feedback on a plan's progress is never 100 per cent accurate but it does act both to reduce uncertainty in planning and to improve the quality of action. Critically the marketer may not be in complete control of the information sources and the speed at which they are delivering quality information back to the marketing function. A great deal of data is often raised elsewhere in the organization but often not in a form which will provide adequate information for the marketer's use. The marketer has two main flows of data. One from the environment and the other from internal operations. Some, but not all, is likely to be under the marketer's direct control, for the rest, other departments need to understand the importance of quality and timely information flows and internal marketing can help this process.

The final, crucial area of marketing and market feedback is market research. In many organizations some market research is carried out but invariably it is insufficient to meet the organization's needs. Market research should not be regarded as a crutch to support weak decision making but as an essential 'investment' in the marketplace and future prosperity of the organization. Unfortunately many organizations, often product, production or planning oriented, do not see the investment aspects of market research but rather consider it as a cost. As competition increases and markets continue to fragment, it is unlikely that investment in market research will decline in the most successful organizations, rather we can expect it to increase as market circumstances become more and more involved.

Drivers for strategic implementation

Rather than simply paint a completely negative picture, organizations and the current market can actively support the implementation of marketing strategy. The astute marketer should be able to use these drivers for change, to enlist help and active co-operation within the organization to implement his or her plans.

Customer expectations Customers in all markets are now starting to demand the 'impossible'. As their needs and wishes are met in very competitive markets such as groceries, consumer goods and motor cars, they see no reason why these expectations should not be met in unrelated fields such as banking, telecommunications and travel. As customer expectations continue to grow, so concepts like 'brand loyalty' tend to diminish with the passage of time. Customers are becoming less and less loyal to brands and organizations if these fail to provide what is wanted, when it is wanted and at a reasonable price. The astute marketer can use the changes in customer demand and forecasts of future demand to drive through changes inside the organization at a rate which internal departments would otherwise possibly consider to be uncomfortable. At this point, customer information and projections are invaluable and form the basis of the marketer's key strength in the organization.

> Consider how BT has used rising customer expectations to transform itself from a 'greedy monopoly' to 'number 1 for customer service' (*Daily Telegraph* survey, 1995).
>
> Think back ten years to what BT was like and the image it had amongst its captive 'subscribers'. It has not changed by cutting price but by continually adding services that customers said they wanted.

Revenue Revenues and profits are the life blood of any organization. The past four or five years of deep recession in the British market (and a slightly lighter variant in other European markets) has meant that many organizations have cut costs dramatically in order to continue flows and returns to shareholders. As the movement out of recession is somewhat slower than expected the potential well of returns from cost savings starts to appear ever more shallow. The only source of continued revenue and profit growth for many organizations is now the marketplace. Customers are the source of all revenues and profits for any organization and satisfied customers have now started to top the agendas of more and more organizations. The marketer needs to use this trend to drive through the message inside the organization that long-term profits do not come from a numbers game (adding more customers at any price) but from a quality game that involves constantly offering customers a solution which meets their needs better than the competition can.

> Often an entire industry will carry on in product-oriented mode, sometimes for years or decades, and no amount of argument will make them change their focus. Eventually the external situation changes, revenue falls and companies either change to customer focus or die.
>
> You can see that this has already happened with computer hardware, and it is now happening in UK financial services. It will soon happen in computer software.
>
> Can you identify industries where change will strike in the next five years?

Competition As technology drives down the barriers to entry into many markets; and markets are beginning to fragment in many and devious ways, competition is intensifying in practically every business sector. Not only are existing players fighting to gain and retain customers but also new entrants from outside the sector are being attracted by more substantial margins than they can gain in their home markets. Brands and products are proliferating and customers are now faced with a greater choice in most markets than they have ever experienced in the past. For most organizations, the only way through this maze is to be able to establish a clear and differentiated image and position in the market in which they operate and to give customers good, simple and relevant reasons why they should come to them rather than the competition. Effective market positioning is not achieved solely by product quality but requires the deft application of all the elements of strategic marketing. Laker first stimulated change in transatlantic air travel, and the trend is being continued by Virgin. Will Daewoo force change in European car retailing?

Innovation A by-product of the increasingly competitive nature of most markets and the application of modern technology, innovation has become the norm in many industry sectors. Innovation for its own sake is unlikely to gain market share or profitably but innovation directed at supplying more relevant products to customers will. In the future, innovation in both product or service delivery and processes and service will be the norm rather than the exception. Unfortunately, many organizations tend to find innovation an uncomfortable experience and many prefer the 'steady state' environment to work in. It is unlikely that such environments will prove profitable in the future and the marketer's role now is to use this tide of innovation to get his or her organization on stream to match, if not to exceed, the competition's offering. The 'Information Superhighway' and the Internet are currently being proposed as innovations that will revolutionize our lives. Is this so, or will the technology languish like the fax did until the customers see a role for it in their daily lives?

Under the headings for the drivers for strategic implementation, can you identify how these factors are influencing your organization?

Are the drivers being properly harnessed to produce real changes? What can be done?

ACTIVITY 8.3

Control systems

Control systems form the second part of the examination title 'planning and control'. If planning is defined as 'deciding what to do' then control is defined as 'ensuring that the desired results are obtained'. Planning without control simply means that the organization has a nice, sophisticated document. The control systems are essential to make sure that the organization drives through the content of the plans and achieves its objectives in the marketplace.

Control systems are many and various and selecting the right method of control will depend very much upon the market that the organization is addressing, the particular goals and objectives which the organization has set itself, as well as the particular organization structure, design and culture. In simple terms the control process can be described as in Figure 8.4.

Control systems then are a matter of balancing four primary issues.

1 Standard setting.
2 Performance measurement.
3 Performance diagnosis.
4 Taking corrective action (if required).

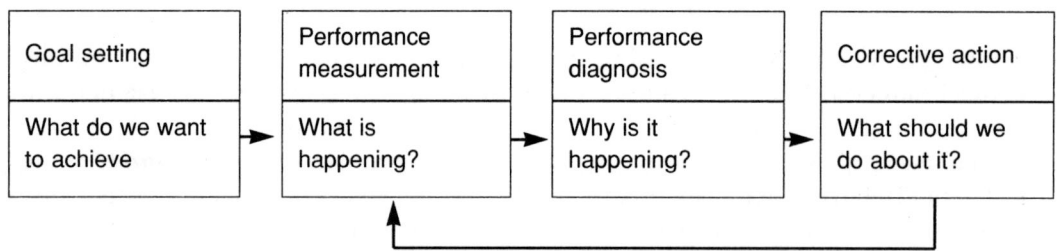

Figure 8.4 The control process

Setting standards

Setting the standards is the role of the planning element of the process and the goals and objectives which fall out of the strategic marketing plan are then translated into standards which drive through the organization and which, if implemented, will determine the successful implementation of the project. Ideally the standards will have been set within an understanding of what the organization is currently able to deliver.

Performance measurement

Performance measurement and reporting of results are the key areas of most control systems. Most discussion then will centre around which performances should be measured and how results should be reported. The measurement activities of the planning achievements can simply be broken down into three broad areas.

1 *Quantity*   How much was achieved? How much should have been achieved?
2 *Quality*   How good was that which was achieved? How good was it meant to be?
3 *Cost*   How much did the achievement cost? How much was it planned to cost?

These basic parameters of the plan can then be quantified through an analysis of one or more of five distinct areas of operation which are:

- Financial analysis.
- Market analysis.
- Sales and distribution analysis.
- Physical resources analysis.
- Human resource analysis.

Audits   One method of assessing strategic marketing effectiveness is by the use of regular marketing audits. The marketing audit (which is described in detail elsewhere) is a robust method of monitoring the successful implementation of marketing plans and policies. No matter which form of marketing audit is taken, marketing management should ensure that all areas of marketing activity are regularly monitored and their performance measured against pre-set standards which, once achieved, will guarantee the successful implementation of the plan.

> 'Marketing Planning is a generally straightforward exercise; the marketer's real problems are those of effective implementation.' (Anonymous).
>
> Identify the nature of the barriers to effective implementation that marketers typically encounter and suggest how, if at all, these barriers might be reduced.
>
> December 1992
>
> (**See** Activity debrief at the end of this unit.)

Budgets Budgeting is probably the most common form of control mechanism in most organizations and, although developed for financial housekeeping and management, is often applied to marketing implementation as well. There are a number of advantages as well as disadvantages to using the budgeting process. Many budgets tend to be short term, typically based on the annual plan for the achievement of that year's profit and turnover forecasts. Short-term budgeting of this nature is not always the most relevant for the measurement and control of long-term strategy. The strategic marketer should note that short-term deviations from plans may require only short-term tactical alterations, but no longer term strategic shifting in direction. Where the budgeting process is longer term and/or continuous rather than periodic in nature the feedback results may be more relevant to longer term strategic proposals. When dealing with budgets it is vitally important to understand that budgeting is not the same as management. Budgeting is an important aid to management decision making but budgets are always based on estimates rather than reality and are always, at best, someone's idea of how the future will happen. Therefore, when deviations from budgeted figures arise marketing must ask itself not only whether the deviations are significant and require corrective action but also how valid were the original estimates incorporated into the budgeting at the outset.

Variance analysis Another analysis and control procedure which falls out of the budgeting process is the detailed analysis of the variance (difference between actual and expected results) that arises from the organization's activities. Variances of a number of different items can be measured and assessed, much will depend upon the key parameters used by the organization to assess its performance overall. Typical variance measures will include sales price variance, sales quantity variance, sales volume variance, profit variance, market size variance, market share variance, etc.

Performance diagnosis

Whatever the method of analysis and evaluation that is deemed the most appropriate for the organization and the strategic marketing plans which you have compiled, it is important to recognize that analysis on its own is rarely sufficient to monitor and implement plans properly. As well as identifying the actual variances or differences from expected results, equal attention has to be paid to understanding the reasons for the variance in the first place. Before any corrective action can be taken (if indeed it is required) the reasons for the variance need to be identified. Corrective action needs to be taken against the reasons for the shortfall (or the overrun!) if it is to be effective. At this point additional feedback is required from marketing intelligence and assessment of the external and competitive situation which may give some clue as to the reasons for the deviation from the expected plan. At the very least it needs to be established whether the reasons for the divergence from the plan have been caused by internal problems or external problems.

> Evaluate the contribution that marketing auditing is capable of making to the marketing planning and control process, and comment upon the problems that are typically encountered in auditing.
>
> June 1992
>
> (**See** Activity debrief at the end of this unit.)

Taking corrective action

Once the control system has been established, and divergences or deviations from the estimated results have been highlighted, the marketer's role is to decide whether corrective action is required and if so how to implement this action in time to bring the plan back on to target. The options open to the organization in terms of corrective action fall into a number of separate categories depending on the reason for the deviation:

Environmental changes   If the reason for the divergence is caused by unpredicted changes in the external environment of the organization the marketer has a number of options open to him or her at this stage. If the environmental factors are deemed to be of a short term nature then a modification in the tactics needed to implement the strategic plan can be considered. If the changes in the external environment or the marketplace are deemed to be fundamental or structural in nature then the marketer may need to revisit the overall strategy and aims and objectives of the plan itself.

Internal problems   If the non-delivery on the estimates of the plan are caused by internal problems the marketer has to decide whether this is a shortfall in performance or is caused by active blockages in other parts or functions of the organization. Corrective action will need to be directed at these points.

Faulty estimating   It may be apparent from a deeper analysis of the variances that the problem lies not in the market nor in the organization's ability to deliver, but that the original estimates set against which the plan was going to be judged were erroneous. In this case the marketer needs to re-estimate the rate at which the organization will achieve its strategic objectives.

The nature of control systems

James Bureau in *The Marketing Book* (Butterworth-Heinemann) describe the nature of good control systems. They must be driven by the following principles:

- *Formality*   Firm rituals that are applied regularly and in a standard manner.
- *Necessity*   Should be seen as useful by the organization and not just a ritualistic process.
- *Priority*   Be concerned with those elements which the organization needs to control, not with everything capable of control.
- *Veracity*   Need to be data-based, not based solely on intuition or subjective opinion.
- *Regularity*   As regular as is affordable and useful, depending on the activity measured and the dynamics of the market situation.

One final note of warning. This book and the two CIM examination papers are all concerned with strategy – not tactics. Strategic decisions will have long-term implications and organizational momentum has to be built over a planned period. Constant change produces uncertainty, confusion, misdirection and wastage – not results. Tactics are designed to change on a weekly or even a daily basis in response to changes in the marketplace caused by customer needs or competitor response. Tactical change causes no problems of uncertainty as long as the strategy, the broad overall direction of the organization, remains constant. Control systems which drive regular tactical changes to keep the strategy on course are a positive boon to any organization. On the other hand, if the control systems allow managers, through ignorance or panic, to make constant changes to strategy and direction the organization will end up achieving nothing and going nowhere.

Summary

In this unit we have looked at the all important step of strategic implementation. We have considered the two main areas critical to implementation, firstly the barriers and drivers to strategic implementation that exist and secondly the control and measurement procedures needed to ensure safe arrival at our destination.

First we considered the barriers to successful strategic implementation that exist for the marketer. These can be seen as originating from the external environment within which the organization must operate and from within the organization, from functions other than marketing itself. We also looked at some of the variables which can, if harnessed properly, actively promote implementation of strategic marketing.

Secondly, we considered the control mechanisms which are necessary to ensure that the strategic plan is implemented and the objectives are achieved. We considered the wide range of analysis and control mechanisms which are used in different organizations, including auditing, budgeting and variance analysis.

Finally, we considered the nature of corrective action that can be taken by the marketer and the form that this should take.

Having completed the unit, consider the following questions as a check on your understanding.

1 Why is implementation so often the cause of strategies proving to be disappointing?
2 What are the three principal causes of poor implementation?
3 Identify the major external pressures on the organization. What are the major internal pressures?
4 How might the internal barriers to implementation be reduced?
5 What is meant by 'drivers for implementation'? Identify the four principal drivers.
6 Why are control systems so important? How would you devise a control system?

For a more detailed explanation of implementation and control systems within Strategic Marketing refer to *Strategic Marketing Management*, Wilson and Gilligan with Pearson, pages 499–615 and *Marketing Strategy*, Fifield, pages 190–204, 240–3.

Activity debrief

Question 8.1 June 1991   This question comes in two distinct parts. Your answer must respond to both parts of the question to be successful. Also, you are asked to cite examples – you must do this to illustrate your understanding of the situation.

Part one of the question asks you to 'comment upon' the 'implications of this trend' for 'both retailers and manufacturers' of 'consumer goods'. (Always be sure that you know exactly what is being asked of you in a question before you begin to write.) If you intend to use Porter's model, make sure you integrate it fully into your answer and that it does not just look like an attempt to avoid answering the real question!

A logical structure is important for the best marks. You might consider the following:

● Brief introduction on the trend to retail concentration (explain what this means).
● What are the implications of the trend for retailers?
    – focused competition
    – price comparisons
    – buying power   cite
    – vertical and/or horizontal integration   examples
    – niche competition
    – power struggle with manufacturers for control
    – own brands
● What are the implications of this trend for manufacturers?
    – fewer buyers
    – pressure on prices
    – buying/bargaining power   cite
    – threat of own brands   examples
    – difficulty of new product distribution
    – market testing

Part two of the question asks you to 'suggest' how 'branded manufacturers', 'intent on retaining the strength of a brand franchise', 'might respond'. Here, the selection of the right example can make all the difference. A good answer might begin by explaining what a branded manufacturer is and why the brand franchise is important (commands a premium price in the marketplace). The key aspect to this question is understanding the difference between 'product-push' and 'customer-pull' strategies and how they can be used, the latter to counteract the increasing power of retailers.

Question 8.2 December 1992 This question comes in two distinct parts, and each must be answered to achieve a pass grade. Part one of the question asks you to identify the principal strategic challenges that marketers are likely to face over the next decade. A question like this seldom has a right or wrong answer and depends to an extent on your ability to argue your case.

Major strategic challenges will, of course, be partly dependent on specific industries, but general aspects might include:

- Globalization.
- Reorganization.
- New technology.
- Demographic change.
- Societal change.
- Consumer needs and motivations.
- Increasing competition.
- Evolution of organizations and structures.

Be sure to explain (at least one paragraph each) the principal challenges that you choose – a simple list of bullet points will not be enough!

Part two of the question asks you to 'comment upon their implications for approaches to marketing planning'. For each of the challenges you have identified in Part one of the question you should now consider the ways in which the planner should amend his or her approach to marketing planning in order to make allowances for these challenges. For example, under the heading of Increasing competition, you might make some of the following comments:

- Broadening use of Porter's five forces model.
- Increasing attention to cost control.
- More attention to changing customer needs and wants.
- Attention to brand building and differentiation.
- Broaden scope of competitor analysis in marketing information system to cover likely new entrants and overseas competition.
- Better contingency planning for defensive retaliation.

Question 8.3 December 1995 This question must be answered in two distinct parts. Part one asks you to explain 'the factors that should be taken into account in the development of a marketing feedback and control system'.

A well developed marketing feedback and control system is capable of contributing in a variety of ways to the more effective management of an organization. However, although it is possible to identify the general characteristics of such a system, there is the need to develop the system against the background of a set of specific factors. The most significant are:

- Complexity of the environment.
- Extent to which information is readily available.
- Information needs of the management team.
- Size of the organization.
- Costs of set-up.

Part two of the question asks you to explain 'in what ways the information generated might be used'. To do this, your answer needs to consider the key outputs of the system:

- Market tidings (market potential, competition, customers, etc.).
- Acquisition leads (for merger, joint venture, etc.).
- Technical tidings (new products, processes, etc.).

- Broad issues (government policy, etc.).
- Other tidings (suppliers, resources, etc.).

Taken together, this feedback should provide managers with a clear understanding of what is happening in the marketplace and how it is likely to develop, the existence and nature of any opportunities and threats, the effectiveness of the current marketing programme and how this needs to be developed. The *control element* then follows from this, and can be seen in terms of providing a (detailed) understanding of absolute and relative performance levels, areas of absolute and relative strengths and weaknesses, and the market, product and delivery development needs.

The information generated is therefore capable of being used in a variety of ways, including the development of the marketing mix, the general profile of the organization, and the competitive stance that is to be adopted.

Question 8.4 December 1992 This question comes in two parts. Part one asks you to 'identify the nature of the barriers to effective implementation that marketers typically encounter'. Your answer should cover (and expand upon) the major areas:

- Environmental barriers (PEST).
- Organizational barriers.
- (Internal) marketing department barriers.

Part two of the question asks you to 'suggest how, if at all, these barriers might be reduced'. Since the barriers consist of both 'hard' barriers and 'soft' (psychological) barriers, they cannot so easily be removed from an organization – at least in the short term. You can consider a number of ways in which the barriers may be reduced, and might include the following:

- Feedback on changing customer demands and expectations.
- Use revenue figures and projections to support the case for change.
- Demonstrate competitive activity and project future impact.
- Innovation created in pockets of the organization to stimulate change.

Question 8.5 June 1992 This question comes in two parts. Part one asks you to 'evaluate the contribution that marketing auditing is capable of making to the marketing and planning and control processes'. You should begin your answer by briefly explaining the concept of marketing auditing – what it is and how it is done. After this brief explanation, you should explain the contribution that auditing can make to:

1 Planning processes.
2 Control processes.

Do not forget the control aspect to the question. The three major elements of an audit are:

- An analysis of the external environment and internal situation.
- An evaluation of past performance and present activities.
- The identification of future opportunities and threats.

Taken together, these outputs can contribute to the planning and control processes in a number of ways, including:

Planning:	focus on:	key strengths
		minimize key weaknesses
		identify major opportunities
		protect against major threats
		resource allocation for future market demands
Control:	focus on:	learning from past experiences and activities
		measuring against the most appropriate parameters
		competitive activity
		other benchmarking exercises

Part two of the question asks you to 'comment upon the problems that are typically encountered in auditing'. For an audit to be worthwhile, it is considered that it should meet four key requirements. Problems are often encountered under these headings:

1   *Comprehensive problems*:   may not cover all major elements of activity.
2   *Systematic problems*:   may not be based on sequential diagnosis.
3   *Independent problems*:   internally assessed audits may contain bias.
4   *Periodic problems*:   if not carried out regularly little tracking can take place.

The mini case study

A mini case study is the first part of the Strategic Marketing: Planning and Control examination. It is a compulsory part of the examination and designed to provide you with an opportunity to apply your knowledge to a particular situation. The purpose of this unit is therefore:

- To help you understand how best to approach the mini case study.
- To highlight the sorts of mistakes that are commonly made.
- To give you an opportunity to prepare a number of practice solutions.

By the end of this unit, you will:

- Be familiar with the sorts of mini case study that have been used over the past few years.
- Have an understanding of the issues that they raise.
- Have gained some practice at approaching these cases.

Although with each of the previous units, it has been a relatively straightforward exercise to identify how long you should spend working on the unit, it is far harder to do this with the mini case. Instead, you should recognize that the more practice you get with the mini case, the more likely it is that you will approach it in your examination with a degree of confidence and an understanding of what is required from you. You should, therefore, spend as much time as you can familiarizing yourself with the format of the mini cases and the sorts of questions that are asked. Practise preparing solutions to the questions and then compare your answers with the solutions that we have included at the end of the unit.

It needs to be recognized that the type of short case (popularly called the mini case) set in the examinations cannot be treated in exactly the same way as the extremely long case set for the subject of Strategic Marketing: Analysis and Decision.

However, far too many students adopt a maxi-case approach, using a detailed marketing audit outline which is largely inappropriate to a case consisting of just two or three pages. Others use SWOT analysis and simply re-write the case under the four headings of strengths, weaknesses, opportunities and threats.

Some students even go so far as to ignore the specific questions set and present a standard maxi-case analysis, including environmental reviews and contingency plans. Others adopt a vague and far too superficial approach. In each case, students are penalized. You should recognize therefore that the mini case is simply an *outline* of a given situation whose purpose is to test whether candidates can apply their knowledge of marketing operations to the environment described in the scenario. For example, answers advocating retail audits as part of the marketing information system for a small industrial goods manufacturer confirm that the examinee has learned a given MIS outline by rote and simply regurgitated this with complete disregard of the scenario. Such an approach cannot be passed. A more appropriate approach to the scenario involves a mental review of the areas covered by the question and the selection by the candidate of those particular parts of knowledge or techniques which apply to the case. This implies a rejection of those parts of the students' knowledge which clearly do not apply to the scenario.

All scenarios are based upon real world companies and situations and are written with a full knowledge of how that organization operates in its planning environments. Often, the organization described in the scenario will not be a giant fast-moving consumer goods manufacturing and marketing company but is instead an innovative, small or medium-sized firm faced with a particular problem or challenge. The cases are often, but not invariably, written from the viewpoint of a consultant and include an extract from a consultant's report.

The examination as a whole lasts for 3 hours. Including your reading time, you therefore have, 1A hours for the mini case.

EXAM TIP

On opening the examination paper, read the mini case at your normal reading speed, highlighting any issues that appear to you to be particularly significant. Having done this, read the questions in Section 1 and then read the mini case again, identifying and highlighting those issues which are particularly relevant to the questions posed. Remember that both questions in the section need to be answered and that the examination paper will indicate the split of marks. Allocate your time accordingly and do not make the mistake of spending more than 90 minutes on Section 1.

The mistakes that candidates make

We have already touched upon some of the mistakes that candidates make in approaching the mini case. We can, however, take these further with the list of the ten most common errors that candidates make.

The ten most common mini case errors

1　Ignoring the specific questions posed and providing instead a general treatment of the case.
2　Thinking that every mini case study demands a SWOT analysis; it doesn't.
3　Not answering in the format asked for. You will normally be asked for a report, a memorandum or a marketing plan and should answer using one of these frameworks.
4　Making unrealistic assumptions about the extent to which organizations can change their working practices.
5　Assuming that unlimited financial resources will be available to you.
6　Failing to recognize the difficulties of implementation.
7　Introducing hypothetical data on costs.
8　Rewriting the case and ignoring the questions.
9　Failing to give full recognition to the implications of what is recommended.
10　Not spending sufficient time on the second of the two questions.

The past cases

Although for the majority of the Diploma papers, Syllabus 94 represented at least a small change in direction and emphasis, for Planning and Control it simply confirmed the sorts of changes that had been made to the syllabus and examination over a three-year period. It is for this reason that we have included ten of the past mini case studies within this unit. These are:

Penton Ltd	June 1992
New Directions plc	December 1992
Anderson Marine Construction Ltd	June 1993
Kanko Ltd	December 1993
Watergate Pumps Ltd	June 1994
RTJ Engineering Ltd	December 1994
Lazy Days Holidays	June 1995
Pentagon Balloons Ltd	December 1995
WGP Industries	June 1996
The Legal Business	December 1996

In reading these case studies, several points should become apparent. The first is that the questions posed cover a spectrum of areas, although in nearly every instance we have a company which has one or several problems. The implication of this is that you will be concerned with addressing all or some part of the solution. The second point that should be apparent is that, in December 1993, we moved away from 2–3 pages of text and introduced some information in the form of tables and figures. There are several reasons for this, the most obvious being that marketing analysts and marketing managers are almost invariably faced with figures on a day-to-day basis and it is not unreasonable therefore for the Diploma examination to require candidates to demonstrate their powers of interpretation. It is perhaps worth emphasizing that you will not be required to *manipulate* any of the data, but instead need to *interpret* it. In other words, what specific and general messages does it convey and what conclusions can you draw?

The questions on the mini case study can realistically be drawn from any part of the syllabus, although insofar as it is possible to identify a general theme, it has to be that of identifying what is wrong with the organization, and what needs to be done in order to overcome these problems. The specific issues covered by each of the mini cases' questions is illustrated in Figure 9.1.

Quite deliberately, although we have included ten mini cases, we have not included solutions for every case. Instead, with some of these we have provided guidelines which should help you to structure your answer.

The mini case study accounts for 50 per cent of the marks available for the examination. If you do badly in the mini case, the pressures upon you to perform at a much higher level in Section 2 are obviously far greater. Make sure, therefore, that you identify clearly and precisely what the examiner is looking for and do not waste time by including unnecessary information.

EXAM TIP

The mini cases
Penton Ltd
New Directions plc
Anderson Marine Construction Ltd
Kanko Ltd
Watergate Pumps Ltd
RTJ Engineering Ltd
Lazy Days Holidays
Pentagon Balloons Ltd
WGP Industries
The Legal Business

Case study	Question areas
Penton Ltd	• The development of a marketing orientation, a stronger planning culture and improved new product process • The implication of these suggestions for control
New Directions plc	• A SWOT analysis • Suggestions for overcoming the organization's problems
Anderson Marine Construction Ltd	• An outline marketing plan • Implementation problems associated with the plan and how to overcome these
Kanko Ltd	• Criteria for how the product and sales and distribution networks should be evaluated and rationalized • Criteria for the selection of a new advertising agency
Watergate Pumps Ltd	• The development and implementation of an environmental monitoring system • Recommendations for future marketing action in order to overcome the organization's problems
RTJ Engineering Ltd	• Portfolio analysis and the implications of the analysis • The development of a customer care programme
Lazy Days Holidays	• The evaluation of market and product opportunities • The preparation of an outline marketing plan
Pentagon Balloons	• The introduction of a stronger marketing orientation • The financial and marketing criteria used to evaluate market opportunities
WGP Industries	• Suggestions on how to improve the new product development process • The development of a brief for a market research agency
The Legal Business	• The marketing audit • Recommendations on how to introduce a strategic marketing orientation to a professional services organisation

Figure 9.1 The mini case question areas

EXAM TIP

Having read the case study, spend a few minutes trying to identify any underlying and fundamental issues. In particular, think about issues of cause and effect. Very often, the sorts of problems that are referred to in the case are the manifestations of something more fundamental. In other words, they are the 'effect', with the 'cause' being something such as a short-sighted management team or an inappropriate managerial culture (this is particularly so in the Penton, New Directions, Kanko, Watergate Pumps, RTJ Engineering and the Legal Business case studies). The significance of this is that any solutions you recommend need to be made against this background and with a full recognition of the implica-tions. In the Penton and New Directions cases, for example, you might think about whether any meaningful and long-term solution can be arrived at with the existing management team still in place.

THE CASE STUDIES

Penton Ltd (June 1992)

Penton is a medium-sized company which manufactures and markets a range of DIY (Do It Yourself) products under the Easi-Way brand name. Its performance over the past ten years, a period during which the market for do-it-yourself products has grown rapidly, has been viewed by those within the industry as steady, but generally unimpressive. In particular, its critics have pointed to performance levels that are below the industry norm, a reliance upon its long-established and now old-fashioned distribution networks, low levels of advertising spend, a failure to exploit the potential strength of the brand name, and a poor profit performance.

Towards the end of 1991, the company was the subject of a takeover bid from a smaller but more aggressive and far more successful competitor. Although Penton's board managed to fight off the bid, the sudden awareness of their vulnerability to further bids has led to a reassessment of their entire manufacturing and marketing strategy.

The problems being faced by the organization were exacerbated by the downturn in retail sales which began to affect the economy at the end of the 1980s. Faced with what was proving to be a static sales curve and a reducing profit margin, the decision was taken to bring in a firm of marketing consultants to conduct a detailed audit of the organization and make recommendations for future strategy. The consultants' initial report highlighted a number of areas of concern which, they suggested, should be the focus of attention:

1 The organization's strong production orientation and a lack of marketing representation at board level.
2 A largely reactive managerial philosophy.
3 Little long-term product or market planning.
4 An over-reliance upon a small number of ageing products.
5 A poorly structured new product planning process.
6 The generally disappointing performance and high failure rate of new product launches over the past few years.
7 A failure to exploit the potential strength of the brand name.
8 Increasing pressure upon margins.

The environmental analysis proved to be more encouraging, with the consultants giving prominence to the size and long-term growth potential of the DIY market, and the major profit opportunities offered by new products. They also pointed to the high level of retail concentration in the market, the need for organizations in this sector to be proactive in their new product development, and for new products to be supported by a strong promotional campaign. In a separate section, the consultants spelled out in detail the implications of the seemingly ever-greater degree of retail concentration, summarizing this with a comment that highlighted the strategic importance of relationship marketing.

The evaluation of the organization's manufacturing capabilities suggested that there was a need for investment in new plant. With regard to the research and development area, the conclusion was that 'whilst the area has potential and the R&D staff are enthusiastic and highly qualified, the activity has suffered from a lack of direction. As a result, the majority of new products have not been related sufficiently directly to market demands.'

Against the background of these findings, the board has attempted to identify the areas of greatest priority and has decided to focus upon the three areas which they believed require the most immediate attention. These are the development of:

- A marketing orientation.
- A far stronger and more effective planning culture.
- A structured and proactive new product development process.

Questions

1 As a member of the team of consultants, you have the responsibility for making recommendations as to how the organization might most effectively achieve this. You are therefore required to prepare a report showing how this might be done.

(35 marks)

2 What are the implications of your suggestions for approaches to management control?

(15 marks)

Required

This is a case study that requires you to be very clear about what is meant by a marketing orientation and how one might be developed within an organization that previously has been product led. Your suggestions must therefore be specific. It is worth remembering that if you can develop the stronger marketing orientation, it is likely that the planning and new product development systems will improve as the result of the stronger external focus.

The second question requires you to think about the nature of the control process and how planning and control are two separate but highly interrelated activities. Again, however, your suggestions must be specific.

What do you think the key issues are in this case?
(The suggested solution appears on pages 208–212.)

New Directions plc (December 1992)

New Directions is a high-street fashion chain which was founded in the late 1950s. After twenty years of slow and generally unspectacular growth, a new Managing Director, Thomas Oakley, was appointed in 1978. Under his very different and aggressively entrepreneurial management style, the company underwent a decade of explosive growth. Many of the old staff left during this period and a far younger team was recruited. The new staff were given considerable operating freedom and high salaries, but were expected to achieve performance levels well above the industry average. By 1988, the company had 400 stores and had become one of the major players in the young (15–25), C1/C2, male and female fashion sectors. Their reputation in the City was that of an ambitious, design-oriented company led by an unconventional, abrasive and maverick figure who inspired considerable loyalty among his employees.

At the beginning of 1987 the company was bought out by a large and cash-rich conglomerate whose financial performance over the preceding decade had proved to be consistently strong. Despite this, the group's senior management was viewed by the City as being generally staid and unimaginative. The group overall was viewed as having a strong financial orientation with an emphasis upon systems and control. Strategy at the group level was perceived as being risk aversive.

New Directions' Managing Director and small senior management team quickly found that operating within a group in which they were accountable to the group's main board constrained their entrepreneurial style and traditional freedom. Not only were they faced with the need to make out a strong written case for anything other than a minor change in strategy but, as they saw it, major restrictions were placed on their ability to capitalize upon short-term opportunities. Profits were remitted to the centre and each division's MD was then required on an annual basis to bid for sums for capital expenditure.

After two years in succession in which his plans for development were rejected by the main board, Oakley resigned. At the heart of the disagreement was his belief that New Directions needed to move up the quality scale and both up and down the age scale. The demographic changes taking place would, he argued, lead to a reduction of at least 20 per cent in the size of the company's traditional target market over the next few years. They should therefore chase the demographic shift by targeting the 30–40 year olds, a sector in which annual growth of 12 per cent was being forecast. At the same time, he suggested, a new chain should be developed that would appeal to the chlidrens' market. 'Children,' he said, 'are the ultimate fashion accessory. We need to capitalize on this.'

He also pointed to the research evidence which suggested that buyers wanted better quality, something for which New Directions had never had a particularly strong reputation. Instead, they had concentrated on developing a strong fashion element at 'popular' prices. While this strategy had undoubtedly been successful, there was now a need to begin the process of making a series of fundamental changes. Oakley also argued for the need for a re-think in the approach to store design. Competition from other retail chains had become ever more aggressive during the 1980s and evidence existed to suggest that buyers were looking for new and more exciting shopping experiences. An essential element in this was the retail concept, something which had taken a significant step forward in the late 1980s in the repositioning and renaming of one of the company's major competitors. Oakley also pointed to the need to begin looking towards opportunities overseas. 'The British market', he suggested, 'offers only limited scope for growth. We need to get into some of the other European markets and particularly Spain.' He went on to point out that the Spanish market was growing at a faster rate than any other. Indeed, without telling the main board or getting their agreement, he had already gone ahead with plans to begin selling into one of the largest chains of Spanish fashion stores.

Each of these arguments was rejected by the group's main board on the grounds of their cost and the perceived risk.

Following Oakley's resignation, the group appointed as his replacement one of their fast-track corporate finance staff. With little direct retailing experience, he set about reorganizing the company. In doing this, he slashed Oakley's plans for development. Largely because of this, a significant number of the team who had worked with Oakley and who very largely saw themselves as his protegés left. In most cases they were snapped up by competitors who placed considerable value on the training and experience they had been exposed to.

As the recession of the early 1990s began to bite, turnover dropped. The new MD's almost desperate response was to pursue an aggressive price cutting policy and to reduce overheads as far as possible.

The annual strategic review at the end of 1991 (two years after Oakley's replacement had taken over) painted a dismal picture. Sales were down, market share was slipping, staff were demoralized and, as a market research report highlighted, the image of the chain in the 15–25, 25–30 and 30–40 age groups was confused. In short, New Directions was no longer a leader or even a serious player in the young fashion market.

Questions

1 Prepare a SWOT analysis of the organization both for the period before the takeover and for the period reached at the end of the case study. Having done this, discuss the implications of *one* of your analyses for methods of marketing planning and control. (30 marks)

2 As a consultant to the organization, and in the light of the findings of the strategic review, what course(s) of action would you recommend should be taken?

(20 marks)

Required

Most Diploma candidates are adept at preparing SWOT analyses and the first part of Question 1 is therefore straightforward. Because of this, the differences between candidates tended to become apparent in the second part of the question when the implications for planning and control were discussed. What is required of you here is a discussion of the *specific* implications.

Refer back to Unit 2 for a discussion of how to conduct a *worthwhile* SWOT analysis.

The second question is perhaps a little deceptive since it is likely to lead candidates towards a set of recommendations which fail to come to terms with the real need to address the underlying managerial culture. It is therefore worth thinking about the extent to which any real change can be brought about as long as Oakley's successor is managing director.

QUESTION 9.2

What do you think the key issues are in this case?
(An outline of the suggested solution appears on pages 212–13.)

Anderson Marine Construction Ltd (June 1993)

Anderson Marine Construction (AMC) is a well-established and financially successful builder of medium-sized, high-performance yachts and power boats. Based on the south coast of England, the company's products have developed a strong reputation for quality and performance, and an intensely loyal and knowledgeable customer base.

The company has traditionally adopted a largely reactive approach to selling, justifying this partly on the grounds that for the past twenty years they have been able to sell every-thing they have been able to make, and partly because the firm's founder and Managing Director, Tom Anderson, saw the firm facing little direct competition in its principal target markets. At the end of the 1980s, however, sales began to drop as demand for expensive luxury goods declined. As a response to this, AMC cut its prices by 6 per cent in real terms for the 1991 season and then by a further 4 per cent for 1992. Despite this, sales remained sluggish.

Faced with this and with no sight of an upturn in demand, Tom Anderson called in a marketing consultant to advise on what AMC should do next. The consultant argued that further price cuts were likely to achieve little and that in the long term they would probably be detrimental to the image developed by AMC. Instead, he suggested, AMC should capitalize upon its reputation and the very strong brand values associated with its name by moving down the size and price scale by developing a new range of smaller and lower priced boats. Although this sector of the market had a greater number of direct competitors, the consultant suggested that patterns of demand would be more consistent and less susceptible to fluctuations in the economy.

Although the idea had an initial appeal, Anderson recognized that the firm's approach to marketing and selling would have to change. Previously, the firm's sales effort had been limited to very occasional advertisements in the boating press and a small stand every other year at a regional boat show. This, together with the strength of the firm's reputation and word of mouth recommendation, had, he felt, been adequate. Boats were made to order with a delivery time of 9–15 months and prices, which were negotiated individually with clients, reflected the specification demanded. Once completed, they were either delivered by AMC or the customer collected the boat himself.

The consultant emphasized that the new range would need to be targeted at buyers for whom the sailing skills and buying motives and processes would be very different from those of AMC's traditional customers. The implications of this were spelled out in a report.

1   Buyers within the proposed target group are less knowledgeable about boats and sailing and would expect a greater degree of what he referred to as 'active selling' of the product's benefits.
2   There would be a need for a structured distribution network with at least ten dis-tributors throughout the country.
3   Buyers would not be prepared to wait for delivery but would expect boats to be available from stock.

4 A communications programme would be required.

5 A formal pricing and distributor discount structure would be needed.

6 Because the new range would bring AMC into more direct competition with other boat builders, a competitive monitoring system should be developed.

7 A marketing budget should be set as a matter of priority and the responsibility for the marketing effort clearly allocated.

Recognizing that these recommendations called for a far more proactive approach to marketing than had previously been adopted, Anderson decided to appoint a marketing manager. As the person appointed to this post, you have the immediate responsibility for developing the marketing plan to support the new range which is scheduled for launch for the 1994 sailing season.

Questions

1 Prepare an outline of the marketing plan for the launch and subsequent market development of the new range. In doing this, you should make specific reference to the nature of any additional information that you might require. (35 marks)

2 In the light of AMC's previous approaches to selling, what, if any, organizational problems might you expect to encounter in implementing the marketing plan? In what ways might these problems be overcome or minimized? (15 marks)

Required

The first question requires a clear understanding of the structure of a marketing plan, something which the answers revealed that far too few candidates have. Without this knowledge, any answer will lack conviction.

The second question addresses the issues of implementation and how a marketing orientation might be developed and fostered (refer to Unit 7).

What do you think the key issues are in this case?
(The suggested solution appears on pages 213–19.)

QUESTION 9.3

Kanko Ltd (December 1993)

Kanko Ltd is a wholly owned subsidiary of a highly diversified listed public company which has traditionally allowed its subsidiaries to operate with a high degree of autonomy.

Kanko markets a wide range of plumbing accessories, heating systems and small air-conditioning units both for domestic and industrial use. Its products are sold through iron-mongers, specialist builders' merchants and, increasingly, very large do-it-yourself (DIY) outlets (see Table 9.1 below). The company's sales force of forty is split fairly evenly into three geographical regions, each of which is headed by a Regional Sales Manager who has the sales but not the profit responsibility for that region. This profit responsibility rests with the Sales and Marketing Director. Each member of the sales team handles the entire range of products and is expected to cover all types of sales outlet in his/her territory.

Table 9.1 Kanko's sales turnover by type of outlet (1987–93)

	1987 %	1988 %	1989 %	1990 %	1991 %	1992 %	1993* %
Ironmongers	28	27	25	22	19	20	20
Builders' merchants	64	63	62	61	63	63	63
Do-it-yourself	8	10	13	17	18	17	17
*Estimate							

Following the publication of the interim results in mid-1993 (see Table 9.2 below), the Managing Director, Finance Director and the Sales and Marketing Director were asked by the parent company to resign. A new senior management team was appointed and far higher levels of accountability than had been the case previously were introduced.

Table 9.2   Selected sales and profit data (1987–93)

	1987 %	1988 %	1989 %	1990 %	1991 %	1992 %	1993* %	1993** %
Sales turnover (£m)	57	63	62	63	55	56	28	53
Profit (loss) net of tax and parent company management charges (£m)	3.4	3.2	3.0	2.6	0.7	0.5	(1.3)	(3.1)
Net profit as a percentage of turnover	6	5.1	4.8	4.1	1.3	0.9	(4.6)	(5.8)
*First six months **Projection for the full year								

Under the new team, an initial review of the entire sales and marketing function was conducted. Although the clarity of the findings was clouded somewhat by the poor costing and control systems that existed, it appeared that the company had previously been run in a highly haphazard fashion. This haphazard approach was manifested in a variety of ways, including:

1   An unstructured and seemingly indiscriminate new product development programme which had led to numerous products being launched with seemingly little real attention having been paid to their sales or profit potential.
2   Poor day-to-day management of the product range with the result that some 30 per cent of the product range appeared to be unprofitable.
3   Rising costs of distribution and an apparent willingness to appoint distribution intermediaries regardless of their sales potential or ability to provide after sales support.
4   A failure to address the rising levels of complaints about variable product quality and inadequate levels of service support.
5   The generally poor sales and profits performance of the sales team, with little attention paid to market development.
6   Uninspiring and tired sales literature and advertising.

Because of this latter point, the decision to fire the existing advertising agency has already been taken.

In 1992, the nature and intensity of competition throughout the industry increased significantly as Kanko's two principal competitors, both of whom have a similar product range to Kanko, used aggressive price competition to gain market share.

In the same period, overall market demand remained stagnant as domestic buyers, affected by economic uncertainties, demonstrated a high degree of price consciousness, whilst sales to industrial buyers were constrained by the downturn in housebuilding and factory construction. In parallel with this, the structure of the distribution networks continued to change, with an ever greater proportion of sales being channelled through the major DIY outlets (see Table 9.3 below). Because of the strength of the latters' buying power, the terms that their centralized buying teams were able to demand from their suppliers, as well as the far higher levels of marketing support they required, meant that margins on the sales made by Kanko to these outlets were, at best, slim. Kanko's penetration of the major DIY outlets is currently lower than that of each of its two principal competitors.

It is against this background that the detailed review of every aspect of the company's sales and marketing operations is taking place.

Table 9.3 Industry Sales by Type of Outlet (1987–94)

	1987 %	1988 %	1989 %	1990 %	1991 %	1992 %	1993* %	1994** %
Ironmongers	25	25	23	20	18	15	10	8
Builders' merchants	65	57	52	52	50	50	47	47
Do-It-yourself	10	18	25	28	32	35	43	45

*Estimated
**Forecast

Questions

1 As a member of the new management team, you have been given the responsibility for recommending how the product and distribution strategies should develop. You are required to prepare a report detailing the criteria by which the current product range and sales and distribution networks should be evaluated and possibly rationalized.

(35 marks)

2 You are also required to make recommendations on the appointment of the new advertising agency. You should prepare a short briefing paper identifying the criteria by which agencies pitching for the account should be shortlisted.   (15 marks)

Required

The first of the two questions requires you to identify a set of *specific* criteria for the evaluation and possible rationalization of the product, sales and distribution networks. Without this specific treatment, it is unlikely that you will gain more than a few marks.

Equally, Question 2 requires you to identify the *specific* factors that should be taken into account. Vague generalizations are simply inappropriate.

What do you think the key issues are in this case?
(The suggested solution appears on pages 219–23.)

QUESTION 9.3

Watergate Pumps Ltd (June 1994)

Watergate Pumps Ltd manufactures and markets a range of water pumps and control systems for domestic and industrial central heating systems. For the past three years total industry sales of domestic pumps have been stable at an average of 1.3 million units per annum (£40 million at manufacturers' average selling prices). Sales are forecast to grow only slowly over the next few years and are expected to reach a peak of 1.55 million units p.a. in 1998.

Within the domestic sector, there are four principal markets for the product: local authorities; the public utilities such as British Gas; regional/national building companies; and small firms of builders/plumbers and individuals repairing their own heating systems.

The company, which is a subsidiary of a far larger organization which has interests throughout the building supplies industry, has three competitors. Selected market data collected from various sources appear in Tables 9.4, 9.5 and 9.6.

Watergate has been taken by surprise by a variety of developments in the marketplace over the past few years, including:

- The entry into the market in 1991 by Pump Suppliers, a Dutch-owned company which set up a factory in southern England.
- The launch by B G Industrial (BGI) and Northern Pumps of several modified and new products.
- A general competitive repositioning (see Figure 9.2).

- An extension by all three competitors of the guarantees offered on their products from one to three years.
- The three-year stagnation of the market.
- A significant shift in customers' buying motives, with quality and ease of fitting having become increasingly important.
- A series of improvements by all three competitors in their control systems.
- The move by BGI and Northern Pumps into a number of profitable overseas markets.

Because of this, there is now recognition that the company's understanding of the market is poor and that some form of structured external environment monitoring is needed.

Watergate Pump – selected market data
Table 9.4

	Market shares within the domestic pumps sector (1990–93)				Total manufacturing capacity (000 units)	Total output in 1993 (000 units)	UK overseas split of sales in 1993
	1990 (%)	1991 (%)	1992 (%)	1993 (%)			
Watergate Pumps	35	29	27	24	475	320	100/0
BG International	50	50	48	48	850	830	75/25
Northern Pumps	15	13	15	16	300	280	74/26
Pump Suppliers	0	8	10	12	300	300	52/48

Table 9.5

	Sales in 1993 by type of buyer (000 units)	Expected percentage increase/(decrease) by 1998	Market position of each company by type of buyer (1993)			
			No 1	No 2	No 3	No 4
Local authorities	400	(25)	WGP	NP	PS	BG1
Public utilities	300	66	BG1	PS	WGP	NP
Regional/national builders	400	25	BGI	PS	NP	WGP
Local builders/plumbers and private individuals	200	25	BGI	NP	PS	WGP

Key: WGP – Watergate Pumps
      BGI – BG International
      NP – Northern Pumps
      PS – Pump Suppliers

Source: Trade Data

Table 9.6 Rank order of the principal buying motives of different customer groups

	Local authorities	Public utilities	Regional/ national builders	Local builders/plumbers and private individuals
Price	1	3	3 =	3
Availability off the shelf	N/A	N/A	3 =	1 =
Reliability	3	1	1	4
Ease of fitting	2	2	2	1 =

N/A: Not applicable, since supplies are delivered in bulk to regional warehouses

Source: Compiled from trade data

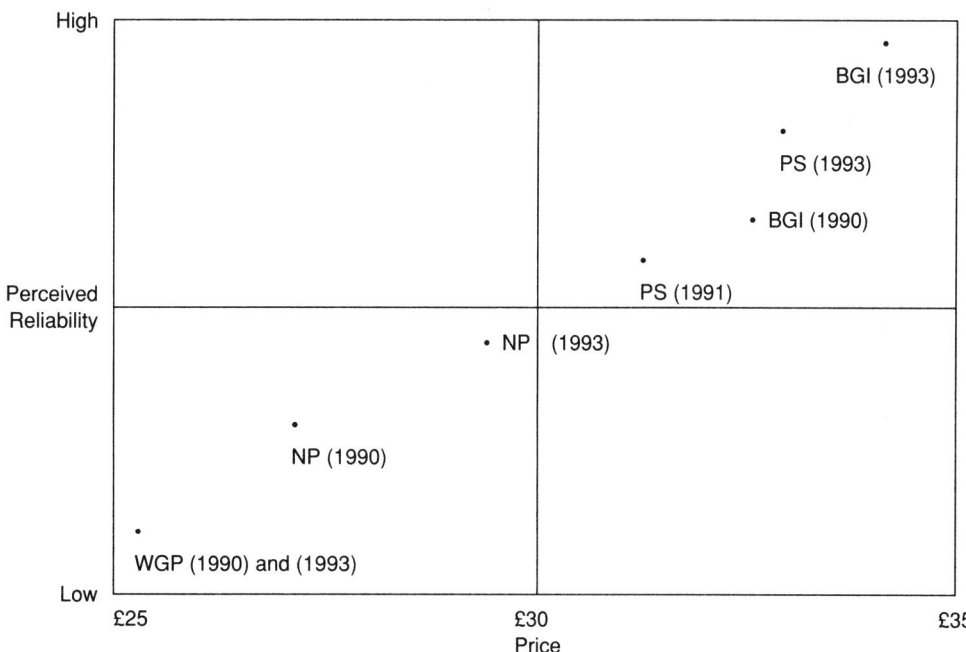

Figure 9.2 Competitive positioning (1990 and 1993)

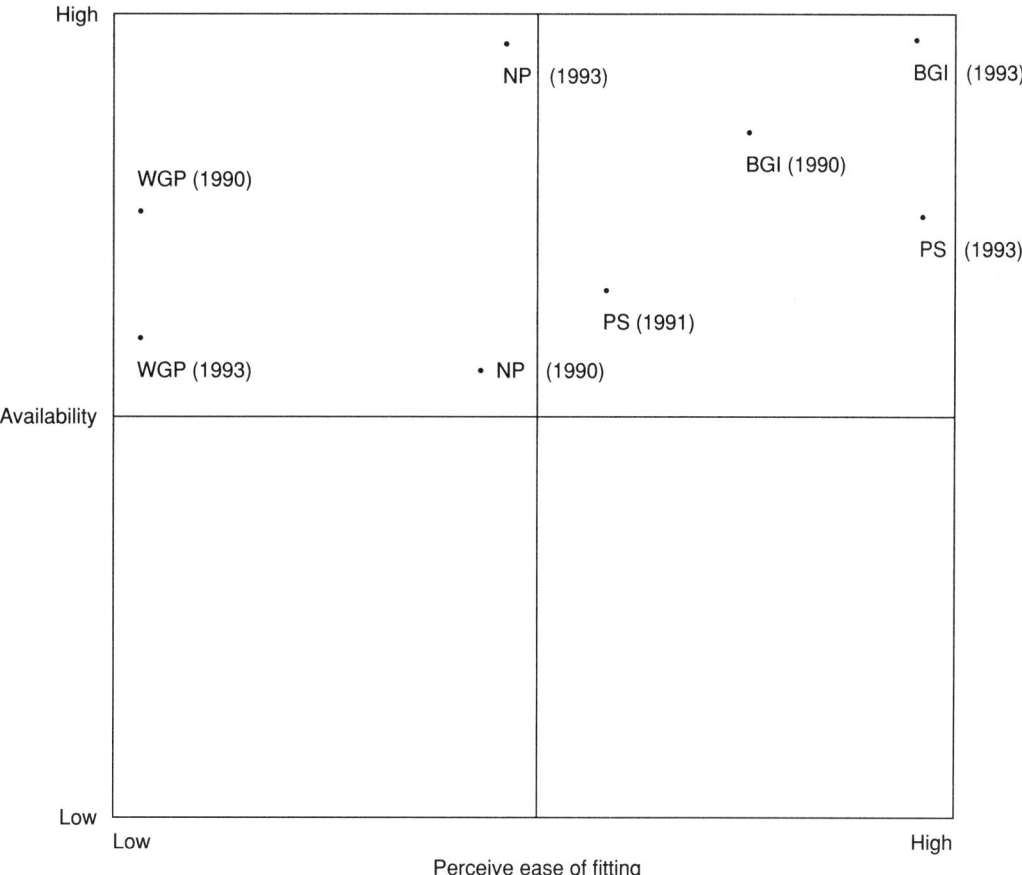

Figure 9.3

Questions

1 As the company's newly appointed market analyst, you are required to prepare a detailed report for the marketing director recommending how an effective external environment monitoring system for the company might best be developed and implemented. Included within the report should be your suggestions on the structure

of the system, the expected inputs and outputs, the probable organizational and resource implications, and the nature of any benefits that should emerge.

(30 marks)

2 In the light of the information contained in the mini case, what recommendations for future marketing action would you make? (20 marks)

Required

The first of the two questions requires you to recommend how an environmental monitoring system might be developed and implemented. In your answer you need therefore to be specific about its structure and how it might be introduced into the organization. The second sentence in the question was designed to provide candidates with guidance on the principal issues that need to be included.

EXAM TIP

Diagrams can play a useful role in your answer, since if they are used properly they can be an effective way of communicating your ideas. This question provides you with an opportunity to draw an environmental monitoring system and illustrate the inputs, outputs and interrelationships that exist.

The second question is one that we have come across before in a variety of guises and requires you to recommend how the organization should overcome its problems.

QUESTION 9.5

What do you think the key issues are in this case?
(The suggested solution appears on pages 223–7.)

RTJ Engineering Ltd (December 1994)

Established in 1952, RTJ Engineering is a fabricator of highly specialized engineering components. Selected sales and financial data appear in Figure 9.5. The company's operations are divided between five strategic business units: Nuclear, Aerospace, Defence, Marine and General Engineering (see Figure 9.6 opposite).

The firm has an international reputation for engineering excellence and prides itself on the very high quality of its work and its ability to tackle projects of extreme technical complexity. However, the sales department within the organization has traditionally operated with a highly reactive approach to selling, relying heavily upon word-of-mouth and repeat business from its established customer base.

In 1992 and 1993, total sales declined partly as the result of a downturn in its core markets, but also because of the loss of three medium-sized and long-standing customers to competitors. Because of this, the managing director hired a marketing consultant who, as part of a programme of activities, conducted a study designed to reveal current and potential customers' perceptions of the firm's three principal SBUs (see Figures 9.4(a) and 9.4(b) for a selection of the results). The consultant's report gave full recognition to the depth and breadth of the firm's technical expertise, but was highly critical of the approaches to marketing and selling. In particular, he pointed to the results of the customer study, arguing that unless a series of changes were made, the company would almost inevitably lose sales and market share to its ever more numerous and aggressive competitors. Against this background, it has been agreed that a far more proactive approach to customer care will be introduced.

	Nuclear		Aerospace		Defence	
	RTJ	Others	RTJ	Others	RTJ	Others
Design skills	8	6	8	7	6	7
Sales expertise	2	4	3	5	3	5
Customer management	3	5	3	6	4	5
Quality of literature	1	4	2	4	2	4
Production flexibility	7	7	7	7	7	7
Ability to cope with complex specifications	9	7	9	8	8	7
Adherence to promised delivery schedules	4	7	4	6	3	6
Price competitiveness	4	6	3	6	4	7
Quality of work	9	6	9	7	9	6
Unprompted technical support	4	6	3	6	3	5
Helpfulness of sales staff/sales support	3	5	3	6	2	5

(1 = Low, 9 = High)

Figure 9.4(a) Customers' perceptions of RTJ Engineering and its principal competitors

'They work at their speed rather than ours.'
'Technically, they're the best in the industry but they haven't got the first idea about marketing or selling.'
'Do they ever deliver on time?'
'They are the most frustrating company that I've ever dealt with, but nobody can match their quality.'
'Have their sales staff ever had any training in anything other than being rude to customers?'
'Have you seen their sales literature? It's a joke.'
'I'd never go anywhere else when I've got a complex job that needs doing.'
'Superb quality, but very expensive.'

Figure 9.4(b) Selected quotations that emerged from the customer research

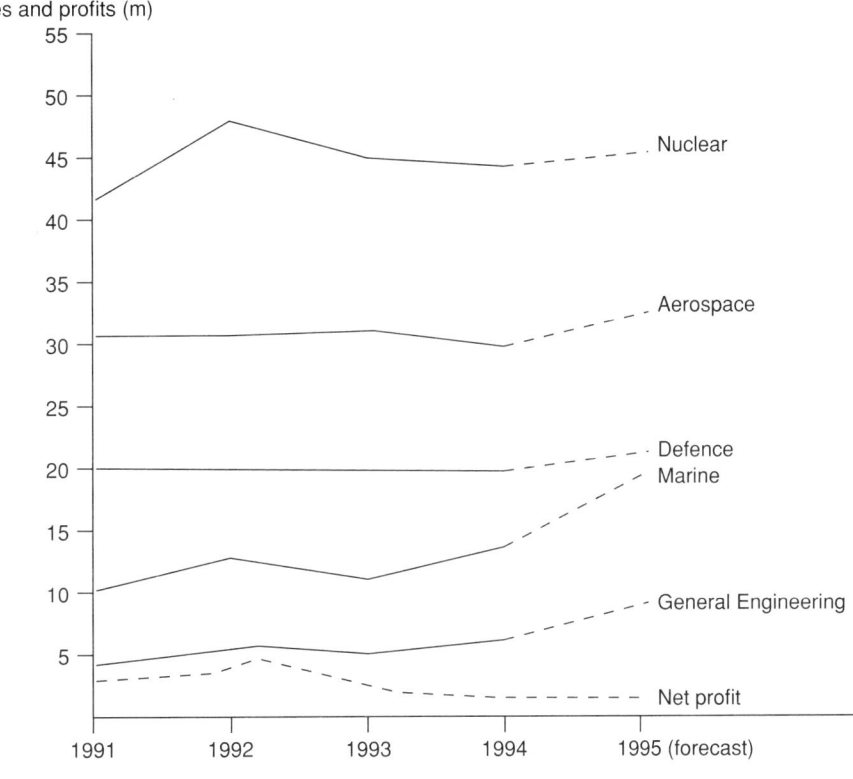

Figure 9.5 Selected sales and financial information

	RTJ's sales 1994 (£m)	Number of direct competitors	Sales of the three largest firms in the sector (£m)	Forecast annual growth rate (%)
Nuclear	13	5	13*, 13, 8	3
Aerospace	12	8	12*, 9, 6	4
Defence	9	12	15, 12, 11	(6)
Marine	6	7	18, 12, 6*	15
General Engineering	4	16	15, 14, 10	8
	44 (forecast)			

Note: Figures asterisked represent RTJ's sales within the sector

Figure 9.6 Selected SBU market data

Questions

1   Using a model of your choice, comment upon the apparent state of the firm's portfolio. In doing this, you should specify any assumptions that you make, the limitations of the model and any other information that you would require before recommending how the firm's portfolio should be developed. You should also identify briefly any other approach to portfolio analysis that might be used to evaluate the portfolio.

(25 marks)

2   In the light of the research findings, prepare a report for the managing director identifying the key dimensions of a customer-care programme and how such a programme might be introduced into the organization. In doing this, you should pay particular attention to issues of implementation. (25 marks)

Required

The first of the two questions asks you to analyse the firm's portfolio. There are several frameworks that can be used for this, but whichever is used, there is a need to make use of the data in the case. Equally, in the second of the two questions, the recommendations for the customer-care programme need to be made against the background of the market research findings rather than in a generalized way.

QUESTION 9.5

What do you think the key issues are in the case?
(The suggested solution appears on pages 227–231.)

Lazy Days Holidays (June 1995)

Lazy Days Holidays is a London-based company offering packaged holidays (flights, accommodation and some meals). Its two primary destinations are North Africa, in which it offers beach holidays in the summer and golfing holidays in the winter, and Eastern Europe, in which it offers low-cost skiing holidays from December to April.

Although for the past three years the company has been relatively successful (see Figure 9.7), the management team believes that its current destinations offer little real scope for growth.

	1992	1993	1994	1995*
Number of holiday makers ('000)	69	82	87	95
Turnover (£m)	15	18	20	22
Gross margin (%)	16	15	13	11
Gross profit (£m)	2.4	2.7	2.6	2.42
Net profit (£000)	450	530	420	390

*Estimated

Figure 9.7   Selected sales and financial data

The company sells its holidays primarily through travel agents. However, because of the growth of the major tour operators and their increased share of the overall market, Lazy Days is now finding it increasingly difficult to achieve shelf space for its brochures in travel agents' showrooms. It is also finding the growing levels of price competition throughout the industry difficult to manage.

Faced with these problems, the company has recently used a marketing consultant to conduct a review of the business. The consultant's final report highlighted several issues, including:

(a)   The firm currently has little detailed information on its customers. What information is available suggests that customers are drawn predominantly from social groups C1 and C2, are between 38 and 60 years old, and see the price of the holiday as being a very important or the most important buying consideration.

(b)   There appears to be little customer loyalty and no real evidence of much repeat business.

(c)   In the absence of a sizeable marketing campaign, the summer destination appears to offer relatively little scope for growth. However, if a campaign was to be developed, it is felt that it might well have the effect of attracting some of the larger players in the industry, who currently view the area as being of only marginal interest.

(d)   Winter golfing holidays are felt to offer significant growth prospects.

(e)   The skiing market is likely to continue growing for at least the next five years, but will become subject to increasing price competition (see (g) below).

(f)   The company currently has a policy of pricing at 5–8 per cent below the average of the industry leaders, and gives emphasis in its promotional material to this.

(g)   With the substantial growth in the capacity of the Austrian, French and Italian ski resorts over the past few years, price competition in these markets has increased significantly. One result of this has been that the price advantage from which the Eastern European market benefited previously has very largely been eroded.

(h)   The firm's sales brochures are uninspiring, and reflect the lack of any real basis for differentiation.

(i)   The company has high fixed costs.

Against this background, the consultant has emphasized the general importance of moving up-market in order to increase the value added element of the holidays and allow for a greater degree of premium pricing. The specific recommendations that have been made are that:

• The company should continue to promote its current destinations, but over the next three years should attempt to reposition these in order to attract clients from higher socio-economic groups.

• It should gradually withdraw from the Eastern European ski resorts and concentrate instead upon higher-margin skiing holidays in the United States.

• A new range of holidays in Africa which would feature ballooning and safaris and targeted firmly at young high-spending customers in social groups A and B should be launched. These should be sold direct to clients and not via travel agents.

Questions

As Lazy Days' newly appointed marketing analyst, you have been given two tasks:

(a) Prepare a report for the managing director, identifying the criteria by which the three recommendations might best be evaluated. (15 marks)

(b) Prepare an outline marketing plan for the launch of a new holiday destination. In doing this, you should make detailed reference to the sort of financial and non-financial information that would be needed to underpin the plan. (35 marks)

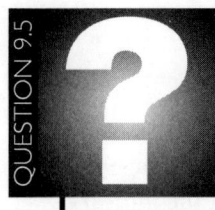

What do you think are the key issues in the case?
(The suggested solution appears on pages 231–7.)

Pentagon Balloons Ltd (December 1995)

Established by three flying enthusiasts in 1980, Pentagon Balloons Ltd started life as manufacturers of hot air balloons capable of carrying up to six passengers. These were sold primarily to a middle-aged and relatively wealthy market of ballooning enthusiasts, and positioned as 'the gift that you always promised yourself'.

In 1984 the company recognized the potential of hot air balloons as a promotional vehicle and began designing and manufacturing hot air balloons for clients in a wide variety of shapes, including various types of clothes, bottles and cans, running shoes, a car, and so on. Although the approach to marketing was largely reactive, this proved to be a highly successful venture and the company developed a reputation both for its high quality and its ingenious, if expensive, designs. Although the recession of the late 1980s had little impact upon sales, the decision was taken in 1990 to sell a 51 per cent stake in the company in order to inject a large sum of cash into the business to fund future growth. This stake was bought by a mini-conglomerate which, until recently, has allowed Pentagon to operate without interference.

In 1991, Pentagon's management recognized that the promotional hot air balloon market had reached what appeared to be a long-term maturity which offered relatively few opportunities for real or sustained profitable growth. Faced with this, the company began looking for new market opportunities. Amongst those identified was the market for micro-light aircraft. These aircraft, which weigh about 150 kg, are made of a tubular framework and the man-made textile, Dacron. Powered by a 500 cc engine, they require a 30-metre runway for take-off and 130 metres for landing. Like a hang-glider, the wing can be folded down to fit into a tube and, with the cockpit loaded onto a small trailer, the machine can be taken and stored almost anywhere. Prices range from £6000–£10,000.

After an initial and admittedly superficial assessment of market opportunities, the company enthusiastically entered the market by coming to a loose and largely informal arrangement with an American designer and manufacturer of very high-quality microlights. Encouraged by their first six months sales results, they then entered into a more formal ten-year marketing licence in late 1992. Under the terms of the licence they import the aircraft and have the marketing rights for Great Britain, Scandinavia, and the Benelux countries, with an option for the French and German markets. The licence requires Pentagon to achieve sales targets that are agreed every five years. Failure to achieve these targets leads to substantial financial penalties.

Although sales of the microlights proved initially to be healthy and profitable, the company has for the past 18 months failed to hit the sales target, and the penalty clause has been invoked. The company therefore employed a marketing consultant three months ago to conduct a detailed marketing audit. The consultant's subsequent report proved to be scathing, and highlighted a series of issues (see Figure 9.8).

1 Despite the firm's initial success in this market, the impression gained is that the company is being run almost as a hobby by a group of flying enthusiasts.

2 Little or no real attention has been paid to structured market development.

3 There has been no sales effort in any of the markets outside Great Britain, even though the company's marketing licence covers several for which there is now hard evidence that a considerable sales potential exists.

4 There is an absence of formal market and marketing planning.

5 The sales effort has been largely reactive and has relied too heavily upon word-of-mouth and the general interest generated by the occasional newspaper feature or television programme.

6 No real segmentation or positioning policy exists.

7 There is little understanding of buyers' motives or where the marketing effort should be focused.

Figure 9.8 Selected extracts from the consultant's report

With regard to marketing and sales (see Figure 9.9), the consultant concluded that 'a significant and underexploited sales potential exists throughout the territories for which you have the marketing rights ... levels of competition are still relatively low ... [and] the product's undoubted quality and performance give you a significant marketing edge. However, given the current approach, this potential will not be realized. .... My biggest single recommendation must therefore be that the organization adopts a far stronger and more proactive approach to marketing'.

Questions

1 Working with the consultant, you have been given the responsibility for preparing a report recommending how a stronger marketing orientation might be introduced to the organization. Within the report you should make reference to, amongst other areas, the organizational and managerial implications of your recommendations, as well as the implications for marketing practice.   (30 marks)

2 Identify the marketing and financial criteria that should be employed to assess the markets identified in Figure 9.9 by the consultant.   (20 marks)

Required

The first of the two questions asks you to recommend how the organization might be refocused so that it has a far stronger external (marketing) orientation and less of an inward-looking approach. As many organizations have discovered, this is not necessarily an easy task, since it requires a major change in the management culture and ways of thinking. The solution is therefore far more complex than simply appointing a marketing director. You should therefore discuss how a change in culture might be brought about, and the sorts of problems that are likely to be experienced. Following on from this, you need to discuss the organizational (structural) implications of your recommendations, the ways in which management practice would need to change, and the consequences for marketing practice.

The second question is relatively straightforward, and asks you to identify the variety of financial and marketing criteria that marketing planners should take into account in assessing the alternatives open to them.

- Police forces, for low-cost traffic monitoring.
- Local authorities, for land surveys.
- Flying enthusiasts, who either cannot afford a 'proper' aircraft or who are attracted by the way in which microlights re-create the early days of flying.
- The military, for a variety of uses.

Of these, it is the third and fourth sectors which offer the greatest potential.

Figure 9.9 Market sectors for microlight aircraft

QUESTION 9.5

What do you think are the key issues in the case?
(The suggested solution appears on pages 237–42.)

WGP Industries Ltd (June 1996)

To: The Group Managing Director
From: The Group Marketing Director
Date: 1 June 1996

Review of WGP Industries Ltd

As you know, in the three months since my appointment as Group Marketing Director I have been reviewing the marketing activities of each of our subsidiary companies. The company that concerns me most is WGP Industries Ltd (referred to hereafter as WGPI).

The firm is currently manufacturing industrial and domestic cleaning machines that are sold in Great Britain, France and parts of Northern Germany. The market, particularly in the volume sector, is dominated by a small number of major international players and so WGPI has traditionally pursued what might loosely be described as a market niching strategy, with an emphasis upon very high quality, high performance, high prices, exclusive distribution, limited advertising, a series of significant product innovations, and strong after-sales support. By contrast, the major players have pursued strategies of price competition, the frequent introduction of small and often cosmetic changes to their products, heavy advertising, frequent trade and consumer sales promotion campaigns, and regular – and often fairly pointless – confrontations with each other.

It is obvious that both the industrial and consumer markets are in long-term maturity and that there is a growing problem of over-capacity. This, coupled with the entry to the European market of a large and aggressive Far Eastern manufacturer, has led to the market becoming highly price competitive. We know that nearly everyone in the industry is now searching for underexploited market sectors and that WGPI's traditional markets are likely to come under increasing attack over the next few years as other firms develop new products for the lower volume but higher quality/higher price/higher margin sectors of the market. The management team first identified this as a possible threat three years ago and a strategy that was designed to safeguard the firm's long-term position was put in place. This strategy has been based upon a four-pronged approach:

1. The early identification and exploitation of market sectors with areas of specialist needs that appear to offer scope for growth (e.g. domestic consumers who suffer from airborne allergies and who need a particularly clean environment).
2. The application of their existing technologies to new markets (e.g. high performance air filtration systems for use in industrial environments where dust pollution must be kept below very tightly defined levels).
3. The entry to a greater number of overseas markets.
4. A programme of product innovation in order to retain and possibly develop further the technological and performance leads that the company's products possess.

Although I am generally happy with the strategy, I feel that we have major problems with how it is being implemented. The company's performance in the areas of new product and new market development has been consistently disappointing, with the firm having found itself beaten to the market by one or more of its competitors on four occasions over the past two years. It appears that there are two major causes of these problems:

(i) The very traditional and sequential approach to new product development that is being used and the consequent length of time between idea formulation and the commercialization of the product.

(ii) An insufficiently detailed understanding of the characteristics of the new target markets.

Because of this, I am about to conduct a detailed review of the firm's new product and new market development activities; I will keep you informed of my progress.

Questions

As the marketing analyst working with the Marketing Director on this review, you have been given two tasks:

1 The preparation of a report suggesting how the current sequential approach to new product development might possibly be improved. In doing this you should make reference to any lessons that emerge from the experiences of other organizations and to the research work that has been carried out into the typical causes of new product success and failure.

(30 marks)

2 The development of a brief for a market research agency explaining what information you require in order to develop a detailed picture of any new markets that the company might be interested in entering.

(20 marks)

Required

The first of the two questions asks you to make a series of recommendations on how the company's new product development (NPD) processes might be improved. Although the problems are most obviously those of it taking too long to get new products to market and that much of the new product development activity is poorly focused, it can be argued that the solution involves tackling a far more fundamental issue, that of the organizational culture. In the event, however, many candidates simply talked about the Booz, Allen and Hamilton framework for NPD and ignored the issues of structure and culture. The question also asked candidates to make reference to any lessons that might emerge from other organizations and to make reference to any lessons that might emerge from other organizations and to the research that has been carried out into the causes of new product success and failure. Far too many failed to do this with the result that marks were often lower than might have been expected.

The second question asked candidates to prepare a brief for a market research agency. In doing this, they had to identify the nature of the information that would be needed in order to develop a clear picture of new markets that the company was thinking of entering. Answers to this question were generally reasonable, although few candidates made use of models such as that proposed by Harrell and Keifer (the model is included in the specimen answer).

What do you think are the key issues in the case?
(The suggested solution appears on pages 242–8.)

QUESTION 9.3

The Legal Business (December 1996)

The Legal Business is an ambitious and growth-oriented medium-sized firm of lawyers with offices in three major cities. The firm operates with 35 partners supported by 97 other fee earners and 100 support staff. The annual fee income is currently around £10 million. The legal services offered include matrimonial, commercial litigation, corporate law and finance, employment law, insurance litigation, insolvency, debt recovery, licensing, intellectual property, and private client work. The fee earning potential and the firm's capabilities in each of these areas varies significantly. Each area is the responsibility of one of the senior partners. Until recently, the managing partner has taken responsibility for the marketing effort, but has found the task to be increasingly demaiding and difficult.

Because of this, the firm hired a marketing consultant to conduct a *brief* and *general* review of the firm's current marketing activities. The results of the review have been summarized for the firm's partners and are as follows:

1 Levels of client satisfaction and client care are far lower that had been expected, with a high proportion of clients suggesting that they were not kept fully or sufficiently informed of the progress of their case.

2 Existing and potential clients appear to have little awareness of the full range of the services that the firm is able to offer. This problem is compounded by the ways in which the individual partners fiercely guard client relationships with the result that although there are often opportunities for the cross-selling of services, this seldom happens.

3 There is no real sense of a long-term direction for the firm or of a true competitive stance.

4 There is little planning and no obvious attempt to capitalize upon the firm's strengths.

5 Although there is some advertising, there is no advertising or promotional strategy.

6 Levels of client retention and new client attraction have dropped significantly over the past two years.

7 Market research suggests that the firm is perceived generally to be rather staid.

8 A number of the younger and more promising staff have been attracted away by competitors over the past two years.

9 A number of the competitors both regionally and nationally have recently become far more aggressive in their search for new business, with the result that the firm's overall share of market is dropping.

In discussions with the partners and staff, the marketing consultant discovered that many were unclear about what is meant by marketing or indeed how it might contribute to the development of the firm. Instead, there was a culture based on a 'professional approach' characterized by a lack of an explicitly commercial orientation and an aptitude which preferred to wait for business to come in rather than going out to get it. This was reflected in comments such as:

'Isn't marketing just a different name for selling?'

'Marketing is a cost and so whatever we spend will reduce our profits for the year.'

'If I had wanted to be a salesman, I would have chosen a different career path. I became a lawyer because I want to practice law. It isn't my job to do all of this selling and marketing, is it? Don't expect me to change how I operate.'

Questions

Given this, the consultant recommended that a marketing manager be appointed to develop and co-ordinate an external and internal marketing programme. As the person appointed to do this, you are faced with two tasks:

(a) Carrying out a detailed marketing audit for the firm. As the first step in this, prepare a briefing paper for the managing partner in which you explain the purpose, focus and components of the audit, how it might be conducted and how the results might be used.

(20 marks)

(b) Against the background of your comments in (a), you are required to prepare a report for the managing partner recommending how a strategic marketing orientation might be introduced to the firm. In doing this, you must make SPECIFIC reference to the particular problems that are likely to be encountered within a professional services organization and how these problems might possibly be overcome.

(30 marks)

Required

The first of the two questions was relatively straightforward and asks you to explain the nature and purpose of a marketing audit, how an audit might be conducted and how the results might be used. In the event, the scripts turned out to be very polarized, with some candidates demonstrating a very clear understanding of the audit, whilst others had little or no knowledge of what an audit is, what it involves and how it might be carried out.

The second question focused upon an issue that concerns many managers, that of how a strategic marketing orientation (SMO) might be developed within an organization. Here, of course, there was an additional twist in that candidates were required to discuss how an SMO might be developed within a professional services organization where you might typically expect a degree of conflict to emerge between marketing and the lawyers' professional culture and those. Unfortunately far too few candidates *really* came to terms with these issues and the examiners were often faced with a series of very general and uninspiring comments. However, where candidates did understand these issues, some very good answers emerged, with an emphasis being placed upon the need to change the culture by introducing marketing at the top of the firm, the importance of training and management development, a programme of internal marketing, and so on (the spectrum of issues is included in the specimen answer that appears later).

What do you think are the key issues in the case?
(The suggested solution appears on pages 248–53.)

QUESTION 9.3

EXAM TIP

Although many candidates refer in their answers to a marketing orientation, the examination scripts illustrated that relatively few understand in detail what such an approach *really* means or how such an approach might be developed within an organization. Given the importance of a marketing orientation, it is almost inevitable that future examination papers will include questions on how managers might introduce a marketing orientation to a business.

SUGGESTED SOLUTIONS

Within this section of the workbook, we have included full solutions to nine of the cases: Penton Ltd, Anderson Marine Construction Ltd, Kanko Ltd, Watergate Pumps Ltd, RTJ Engineering Ltd, Lazy Days Holidays, Pentagon Balloons Ltd, WGP Industries and The Legal Business. It needs to be emphasized that these are solutions which have been prepared by the Senior Examiner without the sorts of constraints of time and examination pressure that the candidates will have faced at the time. They are not designed to be seen as 'ideal' solutions but rather as relatively full answers to the questions so that you might gain an insight into the sorts of issues that might possibly be included.

Deliberately, we have not included a solution to the New Dimensions case but have instead listed the sorts of issues to which you might usefully pay attention in the answer that you prepare.

Penton Ltd: a suggested solution

This case requires you to suggest how the organization might be changed so that a stronger marketing orientation, more effective planning culture and a more proactive new product development process might be developed. It is therefore a useful vehicle for the second of the two questions that underpin many of the mini (and indeed maxi) case studies: knowing what is wrong with the organization, what can we do to improve things?

Question 1

As a member of the team of consultants you have the responsibility for making recommendations as to how the organization might most effectively achieve a stronger marketing orientation, more effective planning culture, and a proactive NPD process. You are therefore required to prepare a report showing how this might be done.

For the Attention of the Main Board of Penton Ltd.

1.0 Management summary

1.1 It has become apparent from our work with the organization that a series of major changes and actions are required. These may be summarized in terms of the need for:

(a) The appointment of a senior marketing person.
(b) A stronger and more obvious focus for the business.
(c) A programme of internal marketing.
(d) A full internal and external audit.
(e) A stronger top-down approach, particularly in the short term.
(f) A clarification of objectives.
(h) A programme of market research.
(i) A more structured planning process which incorporates a mission statement.
(j) Decisions on the competitive stance that is to be adopted.
(k) A programme of monitoring and feedback.
(l) Increased accountability throughout the organization.
(m) A detailed assessment of new product development capability.
(n) Greater exploitation of the brand name.

2.0 Introduction and background

2.1 The suggestions and recommendations made here are based on our findings to date. There is, however, a need for further work with the organization, particularly in the area of implementation.

2.2 The success of much of what is recommended here rests firmly on the appointment of a new senior member of the management team who will have explicit responsibility for marketing activities.

3.0 A marketing orientation

3.1 Penton Ltd has become overly reliant upon a small number of established but ageing products. For the change that is required to take place, there is need for the development of a far stronger marketing orientation which will give greater explicit recognition both to the needs of the customer and to the ways in which, within a changing market, the company might gain – and retain – a significant competitive advantage. This will require a major change in corporate culture. This can best be achieved by:

- The appointment of a marketing specialist at a senior level with the responsibility for the development of a more proactive stance.
- A refocusing of the business.
- A programme of internal marketing so that staff are fully aware of the new direction for the organization and the contributions that they will be expected to make.
- An audit of current activities.
- Market and product development.
- A programme of promotion including public relations and advertising.

3.2 Any change of culture in these circumstances will only be achieved by a 'top-down' approach, with members of the board demonstrating their explicit commitment to customer satisfaction. The marketing and sales departments, led by the new marketing direction, must therefore become the basis from which the organization moves ahead.

3.3 An important part of this will be an understanding of customer and distributors' needs. There will therefore be a need for a programme of market research in order to identify:

- Levels of customer satisfaction.
- Areas of market opportunity.
- Distributors' expectations.
- Competitors' probable moves.

3.4 A degree of refocusing will be needed so that Penton's positioning becomes more meaningful and explicit. The decision on positioning can, however, only be taken following the programme of research referred to in 3.3 above. The refocusing will be designed to achieve several objectives, but most importantly will help to clarify the company's offer.

3.5 A programme of internal marketing will then be needed in order to ensure that staff are made and kept aware of the new direction, the reasons for this, the nature of their expected contribution, and the levels of success being achieved.

3.6 An audit of the current methods of operation underpins all of what has been suggested so far. This will be designed to improve levels of effectiveness and efficiency.

3.7 A programme of market and product development is needed which will reflect changing market needs and corporate capability. Assuming this is conducted effectively, the organization will more effectively be able to develop and sustain a meaningful competitive advantage.

3.8 There will be the need for a programme of advertising and public relations in order to increase levels of market awareness and to support the launch of new products.

3.9 Underpinning all of this should be the development of a mission statement which encapsulates the changed values of the organization (see also Section 4.2).

4.0 A stronger and more proactive planning culture

4.1 The management philosophy has traditionally been reactive. The development of better plans and a stronger and more proactive planning culture will be designed to ensure that:

- Opportunities are more readily identified and capitalized upon.
- Threats will be perceived more readily and action taken to minimize their impact.
- Lead times are reduced.

- Levels of effectiveness generally are increased.
- Levels of accountability are increased.

4.2 This planning process should begin with the development of a mission statement which incorporates the changed values of the business. This will, in turn, require a series of decisions on the direction that the business is to take and the market position to be adopted.

4.3 Other areas in need of clarification are the primary and secondary corporate and functional objectives that are to be pursued.

4.4 A full environmental analysis is required.

4.5 An internal audit designed to identify the true level of corporate capability should be conducted as a matter of some urgency.

4.6 Decisions are required on a variety of areas including:

- The competitive stance to be adopted.
- The product development programme.
- Pricing postures.
- Distribution issues.

4.7 Following on from 4.6, it is essential that work begins shortly on the first drafts of the plans for all key areas, with this being led by members of the board after decisions have been made on the corporate objectives.

4.8 A programme of monitoring and feedback should be instigated with responsibility for co-ordination and ensuring that corrective action is taken being the specific responsibility of main board members.

4.9 Levels of accountability throughout the organization need to be increased.

4.10 Given changes in all of these areas, the development of a more effective and proactive planning culture should begin to emerge. It does, however, need to be emphasised that levels of commitment to planning are only likely to increase if the plans themselves prove to be realistic rather than broad and generally unrealistic statements of intent.

5.0 The new product development process

5.1 The planning process referred to in Section 4 must provide the rationale and direction of any changes to the new product development process. It is, however, apparent from our work so far that the R&D team currently lacks direction. It is therefore essential that the environmental analysis referred to in 4.4, and the clarification of objectives referred to in 4.3, are used as the basis of the development of the new product development strategy.

5.2 Further work is needed on the organization's true NPD capability so that a fuller assessment can be made of:

- What NPD activity might realistically be carried out in the short and long term.
- The particular problems being encountered currently in the process. This can then be set against the background of the findings of the environmental analysis and, in particular, the opportunities that are likely to emerge over the next few years.

5.3 Clarification is also required of the competitive stance that the company wishes to adopt in this area and in particular whether the company, at this stage at least, wishes to be proactive or instead intends to adopt a market follower's approach.

5.4 Given decisions in these areas, work can then be done in order to improve the various stages of new product development, including:

- Market evaluation.
- Prototype development.
- Business evaluation.

- Test marketing.

5.5 It is essential that responsibility for NPD rests firmly at board level and is seen as part of the remit of the new marketing director (see Section 3.2).

6.0 Summary

6.1 A series of changes have been recommended in this report. Deliberately we have not put costings next to them, since these will be the focus of subsequent work. However, for our suggestions to be worthwhile, it is essential that levels of accountability are increased and stronger direction is given from the top.

Question 2
What are the implications of your suggestions for approaches to management control?

The implications for management control of our recommendations are significant and can be seen in terms of the need for changes both in attitude and operating practice.

With regard to attitudes, the key issue is the need for management to recognize that previous approaches to planning and control have been unsatisfactory and that this is due largely to failings in areas such as:

- The setting of objectives.
- The implementation of plans.
- Feedback and follow-up mechanisms.

The attitudinal change required is therefore concerned with recognition of the current inadequacies and a willingness to adopt a more structured and demanding approach to management. Included within this is the willingness to accept the discipline of regular and detailed market analysis and the establishment and implementation of more firmly structured plans throughout the business.

This attitudinal shift can be seen to overlap with the second dimension referred to above, that of changes in operating practice. If the recommendations made in the report that forms the answer to Question 1 are to be implemented, there is therefore the need for a fully integrated planning and control process since the control dimension is meaningless if the planning dimension has not been properly developed. Thus, as we observed above, there is a need for the following:

- A clear statement of objectives.
- A clear statement of the competitive stance.
- A firm positioning statement with an attendant clarification of the target markets.
- An unambiguous and realistic plan which covers both the corporate and the departmental activities.
- A firm allocation of responsibilities and structured delegation.
- A clarification of timescales.
- A programme of staff training.
- An improvement in communication patterns.
- A more collaborative ethos.

Underlying all of this is a far more definitive statement of accountability.

The specifics of the control process follow logically from this and centre around the establishment of intermediate objectives and the development of feedback and control mechanisms. In this way performances can be compared with targets and, where appropriate, corrective action taken.

Against this background, it can be seen that in many ways the implications of our earlier suggestions for the control process are relatively straightforward and can best be summarized in terms of far stronger process of monitoring, feedback, accountability and corrective action. With regard to specific activities, these include:

- Regular customer surveys.

- Trade surveys.
- Competitive monitoring.
- Performance monitoring of both financial and marketing measures.
- Performance against plan.

Although this case study led to some very good answers, far too many candidates produced answers that were unrealistic in that they assumed:

- Unlimited financial resources would be available.
- That management behaviour and customers' perceptions can be changed over night.

The other mistake made involved failing to come to terms with the underlying issue of managerial weakness and adopting what we can call a 'knee jerk' response to the eleven points raised in the consultant's report. In other words, if prices are perceived to be above industry norms, cut them. Only rarely is the answer so simple and instead you need to recognize that the issue of price is a manifestation of a more fundamental problem. Think therefore about whether a solution can realistically be arrived at with the existing management team.

New Directions plc: issues to think about

Question 1

Prepare a SWOT analysis of the organization both for the period before the takeover and for the period reached at the end of the case study. Having done this, discuss the implications of ONE of your analyses for methods of marketing planning and control.

SWOT analysis underpins a great deal of thinking on marketing planning. This case study provides you with an opportunity to construct two SWOTs and discuss the implications of one of them for the planning and control process.

The two questions that you have to answer have a 30/20 mark split. Allowing for 10 minutes of reading time, this means that you have about 50 minutes for the first question and 30 for the second.

The SWOT analyses are relatively straightforward and we have therefore mapped these out on page 213. We have not, however, identified the key features and so you might begin by comparing your SWOT with those on page 213 and then highlighting the points that you feel are the most significant. Having done this, turn to the very significant issue of the implications of one of the SWOTs for planning and control. Probably the best one to use is for Period 2 in which major changes have taken place. Think about the sorts of constraints that the new managerial climate would produce and how this would influence how the organization operates.

Against this background, turn to the second question and map out your recommendations for change.

Do you really feel that the organization has a future under the new MD? If so, what is it likely to be? If not, what are the implications for your recommendations?

Period One *Strengths* • Oakley's entrepreneurial style • A decade of growth • Size (400 stores) • A young, high-performing team • A major player in high-growth markets • The firm's reputation in the City • Employee loyalty and motivation • A proactive managerial culture • High levels of performance *Opportunities* • Scope for further growth both geographically and in emerging market sectors	*Weaknesses* • 20 years of slow and unspectacular growth before Oakley's appointment. In certain circumstances Oakley's style might be a disadvantage • A possible lack of managerial experience? *Threats* • General competitive threats • An attractive target for a takeover?
Period Two *Strengths* • The parent company's financial resources and performance *Opportunities* • Oakley's perception of the scope for improving quality and shifting the demographic focus • The development of a new chain • Store redesign Repositioning New overseas markets Customers' expectations for new shopping experiences	*Weaknesses* • Scope for conflict between Oakley's management approach and that of the new parent • The risk aversive approach of the parent in a fast moving and growing market • Greater bureaucracy • Managerial frustration • Oakley's resignation • Loss of direction • The emergence of a new and seemingly desperate strategy • Reduced turnover • Firefighting (slashing of overheads) • Increasingly demoralized staff • Confused image • Loss of confidence • The loss of staff to competitors *Threats* • A reduced ability to capitalize upon short-term opportunities • Demographic changes and the decline of existing markets • A reputation for price rather than quality when research shows that quality is becoming more important • A stagnating UK market • The competitors' recruitment of New Direction's staff after Oakley's resignation • Competitive inroads (share slipping) • Loss of market leadership

Anderson Marine Construction: a suggested solution

This is a case study of an interesting organization which, because of a series of fundamental environmental disruptions is now faced with the need to make a series of major strategic changes. The decision on which way to go has already been made by the company's owner and the marketing consultant, and the issue that candidates therefore need to address is concerned with the structure of the marketing plan.

Question 1

An outline of a marketing plan covering the launch and subsequent market development of AMC's new range of boats.

The reader should recognize that this is an *outline* of the marketing plan for a new range of boats and, as such, identifies a series of issues without necessarily addressing each in depth. The final and detailed plan can only be produced after further research has been conducted; the areas in which this research is required are referred to in the appendix on page 217.

Structure of the plan

1 Background.
2 Situational analysis.
3 Strategic imperatives.
4 Principal assumptions underlying the plan.
5 Preliminary marketing objectives.
6 The target market.
7 Positioning statement.
8 The marketing mix.
9 Implementation and control.
10 Budgets.
Appendix: areas for further research

1 Background

The recent report submitted by the marketing consultant has highlighted the gravity of our current position and the need to adopt a proactive stance by developing a new range of boats which will broaden our trading base and reduce our vulnerability to the downturn in the custom-built and high price sector of the boat market. With the board having accepted this recommendation, this plan outlines the steps that must be taken to ensure the new range is developed and launched in time for the forthcoming selling season.

2 Situational analysis: a review of the business environment and the company's internal operations.

2.1 The business environment

Market demand for medium-sized, high-performance, power boats and yachts is currently depressed, with sales having dropped steadily over the last four years. Despite a series of price cuts, demand for our products has not risen and this, plus other evidence, suggests that the market is not price sensitive. Instead levels of demand are determined by more fundamental factors such as levels of confidence in the economy. Economic and industry forecasts indicate few signs of an upturn in demand in the premium priced sector of the market over the next two years. Anecdotal evidence and casual observation suggests that our competitors are similarly affected.

By contrast, demand for lower-priced boats appears currently to be rather more buoyant, with forecasts indicating that sales patterns in this area over the next few years are likely to be relatively stable. A larger number of firms operate in this part of the market and a greater emphasis upon prices and costs is inevitable. Preliminary evidence does suggest, however, that with careful positioning, scope exists for AMC to establish itself in this part of the market. (**Note:** these points are summarized as a series of opportunities and threats in the SWOT analysis.)

2.2 Strengths and weaknesses

2.2.1 Strengths

- Well-established manufacturer of high-quality and high-performance yachts and power boats.
- Loyal and knowledgeable customer base.
- Financially successful.
- Skilled workforce with a strong craft orientation.
- Reputation for quality and performance.

2.2.2 Weaknesses

- Reactive selling approach.
- Absence of a proactive marketing culture.
- Recent reductions in margins.
- Absence of a formal distribution network.
- No previous presence or experience in the lower-priced and higher-volume sectors of the boat market.
- Little experience of advertising and promotion.
- Workforce with a strong craft orientation and little experience in volume production.
- Seemingly little emphasis upon cost control and working to a particular price.
- Delivery schedules.

2.2.3 Preliminary assessment of strengths and weaknesses

Although the company undoubtedly possesses a series of strengths, questions must be raised about the management's ability to capitalize upon these in the short term on entering the higher volume sector of the market. It is therefore essential that attention be paid to the issues of managerial expertize and culture, so that gaps might be filled and a more proactive approach developed. Equally, the workforce has a tradition of producing high-quality products but little real experience of volume production in which a strong adherence to cost control is fundamental.

2.3 Opportunities and threats

2.3.1 Opportunities

- Market and sales growth.
- A reduction in the organization's exposure to one sector of the market.
- Scope to capitalize upon the firm's reputation for quality and performance.

2.3.2 Threats

- A greater number of competitors.
- The difficult of establishing a worthwhile market position.
- Possible problems in establishing a firm presence within the distribution network.

2.3.3 Preliminary assessment of the opportunities and threats

Our ability to capitalize upon the opportunities which undoubtedly exist in the higher volume sector of the market will depend to a very large extent upon our ability to move along the learning curve. The threats identified, whilst significant, are very largely predictable. Again our ability to cope with these will depend upon *how* we move into the market and our ability to establish a distinct presence in the short term.

3 Strategic imperatives arising from the SWOT analysis

Given the nature of the findings of the SWOT, it is essential that we address several issues in the immediate future. These include:

- The skills gap in the workforce.
- The absence of proactive marketing skills within the firm's management.
- The development of an appropriate distribution network.
- The development of a communications programme.
- The financial implications of the proposal.

4 Principal assumptions underlying the plan

A number of assumptions underpin this plan, the most significant of which are:

- Demand for the current range will remain depressed.
- AMC will be able to establish itself profitably in the new target sector.

- Sales within this sector will continue to improve over the next 12–18 months.

5 Preliminary marketing objectives

- To capitalize upon AMC's current very strong reputation by developing a new range of smaller and lower price boats offering higher performance levels than the competition.
- To position the new range as *the affordable high quality small yacht and power boat range.*
- To achieve distribution coverage of x per cent (note that this figure can only be finalized in the light of further research).
- To achieve sales in year one of _____*, in year two of _____*, and in year three of _____*, These will translate into the following market share figures:

  Year one _____.
  Year two _____.
  Year three _____.

  * Again these figures can only be determined in the light of further research.

6 The target market

A considerable amount of research is still needed to clarify the size and detail of the buying patterns of the target market (see Appendix, page 217) and at this stage it is therefore possible only to provide a broad picture of the market. In essence, however, the range is designed to appeal to sailing enthusiasts who have several years of experience and who now wish to buy a boat which offers greater performance, albeit within a relatively restricted budget.

Given this, and as the consultant's report has highlighted, the market will require:

- A greater degree of active selling by the distribution network.
- Delivery from distributor's stocks.
- Exposure to an advertising campaign to raise levels of awareness and interest.

7 Positioning statement

The new range will be positioned as *'the affordable high quality alternative'* in the mid-priced sector of the market. In achieving this position, full emphasis will be placed upon the broad values and heritage of our traditional range. The selling propositions will reflect both the performance of and linkages with our current range.

8 The marketing mix

- The product range will consist of small high performance yachts and boats that reflect a high value for money offer.
- Initial distribution will be through a carefully selected number of existing boatyards throughout the south, south east and south west of England. In the light of our experiences in the first year, consideration will be given to broadening this network in years two and three. Distributors will be selected on the basis of their:
  - Current image.
  - Ability to provide sales and technical support.
  - Current sales levels.
  - Geographic location.
  - Existing franchises.

Emphasis will be placed upon the development of long-term relationships with distributors, with this being reflected in the high levels of marketing support provided by AMC and the margins offered.

- Prices will be set at the upper end of the sector in order to reflect the brand values associated with AMC, the quality of the product and the product's performance.
- Advertising and promotion will give prominence to the links with the existing range and will concentrate initially upon creating high levels of awareness and interest amongst the trade, the media and the target customer groups.

9 Implementation and control

Responsibility for refining and subsequently implementing this plan will rest with the marketing manager, reporting in to the main board. Given the significance of the proposed development, it is essential that the necessary level of resources and commitment are allocated to the project. Control will be achieved through monthly and quarterly reports with a series of measures of performance against target.

10 Budgets

These will be set in the light of the findings of further research. At this stage, however, it is possible to indicate several areas of major expenditure including:

- Modifications to the production facilities.
- The recruitment and/or retraining of the workforce needed to produce the new range.
- The development of an appropriate distribution network, including funding of stock levels.
- The funding of the principal dimensions of the marketing plan, including the advertising and research that will be needed.

Appendix

Areas for further research

In order to prepare a detailed marketing plan, a substantial amount of additional information is needed. Included within this is information on:

- Accurate and detailed sales forecasts for the short and medium term.
- The financial implications of the proposed action.
- Competitors: who are they, their size, location, patterns of ownership, resource availability, model ranges, strengths and weaknesses, selling propositions, positioning strategies, levels of advertising, pricing strategies, and patterns of distribution.
- Customers: probable size of each market sector, geographic location, buying motives, sailing skills, approaches to buying and expectations regarding sales support, price sensitivity and readership profiles.
- Distribution: major patterns of distribution network in existence currently, locations, distributors' selling skills, levels of sales support needed, and expectations regarding levels of inventory, terms of payment, margins and advertising support needed
- Trade shows: their relative importance, location, costs of appearance, visitor patterns and levels of media coverage.
- Media availability, areas of specific interest and copy dates.

Question 2

In the light of AMC's previous approaches to selling, what, if any, problems might you expect to encounter in implementing the marketing plan? In what ways might these problems be overcome or minimized?

Given the nature of the business in the past and in particular the relatively informal approaches to marketing that have predominated, I would anticipate a series of problems in implementing a plan which not only targets a new and very different set of customers from those served previously, but which also reflects an infinitely more proactive stance. For convenience, these problems can be categorized on the basis of whether they are essentially internal or external to the organization. Those that are internal are concerned primarily with issues of culture, expertise and resource allocation, whilst those that are external are largely concerned with areas such as customer perception, the nature of the distribution network and the responses of those companies with which AMC will now find itself competing.

Beginning with the internal problems, the most immediate of these is likely to be the question of how best to develop a culture which is more suited to dealing with a higher volume and less specialized market than the one that AMC has previously been concerned with. Because AMC will still be producing boats for its traditional market and can not afford to compromise its methods of operating within this sector, it may well prove to be appropriate to split the organization in such a way that scope exists for a clear focus upon each of the two sectors. Assuming this is done, there will then be a need to begin the process of developing a managerial culture that gives full recognition to the rather different long-term development of the business. It would appear that the current workforce is heavily specialized and, assuming this to be the case, a degree of retraining and/or recruitment will be needed in order to ensure that the firm has the production skills needed for the new range.

At the same time, a rather different set of selling and marketing skills will be needed in order to develop the new product, launch it onto the market and subsequently ensure its success. A question therefore needs to be raised about the ability of the current management team to do this. Where gaps exist, and from a distance it seems most likely that this will be in the market and sales development areas, expertise will of necessity have to be recruited.

Other internal problems that are likely to be encountered include:

- Whether AMC will have sufficient production capacity and flexibility.
- Identifying new suppliers and hence implementing a rather different purchasing policy from that of the past.
- Controlling costs rather more tightly. Given the nature of the comments in the case, it appears that price has not previously been a significant issue. Because of this, it seems likely that elements of tight cost control will not have been important. The new product and market will, however, demand a different approach if the venture is to prove profitable.
- The development and cultivation of new and possibly tighter controls, including those upon the sales and distribution networks.
- The establishment of a more proactive approach to selling, including the development of an internal and external sales team, the advertising campaign and the appearance at selected boat shows.
- A decision on the positioning strategy that is to underpin the market effort.

The probable external problems will stem very largely from coming to terms with the very different market which the company will be dealing with and in particular the characteristics of the new customer base and competitors. Without doubt, one of the most significant issues will be concerned with the company's image, since AMC cannot afford to compromise this in the eyes of its traditional customers, but needs to capitalize upon it for its new market.

In order to overcome these problems, a number of distinct changes will be needed, the most significant and immediate of which involves overcoming the lack of marketing expertise. Perhaps the easiest and fastest way of doing this involves recruiting one or more marketing specialists to support the new marketing manager. Together, these will have the responsibility for:

- Market development.
- The identification and development of an appropriate distribution network.
- The further development and implementation of the marketing plan.
- The recruitment and management of a sales team.

Other areas for action and change include:

- A formal assessment of production capability.
- The development of a modified purchasing policy.
- Instituting a more rigorous climate of cost control.
- Retraining of the appropriate staff.

It is obvious from this that a considerable amount of change is needed if the organization is to capitalize upon the opportunities that seemingly exist. However, without the active support of Tom Anderson and other members of the board, few changes in culture and direction will be achieved, and the effort will have little real payoff.

This case required candidates to prepare an outline of the marketing plan. In the event too many candidates demonstrated that they have little real understanding of what a marketing plan looks like. You should therefore make sure you are familiar with the plan's structure and where the information that the plan needs might come from.

The second question focused upon an issue that has cropped up on several occasions previously: how might you most effectively change the culture of an organization? We commented at an earlier stage that many candidates underestimate the difficulties of changing managerial cultures and well-established methods of operating and you should therefore give detailed thought to the various ways in which this might be achieved. In doing this, you might usefully refer back to pages 169–77 of Unit 8 in which we discussed both the barriers to implementation and the sorts of factors that encourage it.

Kanko Ltd: a suggested solution

This was the first of the mini cases to include a number of tables. You should therefore spend time looking at these tables, and indeed those in the subsequent cases, identifying the messages that they are designed to communicate.

It is very apparent from the case that the company has lost touch with its rapidly changing market. The changes that are needed both to the marketing mix and how the organization operates are therefore significant. The questions put candidates in the position of being a member of the new management team that is faced with the need to evaluate the current offer and decide how to move forward.

What significance do you feel that being part of a larger organization (what the case study refers to as being 'a wholly owned subsidiary of a highly diversified listed public company') might have?

Question 1

As a member of the new management team, you have been given the responsibility for recommending how the product and distribution strategies should develop. Prepare a report detailing the criteria by which the current product range and sales and distribution networks should be evaluated and possibly rationalized.

1.0 Management summary

This report highlights the company's current position and the rationale for a detailed review of the product range and sales and distribution networks. It identifies a wide range of criteria that can be used in the evaluation process and, against this background, explains the basis for possible rationalization of the organization's approach to the market.

2.0 The current position

The initial review of the sales and marketing functions, together with the other information and data available to us, has highlighted a variety of issues that need to be addressed. These include:

- The breadth and depth of the current product range.

- The appropriateness of existing patterns of distribution (refer to Tables 9.1 and 9.3 in the information that was supplied on the company).
- The significance and probable causes of sales and profit decline over the past few years (refer to Table 2 in the information supplied).
- The approaches to new product development.
- Levels of product quality and service support.
- Levels of sales force performance.
- Approaches to advertising and promotion.
- The failure of the advertising agency to capitalize upon our potential brand strengths.

3.0 The criteria for evaluating the product range

Given the nature and magnitude of the problems faced by the organization, it is essential that a full and detailed review of the product range be carried out as a matter of urgency. In doing this attention needs to be paid both to individual products within the range and to the range as a whole. In this way, we will gain a clearer understanding both of the potential of the individual components and of the degree of cohesion across the range. Having done this, we will then be in a far better position to recommend how the range might possibly be rationalized.

3.1 The criteria for the evaluation of individual products

A wide variety of criteria should be used to evaluate individual products within the range, the most important of which are as follows:

(a) The current level of sales by sector, area and region as well as nationally via each form of distribution network.
(b) The current levels of profit or loss and breakeven points.
(c) The levels of gross and net contribution.
(d) The scope that exists for product/market development and the costs associated with this.
(e) The length of time for which each product has been on the market, its apparent position on the product life cycle and the scope, if any, for extending the life cycle.
(f) The levels and costs of sales, service and after sales support needed.
(g) The strengths of any selling propositions and the scope that exists for their further development.
(h) End users, and distributors' perceptions of the product.
(i) The manufacturing, product handling and distribution costs.
(j) The levels of advertising support needed.
(k) The product's comparative competitive position.
(l) The product's position within the product portfolio (refer also to the later comments on the Boston Consulting Group's product portfolio matrix).
(m) The scope that exists for cost reduction.
(n) The product's price sensitivity.
(o) Whether scope exists for increasing the value added component within the product and hence any opportunities for price increases.
(p) Any competitive disadvantages that the product might have, the scope that exists for overcoming these and the costs that would be incurred in doing this.
(q) The level, nature and significance of complaints.
(r) Forecasts of future sales.
(s) Where appropriate, market share and/or position in the market.
(t) The attractiveness of each market served.
(u) Warehousing needed.

3.2 The criteria for the evaluation of the product range

Having evaluated each of the products within the range, we need then to evaluate the range in its entirety. The criteria that should be used for this include many of the points referred to above, although in addition should include:

- The degree of sales and cost interdependencies across the range.
- Issues of synergy.
- The nature of the product portfolio when plotted using a matrix such as that suggested by the Boston Consulting Group.
- Levels of market attractiveness.

3.3 The criteria for the evaluation of the sales and distribution networks

It is apparent from the information made available, and in particular Tables 9.1 and 9.3, that a number of the problems being experienced by the company stem from the ways in which the patterns of distribution that are being used are increasingly at odds with distribution trends within the market. Analysis of Tables 9.1 and 9.3 highlights both the degree of divergence that exists currently and the extent to which this mismatch will increase over the next few years. Given this, the detailed evaluation of the distribution and sales networks should make reference to the following criteria:

Distribution

- Distribution trends. Table 9.3 illustrates the growing strength of the DIY stores and the (continuing) decline of ironmongers and builders' merchants. These trends can be contrasted with the information contained in Table 9.1 which highlights Kanko's traditional presence in and commitment to builders' merchants. Although sales via DIY stores doubled in the period 1987–93, this compares with a 450 per cent increase of industry sales through DIY outlets and a decline of approximately 30 per cent through builders' merchants.
- The costs of distribution via each type of outlet. This should include issues of:
    - Order size.
    - Levels of sales, service and after-sales service support that is required.
- The importance of Kanko's individual products and full product range to each distribution outlet.
- The degree of commitment to Kanko that exists currently and the scope that exists for its development.
- The level of support and exposure that each distributor is willing to give to part or the whole of the range.
- The margins obtained within each type of outlet.
- Distributors' expectations.

Sales

- The costs of the sales force.
- Levels of sales force efficiencies.
- The degree of overlap between territories and/or responsibilities.
- Levels of sales force capability and the scope that exists for their development.

4.0 The application of these criteria

This report has so far identified a considerable number of the criteria that might be used to evaluate the product range and sales and distribution networks. However, although each criterion is undoubtedly of value, they need to be placed within the context of a framework which will allow for any rationalization that is needed to take place. The key dimension of this framework can be seen in terms of the sort of organization that it is intended that Kanko should become and should therefore include:

- The nature of the corporate objectives that are to be pursued.
- The competitive stance which it is felt that Kanko should attain and is capable of retaining.
- Levels of financial availability.

In deciding upon these, reference must also of course be made to competitors' stances. It is against this background that the shape of the future organization can then be decided.

Given this, decision on rationalization can then begin to be made, but should be based upon a clear understanding both of customer needs and distribution trends. It is a knowledge of these that will then provide a platform for a far greater degree of organizational focus and clarification of purpose. Thus in the case of the sales force, scope might well exist for rationalization by the development of key account managers to service the major DIY outlets.

Question 2

Make recommendations on the appointment of the new advertising agency. Prepare a short briefing paper identifying the criteria by which agencies pitching for the account should be shortlisted.

Background

Having operated with the same advertising agency for several years, the decision to fire the agency and appoint a replacement has been made. The basis for dispensing with the services of the old agency was primarily the uninspiring and tired sales literature and advertising that they were producing and hence the failure of the organization to capitalize upon the potential strength of its products and brand name. In appointing a new agency it is therefore essential that we develop a relationship with an organization that is capable of developing a promotional strategy that will contribute firmly to the overall marketing campaign and reflect a far higher degree of creativity. In this way, we are likely to restore some of the brand values that have been eroded over the past ten years.

The shortlisting criteria

Although a wide variety of criteria might be used in shortlisting potential candidates, arguably the most significant are:

- The *type* of agency that we require and the breadth of service needed. The alternatives open to us range from a full-service agency that is capable of handling all aspects of any promotional campaign, through to creative hot-shops which will concentrate upon the development of any creative appeal leaving us to organize, either directly or indirectly, other elements of the promotional task such as media buying. Given the size of our organization, it is recommended that we opt for a full-service agency, since this will allow us to concentrate upon more pressing issues.
- The agency's size and the relative importance of our account.
- Their current and past client portfolio, since this will give us an understanding not just of the breadth of their client range, but also the types of promotional work that they have undertaken.
- Their understanding of the marketing problems that we face and their views of the ways in which a new promotional campaign might possibly contribute to their resolution.
- Their apparent levels of creativity. These can be assessed, in part at least, by reference to previous campaigns.
- Their reputation.
- The nature of their pitch and the extent to which it appears to reflect an understanding of the organization and its market.
- The costs that are likely to be incurred.

An additional and possibly very important factor which should be taken into account is *the degree of empathy* which exists between the agency and Kanko, since it is essential that we develop a fruitful and profitable relationship. Other factors to which consideration might possibly be given include any areas of specialist expertise and their financial stability.

However, in doing this, we need to be very clear about the role that we expect advertising and promotion to play, the marketing and promotional objectives that will be pursued, and the levels of spend that we are willing to make.

Marketing strategists are often faced with the need to rethink their strategies, tactics and methods of implementation. This case study proved to be a useful vehicle for getting candidates to identify the sorts of criteria by which the product range and sales and distribution networks might be evaluated and possibly rationalized. Many candidates handled this well, but too many focused just upon marketing criteria rather than a series of marketing, financial, production and general organizational criteria.

Question 2 focuses upon the criteria for shortlisting potential advertising agencies. Recognize, however, that similar criteria might also be used for appointing, say, a new market research agency.

Watergate Pumps Ltd: a suggested solution

This case focuses upon an organization which, in common with others such as kanko, Anderson Marine Construction and Penton, has lost touch with its market. It has been decided therefore to develop an environmental monitoring system so that the management team might gain a greater – and ongoing – understanding of the marketplace. Candidates were put into the position of having to suggest how such a system might be structured and implemented.

What pictures emerge from the tables and figures? What is their significance?

Question 1

As the company's newly appointed market analyst, you are required to prepare a detailed report for the marketing director recommending how an effective external environmental monitoring system for the company might best be developed and implemented. Included within the report should be your suggestions of the structure of the system, the expected inputs and outputs, the probable organizational and resource implications, and the nature of any benefits that should emerge.   (30 marks)

A report recommending the development and implementation of an environmental monitoring system for Watergate Pumps Ltd.

1   Management summary

This report makes a series of recommendations concerning how an effective environmental monitoring system might be developed and implemented with Watergate Pumps. It makes reference to:

- The structure of system.
- The expected inputs and outputs.
- The probable organizational and resource implications.
- The nature of the system's likely benefits.

It does not include a costing of the system.

2   Introduction and background

It is apparent from the information provided that Watergate Pumps currently has an insufficiently detailed understanding of its external environment. The implications of this have been highlighted by the way in which the company has been taken by surprise by a series of market developments (for the detail of these, refer to page 195–6 of the information supplied and the series of bullet points) and by the subsequent decline in our market share (see Table 9.4). In addition, we have a heavy presence in the declining local authority market and a weak market position in the three other sectors of the market (see Table 9.5). Additional evidence of our poor understanding of the market is reflected in Table 9.6 (the buying motives of the different customer groups) and our failure to reposition between 1990 and 1993.

3   The purpose and benefits of the system

The proposed system will be designed to provide the management team with a clear and ongoing picture of the market. It will focus upon a number of areas, including:

- Competitors' strengths, weaknesses, resources, strategies and performance levels.
- Customers (existing and potential) and their current and developing demands.
- The general trading environment.

The benefits of the system should be seen in terms of a far clearer understanding of the market and, in particular, of customers and competitors. This should in turn lead to the development of far clearer, more focused and appropriate strategic and tactical behaviour. Given this, it should then be far less likely that the organization will be taken by surprise by developments within the market (see, for example, our failure to anticipate the entry of Pump Suppliers in 1991, the launch of new and modified products by BG International and Northern Pumps, the general competitive repositioning, and so on). In addition, the system should provide a basis for a more proactive approach and a general strengthening of our competitive position.

4   The structure of the system

It is proposed that the system consists of four principal dimensions:

- Internal records.
- Marketing research.
- Marketing intelligence.
- Marketing decision support analysis.

The relationship between these areas and the overall structure of the system are illustrated in Figure 9.10 on the next page.

To ensure that the system is of the greatest value to the organization, it will be based very firmly on an analysis of managers' information needs. It is therefore recommended that we begin by examining in detail:

- Information needs.
- Information gaps.
- The ways in which information generated by the system might best be used.

It is essential, therefore, that in developing the system we ensure that we satisfy a number of conditions, including:

- The system must be user friendly.
- It must be manageable.
- It must provide the information that is needed for effective marketing decision making.
- It must avoid the problems of information overload.

Recognizing this, it is proposed that the system be developed and implemented over a predetermined time period. Given that the organization has not had such a system in place previously it is unrealistic to expect that the full system can be developed and introduced to the company in one move. It is therefore recommended that a timetable be established with the system being introduced over a 12 month period. As part of this, it is essential that the responsibility for the system is clearly allocated and that this is at a senior level in the organization. The progress of the system's development will also need to be monitored.

5   The expected inputs and outputs

Although brief reference has already been made to the inputs and outputs, they can be identified more specifically as being:

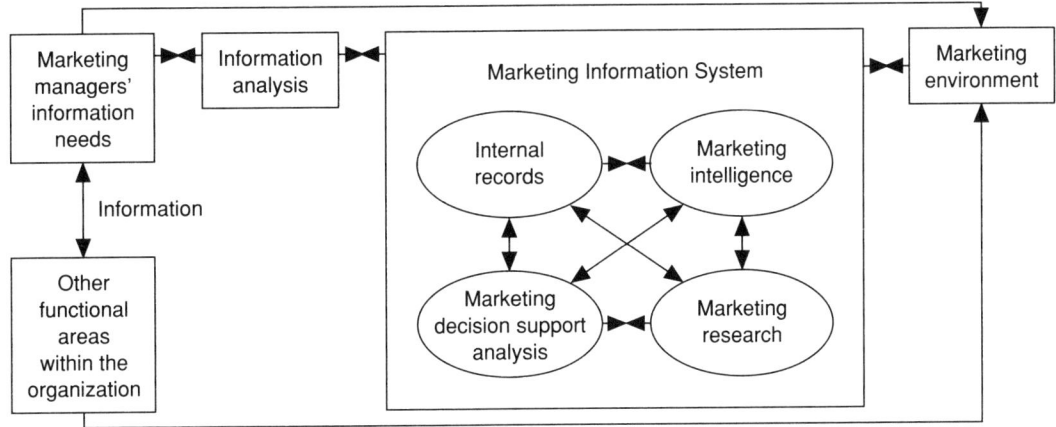

Figure 9.10 The marketing information system

Inputs

- Competitive information.
- Customer information.
- General market information.

These inputs will be obtained from a spectrum of sources including the trade press, the sales force, exhibitions, and distribution intermediaries. In order to collect this information, it is essential that staff are made aware of the nature of the information needed and how it will be used. It is recommended that, initially, a relatively unstructured approach is used (i.e. collect whatever information we can) and that this is gradually refined over time.

A fundamental part of the system is, of course, that of the analysis stage; again, it is imperative that the responsibility for analysis *and dissemination* is clearly allocated.

Outputs

The output from the system will take the form of a monthly report summarizing the key market developments and highlighting the apparent opportunities and threats. The monthly report will be supplemented by a weekly briefing paper.

It needs to be emphasized, however, that these reports need to form the basis for subsequent marketing action and again, the responsibility for this will rest at board level. The circulation list for the reports will therefore need to be carefully determined.

6.0 The organizational and resource implications

The costs of the system cannot be determined at this stage. However, it needs to be recognized that the costs of *not* developing such a system are already apparent. It is therefore essential that there is a full commitment to the system – and its use – at senior management level. In terms of the immediate resource implications, it is evident that, as the newly appointed marketing analyst, I will need to spend a considerable amount of my time over the next few months developing the system. However, perhaps the most significant organizational implication can be identified in terms of the need for a far more obvious, a stronger and much more consistent external focus on the part of management, with a commitment to use the outputs. Without this, the system is likely to be of little value. This can perhaps best be summarized in terms of the need for a new and much more market-oriented management culture.

7 The benefits of the system

These have been alluded to in Section 3, but are in essence related to the scope for a far more proactive stance. This should be reflected most obviously in terms of:

- Better market positioning.
- A clearer and more focused new product development process.
- Better pricing.

- Clearer market targeting.
- Higher levels of customer satisfaction.
- A far stronger competitive stance.

8 Summary

Within this report, I have highlighted the need for an environmental monitoring system and the form that such a system might take. It must be emphasized that the development of the system will take considerable time and effort but that the benefits will be considerable. The consequences of *not* developing the system are likely to be significant and reflected in a further worsening of market position.

Question 2

In the light of the information contained in the mini case, what recommendations for future marketing action would you make?   (20 marks)

It is apparent from the case study that the organization's market and competitive position has weakened considerably over the past few years. It is therefore essential that the current decline in market share is stopeed and that the organization begins targeting those parts of the market which offer significant growth opportunities (see Table 9.5, page 196 in the mini case). Other issues which need to be addressed include the following:

1 The price/perceived reliability relationship (see Figure 9.2).
2 The issues of availability and perceived ease of fitting (see Figure 9.3).
3 The significance of the different buying motives of each of the customer groups (see Table 9.6, page 196).
4 The failure to make full use of the company's manufacturing capacity (see Table 9.4, page 196).
5 The possibilities for exporting (see Table 9.4, page 196).
6 Product modification and new product development.
7 The quality of the products' control systems.

Underlying these points is the question of the competitive stance that the organization wishes to adopt over the next few years. It is evident from the information in the case that the three principal competitors have all given greater emphasis to the issues of price, perceived reliability, ease of fitting, and availability. Watergate's management needs to decide whether it will adopt a broadly similar stance or deliberately adopt a low-price posture in order to achieve a degree of differentiation. There is, however, a danger in this in that evidence from the market suggests that price is not an important factor in the growing market sectors (see Table 9.6, page 196).

It is therefore recommended that the company increases its price, but only against the background of a series of product modification/new product actions designed to:

- Improve reliability.
- Improve the ease of fitting.
- Improve the control systems.

Without these three supporting actions, the company's sales will inevitably suffer. However, taking action in these areas is unlikely to prove sufficient by itself, since the improvements will need to be communicated to the market. It is therefore recommended that a clearly focused advertising campaign be developed, with emphasis being given to these improvements. The target markets for the campaign will be the growing market sectors.

At the same time, attention needs to be paid to issues of availability (see Figure 9.3, page 197). The information supplied provides little information on the sales and distribution approach and it is therefore difficult to make firm recommendations. It is, however, essential that a stronger, more proactive and more firmly focused approach be adopted in order to reach buyers and the appropriate decision making units (DMUs).

Table 9.4 illustrates the extent to which competitors are operating in markets other than the UK and this, coupled with Watergate's failure to use its full manufacturing capacity, suggests that exporting might well be attractive. It is recommended, however, that the company views this as a medium to long-term development rather than something for the short term. The reason for this is that the firm has really consolidated its domestic market, it is likely to overstretch itself by moving overseas. Thought might therefore be given to how costs might be reduced and revenues increased by alternative usage of the excess capacity (one measure, of course, might be to sub-let this part of the premises).

The success of the recommendations made to so far will, of course, be heavily dependent upon a clear programme of implementation and a question that must therefore be asked concerns the quality of Watergate's management. Given that the current management team has been responsible for the organization's competitive decline over the past few years, reservations might possibly be expressed about issues of commitment and/or ability. However, without a far more proactive stance, it is unlikely that the recommendations made here will be implemented to the extent that is needed.

EXAM TIP

Question 1 was written in such a way that it provides a framework for the answer. It did this by stating that the report should make reference to the structure of the system, the expected inputs and outputs, the resource implication, and the nature of any benefits. Where these guidelines are provided, make full use of them. In the event, many candidates chose to ignore them.

RTJ Engineering Ltd: a suggested solution

The company operates with five strategic business units, three of which – nuclear, aerospace and defence – are in market sectors which, because of changed government and social thinking, are unlikely to grow at any real speed over the next few years. At the same time, three long-standing customers have been lost to competitors. The text of the case highlights several of the issues faced by the management team, but much of the information is in the form of the three figures.

QUESTION 9.3

What pictures emerge from the figures on pages 199–200? What is their significance?

Question I

1   The state of the firms portfolio

A variety of frameworks can be used to evaluate a firm's portfolio, including the following:

- The Boston Consulting Group's growth-share matrix.
- The General Electric multifactor portfolio model.
- The Shell Directional Policy Matrix.
- Abell and Hammond's 3×3 matrix.
- The Arthur D Little strategic condition matrix.

Given the information that appears in Figure 9.6 of the case study (see page 200), we will use what is in many ways the most straightforward and probably the best known of these, the Boston Consulting Group's growth-share matrix; the results are illustrated below.

It can be seen from this, that there is a degree of imbalance within the portfolio and that given how the various markets are moving, the organization is likely to find itself exposed and potentially vulnerable over the next few years. The justification for this comment is that:

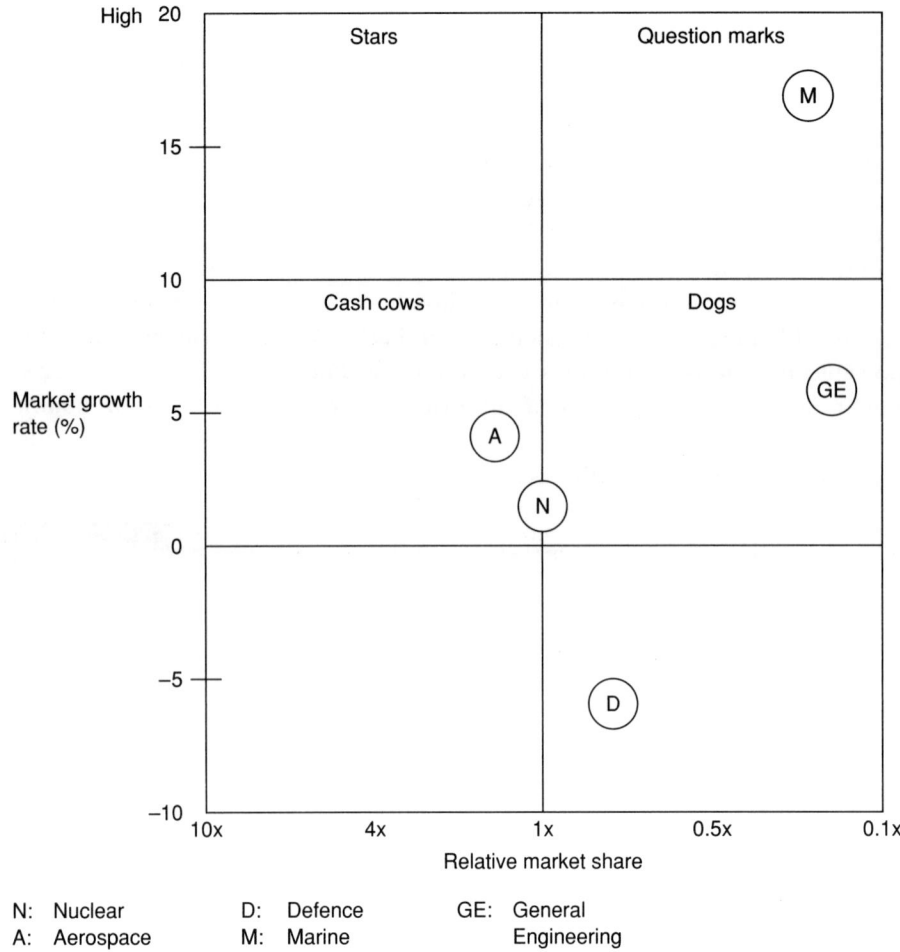

N: Nuclear   D: Defence   GE: General
A: Aerospace   M: Marine   Engineering

Figure 9.11 RTJ Engineering's product portfolio based on the BCG matrix

- Defence, which currently accounts for 20 per cent of RTJ's turnover, is forecast to decline at 6 per cent.
- The marine sector is growing at 15 per cent and it is therefore likely that large sums of cash will be needed to fund the continued growth of what is currently a Question Mark SBU.
- General engineering, which with 8 per cent has the second highest growth rate, is a small SBU (9 per cent of turnover) and is faced with a large number of competitors.
- Aerospace and Nuclear, both of which are cash cows (although perhaps less obviously in the case of Nuclear) currently have relatively low growth rates and given what is happening to these sectors of the economy may well find themselves faced with negative growth over the next few years.
- There is an absence of stars.

2   The assumptions made

It can be argued, however, that the picture that emerges from BCG analysis is relatively limited, since it focuses upon just two factors: the market growth rate and the relative competitive position. A number of writers in recent years (see, for example, Kotler, McDonald, Stacey and others) have argued that portfolio analysis (PA) of this type can be criticized both on general grounds (it provides a very limited snapshot and, in the case of BCG, uses two dimensions which arguably are not the most relevant for true analysis) and specific grounds (a far greater spectrum of factors need to be taken into account). The results should, it is therefore argued, be treated with a degree of caution.

In the case of BCG analysis, however, its advocates claim that the two variables used are capable of providing a valid basis for assessment, and it is this thinking, together with the limited information that is available, which underpins our choice of this particular model. Given more information on the market, we might have used other approaches to portfolio analysis, including the General Electric model which uses the rather broader ideas of *industry attractiveness* and *business strengths* as the basis for plotting SBU positions.

Industry attractiveness is arguably a more valuable dimension than market growth rate, since it encompasses market size, the growth rate, the degree of competition, the pace of technological change, the nature and extent of legislative and/or government constraints, historic profit margins, and so on. Equally, business strength is influenced by factors such as market share, product quality, the brand's reputation, the distribution network, production capacity, and production effectiveness.

Quite obviously, however, for the GE matrix to be used, we would need access to far more information than is in the case. Because of this, it needs to be emphasized that the picture of the portfolio that emerges from our BCG analysis is likely to have some value, but that this value is perhaps limited.

3 Additional information and the development of the portfolio

It follows from what has been said that, before making recommendations on how the portfolio should be developed, we would need far more information of the sort that is identified above. In addition, we would require:

- Forecasts of how each market sector is likely to develop.
- The patterns of ownership of competitive organizations.
- Their probable response patterns.

The other types of information that would be useful include:

- RTJ's resource capabilities under the headings of finance, marketing, management, and so on.
- Stakeholders expectations and attitudes to risk.
- Market information highlighting the patterns of opportunity and threat.

4 Other approaches to portfolio analysis (PA)

Reference has already been made to other models of portfolio analysis, although in each case, the information needs are greater than is the case for BCG.

In calculation, it is perhaps worth commenting that major reservations have been expressed recently about PA, since there is an implicit assumption that the environment of tomorrow will bear at least some relation to that of today. Stacey, amongst others, questions whether such an assumption can indeed be justified.

Question 2

Subject:	**The development and implementation of a customer care programme for RTJ Engineering**
Prepared by:	ABC Consultants
Circulation:	RTJ's main board
Date:	December 1994

1 Background

It is very apparent from the research that we have conducted that, whilst RTJ's design and manufacturing skills are highly regarded within the marketplace, the organization is perceived not to be sensitive to customers' needs and expectations; the details of these findings are summarized in Figures 9.4(a) and 9.4(b) of our report. It is for this reason that we recommend the development and implementation of a customer care programme.

2 The scope of this report

This report identifies the principal dimensions of a customer care programme and suggests how it should be implemented. Details of the costs are not included and will be the subject of a separate exercise.

3 The dimensions of the proposed programme

The research has highlighted several areas of concern, the most significant of which emerge from Figure 9.4(a) in the case and include the following:

- Sales expertise.
- The quality of the sales literature.
- The failure to adhere to promised delivery schedules.
- Price competitiveness.
- Unprompted technical support.
- The ways in which the sales staff and sales support functions are operating.

These areas of concern are reinforced by the comments that emerged from the programme of qualitative research that was conducted (see Figure 9.4(b)).

Given that the organization has a number of competitive advantages in its technical operations, it follows that if the 'soft' side of the operation can be strengthened, the competitive advantages enjoyed by the organization should increase substantially.

It is therefore proposed that a programme of research be conducted to identify in greater detail the specific needs and expectations of different customers and customer groups. With this information, the organization, will then be in a position to identify the specific service levels that should be established and how stronger relationships might be developed in order to foster the idea of lifetime customers.

It is apparent that the organization's handling of enquiries is currently weak and that these weaknesses are continued through the chain of manufacturing (see, for example, late delivery rates) and into the levels of after-sales service. A fundamental reorganization is therefore needed in order to overcome these problems, although underpinning all of these is the need for the following:

- Senior management commitment.
- A willingness to change existing work practices.
- A significant degree of training.

In doing this, we will be aiming to develop what is loosely referred to as a right-side-up organization or a customer-led rather than a product-led business.

Quite obviously, this will require a major change to the organizational culture which currently focuses upon manufacturing excellence rather than customer needs. In arguing for this, we are not suggesting that the levels of design and manufacturing excellence are compromised in any way, but that they are refocused so that customers' needs are met far more directly and immediately than is the case at present.

It needs to be emphasized, however, that change is needed throughout the organization and not just amongst, for example, the sales staff. RTJ is currently failing to perform adequately across a spectrum of areas, but appears to be taking refuge in the quality of its products and its design skills. If, however, a totally integrated programme is to be developed, it will involve staff throughout the organization working in a far more concerted and co-ordinated fashion.

4 Responsibilities

Such a programme will only work if there is total and sustained commitment from the main board. Without this, any subsequent moves are likely to be of little value. The programme must therefore be driven by a named main board direction (ideally the Managing Director) who, together with the other directors, will be held responsible for its success.

Further down the organization it is recommended that we introduce the idea of account managers who will have both the responsibility and authority for working closely with customers and RTJ. In effect, they will act as the interface between the two.

5 Training

It is evident that a full programme of training and development will be needed to heighten the levels of awareness and consequences of customer dissatisfaction. Of necessity, this training and development needs to be a top-down programme.

6   Performance targets

Against this background, a series of performance targets needs to be established. These will be both qualitative and quantitative in nature. It is also recommended that as part of the programme we include a variety of initiatives such as quality circles.

7   Summary

In the light of the research findings, it is apparent that the failure to work closely with customers is creating an increasing number of problems for the organization. In order to overcome this there is a pressing need to develop a practice customer care programme, led by the board, in which RTJ works far more closely with its customers in order to develop long-term and more productive relationships. It needs to be recognized, however, that the negative perceptions that exist can only be changed over what will probably be a lengthy time period and the effort must therefore be sustained. Without this, it is likely that the consequences will be significant.

> As with a number of the previous cases, think in detail about the significance of managerial cultures and the ways in which they might possibly be changed.

> The question of how best to evaluate the alternatives open to an organization is something that many marketing planners face on a regular basis. It is for this reason that a number of the examination papers over the past few years have included one or more questions that ask you to demonstrate your understanding of how this might be done (see, for example, Question 9, December 1994; Questions 1(a) and 2, June 1995; and Question 2, December 1995). In evaluating alternatives, think not just about the range of marketing criteria, but also about the financial, human resource, distribution and manufacturing criteria that need to be considered if a truly worthwhile decision is to be arrived at.
>
> Given that an important focus of this syllabus is marketing planning, it is essential that you understand the structure and components of the marketing plan.

Lazy Days Holiday: a suggested solution

The case focuses upon an organization which is suffering from a series of problems. Some of these are internal (generally limited levels of marketing ability and declining profitability), whilst others are external (changing markets, different customer expectations, and higher levels of competition). In reading the case, you should take note not just of the specific points that are made, but you should also try to identify the more fundamental and underlying causes of the problems.

> What picture emerges from Figure 9.7 in the case?

How confident are you that the existing management team will be able to solve the company's problems?

(a) An evaluation of the proposals for the strategic development of Lazy Days Holidays

1.0 Scope of the report

This report attempts to identify the principal criteria by which the three recommendations contained within the recent consultancy report dealing with the strategic development of Lazy Days should be evaluated. In identifying these criteria, we have deliberately adopted a broad rather than a narrow perspective, in that reference is made not just to the marketing criteria to which consideration should be given, but also to a series of financial and human resource issues.

2.0 The background to the recommendations

Given the nature of the consultant's report and the picture that emerges from points (a)–(I), it is apparent that the three recommendations cannot be looked at in isolation, but that a series of remedial actions are needed so that the organization's future marketing activity will be supported far more firmly. Perhaps the two most obvious examples of this are the consultant's observations that we currently have little detailed information on our customers and that there is little real evidence of customer loyalty (points (a) and (b) of the report respectively). Recognizing this, we need not only to evaluate the recommendations and decide upon the future direction of the business, but also develop a far more effective environmental monitoring system and a generally more proactive marketing stance. Without this, it is almost inevitable that the organization will fail to exploit the apparent potential of the new market opportunities. The consequences of this would be that we will be in a broadly similar position yet again in a few years' time.

3.0 The nature of the recommendations

The recommendations that have been made can perhaps best be categorized in terms of risk and the extent to which they move the organization away from its current product/market combination. Although it is apparent that there is little real future in the current markets, it needs to be acknowledged from the outset that different degrees of risk are associated with each of the recommendations. Ultimately, therefore, the degree of success that is achieved will be determined by managerial perceptions of this risk, together with the management team's ability to handle it effectively.

With this as the background, we can identify the principal criteria that should be taken into account as being:

Marketing criteria
- The size of each of the three markets identified.
- Their probable patterns of growth.
- The nature and intensity of competition.
- Possible patterns of competitive response to our entry.
- Competitors' positioning strategies.
- Competitors' performance levels to date.

- Current and potential buyers' buying motives.
- Levels of customer loyalty.
- Patterns of buying.
- The likelihood of new competitors emerging.
- The scope for developing meaningful – and sustainable – selling propositions.
- The ability to develop a sustainable market position.
- The market's perceptions of Lazy Days currently.
- The ability to reposition the organization.
- The opportunities for further market development.

Financial criteria
- Market entry costs.
- The levels of investment needed.
- Day-to-day operating costs.
- Profit margins.
- The probable costs of repositioning the organization.
- The financial strengths of each of the competitors.
- The implications of currency fluctuations.
- The level of financial resource available.

Human resource criteria
- Managerial abilities.
- The willingness to accept risk.
- Levels of expertise.
- The willingness and ability to adopt new managerial approaches and a more Pro-active management culture.

It should be apparent from this that a wide spectrum of factors needs to be taken into account. However, without this, any decision will inevitably be taken with too little understanding of the risk–return equation.

(b) An outline of the marketing plan for the launch of a new holiday destination

The reader should recognize that this is an *outline* of the marketing plan for a new range of holidays and, as such, identifies a series of issues without necessarily addressing each in depth. The final and detailed plan can only be produced after further research has been conducted; the areas in which this research is required are referred to in the appendix.

Structure of the plan

1 Background
2 Situational analysis
3 Strategic imperatives
4 Principal assumptions underlying the plan
5 Preliminary marketing objectives
6 The target market
7 Positioning statement
8 The marketing mix
9 Implementation and control
10 Budgets
Appendix   Areas for further research

1.0   The background to and focus of the marketing plan

The recent report submitted by the marketing consultant has highlighted the gravity of our current position and the consequent need to adopt a more proactive stance by repositioning our current offer and/or by launching one or more new holiday destinations. This plan focuses upon the third of the consultant's recommendations, that of the launch of a new range of holidays in Africa which would feature ballooning and safaris, and targeted firmly at young high-spending customers in social groups A and B. These will be sold direct to clients and not via travel agents.

2.0 Situational analysis: a review of the business environment and the company's internal operations

2.1 The business environment

Although the holiday market is generally buoyant, the market has changed in a variety of ways over the past few years. The principal changes that have taken place include:

- The emergence of new holiday destinations.
- An apparently greater willingness on the part of holidaymakers to venture further afield.
- Increased customer expectations.
- A greater degree of direct competition between the holiday companies.
- An increased emphasis upon price competition, particularly at the bottom end of the market.
- A growth in second holidays.
- A general increase in the marketing costs required for an organization to compete effectively.
- The beginnings of a shake-out within the industry, with the larger companies adopting an increasingly predatory approach.

2.2 Opportunities and threats

Taken together, these various factors can be seen to create a series of opportunities and threats; these are illustrated in Figure 9.12 below.

Opportunities	Threats
• A general growth in the market	• Increased levels of (price) competition
• Increased customer expectations	• The possibilities of a shake-out within the industry
• A greater customer willingness to experiment	• Mass-market destinations increasingly being viewed as a commodity
• The emergence of new holiday destinations	• The organization's current markets offer little medium- or long-term potential for development
• The scope for differentiation and premium pricing	
• Winter golf holidays that offer growth prospects	• Current markets are price-sensitive
• The new markets identified by the consultant	• It is becoming increasingly difficult to achieve shelf space for brochures in travel agents

Figure 9.12

2.2.1 A preliminary assessment of the opportunities and threats

It is apparent that the market is currently changing in a number of significant and far-reaching ways. Given this, the organization needs to adopt a far more proactive stance in order to capitalize upon the opportunities that exist, but particularly those identified in the consultant's report.

2.3   Strengths and weaknesses

Strengths	Weaknesses
• Lazy Days is reasonably well established • The awareness that now exists amongst the management team of the problems and consequent need for change	• There is little detailed understanding of the current customer base • Little customer loyalty exists • The company is currently targeting the low-spending C1 and C2 socio-economic groups and 38–60-year-olds • Price has become an overly important element of the marketing programme • Uninspiring sales brochures are used • High fixed costs • The gross margin has dropped consistently since 1992 • There are low levels of profitability • Net profits have dropped consistently since 1992 • No real knowledge exists of selling directly to clients • What were previously competitive advantages have been eroded • There is little understanding of the African market • There is no understanding of the safari or ballooning holiday market • The firm has a down-market image as a supplier of low-price holidays • The average price of the firm's holidays has declined since 1992 towards the smaller firms

2.3.1   *Preliminary assessment of the strengths and weaknesses*

The analysis highlights the imbalance between the organization's strengths and weaknesses, and hence its vulnerability. Looking beyond the individual weaknesses, it is apparent that the organization is suffering from the legacy of a high degree of complacency and the failure on the part of management to provide a true sense of direction. Because of this, thought needs to be given to the question of managerial capability, and whether the opportunities that have been identified by the consultant, particularly in the African market, can realistically be capitalized upon.

3.0   Strategic imperatives arising from the SWOT analysis

Given the nature of the findings of the SWOT analysis, it is essential that we address several issues in the immediate future. These include:

- The absence of proactive marketing and selling skills within the firm's management.
- A lack of any detailed knowledge both of the current and the potential markets.
- The financial implications of the move into new markets.
- The type of market offer that will be needed, how this might be needed, and how this might be differentiated from that of other firms.
- The erosion of margins.
- The firm's current down-market image.
- How any strategy might best be implemented.

4.0 Principal assumptions underpinning the plan

A number of assumptions underpin this plan, the most significant of which are that:

- The firm's current skiing holiday markets will continue to be hit by increasing price competition from Austrian, Italian and French ski resorts.
- The firm will be able to establish a significant and profitable presence in the ballooning and safari market.
- Sufficient financial resources will be made available to launch the new range of holidays.

5.0 Preliminary marketing objectives

- To develop and launch a new range of safari and ballooning holidays in Africa.
- To price these holidays at premium levels (note that the extent of this premium will be determined at a later stage).
- To position the new holidays as the first choice for customers seeking such a holiday.
- To achieve sales in year one of_____*, in year two of_____*, and year three of _____*. These will translate into the following market share figures:
  Year one _____*
  Year two _____*
  Year three_____*
  *Note that these figures can only be determined in the light of further research and analysis.

6.0 The target market

A considerable amount of research is still needed to clarify the size and detail of the buying patterns of the target market, and at this stage it is therefore possible to provide only a broad picture of this. In essence, however, the new range of holidays is designed to appeal to younger customers in socio-economic groups A and B who have a sense of adventure.

7.0 Positioning statement

The new holidays will be positioned in order to appeal to young and high-spending customers in social groups A and B. Emphasis will be given to the quality of the product, levels of service, and the once-in-a-lifetime experience.

8.0 The marketing mix

- The *product* will be ballooning and safari holidays in Africa.
- *Pricing* will reflect a premium strategy.
- *Direct distribution* will be used, in the form of newspaper advertisements and the targeting of potential customers via direct mail.
- The product will be *promoted* via direct-response campaigns in the press.

9.0 Implementation and control

Responsibility for refining and subsequently implementing this plan will rest with the marketing manager, reporting in to the main board. Given the significance of the proposed development, it is essential that the necessary level of resources and commitment are allocated to the project. Control will be achieved through monthly and quarterly reports, with a series of measures of performance against target.

10.0 Budgets

These will be set in the light of the findings of further research. At this stage, however, it is possible to indicate several areas of major expenditure, including:

- Customer and competitor research.
- The development of new promotional material.
- Media buying.
- Marketing training.
- The costs of developing the necessary infrastructure in Africa.

Appendix

Areas for further research

In order to prepare a detailed marketing plan, a substantial amount of additional information is needed. Included within this is information on:

- Accurate and detailed sales forecasts for the short and medium term.
- the financial implications of the proposed action.
- competitors: who they are, their size, location, patterns of ownership, resource availability, strengths and weaknesses, selling propositions, positioning strategies, levels of advertising, pricing strategies, and patterns of distribution.
- customers: probable size of each market sector, geographic location, buying motives, approaches to buying, their expectations, price sensitivities, and readership profiles.
- media availability, areas of specific interest, costs, and copy dates.

Pentagon Balloons: a suggested solution

Question I

Working with the consultant, you have been given the responsibility for preparing a report recommending how a stronger marketing orientation might be introduced to Pentagon Balloons. Within the report you should make reference to, amongst other areas, the organizational and managerial implications of your recommendations, as well as to the implications for marketing practice.   **(30 marks)**

For the attention of the main board of Pentagon Balloons Ltd

Prepared by:
Date: December 1995

1.0   Management summary

1.1   It has become apparent from our work with the organization that a series of major changes and actions are required. Prominent amongst these is the need for the introduction of a stronger marketing orientation. This can best be achieved by:

(a)   The appointment of a senior marketing person.
(b)   A stronger and more obvious focus for the business.
(c)   A full internal and external audit.
(d)   A clarification of objections.
(e)   A stronger top-down approach, particularly in the short term.
(f)   A programme of market research and the development of a far more detailed understanding of the market.

(g) A more structured planning process which incorporates a market-oriented mission statement.

(h) Decisions on the competitive stance that is to be adopted.

(i) A programme of internal marketing.

(j) A programme of monitoring and feedback.

(k) Increased accountability throughout the organization.

(l) More effective implementation.

However, it needs to be recognized that the development of a marketing orientation is typically a long-term process and needs to be thought of as a form of investment. To a large extent, this investment is in changing the organization's culture so that common values relating to the need to achieve high levels of customer service, a concern for quality in all activities, and so forth are shared throughout the organization. It needs to be recognized that this is not an appropriate target for the 'quick fix' and that any changes will take time to achieve.

This report highlights the ways in which the marketing orientation of Pentagon can be improved and includes recommendations for its implementation. However, before doing this, we need to clarify what is meant by a marketing orientation and why action is needed in this case.

1.2 Why is a marketing orientation necessary?

Our audit of Pentagon's marketing effectiveness has highlighted a generally poor level of marketing performance. This can be seen to be having a significant effect on the company's performance in several areas, including:

- Sales revenue.
- Profits and profitability.
- The relationships with owners/investors.
- The failure to meet or exceed the licensor's expectations and the terms of the licence agreement.

A changed focus and culture of the organization should result in significant improvements in all of the above areas.

1.3 What is a marketing orientation?

A marketing orientation is a combination of marketing and organizational factors which contribute to greater effectiveness and form the basis of sound organizational performance in its chosen business areas and markets. It is made up of several elements:

1 A customer-oriented philosophy.
2 An integrated marketing organization.
3 Adequate marketing information.
4 A strategic orientation.
5 Operational efficiency.

The suggestions and recommendations made here on how to achieve a marketing orientation are based on our findings to date. There is, however, a need for further work within the organization, particularly in the area of implementation.

It must be emphasized that the success of much of what is recommended here rests firmly on the appointment of a new senior member of the management team who will have explicit responsibility for the development and implementation of external and internal marketing activities.

2.0 Recommendations for ways in which a marketing orientation might be developed within Pentagon

This will involve paying attention to each of the five areas referred to in 1.3.

2.1 The introduction of a stronger customer philosophy

This can be achieved by the following:

- A detailed analysis of customers' needs and wants, with this knowledge then being shared throughout the whole organization.
- The creation of a market-led business mission which concentrates on the benefits we are capable of providing, rather than one which is centred around what we want to produce.
- The creation of meaningful and sustainable competitive advantages in the form of product and process benefits.
- An investment in marketing training in order to improve skill levels.

and, very importantly:

- A deep-seated commitment to marketing on the part of top management, with adequate financing for the marketing effort. In the absence of this, any initiative will be doomed from the outset.

2.2 An integrated marketing organization
Against the background of our comments in 2.1, there is a need for:

- Senior management to control and integrate activities throughout the organization in a far stronger fashion.
- The relationships between marketing, R & D, sales, finance, and production to be clarified.
- The product development and market development processes to be organized more effectively.

2.3 Marketing information
In order to improve our knowledge and understanding of the market, there is a need for:

- Regular studies of customers, channels and competitors.
- A greater awareness of the sales potential and profitability of different market segments, customers and territories.
- The measurement of the cost-effectiveness of different levels and types of marketing expenditure.

Given this, we should then have a far better understanding of:

- Current and future market changes.
- Customers' needs and how these are likely to develop.
- Competitors' activities and their implications for us.
- General environmental forces, including political/legal developments, economic factors and technological advances.

This, in turn, should allow for a far more precise – and effective – targeting of the marketing effort.

2.4 Strategic perspectives
The importance of and need for a strategic approach to planning and a firmly structured approach to market development has already been highlighted. In the absence of this, we risk losing direction and heightening our vulnerability to attacks from competitors and downturns in demand. It is essential therefore that:

- The planning process, including feedback mechanisms, be formalized.
- The quality of the thinking that underpins the marketing strategy be improved.
- Thought be given to contingency thinking and planning.
- A more strategic use be made of the elements of the marketing mix.

2.5 Improving operational efficiency
We must ensure not only that sufficient resources are available to achieve the organizational and marketing objectives, but also that they are applied efficiently. Cost

analyses will be required, and attention should be paid to these across all organizational functions. In addition, there is a need to:

- Improve internal communications.
- Develop a more proactive approach to management generally.
- Improve systems of feedback and control.

It should be apparent from what has been said so far that a major change is being demanded of the organization. It is also apparent that the current organization and management style differ significantly from what is required and that a managerial gap exists. Unless this is fully recognized and then filled by the appointment of a marketing professional from outside the organization, it is unlikely that any real change will take place.

3.0 The organizational, managerial and marketing implications for Pentagon of a marketing orientation

This section identifies the organizational, managerial and marketing implications of a marketing orientation.

3.1 The organizational and managerial implications

The main effects can be summarized in terms of:

- The need for the appointment of a senior person within the organization who will have explicit responsibility for the development and implementation of a marketing strategy.
- A restructuring of the organization so that the marketing director has a high degree of control/influence over other parts of the organization.
- A commitment to marketing from other members of the board.
- A programme of marketing and customer awareness training for staff throughout the business.
- A clearly identifiable marketing budget.
- A recognition throughout the organization of the importance of the customer and the consequent need for a customer-oriented philosophy (refer back to Section 2.1).
- A programme of internal marketing.
- The development of strong feedback mechanisms.

3.2 The marketing implications

The marketing implications of the revised approach can be viewed under several headings, but most obviously in terms of the greater understanding of the market that should emerge and the consequently greater scope for the more precise and effective targeting of the marketing effort. This should therefore allow for:

- A greater understanding of opportunities and threats and hence how the marketing strategy should develop.
- More precise segmentation.
- A more effective management of the marketing mix.

Conclusion

Without the development of a stronger marketing orientation, it is almost inevitable that the marketing effort will remain unfocused and of little real value.

It needs to be emphasized, however, that a marketing orientation is not an easy status to attain, particularly given that the company has not previously focused its attention on this area and little evidence exists of marketing expertise. It should not therefore be viewed as a target for a 'quick fix', but something which requires effort, commitment and input from management, a significant allocation of resources, and an assessment at regular intervals to see if the recommendations are being successfully implemented. It is therefore recommended that we maintain the momentum of change by means of a continuous monitoring of marketing performance to ensure that inertia does not set in. The company's progress towards an improved marketing orientation can be measured by regularly asking questions of the following type:

- Are we easy to do business with?
- Do we keep our promises?
- Do we meet the standards we set?
- Are we responsive?
- Do we work together?

2 Identify the marketing and financial criteria that should be employed to assess the markets identified in Figure 9.9 by the consultant.

> **Rationale**
> Marketing planners are frequently faced with the need to evaluate and choose between the product, market and strategic alternatives with which they are faced. In doing this, it is essential that they take account of a spectrum of factors so that the decision is made as objectively as possible. This question was designed to encourage candidates to think about the sorts of financial and marketing criteria that should be used by Pentagon's management in assessing the four markets identified by the consultant.

The factors that should be used to assess each of the four markets can be viewed loosely as financial criteria and marketing criteria. Included within these are:

Marketing criteria
- The size of each of the four markets identified.
- Their probable patterns of growth.
- The nature and intensity of competition.
- Possible patterns of competitive response to our entry.
- The pricing strategies that might be pursued.
- Competitors' positioning strategies.
- Advertising and promotional needs.
- Competitors' performance levels to date.
- Current and potential buyers' buying motives.
- The sales and distribution approaches that will be needed.
- Levels of customer loyalty.
- Patterns of buying.
- Product development/product modification needs.
- The likelihood of new competitors emerging.
- The scope for developing meaningful – and sustainable – selling propositions.
- The ability to develop a sustainable market position.
- The market's perceptions of Pentagon currently.
- The opportunities for further market development.

Financial criteria
- Market entry costs.
- The level of manufacturing/assembly investment that will be needed.
- The levels of investment needed.
- Day-to-day and long-term marketing costs.
- Profit margins.
- The probable costs of achieving a sustainable competitive position.
- Stockholding costs.
- The financial strengths of each of the competitors.
- The implications of currency fluctuations.
- The level of financial resource available.

However, in addition to the marketing and financial criteria that we have identified here, it is often useful to take account also of the abilities of the managerial team, since it is these which ultimately will determine how effectively the organization will operate. Thus, we might add to the two lists that we have developed so far the following three factors:

- Managerial skills and abilities.
- Managers' knowledge and experience of market development.
- The extent to which a proactive management culture exists.

A number of the mini cases have focused upon the ways in which the case study organization needs to be refocused and a far stronger external/marketing orientation developed. You should think in some detail about the ways in which this might be done and a culture change brought about.

WGP Industries Ltd: a suggested solution

The mini case study is an important part of the Planning and Control examination and is designed to provide you with an opportunity to apply your knowledge to a practical problem faced by an organization. In this instance the organization – WGP Industries Ltd – is encountering a series of market-based problems and, because of its internal structure and culture, is losing ground. Question 1 requires you to evaluate the current and rather traditional approach to new product development and, by drawing upon the lessons that have emerged from elsewhere, make suggestions for the ways in which the process might be improved. In the event, however, many candidates chose not to address each of the areas asked for in the question, but talked instead in rather general terms about the role of new product development. Others produced SWOT analyses or marketing plans. Overall, therefore, far too many of the answers proved to be unfocused and lacking in the detail that was required.

Question 1

As the marketing analyst working with the Marketing Director on this review, you have been given the task of preparing a report suggesting how the current sequential approach to new product development might possibly be improved. In doing this you should make reference to any lessons that emerge from the experiences of other organizations and to the research work that has been carried out into the typical causes of new product success and failure.

A review of the new product development process within WGP Industries Ltd

1.0 Introduction

This report focuses upon the ways in which the new product development process, currently employed within WGPI Ltd, might be improved. It will include suggestions for improvements to the current methods employed, a review of the research that has been conducted elsewhere into the causes of new product success and failure, and how an innovatory culture might possibly be introduced. In doing this, it will also make reference to the lessons that emerge from the experiences of other organizations.

2.0 An evaluation of the current approach to new product development

The current approach to new product development (NPD) is sequential and reflects the approach advocated by Booz, Allen and Hamilton in the 1960s. As such, ideas for possible new products are identified, these are then screened, the most promising are subjected to a detailed business analysis, the most promising of these is then sent to engineering for prototype development, a small production run is test marketed and, assuming the results are sufficiently positive, the product is finally launched.

Although the approach has a number of advantages (e.g. assuming that each stage is conducted thoroughly, the process has an obvious rigour), it also suffers from a number of significant drawbacks. The most obvious of these are that it is costly, slow and time-consuming, with each element being dependent upon the former having been completed. Because of this, a delay at any stage has an obvious knock-on effect to each subsequent stage. Planning is therefore made more difficult and this, in turn, tends to lead to a lack of urgency and little real feeling of 'ownership' of the process. In the case of WGPI, this is obviously now causing difficulties, with these problems being exacerbated as the result of an increasingly competitive and fast moving market. However, it needs to be recognized that a sequential approach is, by itself, not necessarily a 'bad' process. Instead, it is a question of how this process is managed.

The second and interrelated fault or weakness that WGPI is suffering from is the lack of an innovative culture. Although the research and development department staff are very obviously involved in and have a responsibility for innovation, the development of an innovatory culture is far more fundamental and, of necessity, must pervade the whole organization. The responsibility for developing, maintaining, reinforcing and implementing this culture lies therefore not in the R&D department but at the level of senior management. In the absence of this, it is unlikely that significant long-term change will take place within the business.

3.0   Lessons from other organizations

Before going on to suggest how WGPI's current approach to NPD might be changed, it is worth looking at other organizations with a view to identifying whether any lessons from good practice might be learned. However, in doing this, a word of caution needs to be uttered in that although an organization might well succeed with a particular approach, it does not necessarily follow that another organization will either be able to adopt the same approach or that if it does it will achieve the same degree of success. Nevertheless, it is possible to identify a number of *general* lessons that might be learned. Included within these are that:

1   Top management is ultimately accountable for new product success. It is not sufficient for senior managers to demand new products without providing a clear focus for NPD activity, consistent support and adequate funding.
2   Success breeds success. The organizations which have the greatest success with new products tend to be those in which there is a recognition that new product development involves a series of skills which have to be learned and developed over time. It is therefore an activity which needs to be managed over time and is not something which can be turned on and off as circumstances change.
3   New product strategy must be linked to and be an integral part of the strategic planning process.
4   There must be formal and sophisticated organizational arrangements for managing the new product and development process.
5   Teamworking is essential, with marketing, sales, R&D, engineering, manufacturing, purchasing and finance all working together with a clear sense of purpose (see, for example, Japanese companies)
6   Product ideas must be researched from a *marketing* viewpoint.
7   Customers should be brought in at an early stage in order to give their views on what is being developed.
8   'Me-too' approaches and ideas are of only marginal value.
9   There is a need to recognize that the failure rate of new products and new product ideas is typically high and that if failure is punished, staff will prove to be reluctant to take risks.

Many of these ideas or lessons are brought together in the organization which is regarded by many as one of the most innovative in the world, 3M. 3M's approach to innovation rests on the expectation – which is met – that each of its forty divisions will generate at least 25 per cent of its income from products introduced within the preceding five years. Because of this, the company has a history of launching at least 100 new products each year.

The company's success stems from an innovation-driven culture in which everyone is encouraged to be a 'product champion'. Thus anyone who has an idea for a new product is encourage to do some research in order to:

- find out what knowledge exists inside and outside the organization;
- find out where within 3M the product might be developed;
- establish whether it is patentable; and
- how profitable it might be.

If the idea then finds support, a venture team consisting of people from R&D, marketing, sales, manufacturing and the legal department is formed. Each team is headed by an 'executive champion' who helps the team and protects it from bureaucratic intrusion. If the product ideas prove to be commercially viable, the team says with it. If it fails, team members return to their jobs without any stigma of failure.

4.0 Research into new product success and failure

A considerable amount of work has been conducted over the past thirty years into the causes of new product success and failure, some of the results of which can be seen to have been influenced by the sort of thinking reflected in the section 3.0 above. However, we can identify some of the principal findings in terms of:

Successful products almost invariably exhibit one or more of three characteristics:

- a significant price or performance advantage;
- a significant difference from existing products; and
- they are first into the market.

At the same time, it has been found that **failure** tends to be the result of market-related rather than technically-related factors. Included within this are the problems of:

- competitors proving to be too firmly entrenched with the result that the necessary levels of sales prove difficult to achieve;
- overestimations being made of the numbers of potential users;
- prices being set at too high a level; and
- the marketing effort being misdirected.

This has led Cooper to suggest that the major contributors to failure are:

1   the absence of detailed marketing studies;
2   poor test marketing; and
3   inappropriate product launch activities.

A broadly similar pattern of results emerged from work in the United States by Hlavacek, with the causes being identified as:

- inadequate market size;
- distribution problems;
- internal conflicts;
- impatience and resistance on the part of marketing staff; and
- poor marketing research.

Returning to the contributors to **success** the market researchers AC Neilsen have suggested that:

1 The product should be of demonstrably higher quality than those that it will be competing against.
2 It must compare favourably with the competition in terms of:
   - the new product idea;
   - packaging excellence;
   - price/value for money;
   - advertising support;
   - sales support;
   - benefits for the distribution network.
3 It should be capable of bidding for a strong position in the market if levels of brand loyalty are low.
4 Care should be taken to guard against distribution hiccups, particularly in the early stages of the product's life.
5 It should not be too far ahead of its time.

Rothwell (1972, 1974, 1977) and Project Sappho highlighted several other significant elements:

- successful companies had a higher than average understanding of user needs;
- greater attention was paid to marketing;
- development work was performed effectively, but not always quickly;
- use was made of outside technology and advice;
- the individuals involved in NPD held senior positions and had significant authority.

5.0 The development of an innovatory culture

Underpinning much of what has been said so far is the need to develop an innovatory culture within the organization if new product development is to have a higher priority and the likelihood of success is to be increased. However, it needs to be recognized that as with all aspects of cultural change, this is neither an easy nor a short-term issue. Instead, there needs to be a fundamental acceptance that there must be a change in priorities within the organization, with a much clearer and much longer term focus upon a new product activity. In order to achieve this, we can make a series of recommendations, including:

- There must be a full-blooded commitment to new product development on the part of the senior management.
- Support for new product development must be of a continuing nature rather than spasmodic and a reflection of company fortunes.
- New product development expertise must be recruited.
- There must be a recognition that not all new ideas will succeed and that failure must be accepted and learned from, not punished.
- Teamworking must be encouraged.
- Clear targets and priorities must be established.
- Full funding must be provided.
- The company must be close to its markets.
- Structures must be much more fluid with the introduction of, for example, venture teams.
- The organization must learn from – and applaud – success.

6.0 Recommendations for WGPI

It follows from what has been said that a series of changes need to be introduced to WGPI. Perhaps the most obvious of these is that new product development needs to take on a far higher priority than has been the case in the past. The impression gained is that the organization has failed to recognize its true strategic significance, resulting in a lack of focus, urgency and funding. My recommendations are therefore as follows:

1   There is a need for the board to decide far more clearly what is expected from new product development and how WGPI is to be positioned. If it is to be a 'me-too' or 'also-ran' organization, the current approach is adequate. However, given how the market is changing and the previous performances and positioning of the organization, this seems inappropriate and it is therefore suggested that a far more proactive approach be developed.

2   A sequential approach to new product development has merits, although in the case of WGPI, there needs to be a far greater degree of urgency injected to the process, with a greater sense of ownership, with this being driven by a senior management champion.

3   There is a general need for greater new product development expertise. This may well involve the recruitment of new staff at a senior level.

4   The scope for the parallel performance rather than the purely sequential performance of activities within the new product development process should be investigated.

5   The importance of the 'ownership' of new product ideas should be recognized; again this highlights the importance of one or more new product champions.

6   Clear expectations, targets, timescales and budgets should be established.

7   Where appropriate, venture teams should be established.

8   Teamworking should be encouraged and developed.

9   There should be a more detailed understanding of the market so that gaps can be identified and their potential evaluated.

10   Adequate funding is essential.

11   Staff throughout the organization should be encouraged to develop a more innovatory approach, with this being reflected in a willingness to give them time – and the resources – to develop ideas.

12   Greater use should be made of outside bodies such as research associations.

13   Attention should be paid to developments in other companies in the UK and overseas, with a view to learning from them.

14   The possibilities of joint ventures should be examined.

Taking these ideas together, it can be seen that there is a need for this new product process to be driven to a far greater extent than is currently the case. Whether this is really possible with the current senior management team is perhaps questionable.

Question 2

You are required to prepare a brief for a market research agency explaining what information you require in order to develop a detailed picture of any new markets that the company might be interested in entering.

The development of a brief for a market research or advertising agency is the sort of activity that the majority of marketers are involved with on a reasonably regular basis. This question required you to focus upon a very typical area, that of the information needed in order to develop an understanding of a new market. Overall, candidates answered the question reasonably well, although there was a tendency to produce answers which simply listed a series of points rather than putting them into a framework and context.

To: ABC Market Research
Topic: The information requirements for an understanding of potential new markets.
Prepared by: Market analyst, WGP Industries Ltd
Date: June 1996

Introduction and background

WGP Industries Ltd is a manufacturer of industrial and domestic cleaning machines that are currently sold in Great Britain, France and parts of Northern Germany. The company pursues a market niching strategy, with an emphasis on very high quality, high performance, high prices and exclusive distribution. These markets, which are highly competitive, are now in maturity and there are growing problems of over-capacity.

Organizational objectives

The company has developed a strategy which involves moving into a series of new markets both domestically and internationally.

The purpose of the research programme

Although we have considerable experience and knowledge of our current target markets in Britain, France and North Germany, we have little understanding of the size, structure and potential of other markets either domestically or overseas. The programme of research is designed to overcome this.

Information requirements

The research must provide the basis for decisions on market entry and marketing strategy. As such, it is essential that two key issues are addressed:

1 the size and potential of each market; and
2 the bases for operating within each of these markets.

It seems likely therefore that information will be needed under each of the following headings:

- The overall market size currently by volume and value.
- The nature and size of each sector or segment within each of these markets.
- Probable patterns of growth.
- The nature, sources and intensity of competition.
- The ways in which the bases of competition are changing.
- The commitment of each organization to their current markets.
- The existence of any relationships between existing players in the form of, for example, joint ventures.
- Competitive response profiles.
- Patterns of distribution.
- The criteria for achieving access to distribution.
- Distributors' expectations.
- Patterns of income distribution (consumer markets).
- Purchasing patterns and criteria (organizational markets).
- Current patterns of marketing behaviour.
- Patterns of economic growth.
- Inflation levels.
- Tariff and non-tariff barriers.
- Critical success factors.

Although this is not an exhaustive list and we would welcome any suggestions that you might make for adding to this. It is felt that the information generated will provide a basis for determining the attractiveness of each market and our ability to take advantage of any opportunities that exist. The framework we intend using for this is illustrated in Figure 9.13.

Timing

It is expected that the results will be made available to us within a six-week period.

Budget

This will be agreed in the light of your quotation following this brief.

Report format

We require a full breakdown of your findings and your preliminary conclusions/recommendations.

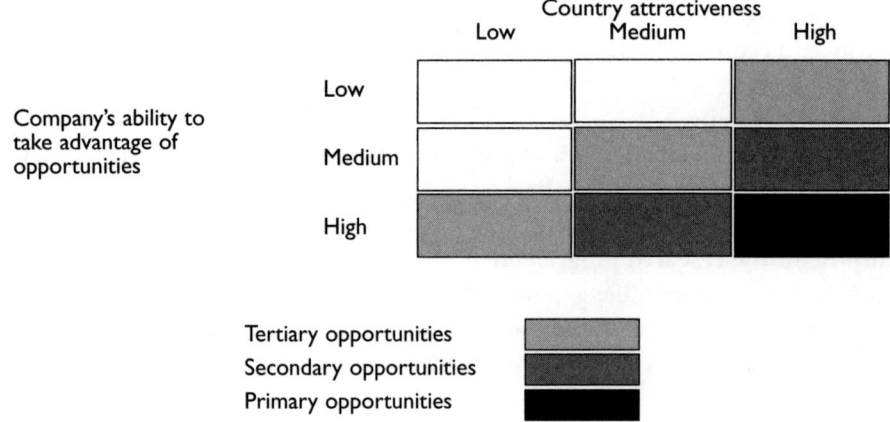

Figure 9.13

The Legal Business: a suggested solution
Question (a)

This question required a candidate to explain how an audit of the organization might be conducted and how the result might then be used to improve the firm's performance. It is therefore, realtively straightforward and concerned with an area that all candidates should be familiar. In the event, however, performances were very patchy, with some candidates demonstrating that, at best, they had only a limited knowledge of the audit. Others just explained what an audit is, but failed either to relate their comments to The Legal Business or explain how an audit might be conducted and the results used.

1.0 **A briefing paper for the managing partner on the purpose and benefits of marketing auditing**
     (prepared by CIM Consultants, December 1996)

As our initial report has shown, The Legal Business needs to adopt a stronger and far more proactive approach to marketing. As a first step, we recommend conducting a detailed marketing audit of the firm.

2.0 **The nature and purpose of the audit**

The marketing audit is in a number of ways the true starting point for the strategic marketing planning process, since it is through the audit that the strategist arrives at a measure both of environmental opportunities and threats, and of the organization's marketing capability. The thinking that underpins the concept of the marketing audit is straightforward: it is that corporate objectives and strategy can only be developed effectively against the background of a detailed and objective understanding, both of corporate capability and environmental opportunity. The audit is, therefore, as McDonald has suggested, 'The means by which a company can identify its own strengths and weaknesses as they relate to external opportunities and threats. It is thus a way of helping management to select a position in that environment based on known factors'.

Definitions of the audit have also been proposed by a number of other writers, including Kotler:

'A marketing audit is a *comprehensive, systematic, independent* and *periodic* examination of a company's – or business unit's – marketing environment, objectives, strategies and activities with a view to determing problem areas and opportunities and recommending a plan of action to improve the company's performance.'

and Schuchman:

'A systematic, critical and impartial review and appraisal of the total marketing operation: of the basic objectives and policies and the assumptions which underlie them as well as the methods, procedures, personnel and organization employed to implement the policies and achieve the objectives.'

Taken together, these definitions highlight the three major elements and potential benefits of the marketing audit:

1 The analysis of the external environmental and internal situation.
2 The evaluation of past performance and present activities.
3 The identification of future opportunities and threats.

3.0 The structure and focus of the audit

In terms of its structure, the marketing audit consists of three major and detailed diagnostic steps. These involve a review of:

1 The organization's environment (opportunities and threats).
2 Its marketing system (strengths and weaknesses).
3 Its marketing activities.

This is illustrated in Figure 9.14.

The first of these three steps is designed to establish the various dimensions of the marketing environment, the ways in which it is likely to change and the probable impact of these changes upon the organization. The second stage is concerned with an assessment of the extent to which the organization's marketing systems are capable of dealing with the demands of the environment. The final stage involves a review of the individual components of the marketing mix.

It should be apparent from this that in conducting an audit the strategist is concerned with two types of variable. First, there are the *environmental* or *market variables* over which the strategist has little or no direct control. Second, there are the *operational variables* which can be controlled to a greater or lesser extent. This distinction can also be expressed in terms of the *macro-environmental PEST forces* (Political/legal, Economic/demographic, Social/cultural, and Technological) that affect the business, and *micro-environmental actors* (customers, competitors, distributors and suppliers) who subsequently influence the organization's ability to operate profitably in the market-place. Regardless of which approach to categorization is used, the process and purpose of the audit is the same. It begins with an *external audit* covering the macro-environmental forces referred to above and the markets and competitors that are of particular interest to the company. The *internal audit* then builds upon this by assessing the extent to which the organization, its structure and resources, relate to the environment and have the capability of operating effectively within the constraints that the environment imposes.

In doing this the auditor should not view the marketing audit and its result in isolation but, as we observed earlier, should instead give full recognition to the way in which it sits within the general framework of the overall management audit and alongside the audits of the other management functions. In this way the strategist should arrive at a true measure not just of environmental opportunity but also of the ability of the organisation as a whole to respond effectively.

4.0 Conducting the audit

The auditing process should begin with agreement being reached between The Legal Businesses' managing partner and the marketing auditor regarding the specific objectives, the breadth and depth of coverage, the sources of data, the report format and the time period for the audit. Included within this should be a plan of who is to be interviewed and the questions that are to be asked.

With regard to the questions of *who* is to be questioned, it needs to be emphasized that the audit should never be restricted just to the firm's partners; it should also include clients and the other outside groups. In this way, a better and more complete picture of the firm's position and its effectiveness can be developed. In the case of clients, for example, the auditor should aim to develop satisfaction ratings which are capable of highlighting areas in need of attention.

Once the information has been collected, the findings and recommendations need to be presented with emphasis being given to the type of action needed to overcome any problems, the timescale over which remedial action is to be taken, and the names of those who are to be responsible for this.

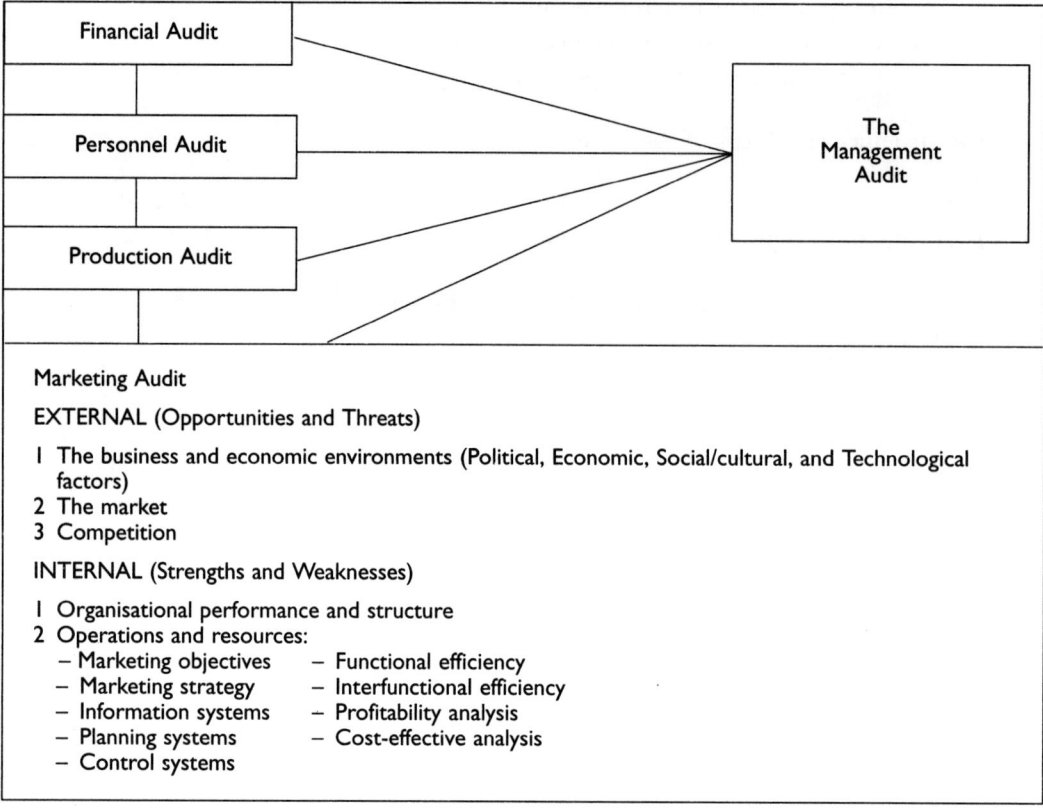

Figure 9.14

Within the general framework of the external and internal audit, Kotler et al. suggest there are six specific dimensions that are of direct interest to the auditor. These are:

1 The marketing environment audit.
2 The marketing strategy audit.
3 The marketing organization audit.
4 The marketing systems audit.
5 The marketing productivity audit.
6 The marketing functions audit.

5.0 How are the audit results used?

Having conducted the audit the question that then arises is how best to use the results. In some organizations a considerable amount of time, effort and expense is given over to the auditing process, but the corrective action that is then needed simply falls by the wayside. To ensure that the results are incorporated most effectively within the strategic planning process of The Legal Business, the major findings of the audit need to be incorporated within an appropriate framework. This can be done in one of several ways, although undoubtedly the most useful is the SWOT framework. This should focus on the *key* internal strengths and weaknesses in relation to the *principal* external opportunities and threats, and include a summary of the reasons for good or bad performance. It is then against the background of this document that the partners, together possibly with the consultant, should begin planning at both the functional and the corporate levels.

Question (b)

The question required candidates to explain what is meant by a strategic marketing orientation and how such an approach might most readily be developed within The Legal Business. Although some candidates produced very competent answers, many decided to prepare a SWOT analysis or an outline marketing plan, neither of which had been asked for. Because of this far too many candidates performed far less well than they might have expected.

1.0 Recommendations on the development of a strategic marketing orientation within The Legal Business

Background

From the audit that has been conducted it is apparent that The Legal Business reflects a strong professional rather than a commercial orientation and that because of this the full potential of the organization is not being realized. This is illustrated in a general sense by the nine key points highlighted by the consultant (see p. 206) but in particular by the apparent absence of strategic direction; the lack of an obvious competitive stance; the failure to cross-sell services and capitalize upon the firm's full asset base; and the loss of clients. Given this, and that the marketing consultant has highlighted the need for a far stronger and more explicit strategic marketing orientation, a series of significant changes will have to be made within the firm. In order to do this we need to take a number of steps. However, it needs to be recognized that although organizations typically experience problems in developing a strategic approach to their operations, these problems are often magnified in the case of professional services organizations made up of lawyers, accountants, medical practitioners, architects and so on. There are several reasons for this, the most obvious of which is the perceived scope for conflict between *the professional ethos* (that of a lawyer in this case) and that of an apparently *overtly commercial orientation*. This, it is argued, offers scope for a clash of interests. As an example, a lawyer or medical practitioner might argue that an action which is in the best legal or medical interests of *the client* is not necessarily the most obvious or sensible in purely commercial terms for *the lawyer or doctor*. To argue this does however show a fundamental misunderstanding of the nature and purpose of marketing. It is essential therefore that the partners and staff within the firm recognize there are two principal dimensions to marketing:

1   It involves a series of tools that can be used both strategically and tactically (these are the elements of the marketing mix).

and more fundamentally:

2   It is a philosophy of how the business operates and interacts with its markets.

Until this misunderstanding is overcome, it is inevitable there will be a high degree of suspicion and that any attempt to develop a strategic marketing orientation will be doomed to failure.

2.0 Moving towards the development of a strategic marketing orientation (SMO)

A considerable amount of work has been done over the past ten years in order to identify how an SMO might be developed, the sort of barriers that exist and how these barriers might best be overcome. However, before we consider these we need to be clear about what is meant by an SMO. In essence, an SMO reflects a long-term perspective in which customer or client satisfaction, a clear offer, an explicit positioning strategy, and high levels of resources co-ordination are all seen to be paramount to the firm's success.

In discussing this, Wilson and Gilligan suggest that the extent to which an SMO exists within an organization can be identified by posing a series of questions.

1   Is there a good understanding within the organization of the needs, wants and behaviour patterns of targeted customers or clients?
2   Is the organization profit-directed rather than volume-driven?
3   Does the chief executive or managing partner see himself as the firm's senior marketing strategist or 'marketing champion'?

4   Is there a market-driven mission?
5   Do the strategies reflect the realities of the market-place including the competitive situation?
6   Is marketing seen as being important by managers and/or partners?
7   Is the firm organized in such a way that it can be more responsive to marketing opportunities and threats than its less successful competitors?
8   Is there a well-designed marketing information system?
9   Do managers and partners make full use of marketing research inputs in their decision-making?
10 Are marketing costs and revenues systematically analysed in relation to marketing activities to ensure that the latter are being carried out effectively?
11 Is there a strong link between the marketing function and the development of new products/services?
12 Does the firm employ staff in the marketing area who are marketing professionals?
13 Is it understood that marketing is the responsibility of the entire organization if it is to be effective?
14 Are decisions with marketing implications made in a well-co-ordinated way and executed in an integrated manner?

In the case of The Legal Business, it is apparent the answer to nearly every one of these fourteen questions will be 'no'. Given this we can identify a series of *broad* issues which needs to be faced up to in the development of the SMO that The Legal Business requires if it is to compete more effectively in the future. These include:

1   Securing deep-seated support from the senior partners, since a bottom-up approach would be doomed from the outset given the firm-wide implications of a marketing orientation.
2   Specifying a mission relating to the development of a marketing orientation.
3   Setting up a task force as part of the plan to bring together partners and staff from across the firm to carry out tasks such as

- identifying the current orientation of the firm;
- carrying out a training needs analysis as a basis for a partner and staff development programme to change the firm's culture in the desired way;
- advising on structural changes within the firm to support marketing activities; and
- ensuring commitment to change via the system of rewards (such as bonuses and promotion) that will apply to facilitate change.

4   Maintaining the momentum of change by means of continuous monitoring of marketing performance to ensure that inertia does not set in. Progress towards improved marketing orientation can then be measured by regularly asking questions of the following type:

- are we easy to do business with?
- do we keep our promises?
- do we meet the standards we set?
- are we responsive?
- do we work together?

3.0   The specific changes needed

3.1   In the light of what has been said so far, we can now identify the types of *specific* changes and developments that are needed if The Legal Business is to develop an SMO. These include:

- The appointment of a senior marketing specialist at a senior level within the firm who will work with the senior partners in order to provide a focus for marketing and who will be responsible for developing the marketing ethos and skills, initially at a senior level, but increasingly throughout the firm.
- A full internal and external audit.

- A stronger and more obvious focus for the business.
- A programme of internal marketing.
- A stronger top-down approach, particularly in the short-term.
- A programme of market research.
- A structured planning process which incorporates a mission statement.
- Decisions on the competitive stance that is to be adopted.
- A programme of monitoring and feedback.
- Increased marketing accountability throughout the firm.
- Greater exploitation of the firm's name.

3.2   It needs to be recognized that these suggestions and recommendations are based on our findings to date. There is, however, a need for further work within The Legal Business, particularly in the area of implementation. Very obviously, though, the success of much of what is recommended here rests firmly on the appointment of a new senior member of the management team who will have explicit responsibility for marketing activities. Without this, it is likely that few changes will be made

3.3   An important driver of the changes will quite obviously be an understanding of clients' needs and competitors' strengths and patterns of behaviour. The programme of market research referred to above will therefore be designed to identify:

- levels of client satisfaction;
- areas of market opportunity;
- competitors' probable moves.

3.4   A degree of refocusing will also be needed so that The Legal Businesses' positioning becomes more meaningful and explicit. The decision on positioning can, however, only be taken following the programme of research. The refocusing will be designed to achieve several objectives, but most importantly will help to clarify the firm's offer and distinctive competencies.

3.5   A programme of internal marketing will then be needed in order to ensure that partners and staff are made and kept aware of the new direction, the reasons for this, the nature of their expected contribution, and the levels of success being achieved.

3.6   An audit of the current methods of operation underpins all of what has been suggested so far. This will be designed to improve levels of effectiveness and efficiency.

3.7   A programme of market and product/service development is needed which will reflect changing market needs and corporate capability. Assuming this is conducted effectively, the firm will more effectively be able to help develop and sustain a meaningful competitive advantage in the market-place for legal services.

3.8   There will be the need for a programme of advertising and public relations to increase levels of market awareness.

3.9   Underpinning all of this should be the development of a mission statement which encapsulates the changed values of the organization.

Summary

It is apparent that a series of major changes are needed if an SMO is to be developed. However, if this is to be achieved, full recognition needs to be given to the potential for conflict between the professional and commercial ethos referred to in 1.0. It is essential therefore that the reasons for this are recognized and that the process of introducing an SMO is managed sensitively. Amongst the ways in which this might be done is to ensure from the outset that partners and staff throughout the firm are made fully aware of the reasons for the changes, the consequences of failing to change, the nature of the changes being made, the implications of these and the progress that is being made.

The major case study: marketing strategy – analysis and decision

This final unit of the Marketing Strategy Workbook will look not at any specific part of the syllabus, but at the final question paper in the Diploma series. In this unit we will consider what the case study exam is and why the Institute uses this particular method of examination.

We will also look at what you can expect in the examination itself, how to prepare for the examination and, finally, how to answer the examination without throwing away marks! We will also look at current trends, both in the examination itself and in marketing more generally, that you might want to take into account in your preparations for this examination.

Finally, we will consider the last two examination papers in the series which you can treat as a mock examination process. The two papers will be followed by a review of the case against which you can assess your own individual answer.

The most important aspects of this unit of the book are the two past examination papers. As in all things there is no substitute for experience and you are strongly advised to prepare for and to sit the two papers under examination conditions – or as close as you can approximate to examination conditions. Try if you can to consider the cases without looking at the questions or the additional information which is included. This will give you a better understanding of the examination process and prepare you for the examination day itself.

As there is no right answer to a case study no specimen or ideal answers have been included in this unit. Instead, each case is followed by a short review section which highlights the main points which the examiners were looking for when examining the cases.

It is difficult to place a time commitment on this unit. Nevertheless it is clear that a large proportion of case examination failures are produced by a lack of preparation.

To improve your chances of success you should attempt at least one full 'mock' case under examination conditions.

What is the case study exam?

Case studies as a method of learning an examination, have played a major role in management education since the method was first introduced in the Harvard Business School in America. The main reason for using case studies was, and still is, to create a scenario o context within which academic theory can be practically applied to a real life business situation.

Most students find case studies far more difficult to tackle than the more traditional examination papers with a number of questions. Case studies are not necessarily more difficult, but they certainly are different from the traditional methods of examination that perhaps we have all been used to since school days. Nevertheless, if you follow the rest of this chapter carefully it should cause you no undue problems.

Candidates hoping to pass the Analysis and Decision paper should bear in mind that as the Institute of Marketing Diploma becomes more widely recognized as the premier marketing qualification in the UK and Europe, this final paper must be a true test of the holder's ability to practise his or her trade. In the interests of both holders and employers, the Analysis and Decision case will continue to strive to be a rigorous test of the candidate's ability to apply marketing theory in real business situations.

Finally, the CIM Diploma has recently been submitted to the Open University validation service (CATS) scheme and has been awarded 70 'M' points that can be used as credit towards a Masters or other higher degree at the discretion of the awarding university. This award, significantly, makes the CIM Diploma equivalent to a post-graduate diploma. Obviously the examiners have the task of ensuring that this post-graduate level is maintained in the Case Study paper. Candidates should note that they should be submitting papers that are *beyond degree level* to ensure success.

Don't panic!

The Analysis and Decision paper has no set syllabus as such. It is a test of the student's ability to apply marketing theory from its sister paper, Strategic Marketing – Planning and Control, as well as the other two Diploma subjects Marketing Communication Strategy and International Marketing Strategy. As well as testing the candidate's ability to apply theory in all these four related areas, the major case study will also expect a solid and practical understanding of various issues which are covered in the Institute's certificate and advanced certificate papers. Topics such as financial implications, organization structure and design and the broader human resource implications of marketing strategy will also be rigorously tested in the case study.

It should also be understood that the very nature of the case study examination means that there is never one single 'correct' answer. In any complex business situation there will always be a number of alternative scenarios and strategic directions which can be identified by a manager. In the real world clear-cut cases are extremely rare too! What the examiners will be looking for in the case study, as will be shareholders in the real world, is a sound understanding of the situation facing the company described in the case study, an analysis and review of the strategic options open to the company and a clear recommendation as to the route that you believe the organization should take – with clear and reasonable justification.

What to expect from the case

Case studies can be anywhere from half a page to a hundred pages including appendices and additional information. The CIM Analysis and Decision case study typically extends to between twenty and fifty pages and will normally contain a section of text describing the situation faced by the particular company portrayed, plus a number of appendices.

The case study is always based on a real life business situation but will often be disguised in order to protect commercial confidentiality. On examination day the examination paper will consist of between two and four questions related to the case, normally carrying unequal marks. The examiner also reserves the right to include some additional information with the examination questions on the day. There are two reasons for including additional information. They are:

- To stimulate new and creative thinking on the day.
- To prevent the presentation of pre-prepared group answers.

It is important to take account of the additional information and to incorporate it into your answer wherever possible. Remember that the application of the additional information can be worth up to 20 per cent of the total marks awarded.

The case itself will often contain a wealth of data and information. As in the real world it is unlikely that the case material will contain all the data or information that ideally would be needed in order to solve the situation. So some assumptions or intelligent gap filling will be required. Also, not all of the data will be either useful or relevant to the situation in hand. Not only that but you are likely to uncover some contradictions or anomalies in the data material. All this has been designed, not to trap students, but rather to force them to think independently and creatively about the company described. In the real world data is not always clear cut nor are the solutions self evident. The case study does its best to replicate the real world with all its problems and challenges.

How to prepare

As has already been stated there is no single correct answer to any case study. Neither is there one guaranteed way of analysing a case study. A number of processes have been recommended which lay out the logical sequence of analysis and decision steps. Some of the more popular approaches are:

Process 1

1 What is wrong?
2 What are you going to do to put it right?

Process 2

1 Problem identification.
2 Problem definition.
3 Solutions generation.
4 Solution choice.
5 Solution implementation.
6 Solution monitoring.

Process 3

1 Situation audit.
2 Problem/decision statement.
3 Alternative identification.
4 Critical issues.
5 Analysis.
6 Recommendations.

Process 4

1 Comprehend the case situation.
2 Diagnose problem areas.
3 State problem.
4 Generate alternatives.
5 Evaluate and select.
6 Defend implementation.

In addition to the above, two more detailed processes of case preparation and analysis are recommended by the Institute and the senior examiners. The first is a process which breaks down into 28 identifiable stages and is the suggested route for the group process applied to case studies. The second is a derivative of the first, but a less detailed approach which tackles the case in six separate stages and is useful for group work and candidates working alone.

RECOMMENDED METHOD ONE
SUMMARY OF THE 28-STEP METHOD

Step 1   Read the case.
Step 2   After an interval, re-read the case.
Step 3   Reflect on the instructions and candidates' brief.
Step 4   Think yourself into the role and the situation.
Step 5   Re-read the case and write a precis. Discuss with colleagues.
Step 6   Conduct a marketing audit. Discuss with colleagues.
Step 7   Do a SWOT analysis. Discuss with colleagues.
Step 8   Conduct analyses/cross-analyses of appendices. Discuss with colleagues.
Step 9   Reconsider your precis, marketing audit and SWOT analysis.
Step 10   Conduct a situational analysis. Discuss with colleagues.
Step 11   Decide key issues. Discuss with colleagues.
Step 12   Develop a mission statement. Discuss with colleagues.
Step 13   Decide broad aims. Discuss with colleagues.
Step 14   Identify and analyse major problems. Develop and analyse alternative solutions. Discuss with colleagues.
Step 15   Develop quantified and timescaled objectives. Discuss with colleagues.
Step 16   Consider alternative strategies and select those most appropriate. Discuss with colleagues.
Step 17   Draw up detailed tactical plans covering the marketing mix. Discuss with colleagues.
Step 18   Draw up a marketing research plan and MkIS (Marketing Information System).
Step 19   Consider organizational issues and make recommendations for changes towards complete marketing orientation as felt necessary. Discuss with colleagues.
Step 20   Consider the organization's culture and make recommendations for internal marketing programmes as felt necessary. Discuss with colleagues.
Step 21   Consider the financial and human resource implications of your plans/recommendations. Discuss with colleagues.
Step 22   Assess costs and draw up indicative budgets. Discuss with colleagues.
Step 23   Draw up schedules showing the timing/sequence of your plans/recommendations. Discuss with colleagues.
Step 24   Specify review procedures and control mechanisms. Discuss with colleagues.
Step 25   Outline contingency plans. Discuss with colleagues.
Step 26   Review your complete marketing plan.
Step 27   Draw up your examination plan.
Step 28   Practise writing in true report style.

The process in detail is as follows:

Step 1   Read the case.

When the case arrives read it at normal reading speed and simply try to gather the gist of the situation and what is going on. You should avoid trying to go through the case too slowly at this stage or even making notes. Let the subconscious do the work for you.

Step 2   After an interval, re-read the case.

After a decent interval re-read the case once or twice again, not making too many detailed notes but to try and cover anything you may have missed first time through.

Step 3   Reflect on the instructions and candidates' brief.

Now that the content of the case is bedding down gently in your mind, it is time to turn to the important page of instructions which come along with the case and give you a clear indication as to what is expected of you. There are two sections to read. Firstly, the candidates' brief and secondly, the important notes which accompany the case study. The important notes remind you what will earn marks and what will not earn marks in the examination and that the data contained within the case will be split into the useful and the irrelevant. The notes also remind candidates not to bother contacting companies in the industry as this is unlikely to result in additional marks on the day. The candidates' brief is important in that it describes the role that you will be expected to play when framing your answer.

Step 4   Think yourself into the role and situation.

Without re-reading the case at this point consider the role which you will be asked to take in the examination and start to look at the case and possible alternatives from this point of view. Sometimes candidates are positioned as an employee in the company and other times as an external consultant. The role described will give strong indications as to the nature of the recommendations which will be required in the examination questions.

Step 5   Re-read the case and write a precis. Discuss with colleagues.

Writing a precis (this means shorter than the original!) of maximum one page A4 typed will force you to condense the details of between 30 and 50 pages of data into a very concise form. Precis writing is a useful discipline for identifying the really important facts from the case. Remember that in a short precis you have no space for opinions or interpretations. Once you have prepared your precis you should discuss this with your colleagues or group members and see how your opinion of the most important facts compares with other peoples.' In the light of other people's precis you may wish to refine your view of what the most important facts are.

Step 6   Conduct a marketing audit. Discuss with colleagues.

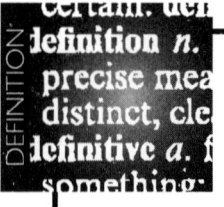

Marketing audit is described as 'a situational analysis of the company's current marketing capability.' (McDonald)

The marketing audit is the primary analysis tool of the case and is directed at analysing the current state of the organization's marketing as described in the case. A robust marketing audit should consider both external/uncontrollable factors including political, economic, sociological and technological factors (PEST) but candidates should note that this external analysis also includes a review of the most important marketing variable – customers (their needs, wants and aspirations) and competition. The internal element of the audit should be an analysis of how well the organization currently meets the market's requirements and should review mission and statements as well as marketing objectives, strategies and mixes if these are described.

It may also be relevant in this audit stage to consider other audits such as human resource, production, and financial audits if there is sufficient data and the analysis is considered pertinent. Once the audit has been completed, it is invaluable to discuss your findings with colleagues and compare notes on the different analysis routes and results obtained.

Step 7 Do a SWOT analysis. Discuss with colleagues.

SWOT analyses are well known analytical tools and, while they can be quite powerful, they are also prone to misuse. The SWOT analysis allows the investigator to identify the key strengths and weaknesses of the organization (internal) and the opportunities and threats which the organization may face from its external marketplace. Unfortunately the SWOT analysis is essentially a subjective process so comparison with colleagues and peers is essential. Also a variable is likely to feature in more than one category depending upon your point of view.

Too many SWOT analyses stop at the point of listing the various factors under one of the four headings. The real benefit from a SWOT analysis comes from discussion about what the classifications mean for the organization and what can be done. Many, more elaborate strategies have sprung from the simple idea of converting threats into opportunities, converting weaknesses into strengths and matching strengths to opportunities.

- Have you ever carried out a SWOT analysis in your organization? Most organizations have.
- What use was made of the SWOT? Most organizations carry out the analysis and then move on.
- How might the SWOT be used strategically in your organization?

ACTIVITY 10.1

Step 8 Conduct analyses/cross-analyses of appendices. Discuss with colleagues.

Case study appendices normally come in a variety of forms, from financial statements through tables to memos and examples of current advertising. The task before you in this step is to analyse the various tables in their various forms and pull out the various data sets that could be useful information to add to your understanding of the main text. Cross analyses of appendices also tend to highlight facts that will not be evident by looking at one table in isolation.

A word of warning, when confronted with financial data in a detailed form, you should be aware of the indiscriminate use of computer driven spreadsheets and always look for the meaning behind any financial calculations or ratio analysis.

Step 9 Reconsider your precis, marketing audit and SWOT analysis.

Putting the various analyses you have carried out so far together what can be learned? Are there any anomalies which appear? Have some of your earliest thoughts now been either confirmed or rejected?

Step 10 Conduct a situational analysis. Discuss with colleagues.

Based on the analyses now carried out, you should be ready to place all of this within a situational analysis which is capable of positioning the company within the broader industry and economic environment in which it must operate. Using the detailed analytical models at your disposal as well as some creativity and intuition, now is the time to step back from the detail of the case and consider where the company really is. The marketing audit data which reviewed the internal and external analysis of the organization can be developed further and now is the time to step back to one of the earlier writings in the marketing area, 'Marketing Myopia'. You should now have a much better idea about what the organization is able to do particularly well (competence), and the nature of the customer needs, wants and aspirations in the market being served. Looking at the problem from a customer rather than an internal perspective, can you decide what business the organization is in and what real competition faces – including substitutional competition? At this point it is essential to discuss your findings and your conclusions with colleagues. You will need a frank exchange at this point in order to sharpen your understanding of the real marketplace opportunities and threats which face the company.

Step 11   Decide the key issues. Discuss with colleagues.

There has to be a point at which the analysis stops, remember that no amount of analysis on its own – no matter how elegant – will be enough to achieve a pass mark in the examination. Decision is the only reason for carrying out analysis and we are now moving into that stage of the process.

   If you have carried out your analysis properly then the key issues confronting the organization will start to become apparent. Further discussion with peers and colleagues will start to crystallize these key issues.

Step 12   Develop a mission statement. Discuss with colleagues.

The mission statement is a key element of any marketing strategy for any organization. A good mission statement is one which works for the organization. It should be clearly understood by everybody in the organization and should provide a focus for everyone's activity within the business.

   A mission statement typically is unquantified but should do two things:

1   Clearly define what business the organization is in. In customer benefit rather than product terms.
2   State the organization's desired position within that business, for example biggest, most innovative, most recognized etc.

1   What is your company's mission statement?

2   What are the mission statements of your principal competitors?

Step 13   Decide broad aims. Discuss with colleagues.

This step takes the previous stage of the mission statement and develops it forward within the context of the case with which you are provided. Looking at where the organization is now and the mission statement of the organization, the broad aims would show how the organization might get from 'A' to 'B'.

   The advantage of looking at broad aims at this stage is that you can get a clear and uncluttered view of the organization and its strategy before you take on detailed analysis of the data. Obviously broad aims have to capable of being turned into objectives and milestones at a later stage (with quantification and timings) but this step helps put the various data provided in the case into context. Remember that not all of the data will be useful to the organization and its strategy!

Step 14   Identify and analyse major problems. Develop and analyse alternative solutions. Discuss with colleagues.

Bearing in mind the work you have done on identifying the organization's mission statement and broad aims, your job now is to identify those key and major problems which may stand in the way of the organization achieving what it wants to achieve.

   You would be well advised at this stage to try and differentiate between 'problems' and 'symptoms'. Look at all the apparent problems in the case and try and identify what are the major areas of concern (the strategic problems) that the organization needs to tackle and to solve in order to find a way forward. Before you jump to tackle what appear to be the biggest problems always look behind these to find out whether there isn't a bigger, more strategic, problem behind what are, in fact, just simply painful symptoms.

Remember, when you a look at a flat tyre, the puncture is not necessarily to be found where the tyre is flattest!

Step 15 Develop quantified and timescaled objectives. Discuss with colleagues.

Marketing, in common with all other business functions, requires objectives and time-scales in order to control and monitor its activity. Now that you have identified the most likely mission statement for the organization and have identified its broad aims and its major (strategic) problems, you must decide what the marketing function now needs to take the organization forward in order to achieve its aims. Without objective timescales no one in the organization will know what needs to be done, by when it needs to be done and how we measure success or failure.

Your answer should clearly define and differentiate between corporate objectives and marketing objectives (this has been covered elsewhere) and also between objectives and strategies. Marketing is essentially about harnessing the resources and capabilities of the organization to satisfy its markets/customers needs. In other words the marketing activity will tend to revolve around products and markets and the marketing objective ought to be couched in these terms.

The best way to understand the difference between objectives and strategies, on the other hand, is to always remember that an objective is an aim or a goal and therefore should be preceded by the word 'to'. Strategy, on the other hand, is defined as the means by which the objective is to be achieved, it should always therefore be preceded by the word 'by'.

Tactics then cover all the rest of the day-to-day activity in the marketing function and include the whole range of marketing detail from research and development, new products, market research, advertising schedules, training etc. Remember that no matter how important these various tactical activities may appear on the day (or even in the case study) they are only tactics. To pass the analysis and decision case study successfully you need to be able to step back from these tactics to be able to take a broader view of the organization, its strategic situation and develop a strategic solution for the future.

Step 16 Consider alternative strategies and select those most appropriate. Discuss with colleagues.

Having decided on the most appropriate marketing objective for the organization described in the case, your next step is to decide the most appropriate way of achieving that objective. The Ansoff Matrix often provides the most useful first step in this process and, usually (leaving out diversification) market penetration, market development and product development, will normally contain the broad strategic approaches open to the organization. After Ansoff consider Porter or GEC McKinsey.

Remember that Ansoff is only a tool to be used and you should make your selection of the most appropriate strategy for the organization based on your understanding of the case and the problems facing senior management.

Too many examination failures are caused by candidates' apparent inability to take into consideration competitor activity when selecting from strategic alternatives. No organization exists or operates in a vacuum and competitors' strategic positions need to be analysed and understood. There are two important aspects of competitor analysis which need to be brought into play at this stage:

1 Predicting competitor strategic action. Where is the competition going – what are they likely to be doing and what do we believe their plans are for the future?
2 Competitor response. How is the competition likely to respond to any strategic activity on our part?

'Analysis Paralysis' can be dangerous. Don't become obsessed with the minute detail in the case. Look beyond this to what the data is telling you. Search for the 'Big Picture'.

EXAM TIP

Step 17 Draw up detailed tactical plans covering the marketing mix. Discuss with colleagues.

Now that you have a broad strategic option which you have discussed with colleagues and agreed is the most sensible way forward for the organization, you should be able to expand this strategic approach into a more detailed marketing plan covering the basic elements of the marketing mix. You should consider both McCarthy's 4P approach to the marketing mix (product, price, place and promotion) but also the extended marketing mix proposed by Booms and Bitner (product, price, place, promotion, people, process and physical evidence). The latter is especially useful when considering services organizations.

It is vitally important at this stage that your detailed tactical plans (the marketing mix) are seen to support completely the strategic approach which you have devised as a solution for this organization's problems. A marketing plan is only practical and useful if it takes the organization towards the achievement of its strategic objectives. Try not to get carried away at this stage by particularly large tactical problems facing the organization, nor your particular desire to develop an elegant promotional strategy for the business. Remember the analysis and decision case study will be testing candidates' ability to think strategically not just tactically.

Step 18 Draw up a market research plan and a marketing information system.

At this point in the process you should have started to uncover critical information gaps that face the organization and without which it will find moving towards its strategic objectives much more difficult. It is also important at this stage to differentiate between strategic research and tactical or operational research.

You may find that strategic marketing often requires information which is not normally covered in regular day-to-day tactical market research activities. Research of a strategic nature may cover items such as customer needs, market segmentation and competitor analysis as well as distribution channel availability and various internal performance measures.

At this stage you should be able to define clearly what information the organization needs to move forward – where it might be obtained and how it might be gathered. It is unlikely in the examination that you will be asked to present a detailed market research plan itself. However, you should be very conversant with the particular methodologies open to the business.

Step 19 Consider organizational issues and make recommendations for changes towards complete market orientation as felt necessary. Discuss with colleagues.

Here you should review the organization's structure and design with particular emphasis on its current ability to satisfy customer/market needs. Having developed a mission statement, broad aims, marketing objectives and strategies etc., you need to be looking at the organization to identify potential blockages which may stop management delivering on market needs.

Many organizations, of all types, tend to be organized along functional lines for their own internal efficiency and convenience. Often these hierarchical structures make delivering customer satisfaction quite difficult. What changes would you suggest to this structure?

The second important area under this step is to try and identify the level of market or customer orientation which exists in the business. To what extent do the people in the organization (in all the functions) understand that the customer is king? To what extent is the focus of the organization on the internal activities or on the external (market) activities? What changes would you suggest are made to make the organization more market and customer focused?

Step 20 Consider the organization's culture and make recommendations for internal marketing programmes as felt necessary. Discuss with colleagues.

If the culture is not customer focused how does this need to be changed? You should be aware of recent emphasis in the business literature on TQM, BS5750/ISO9000 and

Re-engineering. These are all useful activities but only if customer focused. (Remember that BS5750/ISO9000 is all about efficiency of process and makes little or no mention of customers and customer needs!)

All organizations can say they are changing and can even make changes to managers' titles. Real culture change is a long and complicated process but often necessary. If culture change is a major issue in the organization described in the case how might you go about this process?

Step 21 Consider the financial and human resource implications of your plans/ recommendations. Discuss with colleagues.

Marketing does not operate in a vacuum – much as many marketers would like it to do so! Whatever strategies and plans you propose for the organization they will always have both financial and human resource implications. It is unreasonable and unprofessional not to predict and understand these implications fully before such strategic plans are proposed.

Financial implications: whatever activities the marketing function undertakes, including strategic plans for the future, the objective is always to improve the profitability of the organization. Marketing strategy is not about buying market share but improving longer term return on the organization's assets. At the very least you will be expected to understand the financial implications of your proposed strategy in terms of a small number of key financial measures – for example, what effects will it have on revenue, gross margins, costs and cash flow?

Human resource implications: nobody should ever forget that whatever an organization decides to do has to be carried out by people. Your proposed marketing strategy will have implications on the human resource function in an organization as well as the culture of the organization. Your strategy will probably have implications on the skill base required by the organization and may even require the acquisition of completely new skills. At the very least you should understand the implications of your proposals in terms of training and of longer term recruitment. Any such measures require time and money both of which will need to be budgeted.

Step 22 Assess costs and draw up indicative budgets. Discuss with colleagues.

A period of four weeks is given and it is felt this is sufficient time for you to uncover most reasonable costs of the actions and activities of which you are proposing. It is also expected that candidates will be able to develop an outline marketing budget and therefore will be able to cost their proposals fully. Advertising and promotion is often a major marketing cost but it is not the only one. Don't forget to allow for and budget for the other marketing costs which will be implied within your strategic proposition.

Step 23 Draw up schedules showing the timing/sequence of your plans/recommendations. Discuss with colleagues.

This stage allows you to build in some realism to your strategic proposals by working out just how long the various proposed activities are likely to take. In some instances case studies show a situation where time is of the essence, in other case studies the organization may be less pressed by competition and have time to plan more carefully for the future. Whichever case, your planning needs to incorporate this data.

Again, any strategic proposition needs to be accompanied by more than a simple promotional plan. There are likely to be a wide range of activities which you proposed and some will be dependent upon other activities before they can be started. Your schedules will need to cover all such activities including new product development, market research, internal recruitment and training as well as advertising and promotion.

Step 24 Specify review procedures and control mechanisms. Discuss with colleagues.

The detail of control mechanisms is discussed elsewhere. It is essential with any plan or strategic proposal that management understands exactly how progress towards (and deviation from) the strategy is both identified and corrective measures taken as required.

Here you will need to decide exactly which measures should be used to control the progress of the plan and how they will be used in detail. Remember, a plan without a control mechanism is not called a 'plan' – it is called a 'hope'.

Step 25   Outline contingency plans. Discuss with colleagues.

In the real world nothing ever goes to plan. It is the one thing we can be certain of! In the real world customers change, competition changes and organizations change and, however we see the world at the moment, is likely to have changed by the time any strategic proposals start to get implemented. Therefore it is useful at this stage to run one or two 'what?' scenarios to test the rigour of your strategic proposals. For example, in the Purbeck case what would be the scenario if the Government decided to levy VAT on motor insurance?

In the modern world, with its uncertainties, no plan is complete without contingency thinking and some level of contingency planning. Remember you are never quite sure what the additional information will be on the day!

Step 26   Review your complete marketing plan.

Now is the time to go right back to the beginning. Look at all the elements of your plan from analysis of the problem through mission statements, broad aims, marketing objectives and plans – do they all make sense when put together?

You must ensure that where you started and where you finished still makes sense given the structure and situation outlined in the case study. If your overall strategic selection was in the area of market development make sure that in developing your market plans you haven't spent most of your time talking about product development!

Step 27   Draw up your examination plan.

Now that you have completed the main thinking work and have discussed your thoughts with colleagues and refined your ideas in the light of their observations, it is time to plan carefully how to use your available resources between now and the day of the examination.

It is probably fair to say that one of the major reasons for failure in the case study is lack of examination technique. You have some four weeks between the time you get the case study and the examination. You should use this time carefully to prepare, analyse, view the situation from different angles and to share your observations with peers and colleagues. On the examination day you have but a scant 3 hours to incorporate the additional information into your thinking and your analysis and to get all your thoughts and explanations down on paper in a form that will acquire the maximum number of marks. You should talk to your tutors and your colleagues about exam technique but in the end there is no substitute for practice, practice and more practice. Two of the most recent cases have been included in this book for you to test your approach. Other cases are available from other sources. You are strongly advised to take the cases as dry-run experience and to time yourself. Time on the examination day is strictly limited so use it wisely.

Step 28   Practise writing in true report style.

The answers to the major case study are required to be written in business report format. There is a clear difference between report style and essay writing and you should practise to make sure that you are able to write in a clear report format. As with examination technique there is no substitute for practice.

The 28 step method is a good, if detailed, approach to the case study and is ideal when working with a group of other students. This method relies strongly on gathering feedback from others and modifying your approach in the light of contribution from peers. Unfortunately, not all candidates wish, or are able to analyse the case with others. Whenever possible you are urged to do so. If you cannot work in a group with others taking the exam you should try to enlist the help of someone else to talk over the case with. Maybe a friend or a colleague at work.

For those candidates who are not able to tackle the case in the group process, or who only have a short amount of time in which to do so, the second method may be more appropriate.

> **RECOMMENDED METHOD TWO**
> **SUMMARY OF THE 6-STEP METHOD**
>
> Step 1   Where are we now?
> Step 2   Where do we want to be?
> Step 3   How do we get there?
> Step 4   How can we make it happen?
> Step 5   How can we ensure arrival?
> Step 6   Putting it all together.

The process in detail is as follows:

Step 1   Where are we now?

Begin with detailed audits and analysis of the case material to establish the current position as described. You should be able to produce a succinct summary highlighting the key strengths, weaknesses, and constraints affecting the organization.

Step 2   Where do we want to be?

At this stage you should critically review the organization's mission, forecasts of likely future demand, objectives and be able to calculate gaps in achieving the set goals. At the end of this stage you should be able to produce a short statement of objectives for the organization, quantified over time. These could be illustrated by market, product, image, activity and competitive gap analyses.

Step 3   How do we get there?

Step 3 involves identifying alternative ways (strategies) that the organization might have of achieving the objectives which it has set. You should also consider the key criteria for selection between these strategies – and you should make a choice. Once completed you should be able to write a brief summary of the organization's 'strategic intent'. Typically this could be illustrated by models such as Ansoff and positioning maps.

Step 4   How can we make it happen?

This step takes the analysis into the tactical and operational level of planning. Developing your strategic thinking into areas such as product policy, pricing, distribution, promotions, finance and organizational design. At the end of this stage you should be able to draft an outline marketing plan to support your choice of strategy.

Step 5   How can we ensure arrival?

This stage will include the important control measures required to monitor and modify (if required) the implementation of the plans. You should consider aspects such as budgets, timescales, management and marketing information systems and contingency planning. You should consider both financial and non-financial controls. Your report at this stage might include budgets, gantt charts and cash-flow forecasts to support the implementation of your proposed plan.

Step 6   Putting it all together.

This final step is essential. Although we have broken down the strategic process into separate steps, these are only to permit us to understand better how to approach the problem. The customer may be effected by our activities in different audits and in different situations. For the customer the presentation must be seamless. At this stage you must review the steps above from the customer's point of view. Does it make sense? When it is implemented will it appear sensible? Do all the plans/actions piece together in a way that makes sense to the marketplace? Will the totality of the approach make this a more attractive proposition than the competition?

If not you may need to modify elements at different steps. Marketing is an iterative process.

How to answer the case

The marketing strategy, analysis and decision paper is examined as a three hour 'open book' case study examination. Open book means you may take as much material into the examination room as you please to include pre-prepared material and text books in order to help you frame your answer. If you have any precise questions about what is allowed in the examination and what isn't you are advised to check with the CIM or your local tutors. You should remember though that open books examinations are not always the great boon that they appear to be. Three hours is a limited time and the more information and data which you take in with you the more time you could waste looking through it to find the last final quote or analysis that you require. It is far better to carry out analysis prior to the examination and take in a clearly marked binder or folder with all the pages that you might need in predetermined order.

Whilst the open book examination allows you to take in additional materials, you are expressly forbidden to append materials to your script which have not been produced during the examination on paper provided by the CIM invigilator. Any prepared pages or appended material will be treated as invalid by the examiners.

Read the questions and the additional information carefully: as soon as you see the paper on the day take time to read the questions carefully and the additional information to find out what new perspectives this might throw on the case and the analysis which you have carried out on the case prior to the examination. Remember the additional information can carry marks up to 20 per cent of the total for its inclusion in the answer so don't throw this opportunity away. Once you have read the questions re-read them another second and third time to make sure that you understand exactly what the examiner is asking from you in your separate answers to the various sections. Remember that examiners are not trying to trick you or mislead you with the questions but often a degree of anxiety makes interpreting the plainest of English a problem. Take your time.

Make notes before you start to write the answer proper look at each of the questions in turn and the additional information and carefully plan out your answer to each one of the questions. Make sure that your answer follows a logical flow of argument and that it answers the question as stated as completely as possible. Make sure that wherever feasible you have managed to incorporate additional information into your answer. Once you have done this, review your notes and find out whether anything is missing and whether you need to add any additional thoughts at this stage. Now you may be ready to write.

Take on the role in the case study you will have already been assigned a role to play, this might be as an internal manager or an external consultant. You are strongly advised to take the role and to frame your answer from this persons point of view.

Write in report format if you have been successful and spent at least 15–20 minutes at the beginning of the examination understanding clearly and precisely what the questions are asking from you and you have made copious and logically ordered notes you should now be ready to start writing in clear, concise report format. Report format is not the same as essay writing and requires a logical flow of arguments and the use of headings and sub-headings wherever possible to support the sequence of argument. Clearly, logically thought out notes and a planned answer will make the report writing of the examination a fairly straightforward task.

While we are on the subject there are a number of things that you should certainly NOT do when answering the examination. If you wish to pass the examination the following should be noted:

Don't start writing as soon as you open the question paper.

Don't ignore all the planning and analysis which you carried out prior to the exam.

Don't write out the questions on the answer paper again (it just wastes more time).

Don't simply re-state the data contained within the case study.

Don't write pages and pages of essay text unbroken by headings.

Don't submit pages and pages of analysis (decisions gain marks).

Don't write beyond the allotted time on each question.

Don't forget to leave five minutes at the end of the examination to check your answer all the way through.

Don't run out of time.

Don't panic!

Trends in the examination

As with all areas of contemporary marketing, the analysis and decision case study tries hard to keep up to date with modern developments in the field. Since there is no set syllabus for the case study you can of course take advantage of many new developments and incorporate them easily into the required answers. Senior examiners also change over time but this should influence the tone of the case study less than the development of academic and practitioner thinking in the area of marketing generally. There are a number of key areas where the case study has changed over recent years and will continue to develop in the future. The following are worth noting:

Longer term thinking Despite a current emphasis on financially driven shorter term thinking, strategy is about the longer term. Managers must think beyond the short-term financial drivers of an organization and must have a clear driving vision or mission statement that looks at least five years forward. The case study will be looking for answers which take into account this longer term view and have a good understanding of what the organization needs to do in a longer time frame.

Financial awareness It is true to say that in the past one major criticism levelled at marketers was that they tended to be financially illiterate. If marketing is ever to achieve its destiny in organizations then it is clear that financial awareness is a skill that marketers simply have to acquire. The analysis and decision case study will continue to contain more and more searching financial analyses of an organization's situation and successful candidates will need to demonstrate a clear understanding of financial matters.

Organizational implications Apart from finance, human resource is a key area which will be affected by and will affect marketing strategy. Human resource is a key element in every organization and having the right people and organizational structure can often make the difference between a successful marketing strategy and a failure. Marketers in the future will need to be much more aware of the human resource implications of their proposed strategy as well as the role of people in implementing strategy into the marketplace.

Internationalization The world is shrinking, globalization is a major issue, fewer and fewer organizations are now able to survive in a purely local market facing local competition only. The UK is not outside but is a full member of the European Union (EU) and, as we move slowly towards a single market, European marketing will start to become the norm rather than the exception.

The importance of customers As the British and European economies continue to realign from the 1980s to the new realities of the 1990s it is clear that a major factor in organization success in the future will be the ability of senior management to focus their attention on customer needs as well as internal cost control and efficiency drives. Marketing strategy needs to be at the forefront of this movement and must ensure that the development of strategy is based on clearly defined and understood customer need. Scientific marketing, modelling and analysis are useful tools but are no substitute for empathy with our customers.

From analysis to decision Now that the two papers covering Strategic Marketing, Planning and Control and Analysis and Decision are both required compulsory papers for every candidate wishing to obtain the diploma, it has become easier to refine more closely the focus and objective of each paper. The Analysis and Decision paper will, in the future, concentrate much more on the practical application of marketing strategy within the real business world. All candidates should note that the use of marketing theory and analysis, no matter how eloquent and accurate, will not be sufficient to obtain a pass mark in the case study examination. The examiners place their emphasis clearly on the application of theory rather than simple analysis and this focus can be expected to increase over the coming years.

Trends in marketing

As the case study has no formal syllabus to follow it makes it a relatively easy task to incorporate new ideas and thinking into the appropriate case answers. For example, there has been much talk over recent years about issues such as 'quality', 're-engineering/business process redesign' and 'relationship marketing'. Wherever relevant to the case study in question, candidates should always attempt to bring this latest thinking into their answers and apply it in a relevant and practical manner.

A note of caution, however, needs to be made at this point. There is a difference between modern marketing thinking and management 'fads'. Answers to a case study which content themselves with a long exposé on the benefits of re-engineering (just because it happens to be current in the candidate's organization) are unlikely to gain a pass grade. If re-engineering or relationship marketing, for example, are seen as relevant activities given the overall approach proposed in a marketing strategy then they should be included – but always in context.

Past cases

This unit concludes with the two most recent case studies, Firstrate and the Leffe. You are urged to use these two cases as practical, timed 'dry runs' for the case study you will face in your examination.

Since there is never a right or a wrong answer to a case study the cases and questions have been included as they were presented to candidates in 1994 but, rather than a specimen answer, each case has been followed by a series of notes against which you should mark your own answer. These notes are intended for guidance only but cover the main points which you should have included in your answer.

A final note

A note is now sent to all candidates with their copy of the major case study:

STRATEGIC MARKETING MANAGEMENT:
ANALYSIS & DECISION

A MESSAGE FROM THE SENIOR EXAMINER

As you receive your copy of the case study for the forthcoming examination, I thought it would be worthwhile writing to you before you begin your preparation on the current case.

The case study examination is a new style of examination for most candidates, and those who have not sat case exams before need to prepare carefully both before the examination and no the day itself. The case study, unfortunately, has the lowest pass rate of all the Diploma subjects – not because it is more difficult but, perhaps, because it is different!

Any wise marketer always learns from the mistakes of others. I urge you to read this paper carefully. Your can avoid the most common mistakes made by previous candidates when you sit your examination next month.

As you begin your preparation this month, you should think about the following points. Together these account for the majority of the failing scripts – every year!

I   Do you know what the case study is looking for?

The Analysis and Decision case study, as with all Diploma subjects, is testing your ability to apply the marketing theory that you possess. The examination is not a simple test of knowledge – that is tested at Advanced Certificate level. To be sure of a pass in this case study you will need to convince the examiner not that you know (for example) what the Ansoff Matrix is, but how you would apply it in the confines of the case study. Do you know what 'market penetration' means? Can you explain it in terms of the marketing mix required to implement it? The same applies to any models you think may be relevant.

The second problem candidates face is separating 'Analysis' from 'Decision'. Some marks will be acquired in the examination for analysis of case material, but certainly the majority of the marks will be reserved for clear recommendations of action. It is always sad to see answers containing four or five pages of detailed SWOT or PEST analysis that might, at best, acquire 5 marks. The time spent writing out detailed analysis could often be much better employed describing recommendations for marketing objectives, strategy evaluation and strategy choice, with justifications, where far greater marks can be obtained.

2 Do you understand marketing?

The very core of marketing is the customer. The customer is the reason for an organization's existence, and customer satisfaction is the source of the organization's profits.

Following this basic tenet of marketing, any strategy document needs to be based on an understanding of customer needs. Far too many papers are presented that ignore customer needs completely, preferring to identify short-term methods of selling more product. The resulting 'product-push' or sales plans regularly fail to achieve a pass grade.

Do you understand what the customers in the case want? Can you differentiate between product features and benefits? Can you identify what makes the customers buy?

Remember too that, unlike other Diploma subjects, the Analysis and Decision case study has no set syllabus. Questions can span the subject matter of the entire Diploma syllabus (Planning and Control, Communications Strategy, International Strategy), and *the full range of CIM Certificate and Advanced Certificate are all assumed knowledge.*

3 Do you understand strategy?

Can you spot the difference between a strategy and a tactic? Remember that this is an examination of your ability to apply *marketing strategy* to the organization described in the case. Quite simply, there are more marks to be obtained by your recommendations on the strategic issues (segmentation, differentiation, positioning, targeting, strategy evaluation, strategy choice, etc.) than there are to be gained from long explanations of the marketing mix.

Secondly, strategy is, by its very nature, longer-term. You will normally be given a time frame in the case (often 5 years or longer) within which to base your answers. Short-term plans (1–2 years) are much more tactical in nature and tend not to gain pass grades. To be sure of success you must be thinking in the longer term.

4 Do you understand your role?

In each case study you will be given a clear role to play. You may be asked to assume the role of chief executive, director, marketing manager or external consultant. It is important that you answer the case questions from that role consistent with the terms of reference that would normally apply in that role. For example, if you are placed in the role of marketing manager you can question certain aspects of the organization (for example, the mission statement, if provided), but you cannot be expected to change them. If, for example, you are placed in the role of external consultant you can advise the organization, but you have no executive control.

5 Can you present your answer in a definite structure?

You do not know the questions until the day of the examination, but you may be able to see the areas that the questions will address. You are required to lay out your answer in *report format*. That is, you should work to construct a logical sequence to your thinking and use appropriate headings/sub-headings. There are a number of recommended approaches to the problem; you should choose one that suits you best. At the very least you should have very clear ideas about these two questions before the examination day:

1   What is wrong in the situation described?
2   What are you going to do to put it right?

6 Are you presenting your own work?

The Analysis and Decision examination is a test of *your* ability to apply marketing strategy. Only work which is clearly the individual work of the candidate will be marked.

A number of candidates prepare for the case study examination is groups. This is encouraged. Unfortunately, too many students then simply copy down the group answers prepared before the examination and hope that this will be enough to pass. Such papers are quite easily identified by the examiners and they are *failed en masse.*

By all means use the strength of the group to make sense of the case study, but be careful to develop and present your own solutions, in your own words, if you wish to pass.

The Additional Information is presented on the day of the examination precisely for the purpose of discouraging pre-prepared answers. The additional information will be extremely difficult to predict and will force you to think independently about the case organization's strategy. *The additional information can be assessed separately and can account for up to 20 per cent of marks awarded – do not ignore it.*

7 Are you prepared for examination day?

Finally, it must be said that any amount of good preparation can easily be destroyed by bad examination technique on the day. If you have taken a 'mock' examination of a previous case study as part of your preparation, you will know how difficult it is to read and understand the questions, plan your answers and write down all you need to say – in just 3 hours. If you have not tried to do this under 'mock' examination conditions, be warned that probably one third of all failures are caused by bad time management.

When you arrive in the examination room you should spend at least the first 20–5 minutes reading the questions and planning your answers before you start writing. You should:

- Read the questions and the additional information.
- Understand what the additional information means.
- Understand what the questions are asking – precisely.
- Plan your answers to each of the questions (based on your preparation but now incorporating the additional information).
- Plan your time, by question, according to the marks allocated to each question.

Only when you are clear what you want to say and how you are going to say it should you start writing.

I and my examiners wish you every success.

Paul Fifield

Case Study

MAY 1995, FIRSTRATE TECHNOLOGY SUPPORT CENTRE, FRANKFURT

"Oui.....oui.....non.....d'accord. A la prochaine. OK. Au revoir."

Thijs put the telephone down thoughtfully and turned to Claus, his new assistant, who had been waiting patiently for his attention. "You know, I do believe we are making some progress with the French at last! That was Pierre Marchand and not only was he pleasant to me but he actually suggested that we have dinner together the next time I am in Paris. I never thought I would crack that problem, he has always been so off-hand and when I first joined he went out of his way to embarrass me in front of a customer. It's fortunate I don't have a similarly Latin temperament or I would have walked out then. You should know that the Paris office has been behaving so badly since the reorganisation but perhaps this is the turning point. I just wonder what has happened to change his attitude.

"Claus, I am going into a meeting now and unfortunately I shall be tied up for the rest of the morning. Why don't you take a look at this report which Gareth Hall wrote for me when I joined the company. It will give you some good background so that later on today we can make a start on the 1995/96 marketing plan. We only have a month before the board meeting and there is so much to do. I have been tied up with so many promotional activities since I joined that I haven't had a chance to start thinking strategically yet."

As Thijs left the room, Claus settled down with a cup of coffee to try to understand something about this company he had joined...

MEMORANDUM

To: Thijs Van der Vliet   From: Gareth Hall

Subject: Internal report on FirstrATE Europe

Date: 13th September, 1994

So sorry that I cannot be with you for your first fortnight at work. This is the first holiday we have taken for two years now - it really has been extremely busy here recently, implementing the re-organisation. I have written the attached report an introduction for you to FirstrATE Europe. We discussed some of this at interview, but I felt that you would need further depth and clarification.

James Duncan, European Finance Director, who is also based here in Thame, will be in touch shortly and will organise a European tour for you to visit all the Customer Centres (CC). In the meantime, I hope you will find your way around the Technical Support Centre and venture out to meet everyone in the Frankfurt CC.

Good luck! I look forward to seeing you in a fortnight.

Garett

INTERNAL REPORT by GARETH HALL

PRIVATE AND CONFIDENTIAL - DO NOT COPY

FirstrATE EUROPE

1 History and US parent

FirstrATE Inc. was founded as First Electronic Components Inc. in 1954 and has just celebrated its 40th anniversary. It has always operated in the field of supplying test equipment to electronic systems manufacturers and changed its name to FirstrATE Inc. in 1974. The company used to pride itself in providing a unified corporate "total solution" to the electronics world supplying test equipment at every stage of a production process - from design through manufacture to service.

However against a background of falling revenues and increasing losses, the recently appointed Chief Executive of FirstrATE Inc., John Leyton, reorganised the company into divisions which for the first time are accountable for their performance. This global reorganisation took place in 1991.

Since then, two of the divisions whose activities were seen to be peripheral to the main business have been sold off, leaving only the ATE Division and the Repair Equipment Division.

The ATE Division, which provides automatic test equipment products, software and service is by far the largest part of the business, accounting for 80% - 85% of revenues. The Repair Equipment Division (RED) provides test equipment which is used in the servicing of faulty printed circuit boards (PCBs), which are found, for example, in personal computers.

FirstrATE Europe is the European division of the ATE Group with offices in five countries as follows:

UK	Thame
GERMANY	Frankfurt
FRANCE	Lyons
ITALY	Milan
SWITZERLAND	Geneva

Historically, management control of each division was based around R&D centres, so that FirstrATE Europe was controlled out of Princetown because that is where the R&D takes place on ATE products. Each of the European offices had complete functional organisation structures including sales and service, customer support, finance, personnel and logistics. However the reporting structure was somewhat idiosyncratic. Some functional heads had management control of that function in other European offices - so for example I was in charge of sales in Thame as well as being European Sales and Service Director. The sales managers of all the other countries reported to me and had dotted line relationships with Princetown. In contrast, the regional service managers reported to Princetown with only dotted line relationships to me.

In 1993, the future was looking bleak, since neither FirstrATE Inc. nor FirstrATE Europe had reported an operating profit in five years and there was no evidence of an improvement in trading conditions on the horizon.

2 Restructuring of FirstrATE Europe

While John Leyton was getting to grips with his new position as Chief Executive of FirstrATE Inc. and concentrating his efforts on the United States and the rest of the world outside Europe, I appointed a firm of management consultants (JMB Limited) to take the senior management of FirstrATE Europe through a series of structured workshops. These had the following objectives:

1 To define, document and initiate a 5 year regional strategy for sustained sales growth including an agreed set of optimal solutions to our business problem.

2 To define the organisational implications of such solutions and to identify planning gaps and the means of resolving them.

3 To define and document an agreed implementation plan, covering 1994 in detail and major milestones to end 1995.

After a great deal of thought, preparation and effort the re-organisation of FirstrATE Europe was announced in the spring of this year and is currently being implemented. Unlike many of its competitors, FirstrATE is heavily dependent on the ATE market and, to date, FirstrATE Europe has sourced all its products from the parent company. Because of this situation, the series of workshops concluded that in the short to medium term, FirstrATE

Europe has no alternative other than to carry on with the existing business but to do it better and at less cost.

We identified that this would require:

- the acquisition of more new customers
- the retention and development of the existing customer base
- enhanced levels of customer satisfaction
- improved market intelligence
- more efficient and effective ways of working, with reduced resources

The new organisation structure involves a change in status of the country subsidiaries and a head-count reduction of some 20%. The objective of the new model is to enable newly formed local units to focus exclusively and cost-effectively on sales and service. The actions being taken to achieve this are:

1. Taking away as much finance and administration activity from the local sales and service operation as possible.
2. Consolidating a critical mass of technical skills in a new centre of technical excellence (Technology Support Centre (TSC) based in Frankfurt).
3. Creating a new European marketing function (hence your appointment).
4. Developing an overall strategy for the European market.
5. Centralising many of the existing devolved financial, commercial and administrative functions. (Finance and HR in Thame).
6. Out-sourcing logistics. (Netherlands? This has not happened yet)
7. Changing the status of the national operations from subsidiaries to customer centres.

The new model requires significant changes in perceptions of FirstrATE staff across Europe but enables the organisation to be in a position to re-start a growth pattern as soon as market conditions and increasing revenues allow.

The whole impetus for change is to ensure that FirstrATE Europe moves from a product-driven sales organisation to a customer-oriented, market responsive one. This is essential for survival in the increasingly mature and competitive ATE market. The new framework is based around putting the customer at the centre of everything that the organisation does. Each functional activity is now seen as a flow of services towards the customer.

The local units are close to the customer, psychologically as well as geographically. These units are supported by all the other functions which are dispersed across Europe. The absence of a head office has been achieved by having the senior members of FirstrATE Europe's management team geographically spread. The directors of Sales, Service, Finance and Human Resources form the European management team which reports into FirstrATE Inc.

The primary interface is now between the local unit, called a Customer Centre (CC) and its customer base. Instead of running and operating a subsidiary operation with all its administrative, legal, regulatory and financial requirements, these units will be devoted almost entirely to serving the customer.

3   The European ATE Market and FirstrATE's Product Range

The ATE market is in decline for a number of reasons:

Because of the cost of ATE, electronic equipment is being designed specifically to be self testing or at least testable in simpler, cheaper testers, for example using Boundary Scan techniques.

The drive for quality in electronics, Japanese style, says that a fault detected by ATE is a fault detected too late.

It is better to eradicate the cause of the fault altogether. This does not help our salesmen!

PCBs are becoming so dense and multi-layer that traditional test technology cannot access the components. Alternatives up-stream are being sought, for example using software to check out the design more thoroughly.

Within the ATE Group, we address two market segments, namely in-circuit test (ICT) and functional test (FCT). These may be combined in one piece of equipment known as a combinational tester. (CT)

ICT   Testing components in-situ by placing the board on a bed of electrical pins which allow a stimulus and response directly to and from the nodes. This is known as a "bed of nails" and from this test the manufacturer can identify that all the components are in the correct place and working. If a board is shown to be faulty it is routed back onto the production line to have the fault rectified. Because of the complexity of modern boards, this market is in serious trouble. FirstrATE pioneered this technology and are market leaders.

FCT   Testing boards for their full operational function through the edge pins - this is a much slower and more expensive procedure. If the board is shown as faulty, an engineer must be called who, with the aid of a circuit diagram, can analyse the fault. A functional test may take many minutes, whereas an in-circuit test takes a few seconds. Functional tests are much harder to devise and the equipment is very expensive, but they provide a better operational test. A cheaper alternative to functional testing is called Boundary Scan and FirstrATE have also developed this type of equipment.

CT   In some situations, combinational testing is appropriate, using both ICT and FCT. One example would be when performing a system test. The ICT would establish that all the components on the boards in the system were in position and working while the FCT would establish that the boards were talking to each other as they should.

FirstrATE Europe operates in five product areas:

1.   **Omega Series:** Our traditional product range providing both ICT and combinational capabilities, with comprehensive software support.

2.   **Delta Series:** Our new functional verification test series, specifically focusing on the telecommunications market.

3.   **Alpha Series:** Our new low-cost modular test series, the first product offering which we have bought in and not sourced from FirstrATE Inc.

4.   **Service:** A wide variety of value-added services ranging from complete turnkey test solutions to advanced applications support and customer training.

5.   **FirstrATE Extra:** Our brokerage service offers lower-priced factory refurbished FirstrATE test systems to first time customers. Existing users benefit from being able to retire equipment with favourable trade-in allowances.

LATER THAT MORNING

Claus looked up in surprise as Thijs stormed into the room and flung his papers down on his desk.

"You just wouldn't believe how little people understand marketing in this organisation!" he snarled before he thought about who he was talking to. "Oh, sorry! I don't mean to give you a bad impression when you have only just arrived. It's just that whenever I have a meeting with the sales managers from the local units, I feel that I am swimming in treacle. They are so used to being provided with a product from the US, at a given price and going out and selling it as best they can, using their own promotional material - and you can just imagine what that's like. Sometimes I feel that I have fallen into a black hole whenever I need support or feedback from the local units. And as for Princetown, they're no better!

"Anyway, without further ado, I have set aside most of the rest of the day to make a start on the 1995/96 marketing plan. You now realise that this is pioneering but take heart! It will be better once we have established a planning procedure. Now that you have read Gareth's report I thought I would fill you in on what has happened since I joined eight months ago.

"Broadly speaking, 1994 was the year of re-organisation. 1995 is the year of consolidation and hopefully 1996 onwards will make it all worthwhile. We have implemented almost to the letter what we decided to do in the workshops. Incidentally, we discovered in those workshops that our top 12 customers accounted for 60% of business. This is one reason why we have tried to create a truly multinational organisation, particularly from a marketing point of view.

"Have you looked around the outfit here yet? These new premises are excellent, only twelve minutes to the airport, and purpose built for a high tech business like ours. We now have excellent training and demonstration facilities and meeting rooms.

"Most of the local offices adapted to the changes within their existing premises but occupying smaller spaces. Only Thame has moved offices - it took over a year to get rid of that lease. Since the reorganisation, all the sales managers in Europe have changed - some couldn't cope with the cultural differences and others simply were not capable of taking on the additional responsibilities. The financial group is well established in the UK with one person in Frankfurt and a roving person based in Paris. We have also implemented the support structure and most people who are meant to be working remotely are now doing so.

"Overall it has been a great experience. The business is now going well and the reorganisation has overcome previous problems of lack of capital expenditure. The "feel good factor" is still missing, with the sales managers turning in pessimistic forecasts though business has done exceedingly well. Product sales are well up on budget but the service business is still problematic and we are losing business there.

"The resistance to change has been interesting. Each country has different barriers and cultural issues are very important. As I told you earlier, the French are still the biggest problem. The re-organisation was a huge shock. Gareth said that their reaction was one of disbelief. "How could you do this to us?" They are still upset. They have been simply ignoring the centralised functions such as customer training but at last we are seeing some improvement and they are beginning to co-operate. The Italians were also very shocked and when Gareth made the presentation he thought they were going to strangle him! The UK and Switzerland have accepted the reorganisation well and so has the German office because the Technology Support Centre is nearby. The reduction in head-count is saving $2.5m a year which is a huge help. In the long term the geographic location of the European Technology Centre will be re-evaluated but in the short term there was not time to look elsewhere, apart from near the existing FirstrATE centres.

"Within the TSC, technical skills have been provided by staff who are pulled in from different countries and travel home at weekends. Training has not worked out as expected and we have had to create three travelling units to take to the customers. The problems arise because of manager-level jealousy regarding international travel. It is seen to be a perk, especially in the UK. In France, the Lyons office is resisting sending people to Germany. The quality of training has suffered by allowing it to be at the offices and it's a pity this hasn't worked because the environment in Frankfurt is more sales-oriented. We have French and German trainers. The head of training is a Romanian who speaks French but his English is not good. We are now resigned to the fact that we are often not going to manage to get customers to come to Frankfurt. This is a trade-off between quality and cultural issues. We are working on lowering the cost of the training equipment which we buy from the US. This is a political transfer pricing issue and we feel we want to be charged the true cost.

"Don't underestimate the importance of training. It is a huge competitive issue because the users' view of system performance can be low because of poor training; also we have to spend a lot more supporting customers who haven't been trained properly. It gives us another opportunity to get close to the customer."

At this point Claus interrupted. "But what about marketing? How is it going now?"

Thijs continued "You will be pleased to know that after a very shaky start, the marketing function is getting off the ground at last. You have to be very self motivated in a job like this because there is no established pattern to follow. Perhaps I tend to be too aggressive and I have ruffled some feathers. I am not a marketing professional but I have a good solid background in a software company and it really helps to be trilingual. One of the main battles we have to win is to overcome the fragmented image which customers have of this organisation. In the past, sales managers have organised all the exhibitions and advertisements but now they have to hand over this initiative. We must look at the sales manager as our partner in each country. One of our key goals is to create a European image. Our biggest global competitor is Jupiter which is superb at marketing of course. There is no way FirstrATE could afford to compete.

"For the first six months I simply focused on promotions and we are just coming out of that stage now. I have pulled together some market research reports - Friedman & Smith is the best. Recently I ran a two day internal strategy workshop on Jupiter. The conclusion we came to was that the problem is to get access high enough in the customer organisation when competing with an organisation like that.

"Our customers are either pro-FirstrATE or pro-Jupiter but probably not wholly invested in one or the other. We need to know what our customers' customers are doing because the end user is driving our customers. Our only chance is to link up through the sales and service forces. This is a big strategic issue and we are trying to establish a brand franchise in the marketplace. This is why we have been recruiting people who are international and from the end-user industries such as telecoms, not from ATE backgrounds. The cultural barriers are huge but this is changing.

"FirstrATE is smaller and quicker than Jupiter. We can be flexible but we need to be better and we should anticipate customer needs, not just meet them. Having our people on the factory floor is one way of doing this.

"John Leyton has been instrumental in all of this. We couldn't have got off the ground without him. He is now trying to establish a global FirstrATE - the ATE group, including service, and the Repair Equipment Division are moving from being local presences to regional to global. This is where I frequently encounter the worst problems. A global marketing network simply does not exist.

"Going back to the reorganisation, the only thing we did not implement was the plan to centralise logistics, such as parts. We looked at various countries' software packages and even the best is patchy. For example in Scandinavia, Southern France and Sicily we cannot find a 48 hour guaranteed service. So what we did was to analyse the levels of inventory and the traffic of parts which moved regularly - there were very few. Two thirds of the parts in stock turned over only once a year or less and many were old products which could be scrapped. The conclusion we came to was that we should create our own logistics software package. There is a big MIS evaluation taking place in the US at the moment and we are waiting for the conclusions before making a move.

"The action we have taken in the short term is to scrap lots of parts and reduce the inventory to a manageable level. We used to carry 2000 items of which only 100 moved more than twice a year. It will probably be the middle of next year before a solution is in place. In the meantime, customer service is not suffering because with less parts, the local manager can take care of any problems. The paper system controlling parts is based here in Frankfurt.

"Financially, things are really looking up. 1995 is likely to be a record year and as a group, FirstrATE Inc. is forecast to make a profit before tax for the first time in years. Mind you, so it should after the massive provisions taken last year.

"The European economies are mainly improving, except Italy. Market research information says that the ATE market in Italy is worth $25-30m but FirstrATE have only $2.5m. This doesn't sound right and we need to find out who else is there. Perhaps Poseidon, being Italian, is attributing all its European sales to Italy and double counting. Switzerland is doing well because a) the telecommunications industry is booming, a major market segment and b) the Delta series has really caught on there.

"Financial systems have been a real problem and have not enabled the sales managers to provide an acceptable level of service to the customer. The mentality of the finance department has not been service-oriented and managers weren't getting the level of information they needed to do the job. You see, marketing on its own cannot succeed. Incidentally, finance is UK-based because the UK financial services are better than others, the skill set is there and the systems expertise is there.

"We have recently introduced a finance package which we offered selectively to begin with. It works like this: we install a tester for one third of the price then the customer pays per board processed. High usage renders the package inappropriate, however it has grabbed market attention and distracted people from the final price. We have had to do various finance deals - we may have the technical edge but perception and image is very important. FirstrATE is perceived to offer quality at a high price. Jupiter discounts heavily in competition with us and is buying market share. The big money is in the top end of the market and we don't want to get into the lower end. But there are only two of us competing for this market, FirstrATE and Jupiter. FirstrATE must fight back on meeting customer needs, adding value, differentiation, positioning. We have to fight on value because it is almost impossible for us to fight on price.

"There are various non-product attributes which we can provide such as auditing for customers to analyse the efficiency of their production line. If the customer has volume problems we can provide an enhanced programme giving him economic benefit. We just have to be there to know what the customer needs.

"As far as products are concerned, we are very excited about the Delta series. We estimate that this is a $150m market and our three year plan forecasts break-even this year. Overall we are not on track there although sales are going well in some countries.

"Our market focus is something of a matrix. We have moved from a product focus to a vertical (industry) market focus but we can't address everything at once with limited resources. The other dimension of the matrix is the regional focus.

"The Omega series has reached a plateau as far as its life cycle is concerned. This is why we are now looking at vertical markets, modularity, and the telecoms focus.

"The big problem area is service and this is where we are losing customers. Historically, service meant maintenance. Now we offer other services which are software based such as programming services and consultancy. We would like to manage the test site for the customer and so move away from product to benefit. Our aim is to get FirstrATE products to be more useful on the customers' site. We have moved to outsourcing a team of programmers, who are sophisticated applications specialist programmers, and work on a contract basis. We still have problems because of the high pressure environment on the factory floor, so it is difficult to find project leaders.

"One example of this working well is at Z-Boards in Scotland where FirstrATE is permanently on site and gets paid according to the increase in yield. Z-Boards has put in eight manufacturing lines this year and is looking at another £150,000 investment. If we can reach the right level in the customer organisation we can add real value like this.

"A more delicate issue is the reorganisation. We have already come a long way and a lot of managers think that it is time for the business to settle down. I am not so sure. We have managed to get the customer back into focus but there are still too many people thinking product first. If we are going to be really customer focused, and to compete with Jupiter we have no choice, there are still some important changes to be made. We certainly cannot deliver full solutions to vertical markets from our present structure.

"The last subject we should discuss is the new role of Customer Relations Managers. Some have been working well, others have been replaced. It is a very responsible job handling the customer, networking internally, making sure customers don't get dropped and managing two assistants. It was a struggle for the first six months to get them to understand their role and apparently there were lots of problems over disciplines and procedures. This has settled down and is working well now.

"OK, Claus. I hope that hasn't been too much, too soon. Let's break for lunch now and later on this afternoon we will make a start on the strategic marketing presentation. It will be the first ever presentation on this subject within this organisation and we will span an eighteen month period to cover what is left of this year and the whole of 1996 in detail into a review of plans up to 2000. You will find everything else you will need in this file so why don't you start reading that while I attend the weekly sales meeting of the German Customer Centre at 2 o'clock?"

Claus agreed to meet Thijs back in his office at 4 o'clock and left the room for lunch, very much in need of a break.

THIJS'S FILE CONTENTS

A1, A2, A3, A4	Product portfolio
B1, B2	Job description - Thijs Van der Vliet
C1, C2	Objectives - Thijs Van der Vliet
D	New corporate structure
E	1990 - 1994 European sales
F	1994 financial results
G1, G2	Memo re: role of new customer centre
H1, H2, H3, H4, H5, H6, H7, H8, H9, H10, H11	Friedman and Smith report

<u>NOTE TO MARKETING PLANNING FILE</u>
<u>RE: PRODUCT PORTFOLIO</u>

Thijs Van der Vliet   March 1995

1. Omega Series: Our traditional product range providing both ICT and combinational capabilities, with comprehensive software support.

Strong focus towards production line testers and reductions in total test time. Each successive generation of hardware and software improves price/performance ratio. The latest version, Omega Special, allows programmes and fixtures created for existing Omega Series systems to be easily migrated to the new Omega Special so that customers can add Special systems without sacrificing their prior investments in programs and fixtures. The Omega Special systems are designed to help electronics manufacturers meet competitive time-to-market pressures, increase product quality, capitalise on new technologies and reduce costs. The range supports from 256 to 4096 hybrid pins and is ideal for a broad spectrum of manufacturers from consumer electronics to engineering workstations where flexibility, diagnostic accuracy, high throughput and reliability are critical issues. The Omega Special is really a repackaging of the Omega Series.

We have also recently launched the Omega A and Omega B which are smaller and cheaper than the other Omega machines. These support from 256 to 1328 nodes.

The Omega C and Omega D support up to 2000 nodes and the Omega E, Omega F and Omega G support from up to 4096 nodes.

The Omega series is sold as a bundled package of hardware with basic software. There are extra software packages which can be added such as the Omega SW which is test and repair software which allows the customer to manage the data such a production line failure in report form. Not all customers purchase extra software because they do not understand the value or they produce something similar themselves which runs on a PC.

One of the critical issues concerning customers is throughput which depends on the amount of time taken to carry out a test and diagnose a fault. Larger manufacturers achieve a throughput of thousands of boards per day.

A-1

Another critical issue is the "time-to-market" factor which means the time it takes from originating a product (the design engineer designs the card) to getting it to the customer (the product is fully tested and rolling off the production line). For example, time-to-market for a new PC might be two to three months, while time-to-market in the telecoms industry is typically twelve to eighteen months. FirstrATE TEST is another software product which provides a benefit in writing a test programme, again reducing time-to-market.

2. **Delta Series: Our new functional verification test series, specifically focusing on the telecommuncation market.**

The Delta series has specific applications within the telecoms markets, for example, in the testing of line cards which route the calls at the exchange. Line cards need functional testing and with the number of lines per card increasing from 8 to 16 to 64, the testing is becoming more complicated.

The telecoms industry is expanding dramatically, for example, in China 100 million lines are being installed so 6 million line cards will be manufactured. A typical line card manufacturer might have 10 production lines and would therefore need 10 testers. The advantage of the Delta series is that the test time has been reduced from 40 minutes to 15 minutes.

Other developments in the telecoms industry to look out for are ISDN - integrated services data network which, for example, will enable the idea of home shopping to become a reality. Telecoms now operate on a narrow band. Soon this will be broad band so that video telephones will become standard office equipment.

The Delta Series has not taken off in the US but in Germany FirstrATE is doing well with this product. We are driving in hard with a very committed team. We are looking to provide integrated solutions and services we can bolt on, and are moving from hardware to software.

The question is how to leverage off the success of Delta Series? We only have limited resources - where should we focus our effort?

A-2

3. Alpha Series: Our new low-cost modular test series

The Alpha Series is the first product offering which we have bought in and not sourced from FirstrATE Inc. There is no dominant supplier of this low cost product. We picked up this new product line because segmentation analysis had identified a gap in the price/performance spectrum. John Leyton gave us a free hand when politics in the ATE Group would have prevented this previously. The ATE Group used to exist to sell equipment out of the US - now it is customer led.

The channels of distribution which we have been using are telemarketing and direct sales. We can reach our own customers easily but how do we reach the rest of the market? Found product, need channels. In practice, we haven't closed many sales because competitors are there already. What we have done is opened the market to competition. This needs rethinking.

4. Service: A wide variety of services.

As levels of support requirements vary through the tester product life cycle, we provide support to meet specific needs driven by different test situations.

State of the art hardware, software and systems design technology help achieve and sustain product innovation and quality objectives through our Design Consultancy.

Operator and applications training are available to the new user, while engineers are available from the Technical Support Centre to provide technical assistance throughout the product's life.

The customer may choose to have the equipment maintained by FirstrATE, in which case there is a choice of maintenance agreements, remote diagnostics and repair and calibration services. Alternatively, the customer may opt for self-maintenance in which case, training and parts are available.

Value-added services are available to continually enhance the customer's test environment. They range from complete turnkey test solutions from FirstrATE's Custom Products engineers, to advanced applications support to help manage staff overload during peak periods.

A-3

Advanced applications training, based on scores of unique and challenging test solutions, is available. Frequent test technology seminars and user forums serve to exchange test knowledge and to feedback customer ideas to new-product development teams.

FirstrATE's Software Support Program guarantees access to new software releases and revisions. In addition, the program provides toll-free telephone support, software model library updates, an electronic bulletin board, newsletters and application notes.

Clearly there is plenty of scope for growth here so why are we losing business?

5. FirstrATE Extra: Our brokerage service offers lower-priced factory refurbished FirstrATE test systems to first time users and existing customers.

Existing users benefit from being able to retire equipment with favourable trade-in allowances. FirstrATE Inc. run a database on second-hand systems which are available and have one person full time in Princetown plus a roving person in Europe to co-ordinate the service. It is becoming a worthwhile business and is going to turn over $10m world-wide this year.

Apart from the benefits to first time customers and upgrading customers, it is often invaluable to customers who want to increase capacity, perhaps by adding another production line, without having to disrupt the existing production line or introduce any changes as far as their staff are concerned. If they can track down an identical system to their own through FirstrATE Extra, they can replicate the process without having to provide any additional training or support.

A-4

JOB DESCRIPTION

Title: **European Marketing Manager**

Department: European Technology Centre

Reports to: European Sales Director   Date: **October 1994**

BASIC FUNCTION

Directs the European marketing strategy in analysing, planning and implementing plans and programs for various products to meet or exceed profit, volume and market share targets. Responsible for market analysis to determine industry growth, market share and competitive positioning.

PRIMARY DUTIES

Sales and Customer Support

1 Develops, implements and controls marketing programs for current/new products including advertising, product literature, trade shows, exhibits, initial training and seminars.

2 Generates and implements communications campaign plans in support of Divisional/Corporate objectives. Co-ordinates public relations, press releases, presentations and advertising to ensure proper image guidelines conform and are of quality.

3 Monitors effectiveness of programs and campaigns against established objectives and budgets. Provides regular reports on project and budget status to European Sales Director.

4 Formulates strategic marketing plans and approaches for product enforcements, new product introductions and mature products. Develops courses of action to enable FirstrATE to manage product life cycles and ensure continuity of revenue stream.

B-1

5 Co-ordinates and communicates product strategies to European organisations. Participates in local meetings to provide product, update and selling strategies and competitive information as required throughout the product life cycle.

6 Responsible for market, industry growth and share analysis to determine market and segments for new product presentation by collecting, documenting, analysing and disseminating information pertaining to all competitive products and strategies, for tactical and strategic planning.

7 Performs market analysis and research that leads to the generation of new product and market profiles for divisional strategy.

8 Develops methods of reducing sales or marketing related risks defined in product proposals through trial sell programs, additional market research or sales strategy development.

9 Recommends, based on market analysis and new product plans, the discontinuance of products that are no longer good business opportunities.

10 Maintains close contact with other FirstrATE Divisions for the purpose of exchanging market need ideas, promoting synergy in marketing strategies and product support functions.

11 Responsible for developing, recommending and integrating policies, procedures and practices for the Customer Centres.

12 Performs the role of "champion" for European markets.

B-2

NAME: THIJS VAN DER VLIET

JOB TITLE: EUROPEAN MARKETING MANAGER

LOCATION: FirstrATE, FRANKFURT

PERSONAL OBJECTIVES 1995

1 Develop a Pan-European Promotions Program for Sales and support which takes into account the broad-based needs of Europe as well as the needs of the local countries.

This program should include:

- Common theme/booth for all exhibitions, where possible.

    Approved Exhibitions in 1995:
Nepcon - UK	March '95
Forum Mesure - France	September '95
Test'94 - UK	October '95
Electronica - Germany	November '95

- Review of the use of various PR agencies around Europe with recommendation to change where appropriate.

- Development and implementation of Customer/Market communications media as a vehicle to help establish a more dynamic image within the European marketplace.

- . Review procedure with each Customer Centre to enable management of the implementation of local activities.

- Program aimed at improving the press awareness of FirstrATE in each European country.

- Promotions pack which can be used by the distributors.

- Methods by which the success of the various programs can be measured.

Plan to be completed by the end of Quarter 1

C-1

2 Design, develop and implement a Launch and Promotions Program, specifically to support the sale by FirstrATE of the Alpha Series of products in Europe. Program to begin with the introduction of the products at Nepcon - UK in March 1995 and to have a continual 12 month visibility.

- by Quarter 1

3 Establish the Jupiter selling strategy in Europe particularly with respect to pricing. Work with the European Sales Managers to develop market tactics to counter this strategy.

- by end Quarter 2

4 Play an active part in all European Managers' Meetings and Training. Participate in Local Sales Meetings as required.

- on going

5 Ensure all necessary contacts are made with ATE Group personnel in Princetown such that the "Marketing Pipeline" between the USA and Europe grows stronger and becomes more effective in both directions.

- by end Quarter 2

(signed) .... (dated) .....15/12/94.........

C-2

NEW CORPORATE STRUCTURE

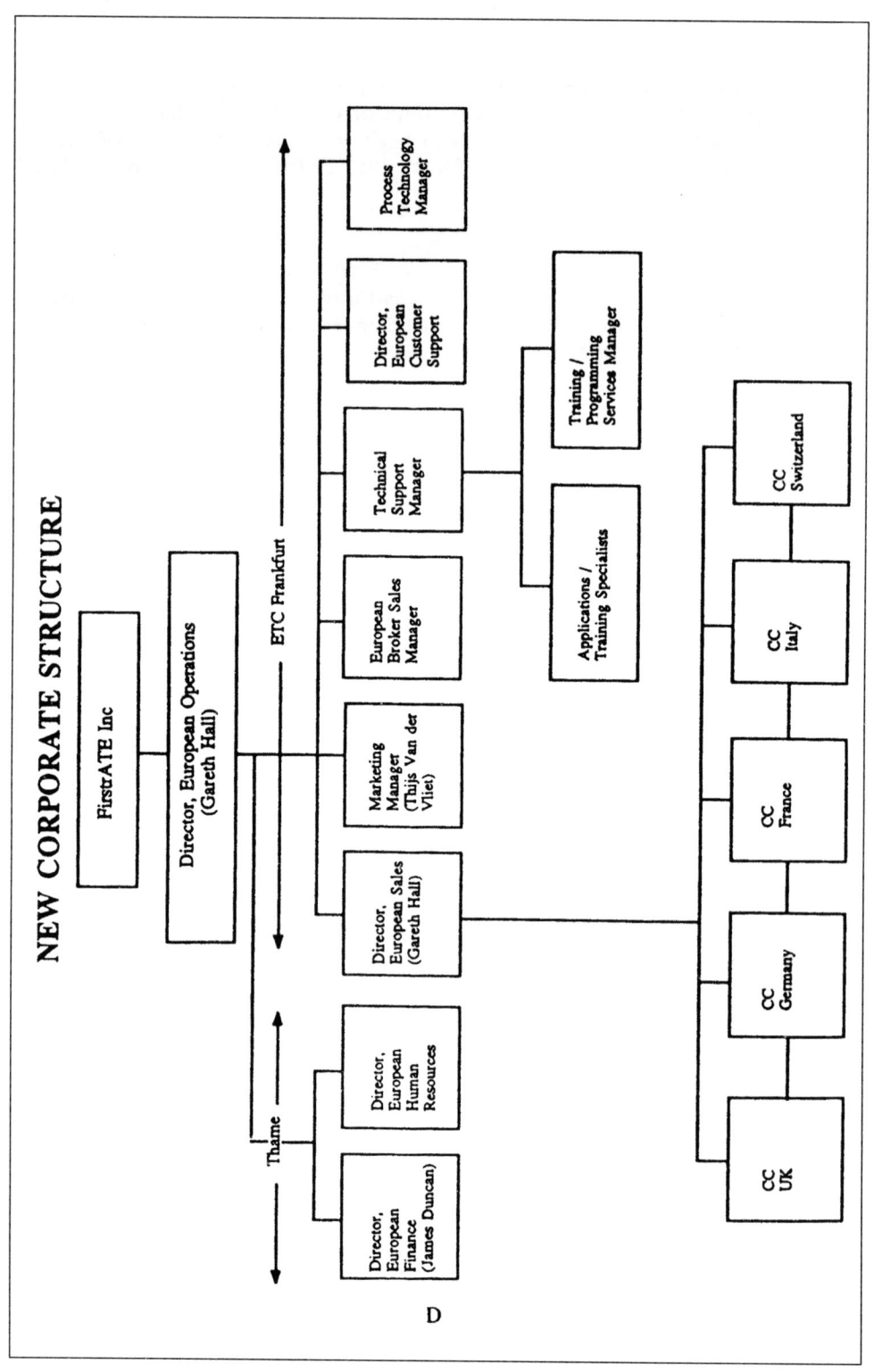

1990-1994 EUROPEAN SALES ($)

	FRANCE	GERMANY	ITALY	SWITZERLAND	UK	TOTAL EUROPE
PRODUCT						
1990	7,272,613	10,149,818	4,243,436	3,787,480	7,843,262	33,296,609
1991	7,295,199	9,182,870	4,871,744	3,802,823	6,579,938	31,732,574
1992	5,803,841	8,176,554	3,852,925	1,905,550	4,319,891	24,058,761
1993	5,654,385	5,383,253	2,311,421	2,763,758	3,791,727	19,904,544
1994	3,577,775	3,861,346	2,589,425	2,229,844	3,177,057	15,435,447
SERVICE						
1990	3,832,240	3,997,550	1,360,622	1,246,566	4,336,966	14,773,944
1991	4,703,292	4,854,524	1,818,530	1,514,878	4,481,303	17,372,527
1992	4,421,712	4,884,098	1,715,262	1,515,872	4,461,259	16,998,203
1993	4,763,840	5,556,379	1,758,303	1,289,224	3,871,252	17,238,998
1994	4,151,733	5,017,475	943,885	1,339,925	2,835,810	14,288,828
TOTAL						
1990	11,104,853	14,147,368	5,604,058	5,034,046	12,180,228	48,070,553
1991	11,998,491	14,037,394	6,690,274	5,317,701	11,061,241	49,105,101
1992	10,225,553	13,060,652	5,568,187	3,421,422	8,781,150	41,056,964
1993	10,418,225	10,939,632	4,069,724	4,052,982	7,662,979	37,143,542
1994	7,729,508	8,878,821	3,533,310	3,569,769	6,012,867	29,724,275

E

FIRSTRATE EUROPE FINANCIAL RESULTS ($) (1994)

	FRANCE	GERMANY	ITALY	SWITZERLAND	UK	TOTAL EUROPE
Net Sales:						
Product	3,577,775	3,861,346	2,589,425	2,229,844	3,177,057	15,435,447
Service	4,151,733	5,017,475	943,885	1,339,925	2,835,810	14,288,828
Other	85,654	135,948	282,257	75,939	1,067,545	1,647,343
TOTAL	7,815,162	9,014,769	3,815,567	3,645,708	7,080,412	31,371,618
Gross Margins %:						
Product	26%	12%	28%	2%	-13%	11%
Service	43%	45%	33%	38%	44%	42%
Other	103%	100%	122%	7%	157%	145%
TOTAL	35%	30%	30%	15%	21%	28%
Expenses:						
Marketing	65,225	190,143	3,731	12,917	75,826	347,842
Selling	1,908,082	2,515,190	872,039	551,465	1,222,478	7,069,254
G&A	207,941	254,370	97,820	72,283	474,530	1,106,944
TOTAL	2,181,248	2,959,703	973,590	636,665	1,772,834	8,524,040
Operating Inc.	578,535	-226,975	154,267	-79,486	-264,902	161,439
Reorganisation Costs	1,687,430	470,782	813,614	168,306	3,288,750	6,428,882
Profit B/f Tax	-1,108,895	-697,757	-659,347	-247,792	-3,553,652	-6,267,443

F

MEMORANDUM

To: John Leyton cc. James Duncan   From: Gareth Hall

Subject: Customer Centres   Date: 23rd October, 1993

As you know, we recently spent two days in a workshop with JMB Limited to finalise some of the details of the reorganisation and we made good progress. We concentrated mainly on the Customer Centres, since we believe it is of paramount importance that these should work well in order to maintain an acceptable level of customer care during and after the reorganisation. We also spent some time on the Technology Support Centre. This is what we came up with:

Different functional roles within local units will have to "think customer" at all times - especially sales and service managers. They will look for the "lifetime value" of each customer. This joint approach will be enhanced by the European marketing manager who will develop Europe-wide marketing and PR programmes. An important part of the sales and service operations will be to find out what the customers need and want and then establish benchmarks to ensure that these expectations are met.

Sales managers will take the lead in helping the team to work together and overcome problems. They will have direct account responsibility, reporting to me, and will work with sales and service engineers to develop a programme of visits. This will entail some training since these responsibilities are well outside the brief of our existing sales managers. Leadership and motivation will be crucial at a time of reduced staffing levels to sustain existing levels of customer satisfaction and then improve customer satisfaction with the lower level of resources over time.

"Customer Relations Manager" - a new and vital role will be played by the present local office managers who will act as the prime point of contact for all incoming customer calls and manage a co-ordination and routing system. As well as dealing with customers, they will handle key communications with the Technology Support Centre as well as with the finance and HR functions. They will report to the local sales managers.

G-1

Sales and service engineers will work remotely, being equipped with PC's, E-mail, answer phones, faxes and mobile phones as required. This will enable all local units to be relocated to smaller premises and will encourage the engineers to spend much more time with customers.

The Customer Centres will have to rely heavily on the Technology Support Centre if they are to be effective. This will be an unfamiliar situation and will need careful attention.

The Technology Support Centre will not become the head office of FirstrATE Europe, neither will it become the main focus of customer contact. It will, however, be a "centre of excellence", allowing economies of scale and offering a highly professional service for new product sales, for demonstrations and training as well as supporting mature products.

Local units are the primary focus for the customer and the TSC should treat the local units as "internal customers". Again, team-working and effective communications will be the key to ensuring that the TSC provides the most appropriate services as efficiently as possible. The TSC will be located near the airport in Frankfurt, the other side of town from the local unit, in order to establish it as a common resource for all the local units to use.

G-2

CIRCUIT BOARD TESTERS
(Millions of Dollars)

COMPANY	1981	1982	1983	1984	1985	1986	1987	1988	1989	1990	1991	1992	1993
NEPTUNE	10.5	16.1	17.8	20.6	23.5	17.9	19.3	21.0	15.8	14.3	13.1	12.8	8.6
FIRSTRATE	80.3	97.5	124.9	132.0	102.4	99.0	107.6	119.6	115.5	114.0	104.6	96.0	98.3
JUPITER	27.8	25.5	31.9	53.3	45.8	43.5	55.5	66.0	79.1	79.5	79.1	81.0	105.8
HERA	0.0	0.0	0.0	0.0	0.0	0.0	1.5	4.1	6.4	9.4	18.0	9.4	8.6
THOR	10.9	13.1	22.5	27.8	29.3	37.1	31.1	30.4	22.5	21.0	18.0	16.9	15.0
ZEUS	1.1	1.5	2.3	3.4	6.0	7.9	9.8	12.0	11.3	10.9	11.6	11.3	9.8
CRONUS	55.1	65.3	75.2	87.8	69.0	64.5	63.8	63.8	63.0	61.1	63.8	54.4	35.6
POSEIDON	2.0	3.4	4.9	9.8	11.6	14.3	17.3	19.9	22.5	27.4	22.1	20.6	15.0
ATHENA	3.8	4.9	5.3	7.1	12.8	12.8	13.9	18.8	15.0	17.3	12.0	10.9	9.8
ATEN	0.0	0.8	1.9	2.6	4.1	6.0	8.6	10.5	12.8	13.9	27.0	22.1	19.9
HEBE	32.3	57.4	85.1	100.5	88.1	89.3	96.0	97.9	96.8	81.0	97.1	87.8	80.3
NEMESIS	3.4	4.9	6.5	8.3	8.3	8.3	7.9	6.0	7.5	8.3	8.6	10.1	12.0
TOTAL	227.2	290.4	378.3	453.2	400.9	400.6	432.3	470.0	468.2	458.1	475.0	433.3	418.7

Source: Friedman & Smith

H-1

FUNCTIONAL BOARD TESTERS
(Millions of Dollars)

COMPANY	1981	1982	1983	1984	1985	1986	1987	1988	1989	1990	1991	1992	1993
NEPTUNE	10.4	14.6	17.0	19.5	21.6	16.4	17.4	19.3	15.6	12.8	10.5	10.1	6.8
FIRSTRATE	39.4	35.3	31.1	30.0	25.9	29.6	30.8	29.3	24.8	24.0	24.8	26.6	25.5
JUPITER	4.5	3.0	1.9	1.5	0.8	0.0	3.0	2.3	2.6	3.0	2.6	6.0	15.0
THOR	2.3	2.6	4.5	5.6	5.3	10.5	10.5	8.6	6.8	7.5	7.9	7.9	7.1
CRONUS	15.8	23.3	23.3	26.6	24.8	28.5	34.9	35.3	34.5	38.6	43.5	34.5	27.4
ATHENA	1.5	1.5	1.5	1.1	3.8	4.1	3.8	4.1	1.1	1.5	1.1	0.4	0.4
HEBE	15.8	33.0	57.0	65.6	64.1	57.4	61.1	56.6	51.0	36.0	51.8	37.5	44.3
NEMESIS	2.6	3.8	5.0	5.3	6.8	6.8	5.6	4.1	5.3	6.8	8.3	8.6	10.1
TOTAL	92.3	117.1	141.3	155.2	153.1	153.3	167.1	159.6	141.7	130.2	150.5	131.6	136.6

Source: Friedman & Smith

H-2

UNDER $25K FUNCTIONAL BOARD TESTERS
(Millions of Dollars)

COMPANY	1981	1982	1983	1984	1985	1986	1987	1988	1989	1990	1991	1992	1993
NEPTUNE	4.0	10.1	12.3	12.9	14.0	10.9	10.1	11.6	6.0	3.0	0.0	0.0	0.0
FIRSTRATE	0.8	3.0	1.9	2.6	5.3	13.5	3.8	0.0	0.0	4.1	4.5	10.1	0.0
TOTAL	4.8	13.1	14.2	15.5	19.3	24.4	13.9	11.6	6.0	7.1	4.5	10.1	0.0

Source: Friedman & Smith

H-3

$25K TO $100K FUNCTIONAL BOARD TESTERS
(Millions of Dollars)

COMPANY	1981	1982	1983	1984	1985	1986	1987	1988	1989	1990	1991	1992	1993
NEPTUNE	0.8	1.0	1.4	1.4	2.4	3.1	5.8	5.8	8.6	9.0	10.5	10.1	6.8
FIRSTRATE	8.3	9.0	10.9	15.4	11.6	8.3	14.3	10.5	7.5	2.6	1.5	1.1	1.1
JUPITER	4.1	2.6	1.5	1.1	0.0	0.0	0.0	0.0	0.0	0.0	0.0	0.0	0.0
THOR	0.0	0.0	0.0	0.0	0.0	1.1	4.1	4.1	4.5	3.8	3.0	4.1	3.8
CRONUS	0.5	0.2	0.4	0.4	0.0	0.0	0.0	0.0	0.8	2.6	8.3	7.1	2.6
NEMESIS	1.9	3.0	3.5	3.8	6.4	6.6	5.6	4.1	5.3	6.8	8.3	8.3	8.6
TOTAL	15.6	15.8	17.7	22.1	20.4	19.1	29.8	24.5	26.7	24.8	31.6	30.7	22.9

Source: Friedman & Smith

H-4

$100K TO $350K FUNCTIONAL BOARD TESTERS
(Millions of Dollars)

COMPANY	1981	1982	1983	1984	1985	1986	1987	1988	1989	1990	1991	1992	1993
FIRSTRATE	15.0	12.8	7.5	3.0	3.0	2.3	2.6	3.4	0.0	1.9	1.9	4.9	6.8
JUPITER	0.4	0.4	0.4	0.4	0.8	0.0	0.0	0.0	0.0	1.5	0.8	2.6	5.3
THOR	2.3	2.6	4.5	5.6	5.3	9.4	5.3	4.5	2.3	3.2	3.8	3.8	3.4
CRONUS	12.6	18.5	17.6	13.5	11.3	13.5	10.9	15.0	3.8	3.0	6.4	16.9	12.8
TOTAL	30.3	34.3	30.0	22.5	20.4	25.2	18.8	22.9	6.1	9.6	12.9	28.2	28.3

Source: Friedman & Smith

H-5

$350K TO $750K FUNCTIONAL BOARD TESTERS
(Millions of Dollars)

COMPANY	1981	1982	1983	1984	1985	1986	1987	1988	1989	1990	1991	1992	1993
FIRSTRATE	15.4	10.5	10.9	9.0	6.0	5.6	3.0	3.4	6.0	5.3	7.9	4.5	15.8
JUPITER	0.0	0.0	0.0	0.0	0.0	0.0	3.0	2.3	2.6	1.5	1.9	3.4	9.8
CRONUS	2.6	4.5	5.3	12.8	13.5	15.0	24.0	20.3	26.6	13.5	9.8	6.0	7.5
HEBE	3.4	12.4	7.9	15.4	17.3	34.5	23.6	16.1	8.6	2.6	6.8	13.5	24.0
TOTAL	21.4	27.4	24.1	37.2	36.8	55.1	53.6	42.1	43.8	22.9	26.4	27.4	57.1

Source: Friedman & Smith

H-6

OVER $750K FUNCTIONAL BOARD TESTERS
(Millions of Dollars)

COMPANY	1981	1982	1983	1984	1985	1986	1987	1988	1989	1990	1991	1992	1993
FIRSTRATE	0.0	0.0	0.0	0.0	0.0	0.0	7.1	12.0	11.3	10.1	9.0	6.0	1.9
CRONUS	0.0	0.0	0.0	0.0	0.0	0.0	0.0	0.0	3.4	19.5	19.1	4.5	4.5
HEBE	0.0	12.4	41.3	41.3	37.1	17.6	33.0	36.8	42.4	33.4	45.0	24.0	20.3
TOTAL	0.0	12.4	41.3	41.3	37.1	17.6	40.1	48.8	57.1	63.0	73.1	34.5	26.7

Source: Friedman & Smith

H-7

IN-CIRCUIT BOARD TESTERS
(Millions of Dollars)

COMPANY	1981	1982	1983	1984	1985	1986	1987	1988	1989	1990	1991	1992	1993
NEPTUNE	0.2	1.5	0.8	1.1	1.9	1.5	1.9	1.7	0.2	1.5	2.6	2.6	1.9
FIRSTRATE	40.9	62.3	93.8	102.0	76.5	69.4	76.9	90.4	90.8	90.0	79.9	69.4	72.8
JUPITER	23.3	22.5	30.0	51.8	45.0	43.5	52.5	63.8	76.5	76.5	76.5	75.0	90.8
THOR	8.6	10.5	18.0	22.1	24.0	26.6	20.6	21.8	15.8	13.5	10.1	9.0	7.9
CRONUS	39.4	42.0	51.9	61.1	44.3	36.0	28.9	28.5	28.5	22.5	20.3	19.9	8.3
ATHENA	2.3	3.4	3.8	6.0	9.0	8.6	10.1	14.6	13.9	15.8	10.9	10.5	9.4
HEBE	16.5	24.4	28.1	34.9	24.0	31.9	34.9	41.3	45.8	45.0	45.4	50.3	36.0
ATEN	0.0	0.8	1.9	2.6	4.1	6.0	8.6	10.5	12.8	13.9	27.0	22.1	19.9
NEMESIS	0.8	1.1	1.5	3.0	1.5	1.5	2.3	1.9	2.3	1.5	0.4	1.5	1.9
TOTAL	132.0	168.5	229.8	284.6	230.3	225.0	236.7	274.5	286.6	280.2	273.1	260.3	248.9

Source: Friedman & Smith

H-8

UNDER $100K IN-CIRCUIT BOARD TESTERS
(Millions of Dollars)

COMPANY	1981	1982	1983	1984	1985	1986	1987	1988	1989	1990	1991	1992	1993
FIRSTRATE	0.4	0.0	4.1	1.5	1.9	3.0	5.3	2.6	6.0	3.0	5.3	0.8	1.9
HERA	0.0	0.0	0.0	0.0	0.0	0.0	1.5	4.1	6.4	9.4	18.0	9.4	8.6
THOR	1.1	1.5	1.5	3.4	8.3	7.1	7.5	6.4	5.3	3.0	2.3	1.9	1.9
ZEUS	1.1	1.5	2.3	3.4	6.0	7.9	9.8	12.0	11.3	10.9	11.6	11.3	9.8
CRONUS	3.8	4.5	6.9	7.9	4.5	1.5	4.9	5.3	7.5	9.8	4.1	10.1	1.9
POSEIDON	1.3	1.9	2.6	4.1	4.5	3.8	3.4	7.7	7.9	7.9	7.1	6.0	5.6
ATHENA	1.1	0.8	1.9	0.0	3.0	3.4	4.1	8.6	7.9	9.0	6.8	6.4	5.6
HEBE	6.0	3.8	3.8	2.3	2.3	3.4	3.4	2.3	9.0	7.5	6.4	10.9	8.6
ATEN	0.0	0.8	1.9	2.6	4.1	6.0	8.6	10.5	12.8	13.9	27.0	22.1	19.9
NEMISIS	0.8	1.1	1.5	3.0	1.5	1.5	2.3	1.9	2.3	1.5	0.4	1.5	1.9
TOTAL	15.6	15.9	26.5	28.2	36.1	37.6	50.8	61.4	76.4	75.9	89.0	80.4	65.7

Source: Friedman & Smith

H-9

$100K TO $350K IN-CIRCUIT BOARD TESTERS
(Millions of Dollars)

COMPANY	1981	1982	1983	1984	1985	1986	1987	1988	1989	1990	1991	1992	1993
FIRSTRATE	38.3	58.5	63.4	63.0	44.6	47.6	49.1	63.0	51.0	53.3	48.8	48.4	46.5
JUPITER	23.3	22.5	28.5	46.5	38.3	31.5	37.5	45.0	52.5	46.5	35.3	37.5	48.8
CRONUS	35.6	33.0	33.8	38.3	28.5	25.5	20.3	19.5	9.0	5.3	2.3	4.5	4.1
POSEIDON	0.7	1.5	2.3	5.6	7.1	10.5	13.9	12.2	14.6	17.3	14.6	14.6	9.4
HEBE	10.5	20.6	23.3	29.6	18.8	15.4	15.8	21.0	20.3	17.3	18.8	17.6	19.5
TOTAL	108.4	136.1	151.3	183.0	137.3	130.5	136.6	160.7	147.4	139.7	119.8	122.6	128.3

Source: Friedman & Smith

H-10

OVER $350K IN-CIRCUIT BOARD TESTERS
(Millions of Dollars)

COMPANY	1981	1982	1983	1984	1985	1986	1987	1988	1989	1990	1991	1992	1993
FIRSTRATE	2.3	3.8	26.3	37.5	30.0	18.8	22.5	24.8	33.8	33.8	25.9	20.3	24.4
JUPITER	0.0	0.0	1.5	5.3	6.8	12.0	15.0	18.8	24.0	30.0	41.3	37.5	42.0
CRONUS	0.0	4.5	11.3	15.0	11.3	9.0	3.8	3.8	12.0	7.5	13.9	5.3	2.3
HEBE	0.0	0.0	1.1	3.0	3.0	13.1	15.8	18.0	16.5	20.3	20.3	21.8	7.9
TOTAL	2.3	8.3	40.2	60.8	51.1	52.9	57.1	65.4	86.3	91.6	101.4	84.9	76.6

Source: Friedman & Smith

H-11

FirstrATE EUROPE – EXAMINATION PAPER

Additional Information – to be taken into account when answering the questions set.

MEMORANDUM

To: Thijs Van der Vliet From: Gareth Hall
Subject: Strategic Marketing Presentation Date: 19 June 1995

You know that we have been wondering what was going on in the Italian market – well now it seems that we have found out. Our Italian CC heard rumours a few months ago and it has been confirmed today. It seems that Poseidon have been developing a major new contract with an Italian volume car manufacturer who is finally about to introduce full computer control and diagnostics in their **whole range** of family cars. If this move is repeated on a Europe-wide basis the whole market will explode.

It seems like we will have a new "vertical market" on our hands that, assuming we can get organised in time, we should be able to dominate. I have already been in touch with R&D and production in Princetown and they assure me that we have the product.

The question then becomes a marketing one. Can we move fast enough to establish ourselves in the Automotive sector? While time is limited I am, as you know, concerned that we don't just sell into the opportunity but this time we do it properly. We must be sure to present ourselves as more than just an ATE provider – full service has got to be the solution.

I know you are working up some strategic approaches for the board presentation, I would like to hear your ideas about how we might attack the automotive industry – strategically, and how it might be developed to be a major platform of our business like telecomms.

See you at the presentation.

Garett

Examination questions

Based on the data you have collected, and working closely with your assistant Claus, you have decided to approach the board presentation on strategic marketing in three discreet parts. Your presentation, IN REPORT FORMAT, will cover the following:

1. A strategic marketing plan for FirstrATE Europe for the period 1995–2000. Justify your recommendations.

   50 marks

2. What changes would you suggest making to FirstrATE's organisational structure to enable it to become more customer focused and meet the strategic marketing objectives you have set?

   30 marks

3. Building upon your recommendations for FirstrATE's long-term strategy, propose a plan for the company's entry into the European Automotive industry. Your plan should aim to develop the new market in such a way that it supports the company's planned market position in Europe and builds the automotive market into a market of equal importance to the Telecomms market by 2000.

   20 marks

Examiner's report

General comments

The FirstrATE case study proved to be a testing paper for very many candidates. Not only were pass rates disappointing, the overall pass rate was lower than the previous paper. There were also fewer distinction passes. This seems to show that candidates are not improving their performance in line with the evolution of the Analysis and Decision paper.

Although there were specific reasons for poor performance relative to the case content, the most important (and worrying) reasons for failure concerned the nature of the subject itself. The A&D case is an exercise in Marketing Strategy. The most common reason for failure was that students were unable to demonstrate sufficient knowledge in either of these two facets of the case.

Marketing: answers needed to be based on customer needs not product features.
Strategy: answers needed to consider the longer term (5 years) not discuss one year tactics.

This failure of basic understanding of marketing has caused the examining team a great deal of concern and we will be looking for a marked improvement in these areas in future scripts.

Two of the three questions were clearly predictable for the prepared candidate. This predictability has unfortunately generated more 'group think' answers or even pre-prepared answers copied on the day. Such answers are quite easy to spot and marks are deducted accordingly. In many cases candidates reproduced group answers they clearly did not understand and were failed easily. Candidates should remember that they will only be awarded marks for individual answers.

Finally, the examiners were hoping that the predictability of Question 1 might improve the quality of answers – this has not happened. Candidates who do not take advantage of the four weeks for which they have the case study will be at a disadvantage no matter how predictable the questions!

Question 1 (50 marks)

The examiners were looking for a detailed strategic marketing plan to guide FirstrATE's progress into profit.

Good marks were obtained by candidates who presented the examiner with a logical argument that followed a pattern such as:

1 environmental analysis
2 corporate objectives/mission statement
3 identification of target market (needs, segments)
4 marketing objectives

5 targeting and positioning
6 marketing strategy (alternatives and selection)
7 marketing programmes (7Ps)
8 budgets, controls, contingency planning.

Major problems which the examiners experienced in this question included:

1 lots of analysis (Ansoff + Porter + BCG + ...) but no decision or implementation
2 entire plans that were tactical not strategic
3 exclusive emphasis on 'product push' rather than 'customer pull'
4 no positioning or targeting
5 no choice – some papers suggesting FirstrATE should 'be differentiated,
   and focus, and cut price' at the same time!
6 little understanding of what comprises a Strategic Marketing Plan or what
   it is intended to do
7 few mentions of the 7Ps despite the service aspect of the case
8 lack of decision (analysis alone is not enough)
9 budgets and control systems omitted or, if included, often meaningless.

Generally we were pleased to see more mention of 'objectives' and 'mission
statements' but often these were then not related to customer needs or
programmes for implementation.

Finally, considering FirstrATE described an industrial marketing situation
there was an alarming lack of awareness about industrial buyer behaviour –
too many candidates opting to treat the case like a consumer marketing
exercise. Automatic Test Equipment is different from frozen peas!

Question 2 (30 marks)

The examiners were looking for an understanding of how organisational
structure and systems can support customer orientation.

Good marks were obtained by candidates who were able to build on their
recommendations in Q1 and propose both 'hard' and 'soft' changes to
FirstrATE's organisation.

Success generally came to those candidates who had spent time preparing
the case and had anticipated the question. Others were obviously surprised
by the question.

Better candidates provided a balanced answer that considered the organisation from the target customers' point of view and then looked at structural
and behavioural solutions to the problem.

Major problems which the examiners experienced in this question included:

1 a keenness to build marketing empires rather than improve customer focus
2 concentration on drawing organisational charts but little on culture change
   or behaviour
3 words like 'internal marketing' and 'relationship marketing' used but
   clearly not understood.

Question 3 (20 marks)

This question proved to be a great test and tended to fail:

1 the weak candidate
2 the badly prepared candidate
3 the bad time managers.

Good marks were obtained by candidates who were able to relate entry into this new market with the strategy proposed in Q1. To do this they needed to:

1 identify the target market's needs
2 extend FirstrATE's position into this market
3 propose a method of market entry
4 propose brief plans on developing FirstrATE's penetration of this market (by meeting customer needs) up to the year 2000.

It might have been the last question but it still carried 20 per cent of the marks!

Major problems that examiners experienced in this question included:

1 answers of just one or two pages
2 little ability to think 'on the day'
3 developed strategy (Q1) completely abandoned in favour of aggressive sales campaigns
4 tactical brain dumps with no strategy.

Conclusions

The FirstrATE case proved a testing case for all candidates. Good answers showed an ability to look beyond the apparent complexity of industrial products to identify industrial buyer and organisational needs and to shape the company accordingly. Failures were primarily tactical marketers who were defeated by the technical nature of the case and reduced to writing short-term sales and promotional plans aimed at moving stock at any price.

In a recent study carried out by the CIM and Cranfield, marketing, as it is conducted in many organisations, was described as follows:

> Organisations fail to understand their customers, provide them with an unsatisfactory product or service and then expect a marketing department to sprinkle a bit of 'magic marketing dust' on at the end of the process.

The CIM, the Diploma in Marketing and the case study examination have a responsibility to change this behaviour.

Professional marketers need to understand that there is more to the job than 'sprinkling magic dust'. They will need to know what marketing is really about before they can expect to pass the A&D case study examination.

CANDIDATES' BRIEF

You are Simon Walker, a consultant with PACE, a well known firm of marketing strategy consultants. Your firm has recently won, in stiff competition with other similar firms, a prestigious assignment to critically review the marketing strategy of a part of Mistral UK Limited, focusing on one of the company's old established product areas.

Mistral U.K. Limited is the UK operating division of Mistral Inc., a multinational healthcare company with head offices in Milwaukee, Wisconsin, USA. Your client at Mistral is John Norland who has recently been appointed as Marketing Manager. He is based in Manchester, in the North of England, and reports directly to May Alexander, Director of Marketing.

John has an informal ("dotted line") relationship with the marketing managers in each of the European subsidiaries of Mistral and with the production managers at the Mistral production facilities in Dublin, Athens and Madrid. These relationships are delicate because, while product development and marketing planning are conducted in the UK, implementation relies on the co-operation of the various European subsidiaries. In particular, John is beginning to form the opinion that the European marketing managers are being reactive to market needs, rather than proactive. Moreover, it has been made clear to him that the European subsidiaries find the involvement of head office in their local markets unnecessary and often misguided.

Your immediate task is to present your ideas about the bandages market to John Norland and May Alexander at the quarterly marketing strategy meeting which is due to take place in December. In order to get started, you have arranged a meeting with John to gather some background information and he has given you a file containing all the papers on the bandages market which were left by his predecessor.

VISIT TO MANCHESTER

NOVEMBER 1996

Simon looked out of the window gloomily as the train sped north and wondered how he, a man steeped in fast moving consumer goods marketing (FMCG), could have landed up with this industrial marketing assignment - and in such a high-tech industry as well. "Still," he muttered to himself in consolation, "a bandage is a bandage. At least I don't have to pretend to understand about replacement joints or catheters - not yet anyway." As he flipped through the sales literature which Mistral had sent him, he began to feel very queasy, and heartily regretted the British Rail breakfast which lay uncomfortably in his stomach as page after page of burns, wounds, operations and intravenous drips were revealed in glorious technicolour.

Simon shuffled his papers together and put them back in his briefcase. He slammed the lid shut, hoping for a few minutes of quiet contemplation before reaching Manchester, only to be startled by the loud fake-melodious electronic ring of a mobile phone in the seat behind him and an even louder voice trying to talk to the caller. Simon sat there and fumed for the rest of his journey.

He cheered up on reaching Mistral's modern offices and was enthusiastically greeted by John Norland. "Simon, I can't tell you how pleased I am that you are going to help us out on this project. When I took over this position I had no idea how little attention had been paid to the whole area of bandages and support and I just would not be able to get around to any kind of serious strategic plan this year, with all the other marketing initiatives I am involved in. Now, I am aware that you do not have long so let's get started right away. You ask the questions and I will try to answer them as best I can. Please just bear in mind that I have not been in the job long myself."

"Well," Simon began "first I must thank you for the most helpful information which you sent me. I have been looking at it on the train but I haven't had a chance to become truly immersed in the figures yet. May we begin with the basics such as the background to the company and the industry before we get down to details?"

Some hours later, Simon found a seat in a first class compartment for the return journey. Heartened by his most interesting and successful day, he decided to pay the extra fare in the hope that he would not meet his friend with the mobile phone again. He pulled out his notepad and began to type:

NOTE TO FILE - VISIT TO MISTRAL UK LIMITED

6th NOVEMBER 1996

Verbatim report of interview with John Norland from Mistral by Simon Walker

---

Firstly, please tell me about the company background.

Mistral UK Limited is a wholly owned subsidiary of Mistral Inc. based in Milwaukee, Wisconsin. Mistral Inc. is a diversified conglomerate with activities spanning the healthcare, chemicals, pharmaceuticals and food manufacturing industries.

The UK business was formed out of an established British company, Beaufort, which was founded in 1878 and acquired by Mistral in 1982. The company still sells some old Beaufort products dating back to the 1920's. Subsequent acquisitions have been made over the past ten years to fit in with the global strategic plan. Some of these acquisitions were made to provide geographic coverage of local markets in Europe. Others were acquired for their state of the art technological expertise.

After some recent rationalisation, Mistral UK Limited and all the continental European subsidiaries of Mistral Inc. now operate principally in the area of medical disposables. The product ranges encompass these areas:

- antiseptic wipes
- bandages
- castings
- catheters
- dressings
- gloves
- splints
- surgical instruments
- swabs
- syringes
- thermometers

Currently each of the European companies is an independent profit centre, reporting to the managing director of Mistral UK Limited. All strategic matters concerning medical disposables are managed from the UK. Strategic issues at the moment include product development, marketing planning for all European markets and the monitoring of sales and profits.

The European companies manage what, to now, have been considered tactical marketing issues such as pricing, distribution and promotion.

And the industry background?

The company's European competitors vary by country but are mainly international conglomerates with medical disposable interests. The competitors vary from one market segment to the next. In the bandages market, for example, there are two German competitors, MTM AG and Brunhoff AG, and two American multinationals, Samuel Inc. and BDG Inc. Apart from some obvious cultural differences, these four main competitors are global operations like us and tend to manage their businesses accordingly.

Having the largest market share in the European bandage market, would you agree that your brands are so well established that they are truly cash cows?

Some of our brands are certainly well established - we have been selling them for more than sixty years! What we need to focus on now is the strategies we should employ to maintain the brand and enhance it in the long term but of course we have to take into account short term profit pressures. For example, should the company try to retain market share or profit margins? Some products are becoming commodities, such as surgical instruments and the less sophisticated end of the bandage market. A further question is how can we differentiate sufficiently to justify premium pricing?

Some of Mistral's bandaging brands have a huge market share, even as high as 60% in some countries, and are years old, having been sold since the 1920's. Others are much more technical and are considered to be an important part of the treatment, rather than merely support.

Continental Europe tends to have more old products than the UK. These are perfectly good but they are not moving us forward. There is some friction between Europe and UK on this because the Europeans are happy to tender on the basis of the existing product range, while the marketing department in the UK is agitating for progress.

One thing that we don't appear to be able to grasp though is the difference between developing new products and developing new brands. I am hoping that we can use your experience in consumer markets to help us with this.

What are the main external factors affecting the business at the moment?

Well, hospitals buy established products by tender and there is very little effort required to sell the products. However in recent years credible competitors have been moving in on many product lines and this poses a threat. We tend to rely on our market share and reputation in the bandages market. Although I have only recently arrived I detect that there is a serious lack of product innovation in old-established lines to the extent that I wonder whether the sales force could even cope with innovation if and when it happens.

In other product areas we have introduced plenty of new products, particularly in the area of dressings; we are very close to the customers in that area and are improving our product offer all the time. Clearly we need to do the same with bandages and with our channels of distribution, it should be possible. It will require a change in attitude though.

Superficially, we appear to be doing better in the bandages market than we are in dressings, where we are joint number three in the market. Incidentally, our definition of dressings includes, as well as traditional non-adhesive surface dressings, the much more sophisticated moist wound dressings, deep wound dressings, post-operative dressings and "incise drapes" which are very clever polyurethane films used throughout long surgical operations to prevent migration of bacteria into the incision. To return to the point, in the dressings market, product development is very important and we are gaining ground. The market leaders are two huge brands which haven't innovated for years - BDG and Samuel - and they are in danger of losing their positions. In bandaging, the situation is reversed and we are in danger of becoming the dinosaur.

BDG and Samuel have a huge advantage with their great expertise in manufacturing and are able to drive the price down by standardising products to achieve economies of scale in production. However as I have indicated already, they tend to be weak on innovation and clinical expertise, which I believe are the important strategic drivers now and will be in the future.

Please tell me about the decision making process which your salesmen face in trying to close a sale.

The salesmen may have had it easy in the past but the process is becoming much more sophisticated. Products are evaluated by buyers on the basis of cost effectiveness as opposed to just price and the factors taken into account are many and varied. They include:
- the type of materials used in the product
- the type of waste generated
- the impact on nursing time
- time in theatre
- durability
- reliability

....and so on, as well as clinical effectiveness.

The order in which these variables are placed depends, of course, on the particular circumstances of the buyer.

Added to this, the user group which has a say in the choice of product is vast compared with other marketing situations. It includes:

- The patient and his visitors
- The patient's peer group (other patients)
- Nurses
- Doctors
- Clinical directorate (who identify treatment regime)
- Hospital manager
- Purchasing manager
- Government (who approve the prescription list)

And in the future, what will the purchasing trends be?

The overriding factor affecting decision making units will be the containment of cost. There are two major issues which will cause the cost of healthcare to escalate in the future. The first is demographics. Currently, approximately 40% - 50% of the population are earning and pay for a little over 30% of the population who are over 65. In only a few years, this situation will reverse. In fact, it will be even worse in Japan, where 20% will pay for 60% - 70%. So the pressures on the workforce to provide care for the elderly will multiply. The second issue is technology. There is an obvious direct effect of technology in medicine, whereby more treatments are being found which keep people alive longer. Then there is the indirect effect whereby technology may save lives, for example in major accidents, but the victims of such accidents are permanently maimed. An example of this would be the driver's air bag. A driver involved in a head-on collision, who would previously have died, may now, with the advent of the air bag, survive but his legs are likely to be crushed and he will require major surgery and rehabilitation. In very blunt terms, it costs a lot less to bury people than to rebuild them! I'm sorry ..... you'll never think of your airbag in the same way now, will you?

Getting back to the point, the purchasing manager will call the tune in future, because we expect to live longer and to be rebuilt if anything goes wrong. I don't want to touch on the ethics of all this, but we continually expect, and receive, ever better healthcare, society in the long run will not be able to bear the escalation of cost.

Are there other trends which will affect your business in the future?

Yes. Another 'mega-trend' is the shift away from hospitals in favour of care at home. For example, if a patient has a cartilage operation, or gives birth, they will stay in hospital for much less time than they would have done before, even ten years ago. They also have much more say in how they are treated and with which products. The 1990's is certainly the decade of consumer choice.

The implication here is that many more healthcare supplies will be bought at the pharmacy and this in turn has a serious effect on the activities of our sales force. Instead of selling to a hospital, which is a "one shot tender", the salesmen must target the wholesalers, the large chains of pharmacies and the supermarkets. There are positive and negative effects of this. The barriers to entry for a competitor with a credible product selling into a hospital are low because they can simply undercut on price in the tendering process. There is more scope for building brand awareness by selling through pharmacies. However this is a much more complex job for the salesmen. The same clinical standards apply in either situation.

Since my expertise is in FMCG, I can't help thinking that you could apply the same principles of building up a brand in this situation.

I'm sure there is some truth in this as the burden of responsibility is moving from the hospital into the community, allowing consumer marketing opportunities in previously closed product areas. However, I fail to see how we can do this on a Europe wide basis as all these initiatives are coming out of the UK. It seems to me that, on the whole, the European sales force is looking for the easy sale - they are content to pump existing product through the traditional channels to meet preconceived clinical indications. How do you suggest we break out of this mould?

I'll certainly be thinking about this for our next meeting. May I just ask you now about the different product groups within the bandages market ?

Of course. Broadly speaking there are four types of bandage:

The first category are known as retention and fixation bandages. These are simply what the name implies - the bandage or tape is there to hold something else in place, such as a dressing or a splint. They are supplied in both adhesive and non-adhesive forms. Our brand name for these products is Victrix.

Next we have light support (crepe) bandages. These are used for the treatment of minor injuries such as sprains and strains and minor sports injuries. These are the Felix group of products

The more robust version of support bandages - the third category - are simply known as strong support bandages. These days, sports clinics and physiotherapists are using strong support bandages as part of their treatment. These are used to prevent sports injuries, players may strap or tape ankles before a game, or support and protect ligaments and tendons following more serious sprains and strains. We group these products under the Venus brand name.

And lastly, we have compression bandages. These are very much part of the clinical treatment of acute and chronic conditions including venous leg ulcers, oedema, varicose veins, varicose ulcers, pre and post vein stripping. These are normally used in wound healing and in conjunction with other Mistral products such as the Alpha wound dressing. You may have guessed that this is of course the Vulcan product range.

The most important point for you to understand here is that these product categories form, in effect, a spectrum. The Victrix products serve a very low tech market which is becoming increasingly competitive and we are finding it very difficult to add value here. But the converse is true of our Vulcan range. Here we are beginning to try to look at various medical conditions and add value by packaging complete solutions, rather than just selling existing product.

The Venus range also provides opportunities in many markets such as the UK to add value to the brand as it is an integral part of high profile sports injury treatment and prevention.

Is this product range uniform across Europe?

A good question. The regional companies use the same generic terms but there is some disparity between the products offered in each country. However, because the regional companies are responsible for their own sales and profits, it is difficult to withdraw a line which head office may believe adds no strategic value to the product portfolio, if it is a good earner in a local market.

And what about promotion?

Again, the regional companies are responsible for this. Their approach varies widely, but they mainly employ all the obvious techniques. Advertisements in the trade press are commonplace and occasionally even television advertising is used.

The more imaginative regional companies run a series of nurses conventions whereby clinical experts are engaged to give an explanation of the benefits of using Mistral products. Recently sports injury experts and physiotherapists have been employed in this role.

Occasionally, when a really new product has been launched, the clinicians involved in the trials may be persuaded to go "on tour". For example, when our Vulcan HP sustained compression bandage was launched in the UK, an eminent vascular surgeon from one of the London teaching hospitals took place in a symposium to which both nurses and physiotherapists were invited.

Since promotion is not a Europe-wide function, we are reliant on the line managers in each of the countries to build up the brand values. In some countries, such as the Netherlands, this is working very well whereas in other countries the promotional activities tend to be "hit and miss". Packaging is controlled centrally but the sales forces, local promotional activity, pricing and customer service are managed locally.

Why do you not bring all the marketing functions under one roof?

You may think this is the obvious thing to do but, even having said all this, the last thing we want to do is to implement the marketing plans centrally. We have always believed that we need locals to understand local issues and that, in order to get close to our customers, we must do a lot of marketing at the regional company level.

For example, healthcare systems are changing quite radically in many countries in Europe at present. But our customers are inclined to be conservative and stick to what they know, particularly if existing techniques work. Why take a risk if you don't have to? It's rather like the old adage that nobody ever got sacked for buying an IBM. Nobody ever got into trouble for buying an established medical product that has a 40% share of its market. But for buying an untried new product - which may be significantly more expensive on the basis of a direct comparison, even though it's much more durable and reliable and therefore more cost-effective in the long run - well, that's a real risk.

Pricing has also been a local issue although we have centrally controlled cost of product from the manufacturing facilities to each local company. We have always believed that by measuring the European companies on both sales and profits would avoid any major problems of price differences between countries but I suspect that there may be trouble brewing soon. Also, the role of pricing in customer perception of quality and building brand value in industrial markets such as ours is not well researched or understood. I am starting to wonder whether pricing is really a strategic issue. But to take away any of the local company control over their pricing activities would likely provoke open revolt among European company managing directors.

New ideas take time and effort and we need to nurture our customers in each country. This is of paramount importance within each country but the situation is very different from one country to the next. However, there is some sign of gradual change here and we are beginning to see possibilities for more international conferences. In time, I think we will begin to find that a good idea will travel, and we can encourage this by sponsoring delegates to attend conferences in neighbouring European countries. We are going to have to work hard to overcome parochialism though.

Simon looked up at the drab suburban landscape as the train slowed to a crawl. A customer announcement informed passengers that the train was going to be delayed due to a line failure and that British Rail regretted any inconvenience caused. The voice added "if you were wanting to get to London by 7:30 it wouldn't be this train that you would be wanting to travel on" which was greeted by wry smiles all round the first class compartment in which Simon was seated.

"Oh well," he thought to himself "at least I can get on with looking at the contents of this file which John has given me". As he flicked through the pages of data he was dismayed to see that it was neither complete nor particularly up to date. It was not the quality of information he was used to dealing with in consumer marketing. "This assignment is certainly going to be a challenge."

FILE CONTENTS

APPENDIX 1: MISTRAL UK LIMITED

ORGANISATION CHART OF RELATIONSHIPS BETWEEN MARKETING, MANUFACTURING AND EUROPEAN SUBSIDIARIES

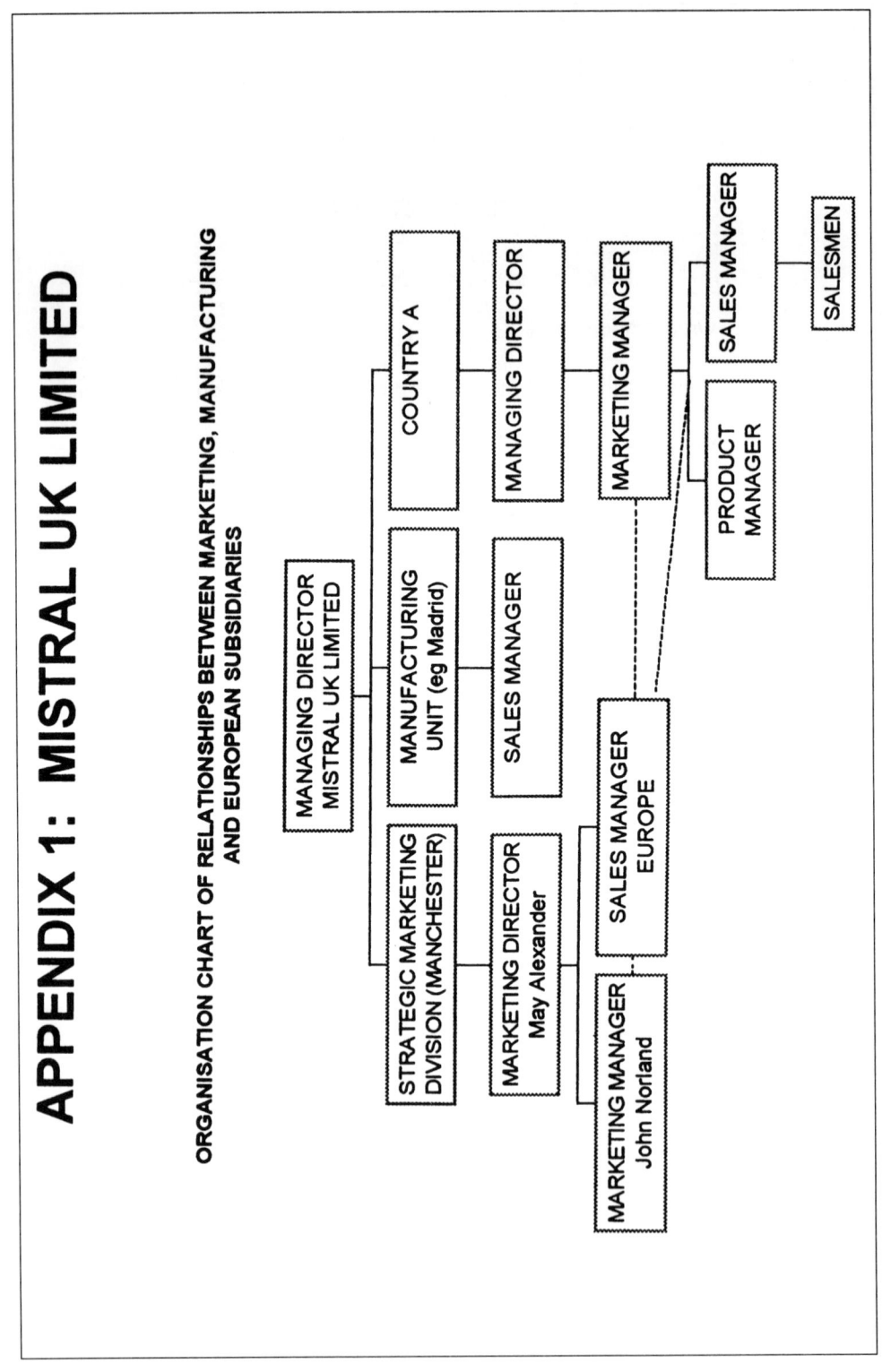

APPENDIX 2: THE WORLD'S MOST INTRACTABLE PROBLEM

Barbara Beck

Here is a prediction with a good chance of coming true. A year from now, if spared by the grim reaper, you will be one year older. And by adding that extra year to your anno domini, you will have made your own tiny contribution to making the world grow older. People are living longer, and the number of births is increasing more slowly.

In 1990 some 18% of the OECD countries' population were over 60 years old. By 2030, say experts at the World Bank, that figure will have risen to over 30%. But it is not just the developed countries that are ageing: in most other parts of the world, too, numbers of over-60s are set roughly to double over the next 30-40 years. Only Africa, on current form, looks likely to remain a young continent for some decades yet.

Why worry if the world is greying? After all, this is happening for reasons that most people would welcome. Families even in many of the poorer countries are getting smaller because parents no longer have to allow for high infant mortality: and also because better educated parents find it easier to see that more might mean worse. Enthusiasm for babies in the former Soviet Union and in Eastern Europe has waned markedly with the advent of a market economy. And most rich countries have long since adjusted their production of new citizens to what they think they can comfortably afford.

Birth rates in Japan and the European Union are well below replacement level. At the other end of life, improved medical care and healthier lifestyles have seen to it that many more people survive beyond the biblical "three score years and ten", and that most of them are a great deal fitter that the Methuselahs of old.

The trouble is that most countries have not been very good at adjusting to this rapid change. The prolonged "baby boom" after the second world war made them think about overpopulation and paying for education rather than provision for old age. Now the debate has changed, but there has been more talk than action.

In most developed countries retirement was originally set at 60 or 65 because people did not live much beyond that age. But life expectancy is rising constantly. In rich countries, a man reaching the official retirement age can now expect to live another 15 years; a woman about 19. In poor countries their post-retirement prospects are even better. And, on present trends, by about 2030 all of them can expect to live ten years longer still. During much of that time they may well be in good shape, spending money on holidays, clothes, housing (perhaps with an alarm bell and a resident warden, just in case things go wrong), entertainments of all kinds, financial products, even going back to school just for fun.

But it also means that in most countries the deal between the generations - pay now, be paid for later - is under severe threat. Most countries' main way of looking after their old folks, the state pension, is becoming too expensive. Already in the OECD countries a quarter of all government spending goes on public-sector pensions. These usually operate on a pay-as-you-go basis, which means that current pensions are paid for by current contributions. In the European Union, for example, at present every five people of working age (not all of whom, remember, will be working) support one pensioner. On present trends, in 30 or 40 years' time they will have to support two. The chances are that this will prove politically impossible.

Already some governments are beginning to wriggle out of earlier promises of ever-bigger pensions, and many have started encouraging their citizens to supplement their state pensions with an occupational or some other kind of private pension.

But the argument between the generations is not just about pensions. Medical expenses too will burgeon as people get older. Already the very old consume a disproportionately large share of the total health-care budget. By one calculation, if people survive into old age, 90% of the cost of medical care they consume over their lifetime is incurred in the six months before their death. New medical techniques and technologies - such a spare-part surgery - seem capable of prolonging life further at ever-greater expense.

Nor is care for the aged just about medical provision. As more people reach a greater age, some of them will need intensive nursing care towards the end of their lives. In the old days, when people became too frail to look after themselves, the family stepped in. In poorer countries it generally still does. But in richer countries the family is not what it was, and women, who used to be the main carers, are increasingly going out to work. So someone will have to foot the bill for expensive professional nursing care.

In Germany, payroll taxes have recently been raised to pay for nursing-home care. In Britain a newly market-oriented National Health Service has made it clear that it is no longer in the business of providing terminal nursing care for the old. Some old people are having to sell the houses they hoped to leave to their children to pay their nursing-home bills.

The problems surrounding what some gerontologists call the "fourth age" - from about 75 onwards - seem intractable. Unless a society is prepared to encourage its old folks to wander off into the snow Eskimo-style (or some modern equivalent), it will just have to pay up. Clearly, though, there is likely to be some rationing of benefits. Not many public-health services, for example, will pay for a heart transplant for an 80-year-old.

But the main expense for most countries will be in providing for the huge numbers who in the next few decades will reach the "third age" - between retirement and infirmity. What can be done to keep that in check?

- Demographers advocate higher birth rates to swell the numbers contributing to the upkeep of pensioners. But before they made a contribution, those extra children would cost money to bring up, putting extra strain on the generation in the middle. Besides, people are not easily persuaded to have more children for the greater good if fewer would be better for them personally.
- A flow of immigrants of working age helps to lower the age profile in the host country. But absorbing such a flow creates its own problems, and eventually the immigrant population gets older like everybody else.
- Reduced pensions would bring down costs. But people can vote until they drop dead, and may voice their disapproval at the polling booth. In countries such as the United States older voters ("Grey Panthers") are already flexing their political muscles.
- Contributions may have to be raised. But the working generation has a vote too, and may demur. Experience in several Latin American countries has shown that if workers get squeezed too hard, they tend to wander off into the black economy.
- Expansion of private provision will have to be encouraged. A number of countries are already doing this, working through occupational schemes. But coverage is patchy, and usually fails to reach the poorest part of the population in greatest need.
- A compulsory savings scheme may be needed to make people put something by for their old age. Some experts now argue that the only way of averting a crisis over provision for old age in the early part of the next century is to spread the load. Three "pillars" - a state pension, an occupational one and a personal nest egg - are much better than one, they say. Obligatory savings schemes would also do the capital markets a power of good.
- Sooner or later, the official retirement age will have to go up everywhere. At 60 or 65, many pensioners are now still in their prime. They themselves do not think of themselves as past it.

All the same, raising the retirement age may not go down well with voters who had looked forward to a long and happy period of leisure after decades of grind. Some countries are running into flak over raising the official retirement age for women, which paradoxically is often lower than that for men even though women on average live longer.

But given appropriate incentives, many senior citizens might well enjoy continuing with some form of work, perhaps in a job that is less demanding or only part-time. Before that happens, though, a lot of ageist prejudices will have to be shed by the corporate world. Over the past decade or two the age at which people retire in practice - as opposed to the official age - has actually come down with a bump. Early retirement has often been used to sweep unemployment under the carpet. In the EU, only about a third of all men aged 60-64, and very few women in that age group, are still at work.

None of the more promising - and rather unpleasant - remedies described above will avert the looming crisis on its own. Only a combination of all of them is likely to work. Sounds grim? Sounds better than ending up, some time in 2030, as a destitute oldie.

World in 1996
© The Economist Publications

APPENDIX 3: MISTRAL UK LIMITED - BANDAGES

Product Portfolio:

Retention and Fixation: **Victrix**

Victrix B bandage: This elastic retention bandage is made of viscose and polyamide. The bandage is soft, lightweight, porous, and very comfortable.

Victrix CR bandage: This retention bandage is made from a latex coated polyester/viscose mixture fabric. The bandage is lightweight and porous, it conforms easily. The cohesive properties of the bandages allow swift application and give economical non-slip dressing retention as only a 30% overlap is required.

Victrix ZO tape: This is a traditional zinc oxide tape for use in dressing retention on patients with normal skin. It is tearable by hand making it practical and easy to use for any kind of dressing. It has excellent immediate and lasting adhesion, ensuring prolonged fixation. It is also water resistant, and will therefore not come unstuck if the dressing gets wet. The larger widths are perforated to avoid skin maceration. The tape can be used for fixation of long term dressings on patients with normal skin, wide post-operative dressings and fixation of catheters, drainage tubes etc.

Victrix LA tape: This is a hypoallergenic tape which adheres firmly to the skin with reduced risk of allergic reaction. It is easy to tear by hand making it ideal for fixing medical equipment and lightweight dressings on patients with fragile skin or who are allergic to traditional tapes. It is permeable to air and water vapour and is easily removable. It can be used for dressing fixation and fixation of needles, probes, catheters and other equipment.

Victrix HM tape: This is a microporous hypoallergenic tape used for dressing fixation. The non-woven microporous substrate allows the skin to breathe preventing maceration in normal conditions. The low allergy acrylic adhesive reduces the risk of allergy and skin irritation on patients with sensitive skin. It is easy to remove and is tearable by hand. It can be used for fixation of long term dressings on patients with sensitive skin.

Victrix TMH tape: This is a transparent surgical tape coated with hypoallergenic adhesive. It has a microperforated backing which allows easy tearing both along its length and across its width.

Victrix DR sheet: This is a self-adhesive, non-woven fabric for dressing retention. Excellent conformability simplifies shaping around joints and awkward body contours and being extensible allows the patient greater freedom of body movement. Complete coverage of the dressing reduces the risks of casual contamination. The broad range of sizes increases convenience and patient comfort.

Victrix ST 1: This is a low allergy adhesive surgical tape which is lightweight, non-woven and porous. It can easily be torn length or width-ways before application, and is effective and comfortable in use.

Victrix ST 2: This top quality waterproof strapping has a very secure adhesive based upon zinc oxide. It will maintain adhesion even in very hot climate conditions, and the plastic exterior surface is resistant to oil, water and grease.

Victrix CB: This is a mix of cotton and nylon fibres woven to produce a product suitable for light levels of support for minor sprains and strains and for dressing retention/cannulae fixation.

Light Support: **Felix**

Felix Prime 2: This elasticated tubular support bandage is made from rib weave stockinette and covered latex rubber. It provides general light support and can be washed and re-applied. No slipping occurs as with traditional flat bandages.

Felix Ace Strapping: An extensible fabric strapping where conformability and comfort are high priorities, when providing secure fixation or strapping.

Felix QUO1: This is a narrow woven cotton, polyamide and elastane bandage. The bandage is conformable, light, strong, durable and suitable for use as a general purpose light support and compression bandage.

Felix QUO2: This is a narrow woven cotton and polyamide bandage with tailored edges. The bandage is light, durable, comformable, washable and re-usable. Light support is provided by the elasticated fibres used in the construction of the bandage.

Felix JAZ: This flexible cohesive bandage is a combination of high strength nylon fibres and elastic yarns, coated with a latex compound, making the bandages ideal for light support bandage functions, particularly in difficult areas.

Felix CARE: This support bandage is a mix of cotton and high strength nylon fibres woven in a way as to produce superior performance over traditional BP quality crepe bandages and making it suitable where support of mild soft tissue injuries is required.

Strong Support: **Venus**

Venus Ace EAB: This is a cotton/rayon bandage with a choice of natural rubber and low allergy adhesives both of which are porous allowing the skin to breathe. Easy application is afforded using the central yellow line as a guide and provides the correct tension for the treatment of sprains and strains, and sports injuries.

Venus Prime 1: This shaped tubular bandage promotes venous and lymphatic return due to its anatomical design. It is a combination of rib knitted stockinette and covered latex rubber threads. Both full leg and below the knee bandages are available in a variety of sizes. The correct bandage size is selected by measuring the leg circumference at the calf.

Venus Maxi: This is a woven product made from high twist cotton/rayon yarns producing the correct tension for the treatment of varicose veins and venous ulcers under rigid compression therapy.

Venus LAZO tape: This is a hypoallergenic tape especially for use in rigid joint support due to its strong adhesion and its capability to stay in position.

Compression: **Vulcan**

Vulcan 4x4 layered: This contains a simple wound contact layer dressing and four bandages for application of the four layer bandaging system developed by a team at Charing Cross Hospital, London.

Vulcan LP sustained compression: These provide for light compression for the treatment of heavy legs, oedema and varicose veins.

Vulcan HP sustained compression: These provide for high compression for the treatment of varicose veins, varicose leg ulcers, pre and post vein stripping.

VulcanEase: This is a narrow woven extensible bandage made from a blend of cotton and nylon, which incorporates elastane to provide elasticity and is therefore suitable for all light compression needs.

VulcanIte: This is a lightweight bandage made from a blend of cotton and rayon which incorporates elastic yarns covered in nylon for patient comfort. It is indicated for the management of superficial early varices, varicosis formed in pregnancy and above and below-the-knee stump bandaging. It is also for use as layer 3 in the 4 layer bandage technique for treating venous leg ulcers.

VulcanOp: These are graduated compression hosiery made of polyamide and elastane. They are lightweight, comfortable, air permeable and washable. Colour coded for easy identification. Used to prevent variscosity, deep vein thrombosis and gravitational oedema.

APPENDIX 3B

KEY: BRANDS AND SALES CATEGORIES

CATEGORY	BRANDS
RETENTION	Victrix (not considered strategic - excluded from analysis)
TRADITIONAL ADHESIVE	Venus Ace
LOW ALLERGY ADHESIVE	No brands mentioned, minor products only so far
TAPES	Venus LAZO, Felix ACE
TAPES ACCESSORIES	No brands mentioned, minor products only so far
NON-ADHESIVE SUPPORT	Felix Prime 2, Venus Maxi, Felix QUO1, Felix QUO2, Felix CARE, Venus Prime 1
COHESIVE SUPPORT	Felix JAZ
COMPRESSION	Vulcan range

SALES OF BANDAGES BY COUNTRY

SALES 1996 (£000)

	United Kingdom		France		Italy		Belgium		Holland		Denmark	
	Hosp	Non-Hosp	Hosp	Non-Hosp	Hosp	Non-Hosp	Hosp	Non-Hosp	Hosp	Non-Hosp	Hosp	Non-Hosp
Traditional Adhesive	5,734	3,238	1,812	592	2,430	7,008	50	73	77	319	284	208
Low Allergy Adhesive	96	12	47	3	0	0	0	1	12	2	8	1
Functional Bandaging	5,830	3,250	1,859	595	2,430	7,008	50	74	89	321	292	209
Tapes	572	340	47	166	54	299	17	54	10	70	28	109
Functional Tapes Accessories	260	300	25	18	141	469	0	3	4	12	14	17
Functional Taping	832	640	72	184	195	768	17	57	14	82	42	126
Non-Adhesive Support	180	108.00	136	122	77	59	168	8	100	8	122	24
Cohesive Support	40	136	44	9	16	247	8	14	31	2	9	6
Support	220	244	180	131	93	306	176	22	131	10	131	30
Compression Bandages	430	1,505	308	2,256	226	72	28	18	1	31	69	12
TOTAL BANDAGES	7,312	5,639	2,419	3,166	2,944	8,154	271	171	235	444	534	377

APPENDIX 5

MARKET ESTIMATED TOTAL SALES OF BANDAGES OF COUNTRY

SALES 1996 (£000)

	United Kingdom		France		Italy		Belgium		Holland		Denmark	
	Hosp	Non-Hosp	Hosp	Non-Hosp	Hosp	Non-Hosp	Hosp	Non-Hosp	Hosp	Non-Hosp	Hosp	Non-Hosp
Traditional Adhesive	7,660	4,040	2868	940	3205	8782	70	102	628	824	345	389
Low Allergy Adhesive	590	260	276	24	0	0	9	13	123	73	65	4
Functional Bandaging	8,250	4,300	3,144	964	3,205	8,782	79	115	751	897	410	393
Tapes	690	470	129	682	62	408	38	312	190	689	71	252
Functional Tapes Accessories	380	525	106	88	152	602	7	53	28	153	39	181
Functional Taping	1,070	995	235	770	214	1,010	45	365	218	842	110	433
Non-Adhesive Support	965	174	864	863	145	77	346	155	1424	270	860	128
Cohesive Support	845	2,595	360	162	297	5892	40	72	132	75	45	144
Support	1,810	2,769	1,224	1,025	442	5,969	386	227	1,556	345	905	272
Compression Bandages	3,740	14,311	2374	23516	2357	5894	223	185	1	276	1988	340
TOTAL BANDAGES	14,870	22,375	6,977	26,275	6,218	21,655	733	892	2,526	2,360	3,413	1,438

APPENDIX 6.1

TRADITIONAL ADHESIVE

COMPETITOR SALES 1994 (£000)

	United Kingdom		France		Italy		Belgium		Holland		Denmark	
	Hosp	Non-Hosp	Hosp	Non-Hosp	Hosp	Non-Hosp	Hosp	Non-Hosp	Hosp	Non-Hosp	Hosp	Non-Hosp
MISTRAL	5,505.60	2,998.75	1,781.87	309.22	2,587.33	7,057.61	52.34	77.55	99.59	226.30	266.02	264.70
COMPETITOR 1	1,006.40	325.60	441.30	189.13	450.35	1,079.02	12.60	16.81	279.93	377.75	73.90	91.57
COMPETITOR 2	521.95	287.30	362.49	157.61	90.07	280.46	4.20	6.30	187.11	147.33	22.49	11.25
COMPETITOR 3	208.85	201.96	0.00	0.00	0.00	245.01	0.00	4.20	0.00	73.66	0.00	0.00
COMPETITOR 4	0.00	99.00	0.00	0.00	0.00	170.37	0.00	0.00	0.00	0.00	0.00	0.00
OTHERS	207.93	93.78	157.61	283.69	30.66	39.00	4.20	0.00	36.83	0.00	4.82	0.00
TOTAL MARKET 1994	7,450.73	4,006.39	2,743.27	939.65	3,158.41	8,871.47	73.34	104.86	603.46	825.04	367.23	367.52
EST. MKT. 1995	7,580.31	4,035.60	2,811.84	939.64	3,190.00	8,782.77	71.89	103.82	615.53	825.05	356.22	378.54
EST. MKT. 1996	7,658.10	4,042.50	2,868.08	939.64	3,205.95	8,782.77	70.45	102.78	627.84	825.05	345.53	389.90
EST. MKT. 1997	7,710.75	4,042.50	2,911.10	958.43	3,221.98	8,782.77	69.74	101.75	646.68	825.05	338.62	397.70
EST. MKT. 1998	7,993.20	4,042.50	2,969.33	958.43	3,238.09	8,782.77	68.35	100.73	659.61	825.05	328.46	409.63

Note: 1) Competitors vary by country so have been listed by size not name. (e.g. Competitor in UK is Samuel Inc, while Competitor 1 in France is Brunholt AG)

2) 1994 date latest available

APPENDIX 6.2

LOW ALLERGY ADHESIVE

COMPETITOR SALES 1994 (£000)

	United Kingdom		France		Italy		Belgium		Holland		Denmark	
	Hosp	Non-Hosp	Hosp	Non-Hosp	Hosp	Non-Hosp	Hosp	Non-Hosp	Hosp	Non-Hosp	Hosp	Non-Hosp
MISTRAL	73.21	6.29	38.46	5.36	0.00	0.00	0.09	0.17	16.79	2.06	4.80	1.43
COMPETITOR 1	326.94	159.75	110.32	7.88	0.00	0.00	5.04	6.30	73.66	36.83	41.77	3.22
COMPETITOR 2	131.92	91.61	69.34	6.30	0.00	0.00	4.20	6.30	20.62	20.62	11.25	0.32
COMPETITOR 3	0.00	0.00	0.00	0.00	0.00	0.00	0.00	0.00	0.00	14.14	0.00	0.00
COMPETITOR 4	0.00	0.00	0.00	0.00	0.00	0.00	0.00	0.00	0.00	0.00	0.00	0.00
OTHERS	0.00	0.00	0.00	3.15	0.00	0.00	0.00	0.00	7.37	0.00	1.61	0.00
TOTAL MARKET 1994	532.07	257.65	218.12	22.69	0.00	0.00	9.33	12.77	118.44	73.65	59.43	4.97
EST. MKT. 1995	550.02	260.03	239.94	23.15	0.00	0.00	9.51	13.02	120.82	73.66	62.39	4.96
EST. MKT. 1996	587.60	258.94	275.93	23.61	0.00	0.00	9.80	13.29	123.24	73.66	65.51	4.96
EST. MKT. 1997	635.92	256.39	317.32	24.09	0.00	0.00	10.10	13.55	126.94	73.66	68.79	4.96
EST. MKT. 1998	685.73	255.00	364.91	24.57	0.00	0.00	10.39	13.82	129.47	73.66	72.22	4.96

TAPES

COMPETITOR SALES 1994 (£000)

	United Kingdom		France		Italy		Belgium		Holland		Denmark	
	Hosp	Non-Hosp	Hosp	Non-Hosp	Hosp	Non-Hosp	Hosp	Non-Hosp	Hosp	Non-Hosp	Hosp	Non-Hosp
MISTRAL	496.30	329.73	25.00	114.00	46.00	271.00	13.00	38.00	11.00	69.00	25.00	113.00
COMPETITOR 1	97.86	44.03	22.00	252.00	2.00	45.00	8.00	75.00	95.00	364.00	28.00	72.00
COMPETITOR 2	0.00	0.00	15.00	126.00	1.00	27.00	8.00	33.00	47.00	228.00	22.00	48.00
COMPETITOR 3	0.00	0.00	0.00	0.00	0.00	0.00	0.00	25.00	0.00	0.00	0.00	12.00
COMPETITOR 4	0.00	0.00	0.00	0.00	0.00	0.00	0.00	21.00	0.00	0.00	0.00	6.00
OTHERS	30.84	34.56	15.00	126.00	0.00	0.00	4.00	100.00	29.00	0.00	0.00	0.00
TOTAL MARKET 1994	625.00	408.32	77.00	618.00	49.00	343.00	33.00	292.00	182.00	661.00	75.00	251.00
EST. MKT. 1995	658.21	439.70	103.00	650.00	59.00	378.00	36.00	304.00	186.00	676.00	73.00	252.00
EST. MKT. 1996	693.75	462.37	129.00	682.00	62.00	409.00	38.00	313.00	190.00	689.00	71.00	252.00
EST. MKT. 1997	726.95	497.45	161.00	723.00	65.00	437.00	40.00	322.00	194.00	707.00	69.00	252.00
EST. MKT. 1998	832.25	531.29	201.00	759.00	68.00	472.00	42.00	332.00	198.00	721.00	67.00	252.00

FUNCTIONAL TAPES ACCESSORIES

COMPETITOR SALES 1994 (£000)

	United Kingdom		France		Italy		Belgium		Holland		Denmark	
	Hosp	Non-Hosp	Hosp	Non-Hosp	Hosp	Non-Hosp	Hosp	Non-Hosp	Hosp	Non-Hosp	Hosp	Non-Hosp
MISTRAL	242.37	263.72	19.86	16.70	133.38	401.58	0.34	1.01	3.83	5.30	12.69	18.70
COMPETITOR 1	99.33	204.39	37.82	28.37	5.27	105.40	2.52	4.20	20.62	105.19	20.88	136.54
COMPETITOR 2	0.00	0.00	18.91	15.76	0.00	0.00	0.00	4.20	0.00	36.83	0.00	0.00
COMPETITOR 3	0.00	0.00	0.00	6.30	0.00	0.00	0.00	0.00	0.00	0.00	0.00	0.00
COMPETITOR 4	0.00	0.00	0.00	0.00	0.00	0.00	0.00	0.00	0.00	0.00	0.00	0.00
OTHERS	28.73	21.79	15.76	12.61	0.00	0.00	4.20	42.02	2.94	0.00	5.62	9.64
TOTAL MARKET 1994	370.43	489.90	92.35	79.74	138.65	506.98	7.06	51.43	27.39	147.32	39.19	164.88
EST. MKT. 1995	375.26	501.39	96.98	83.74	145.58	557.68	7.20	52.45	27.82	150.28	39.20	173.13
EST. MKT. 1996	380.78	523.78	106.67	87.92	152.86	602.30	7.34	53.50	28.37	153.28	39.20	181.78
EST. MKT. 1997	397.32	532.81	117.34	92.32	160.50	644.46	7.49	54.57	28.94	157.11	39.20	190.87
EST. MKT. 1998	412.40	545.92	129.07	96.94	168.53	696.02	7.64	55.66	29.52	160.26	39.20	200.42

NON-ADHESIVE SUPPORT

COMPETITOR SALES 1994 (£000)

	United Kingdom		France		Italy		Belgium		Holland		Denmark	
	Hosp	Non-Hosp	Hosp	Non-Hosp	Hosp	Non-Hosp	Hosp	Non-Hosp	Hosp	Non-Hosp	Hosp	Non-Hosp
MISTRAL	172.97	100.46	106.54	16.70	74.83	73.40	202.33	8.15	88.98	5.60	108.74	19.65
COMPETITOR 1	432.74	62.75	0.00	252.17	42.16	0.00	84.02	25.21	589.32	259.59	220.08	72.29
COMPETITOR 2	0.00	0.00	0.00	145.00	28.74	0.00	33.61	21.01	368.33	0.00	216.86	32.13
COMPETITOR 3	0.00	0.00	0.00	100.86	0.00	0.00	0.00	16.81	235.73	0.00	216.86	4.82
COMPETITOR 4	0.00	0.00	0.00	0.00	0.00	0.00	0.00	0.00	0.00	0.00	0.00	0.00
OTHERS	344.36	0.00	851.06	315.21	0.00	0.00	33.61	84.02	73.66	0.00	72.29	0.00
TOTAL MARKET 1994	950.07	163.21	957.60	829.94	145.73	73.40	353.57	155.20	1,356.02	265.19	834.83	128.89
EST. MKT. 1995	959.72	169.94	909.73	846.54	145.74	75.60	350.04	155.19	1,389.92	267.85	851.54	128.88
EST. MKT. 1996	966.38	174.00	864.24	863.47	145.74	77.86	346.54	155.19	1,424.67	270.52	860.06	128.88
EST. MKT. 1997	968.00	178.32	842.63	880.74	145.74	80.20	343.07	155.19	1,460.29	274.58	860.06	128.88
EST. MKT. 1998	968.00	184.21	800.50	898.36	145.74	82.61	339.64	155.19	1,496.79	277.33	868.66	128.88

APPENDIX 6.6

COHESIVE SUPPORT

COMPETITOR SALES 1994 (£000)

	United Kingdom		Italy		France		Belgium		Holland		Denmark	
	Hosp	Non-Hosp	Hosp	Non-Hosp	Hosp	Non-Hosp	Hosp	Non-Hosp	Hosp	Non-Hosp	Hosp	Non-Hosp
MISTRAL	32.74	99.82	39.72	11.34	11.11	119.30	3.02	5.30	27.40	3.24	1.38	3.81
COMPETITOR 1	582.74	2,218.36	204.89	94.56	258.71	4,662.69	16.81	25.21	58.93	70.42	30.52	77.11
COMPETITOR 2	209.73	161.12	0.00	0.00	19.16	431.67	8.40	16.81	17.68	0.00	0.00	19.28
COMPETITOR 3	0.00	0.00	0.00	0.00	4.31	314.86	6.30	12.60	0.00	0.00	0.00	0.00
COMPETITOR 4	0.00	0.00	0.00	0.00	0.00	124.09	0.00	0.00	0.00	0.00	0.00	0.00
OTHERS	0.00	0.00	94.56	40.98	0.00	11.02	1.68	8.40	22.10	0.00	0.00	0.00
TOTAL MARKET 1994	825.21	2,479.30	339.17	146.88	293.29	5,663.63	36.21	68.32	126.11	73.66	31.90	100.20
EST. MKT. 1995	839.62	252.06	349.34	154.23	296.24	5,776.90	38.02	70.36	129.26	74.40	38.29	120.23
EST. MKT. 1996	844.82	2,600.00	359.82	161.94	297.72	5,892.43	39.93	72.47	132.50	75.14	45.94	144.28
EST. MKT. 1997	852.73	2,687.50	367.02	170.04	299.21	6,069.21	41.92	74.65	135.81	76.27	55.13	173.14
EST. MKT. 1998	887.39	2,790.31	378.02	178.54	300.70	6,190.59	44.02	76.89	139.21	77.03	66.15	207.76

COMPRESSION BANDAGES

COMPETITOR SALES 1994 (£000)

	United Kingdom		France		Italy		Belgium		Holland		Denmark	
	Hosp	Non-Hosp	Hosp	Non-Hosp	Hosp	Non-Hosp	Hosp	Non-Hosp	Hosp	Non-Hosp	Hosp	Non-Hosp
MISTRAL	269.25	98.64	226.63	118.83	153.60	58.26	21.51	8.82	13.85	4.13	37.22	11.38
COMPETITOR 1	926.40	10,673.20	866.82	6,304.18	1,676.85	4,570.61	84.02	50.42	193.89	147.33	819.28	192.77
COMPETITOR 2	732.50	2,025.75	283.69	4,728.14	527.01	1,121.10	33.61	42.02	101.66	88.40	321.29	40.16
COMPETITOR 3	397.20	1,311.13	204.89	2,521.67	0.00	28.74	16.81	33.61	88.40	10.61	144.58	19.28
COMPETITOR 4	391.20	0.00	173.37	0.00	0.00	0.00	16.81	0.00	0.00	0.00	120.48	0.00
OTHERS	870.59	2,807.65	504.34	6,304.18	0.00	0.00	42.02	42.02	73.66	0.00	449.80	48.19
TOTAL MARKET 1994	3,587.14	16,916.37	2,259.74	19,977.00	2,357.46	5,778.71	214.78	176.89	471.46	250.47	1,892.65	311.78
EST. MKT. 1995	3,675.23	14,207.93	2,316.22	21,774.92	2,357.46	5,894.28	219.06	180.41	480.88	262.98	1,939.96	327.36
EST. MKT. 1996	3,741.60	14,309.60	2,374.13	23,516.91	2,357.46	5,894.28	223.44	185.82	490.50	276.14	1,988.46	341.34
EST. MKT. 1997	3,795.72	14,500.00	2,421.62	25,398.26	2,357.46	5,894.28	227.91	191.40	500.31	289.94	2,028.22	354.08
EST. MKT. 1998	3,840.13	14,500.00	2,482.08	27,430.13	2,357.46	5,894.28	232.47	197.14	510.32	304.44	2,078.94	368.24

AVERAGE SELLING PRICES BY SELECTED PRODUCT AND COUNTY (£)

1996 (SPRING)

PRODUCT	United Kingdom		France		Italy		Belgium		Holland		Denmark	
	Hosp	Non-Hosp	Hosp	Non-Hosp	Hosp	Non-Hosp	Hosp	Non-Hosp	Hosp	Non-Hosp	Hosp	Non-Hosp
1. FELIX JAZ												
10cm x 3cm - 'C'	1.22	2.01	1.30	2.21	1.06	1.05	1.27	2.10	1.29	1.95	1.22	1.30
10cm x 3cm - 'M'	1.40	2.30	1.50	2.44	1.22	2.02	1.55	2.41	1.54	2.49	1.45	2.49
10cm x 3cm - 'S'	1.55	2.25	1.46	2.39	1.20	1.79	1.50	2.50	1.87	2.52	1.93	2.63
2. VICTRIX CR												
10cm x 20cm - 'P'	2.90	4.50	3.25	4.60	2.53	3.76	3.10	4.10	2.95	4.05	3.30	4.30
10cm x 20cm - 'S'	2.59	4.95	2.49	5.20	3.26	4.64	3.20	5.20	2.97	5.10	3.57	5.51
10cm x 20cm - 'E'	2.05	2.76	2.11	2.89	1.96	2.64	2.05	2.72	2.10	2.69	2.15	2.99
10cm x 4cm - 'E'	0.40	0.00	0.37	0.00	0.00	0.98	0.42	0.00	0.50	0.00	0.78	0.00
10cm x 4cm - 'P'	0.68	0.72	0.70	0.33	0.57	0.95	0.63	0.78	0.64	0.82	0.74	1.02
10cm x 4cm - 'S'	0.48	0.98	0.39	0.49	0.70	0.98	0.70	0.97	0.72	1.00	0.89	0.98
3. FELIX ACE EAB												
10cm x 4.5cm - 'E'	1.85	2.04	1.78	1.88	1.82	1.96	2.24	2.42	2.32	2.63	2.71	3.22
10cm x 4.5cm - 'P'	3.12	3.12	3.25	3.25	3.25	3.05	3.06	3.06	2.94	2.94	2.66	2.74
10cm x 4.5cm - 'S'	2.97	3.28	3.06	3.44	2.63	2.90	3.02	3.20	2.85	3.05	2.78	3.26
4. VULCAN HP												
10cm x 7cm - 'S'	3.26	4.05	3.02	0.00	0.00	0.00	3.25	0.00	3.62	3.97	4.14	4.26
10cm x 7cm - 'D'	0.00	0.00	3.25	4.38	3.10	4.32	3.70	4.42	3.58	4.06	4.34	4.17
10cm x 7cm - 'E'	3.07	3.27	2.92	3.42	2.10	2.95	3.10	3.59	2.96	3.51	3.33	4.10
10cm x 7cm - 'R'	2.86	2.98	0.00	0.00	0.00	0.00	0.00	0.00	0.00	0.00	3.40	3.70
10cm x 7cm - T	0.00	0.00	2.67	0.00	2.48	0.00	2.73	0.00	2.74	0.00	2.98	0.00

APPENDIX 8

SHARE OF EUROPEAN MARKET BY PRODUCT AND COMPETITOR (1995)

	FUNCTIONAL BANDAGES (34%)	FUNCTIONAL TAPING (22%)	SUPPORT (44%)	TOTAL MARKET (100%)
100%	OTHERS	OTHERS		
90%	MTM		OTHERS	OTHERS 21%
80%	BDG	MTM		
70%	BRUNHOFF / SAMUEL 68.9%	BDG	MTM	MTM (16%)
60%		BRUNHOFF		BDG (11%)
50%			BDG	BRUNHOFF (11%)
40%		SAMUEL 36.7%		SAMUEL (6%)
30%				35.8%
20%			BRUNHOFF	
10%			SAMUEL 9.8%	
0%	MISTRAL	MISTRAL	MISTRAL	MISTRAL

Source: Miles & North; Mistral in-house data

APPENDIX 9:   MEMORANDUM

TO: May Alexander, Director of Marketing

CC: John Norland, Marketing Manager

FROM: Dirk Bradley, Financial Controller

DATE: 20 June 1996

Re: Bandages - financial results for year ending 31 December 1995

I can't give you the precise figures yet, but early indications show that we have increased our 35% market share in taping, despite increased competition. Cohesive bandage sales appear to have risen approximately 24%.

This year seems to be getting off to a good start and with the new manufacturing line for elasticated adhesive bandage in Madrid its over to your department now!

All the best

Dirk

APPENDIX 10

EUROPEAN SALES AND PROFIT
BY COUNTRY 1992 - 1996

£'000

UK

	1992	1993	1994	1995	1996				
Sales		47,730.90	52,451.60	58,279.50	64,755.00	0.91	0.9	0.9	0.9
Gross Profit		23,388.10	26,750.30	30,888.10	35,615.30	49%	51%	53%	55%
Operating Expenses		5,665.70	6,136.80	6,702.10	7,123.10	11.90%	11.70%	11.50%	11%
Sales & Marketing Expenses		9,068.90	11,014.80	13,404.30	16,188.80	19%	21%	23%	25%
A&P		1,217.10	1,416.20	1,661.00	1,942.70	2.60%	3%	2.90%	3%
Net Profit		7,436.50	8,182.40	9,120.70	10,360.80	15.58%	15.60%	15.65%	16.00%

FRANCE

	1992	1993	1994	1995	1996				
Sales		21,411.90	23,529.60	26,144.00	27,520.00	0.91	0.9	0.95	
Gross Profit		11,134.20	11,764.80	10,980.50	11,008.00	52%	50%	42%	40%
Operating Expenses		2,355.30	2,588.30	2,875.80	3,027.20	11.00%	11.00%	11.00%	11.00%
Sales & Marketing Expenses		4,282.40	4,470.60	4,705.90	4,678.40	20.00%	19.00%	18.00%	17.00%
A&P		599.50	611.80	627.50	605.40	2.80%	2.60%	2.40%	2.20%
Net Profit		3,897.00	4,094.20	2,771.30	2,697.00	18%	17%	11%	10%

ITALY

	1992	1993	1994	1995	1996				
Sales		46,549.59	50,597.38	53,827.00	56,660.00	0.92	0.94	0.95	
Gross Profit		21,831.80	22,566.40	22,768.80	22,664.00	46.90%	44.60%	42.30%	40.00%
Operating Expenses		6,051.40	6,577.70	6,997.50	7,365.80	13%	13%	13%	13%
Sales & Marketing Expenses		10,240.90	10,625.40	11,034.50	11,218.70	22.00%	21.00%	20.50%	19.80%
A&P		698.20	759.00	807.40	849.90	1.50%	1.50%	1.50%	1.50%
Net Profit		4,841.20	4,604.40	3,929.40	3,229.60	10%	9%	7%	6%

BELGIUM

	1992	1993	1994	1995	1996				
Sales		1,550.90	1,704.20	1,893.60	2,104.00	0.91	0.9	0.9	
Gross Profit		814.20	852.10	899.50	946.80	53%	50%	48%	45%
Operating Expenses		170.60	187.50	208.30	210.40	11%	11%	11%	10%
Sales & Marketing Expenses		325.70	340.80	359.80	378.70	21%	20%	19%	18%
A&P		31.00	34.10	37.90	42.10	2%	2%	2%	2%
Net Profit		286.90	289.70	293.50	315.60	19%	17%	16%	15%

HOLLAND

	1992	1993	1994	1995	1996				
Sales		1,657.10	2,045.80	2,589.60	3,237.00	0.81	0.79	0.8	
Gross Profit		911.40	1,227.50	1,683.20	2,265.90	55%	60%	65%	70%
Operating Expenses		198.90	245.50	310.80	388.40	12%	12%	12%	12%
Sales & Marketing Expenses		348.00	491.00	699.20	971.10	21%	24%	27%	30%
A&P		54.70	71.60	103.60	161.90	3.30%	3.50%	4.00%	5%
Net Profit		309.90	419.40	569.70	744.50	19%	21%	22%	23%

DENMARK

	1992	1993	1994	1995	1996				
Sales		3,711.70	4,078.80	4,078.80	4,532.00	0.91	1	0.9	
Gross Profit		1,670.30	1,835.50	1,835.50	1,903.40	45%	45%	45%	42%
Operating Expenses		426.80	489.50	448.70	498.50	12%	12%	11%	11%
Sales & Marketing Expenses		816.60	1,305.20	815.80	906.40	22%	32%	20%	20%
A&P		81.70	89.70	89.70	99.70	2%	2%	2%	2%
Net Profit		345.20	-48.90	481.30	398.80	9%	-1%	12%	9%

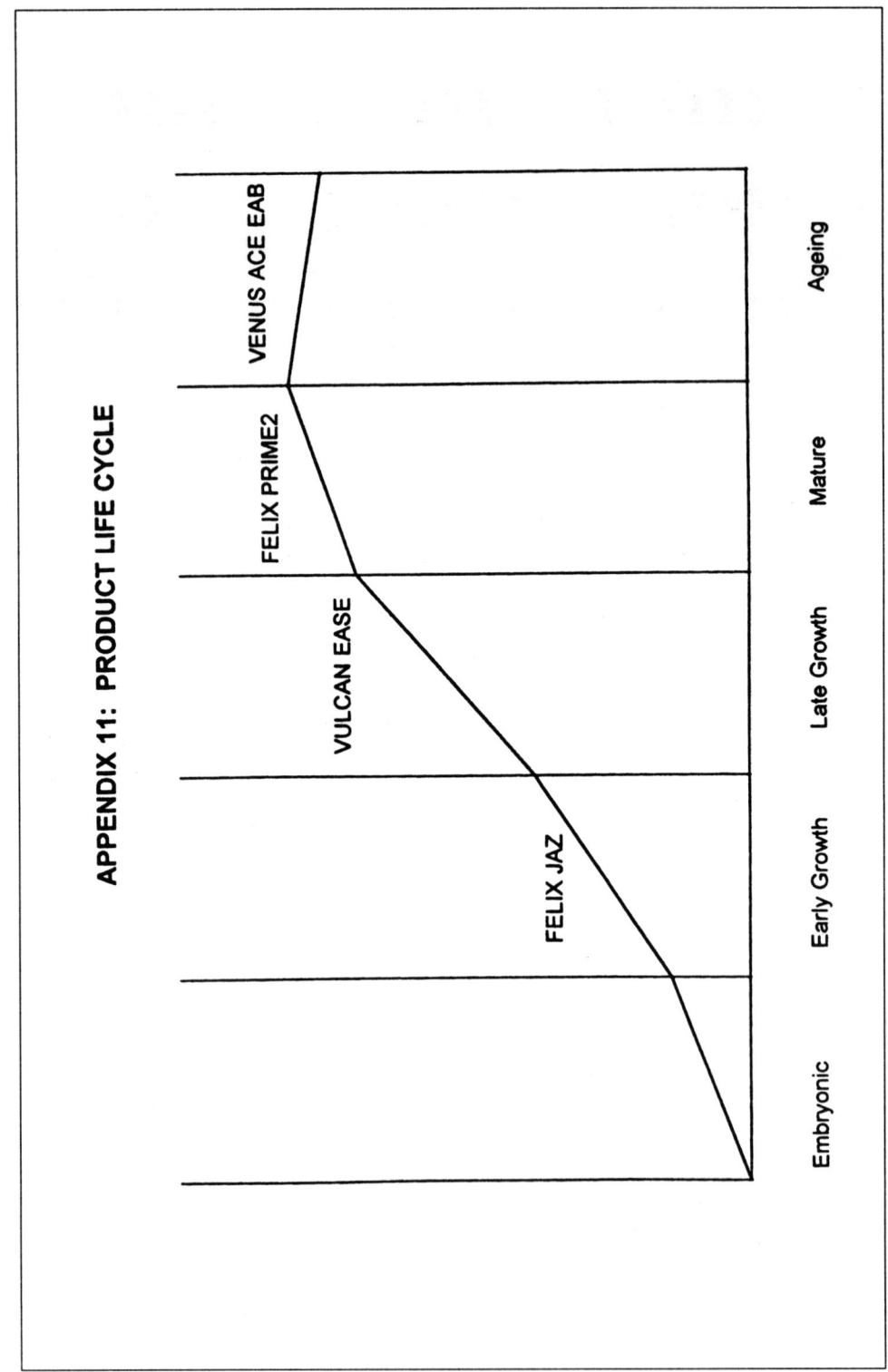

APPENDIX 11: PRODUCT LIFE CYCLE

VENUS ACE EAB

FELIX PRIME2

VULCAN EASE

FELIX JAZ

Embryonic   Early Growth   Late Growth   Mature   Ageing

APPENDIX 12: BANDAGING REPORT

Sales

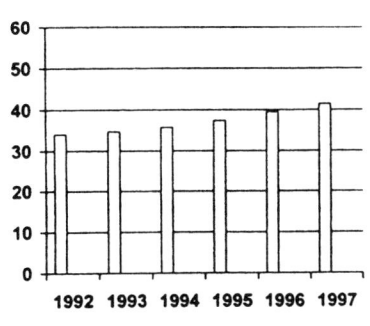

Sales £m   34.08   34.72   35.76   37.36   39.52   41.44

Sales by Region

Profitability

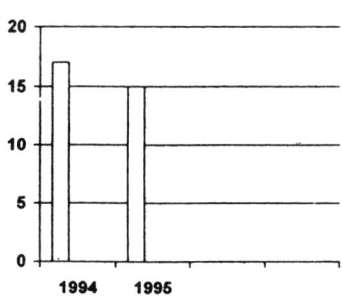

Profit %   17   15

Competitive Situation

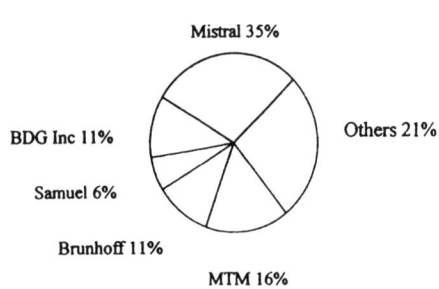

Environment

- The market for support bandages is currently growing by 2.8% per annum

- The emergence of low cost/lower quality general support products is starting but have yet to become significant

Competitor

- The emergence of credible competitors to our adhesive bandages occurred in 1994, eg Spain and France

- The growth of off-the-shelf bracing for sports prophylaxis is eroding our potential in functional bandaging

Profit

- Net profit has fallen from 17% to 15% in 1995 due to:

  The mix change between elasticated adhesive bandages (EABs) and General Support, where General Support and tape products (which have lower net profit levels) now make a greater proportion of sales.

  The expected lower net profit on EABs, in reflection of the increased competitor activity and defending our business against these competitors.

STRATEGIES

- Segment the adhesive bandage market through the introduction/development of product variants:

- and make market supply difficult for our new competitors

  To segment the traditional EAB (via packaging) to enhance its acceptability in all sectors

  - vets
  - sports/activity market
  - hospital
  - OTC (over-the-counter)

- To develop a workshop package to support the range in the key areas of use sports/activity and general physiotherapy

- To aggressively promote a full range of cohesives to strengthen our position in this growing sector

- To manufacture/source a full range of general support bandages to provide a cost competitive range to be offered on hospital contracts to gain substantial growth with minimal investment

- To package some key brands to maximise their OTC potential.

QUESTIONS

You have had a month to analyse the information which John Norlands has given you and to prepare your presentation in discussion with your colleagues at PACE Marketing Consultants. Your presentation, IN REPORT FORMAT, will cover the following:

1 Present a strategic marketing plan for the European bandages business of Mistral, looking ahead five years. Your plan should take into account the major trends affecting the business, including demographics, technology and the switch in influence away from hospitals in favour of the community.

(50 marks)

2 Based on your strategic marketing plan, make recommendations to Mistral for a European pricing policy that will support the company's marketing objectives and overcome problems of parallel importing.

(25 marks)

3 Propose a process by which Mistral can begin to develop new brands in Europe.

(25 marks)

EXAMINER'S REPORT

MISTRAL UK LIMITED - DECEMBER 1996

GENERAL COMMENTS

Unfortunately, results in this paper are still generally disappointing. Too many candidates are still failing to deal with the constraints of a three-hour examination and so failing demonstrate their ability to apply marketing principles.

The Mistral case found far too many candidates unable to address the questions posed on examination day. Work prepared before the examination was too often regurgitated without thinking or taking account of the additional information or the marks allocated on the paper.

The list of reasons for failure in the case were (yet again):

- failure to answer the questions posed on the day
- regurgitation of case material
- presentation of pre-prepared answers regardless of questions set
- lack of knowledge on strategic marketing issues
- inclusion of irrelevant data, numbers and SWOT analyses
- ignoring the additional information
- poor time management

The last point again requires special mention. In this case the questions carried marks of 50:25:25. Question one was rightly anticipated by most candidates but was often answered as if it carried 80% of the marks. Questions two and three were often answered quite superficially and covered in two or three pages each - or even ignored completely!

Examiners try hard to award marks but to do so we need something to mark! Time management is a critical skill for the practising marketer - not just useful to pass exams.

QUESTION ONE (50 Marks)

"Present a strategic marketing plan for the European bandages business of Mistral, looking ahead five years. Your plan should take into account the major trends affecting the business, including demographics, technology and the switch in influence away from hospitals in favour of the community".

Most candidates had properly forecast this question. Having been asked so many times in the past, this question is beginning to focus attention on the contents of a strategic marketing plan and generally the structures (if not the contents) of plans are improving. Unfortunately, for some candidates it is obviously the only thing that they prepare. In this case the strategic marketing plan attracted only 50% of the marks and too few candidates modified their approach accordingly.

One by-product of an easily predictable question is the reliance on group preparation or even completely pre-prepared answers simply copied out on the day of the examination. Such collusion is easily spotted by examiners and always rewarded with a fail grade. Remember, you can prepare with others but the examination is a test of individual, not group, ability. The questions and the additional information are constructed in such a way to make pre-prepared answers difficult to use so candidates should read the questions VERY carefully on the day.

SWOT and PEST analyses continue to take up pages of examination scripts but still attract relatively few marks because they are not applied to strategic action and recommendations.

The major problems in answer to this question on the Mistral case centred around the following:

- concentration on tactics rather than longer term strategy.

- tendency to give top-level views on what should be done without any indication of how this might be achieved.

- inadequate understanding of targeting and positioning although Porter and BCG models were used extensively.

- failure to identify target markets thereby producing a wide range of conflicting objectives and actions and a tendency to produce "product-led" strategies.

- not all candidates submitted budgets and the control aspects were generally weak

- general confusion about the difference between strategy and tactics.

- too many candidates, working to a predictable question, are contenting themselves with a "tick-box" answer that concentrates on getting the headings to a strategic plan right and not worrying too much about the content.

The major comment from examiners is that while many candidates can identify strategic alternatives by using Ansoff/Porter, far too few seem capable of making an informed choice and proposing action. The majority of the marks available to candidates are awarded for decisions not analysis. Once again we found too few opportunities to award marks for this aspect.

QUESTION TWO (25 Marks)

"Based on your strategic marketing plan, make recommendations to Mistral for a European pricing policy that will support the company's marketing objectives and overcome the problems of parallel importing"

This question proved difficult for candidates who had only prepared a strategic plan before the examination. Those who had succeeded in understanding the Mistral situation in a wider, more strategic, context managed better. Those candidates unable to think on the day fared badly.

This question was looking for two things:

Recommendations for a European pricing policy to:

1)   Support Mistral's marketing objectives (Ex question one)
2)   Overcome problems of parallel importing (Ex additional information)

Candidates who thought this simply meant writing out the pricing section they had prepared for the strategic plan tended to fail this question.

The main problems encountered on this question were:

- offering simplistic solutions like "standardised pricing" for all countries without regard to local conditions or implementation.

- not understanding or trying to find out what "parallel importing" means (this is an open book examination so the reference material is available!).

- certificate level explanations of "penetration" or "skimming" without any attempt to relate to the case.

- answers that directly contradicted proposals made in question one, for example reducing prices while proposing a market-leading position!

QUESTION 3 (25 Marks)

"Propose a process by which Mistral can begin to develop new brands in Europe"

This question proved the downfall of far too many candidates. Even allowing for thinking and planning the answer, 25 marks should justify in excess of 30 minutes writing time. Examiners offered just two or three pages found it difficult to award pass marks.

A surprising number of candidates appeared to have little understanding of branding, despite its coverage in Marketing Communications Strategy (Diploma) and the attention given to this subject in the recent marketing literature. The Leffe case was the last case to look at branding as a strategic issue, sadly there is little evidence of progress being made.

The main problems encountered on this question were:

- confusing "brands" with "products" and offering ideas on new product development processes

- not offering a "process" but a textbook definition of what brands are.

- little consideration of the special nature of international branding.

- answers that directly contradicted proposals made in question one.

CONCLUSIONS

Mistral again proved to be a difficult case for too many candidates.

Questions two and three have highlighted the dangerously superficial knowledge held by a number of candidates on key strategic issues such as pricing and branding. Previous cases have also shown this problem in areas such as forecasting and strategic alliances (Gravesend), positioning and promotion (Leffe), marketing organisation (FirstrATE) and segmentation (Australian Tourist Commission)

Future cases will continue to explore these areas.

Glossary

4Ps/7Ps   See the marketing mix.

Advertising   Any paid form of non-personal presentation of ideas, goods or services by an identified sponsor.

Ansoff matrix   A model used for identifying the product and market alternatives open to an organization. This involves focusing upon existing and new products and existing and new markets.

Benchmarking   The analytical process through which an organization's performance is compared with that of its competitors.

Boston Consulting Group (BCG)   The management consulting group which developed the Boston matrix, which makes use of relative market share and the rate of market growth to analyse the product portfolio. Products or SBUs (see below) are categorized as *cash cows, stars, dogs* or *question marks*.

Bottom-up planning   An approach to planning in which individual business units develop their own objectives and strategies. These are then agreed by corporate management, which then adopts a hands-off approach and requires only that the targets are achieved.

Brand/branding   The name, symbol or design used to identify the products or services of a producer and differentiate these from those of competitive producers.

Capability   'A firm's capabilities relate to the distinctive competencies that it has developed to do something well and a company is likely to enjoy a differential advantage in an area where its competencies outdo those of its potential competitors' (Dibb, Simkin *et al*).

Competitors   Those organizations with which the firm interacts, directly and indirectly, in the fight for sales.

Competitive advantage   Those factors which allow the firm to compete (more) effectively in the marketplace.

Competitive information system (CIS)   The formal system that is used to collect, analyse, evaluate and disseminate within the organization information on the firm's competitors.

Competitive stance   The basis on which an organization chooses to operate and compete in the market place. Michael Porter argues that there are essentially only three generic bases of competition: cost leadership, focus (market niching), and differentiation.

Concentrated marketing   The focusing of the marketing effort upon just one or two of the available market segments.

Consumer   The user of the product or service (see also **Customer**).

Contingency planning   A plan of action which will be implemented only if events outside the parameters of the accepted plan begin to emerge.

Cost leadership   One of Michael Porter's three generic strategies, which involves pursuing a strategy based on the development of the lowest cost structure in the industry.

Customer   The buyer of the product or service (see also **Consumer**).

Differentiated marketing   The development of a different marketing mix for each segment.

Differentiation   One of Michael Porter's three generic strategies, which involves making the product or service different from others on the market by developing one or more unique features or by developing a package of benefits which others do not offer.

Effectiveness   The appropriateness of an action or 'doing the right job'.

Efficiency   A measure of how well an activity is performed ('doing the job right').

Environment   The marketing environment is made up of a series of *micro* forces (suppliers, customers, competitors, the public at large and the distribution network) and *macro* forces (political, economic, social, cultural, demographic, legal and technological factors).

Environmental analysis   The process of identifying the various forces within the environment, determining their likely patterns of development and assessing their implications for the organization.

Ethics   The set of moral principles and values that guide an individual's conduct.

Focus   One of the three generic strategies identified by Michael Porter, which involves concentrating the marketing effort upon a particular segment and then competing within this either through cost leadership or a differentiated approach.

Formal organization   The stated and explicit structure of an organization which determines the hierarchy, the division of labour, job specifications and hence the basis of the relationships between individuals and departments.

General Electric multi-factor model   An approach to portfolio analysis which categorizes SBUs on the basis of industry attractiveness and business strength.

Generic strategies   See **Focus, Cost leadership** and **Differentiation**.

Geodemographics   An approach to segmentation which classifies people by where they live. The rationale for this is that 'birds of a feather flock together'.

Goals down/plans up planning   An approach to planning in which corporate management establishes the broad planning parameters in terms of targets, but then allows the business unit to decide how these will be achieved.

Informal organization   The social dimensions and relationships within a business. This is sometimes referred to as 'the oil which allows the wheels to go round'.

Lifestyle segmentation   'A person's pattern of living as expressed in [their] activities, interests and opinions . . . [it] portrays the 'whole person' interacting with his or her environment. Lifestyle reflects something beyond the person's social class . . . or personality . . . [it] attempts to profile a person's way of being and acting in the world' (Kotler).

Managerial culture   The basic assumptions and beliefs that are shared by members of the management team and which determine the organization's view of itself and its environment.

Market challenger   Firms which adopt an aggressive stance by attacking the market leader or others in the industry in order to strengthen their position and possibly gain leadership.

Market follower   Firms which avoid direct confrontation with others in the market are generally willing to accept the current market structure and status quo, and react to the initiatives taken by others (**Note**: followers may follow others closely by responding quickly, or at a distance in that they respond only at a much later stage.

Market leader   Although the market leader is typically seen to be the largest player in the market, an alternative (and, in many ways, better) approach involves seeing the market leader as the firm which, by virtue of its proactive stance, determines the nature, bases and intensity of competition within the market. In this way, others are forced to respond.

Market nichers   Firms which concentrate their efforts upon a small and often specialized part of the market.

Marketing assets   The capabilities possessed by the organization which managers and the marketplace view as beneficially strong. These include customer-based assets (brand image and reputation), distribution-based assets (the density and geographic coverage of the dealer network), and internal marketing assets (skills, experience, economies of scale, technology and resources).

Marketing audit   A formal review of the organization's products, markets, customers and environment.

Marketing channels   The 'sets of interdependent organizations involved in the process of making a product or service available for consumption' (Kotler).

Marketing effectiveness review   A framework for measuring the organization's marketing capabilities and performance by making use of five dimensions: the strength of the customer-oriented philosophy, the degree of integration within the marketing organization, the adequacy of marketing information, the firm's strategic orientation, and levels of operational efficiency.

Marketing information system (MkIS)   'A system which consists of people, equipment and procedures to gather, sort, analyse, evaluate and distribute needed, timely and accurate information to marketing decision makers' (Kotler).

Marketing mix   The set of controllable variables that the organization uses to influence its target markets and determine demand. Although the mix has traditionally been seen to consist of four principal elements (the 4Ps of product, price, place and promotion), others have been added to this in recent years, leading to the 7Ps; the three additional elements are physical evidence, process management, and people.

Marketing planning   The process of identifying, evaluating and selecting the organization's products, services and markets, and how the organization is to operate within each sector of the market.

Marketing research   The process of gathering, recording and analysing market-related information. This typically involves making use of published or secondary data and the collection of problem-specific data (primary research).

Objectives   Measures of desired achievement which are used as the basis of planning and a measure of performance.

Performance-importance grid   A tool used for measuring marketing, financial, manufacturing and organizational performance against the background of the market importance of each dimension.

Personal selling   An oral presentation with one or more prospective purchasers for the purpose of making sales.

PEST   The acronym for the Political, Economic, Socio-cultural and Technological forces within the organization's environment.

Planning   The setting of objectives and the identification, evaluation and selection of the strategic and/or tactical actions needed to achieve them.

Portfolio analysis   The approach to planning and management of the product range, which involves recognizing the nature of the interrelationships between strategic business units and then making investment and marketing decisions that are designed to maximize the performance of the range as a whole rather than that of the individual SBUs.

Positioning   The relative competitive stance adopted within a target market.

Price takers/price makers   Price takers are those organizations which, by virtue of a weak market position, lack of an offensive strategy, absence of distinguishing features, or few resources, simply accept the prices set by others in the marketplace. Price makers, by contrast, are those which, because of their size, competitive stance, aggression, resources, or strong selling propositions, are able to determine not only their prices but also those of other firms in the market.

Primary data   Data collected for a specific market study and designed to help answer a particular question.

Product life cycle (PLC)   A model of product and market evolution which suggests that products and markets have a finite life and that during this life they pass through a number of distinct stages (these are typically *introduction, growth, maturity* and *decline*). As the product goes through these, the nature of the strategy needed to support and develop the product should reflect this, with emphasis being given to different parts of the marketing mix.

Publicity   The non-personal stimulation of demand for a product or service or business unit by planting commercially significant news about it in a published medium or obtaining favourable presentation of it upon radio, television or stage that is not paid for by the sponsor.

Relationship marketing (RM)   The conscious attempt to develop long-term and mutually beneficial relationships with customers. This contrasts with transaction marketing, which tends to view each transaction separately.

Resource audit   The identification and evaluation of the internal and external resources available to the organization.

Sales promotion   Those marketing activities, other than advertising, personal selling and publicity, that stimulate consumer purchase, such as displays, shows and exhibitions, demonstrations and various non-recurrent selling efforts not in the ordinary routine.

Scenario planning   The process of identifying and planning for possible alternative futures.

Secondary data   Market data that is not collected directly by the user nor for a problem-specific purpose. Examples include government and sector reports.

Segmentation   The sub-dividing of a market into distinct and homogeneous sub-groups.

Services   Distinguishable from products in that they are most often produced as they are consumed and cannot be taken away or stored.

Seven-S framework   The model developed by Peters and Waterman which illustrates that strategic capability is influenced not just by the 'hard' Ss (strategy, structure and systems), but also by a series of 'softer' Ss (skills, style, staffing and shared values).

Societal marketing concept   An extension of the traditional definition of the marketing concept in order to take greater and more specific account of the consumer's and society's well-being.

Socio-cultural   The mix of social and cultural factors in the environment (demographics, lifestyle, social mobility, attitudes and consumerism).

Stakeholders   A person or group with a direct or indirect interest in an organization, its activities and outcomes.

Strategic business unit (SBU)   A single business or collection of related businesses which might feasibly stand apart from the rest of the organization and which offer scope for independent planning.

Strategic drift   The gap that emerges between what the organization is offering and what the market wants.

Strategic grouping   The process of plotting the position of the various players within the market on the basis of the similarities and differences that exist in the type of strategy being pursued.

Strategic wear-out   The tiredness or staleness of corporate and marketing strategies.

Strategy   The course of action to achieve a particular objective.

Stuck in the middle   Although Michael Porter identified three generic strategies (see **Generic strategies, Cost, Focus** and **Differentiation**) and argued that firms need to adopt a distinct competitive stance, many organizations fail to identify, develop or exploit a meaningful position. The result is that they end up 'stuck in the middle', in the sense that they have no obvious or communicated selling proposition and hence there is little reason for customers to do business with the firm.

SWOT   The analysis and assessment of the firm's strengths and weaknesses (in essence, the firm's capabilities) and the opportunities and threats in the marketplace.

Tactics   The development of resources within a strategy.

Targeting   The choice of market segments at which the marketing effort is to be aimed.

Test marketing   The process of measuring market response to a new product or service by piloting it within a small area which is seen to be representative of the market as a whole.

Top-down planning   An approach to planning in which corporate management sets the objectives and maintains a close involvement with both the development and implementation of the strategy and tactics.

Undifferentiated marketing   A broad-brush approach to marketing, in which the market is not sub-divided into segments.

Unique selling proposition (USP)   A product/service feature or benefit which others are not currently able to offer. Assuming that the USP is meaningful to customers, it provides a basis for differentiation.

VALS (Values and lifestyles)   An approach to market segmentation which classifies people on the basis of nine value lifestyle groups.

Value chain   The relationships between the value-creating activities within an organization which, if managed effectively, are capable of creating a competitive advantage.

Index